Lecture Notes in Computer Science 603

Edited by G. Goos and J. Hartmanis

J. van Katwijk (Ed.)

Ada: Moving Towards 2000

11th Ada-Europe International Conference
Zandvoort, The Netherlands, June 1-5, 1992
Proceedings

Springer-Verlag
Berlin Heidelberg New York
London Paris Tokyo
Hong Kong Barcelona
Budapest

Series Editors

Gerhard Goos
Universität Karlsruhe
Postfach 69 80
Vincenz-Priessnitz-Straße 1
W-7500 Karlsruhe, FRG

Juris Hartmanis
Department of Computer Science
Cornell University
5149 Upson Hall
Ithaca, NY 14853, USA

Volume Editor

Jan van Katwijk
Delft University of Technology
Julianalaan 132, 2628 BL Delft, The Netherlands

CR Subject Classification (1991): D.2, D.1.2-5, D.3, D.4.7

ISBN 3-540-55585-4 Springer-Verlag Berlin Heidelberg New York
ISBN 0-387-55585-4 Springer-Verlag New York Berlin Heidelberg

Printed in Germany

Typesetting: Camera ready by author/editor
Printing and binding: Druckhaus Beltz, Hemsbach/Bergstr.
45/3140-543210 - Printed on acid-free paper

Preface

The theme of the 11th Ada Europe conference "Moving towards 2000" aims at emphasizing that the turn of the century is approaching very rapidly. The next century will bring an even more dominant position of information technology in our lives than the current period. Software engineering and Ada both play a major role in the development of software and software technology for this information technology.

The 11th Ada Europe conference shows that indeed Ada has matured from a language, mainly for researchers and academics in the early 1980s, into a full-grown tool in software engineering practice. The technical contributions in the conference demonstrate that Ada is very beneficially used in many software development projects and is gradually accepted on the scale it deserves.

In selecting the technical contributions, papers were sought that would show that Ada is indeed ripened in all aspects of software engineering. A variety of topics is addressed: management, economics, practical experiences, as well as numerics and the use of Ada for real-time and distributed systems.

Almost 60 extended abstracts were received; choosing papers for the final programme was sometimes rather hard, due to the outstanding quality of many of the contributions. As an aid in the selection process, each abstract was refereed by three members of an international panel of referees. The final programme was drafted in an attempt to get a balanced programme with high-quality technical papers. Unfortunately, striving for a balance over the various interesting topics caused several technical contributions of good quality to be rejected.

The programme committee for this conference consisted of:

- Prof. Dimitrous Christodoulakis Univ. of Patras, Greece
- At Hijwegen, Data Sciences, The Netherlands
- Toomas Käer, Ericson, Sweden
- Prof. Jan van Katwijk, Delft Univ. of Technology, The Netherlands
- Prof. Karel de Vlaminck, KU Leuven, Belgium

A large number of people contributed by carefully refereeing the extended abstracts. For this conference, apart from the members of the programme committee, the following persons contributed to the refereeing process: A. Alonso, A. Alvarez, J. Bamberger, E.M. Dusink, E.Dürr, T. Elrad, F. Gomez-Molinero, R.D. Huijsman, J. Kok, B. Lynch, B. Maessen, M. Nagl, G.J. van Oosten, C. Pronk, W.J. Toetenel, F. Ververs, P. Wehrum, B. Wichmann, and C. Wojahn. Finally, we would like to express our gratitude to our sponsors and to the other members of the organizing committee of the conference: Rob Westermann (chair), Pieter Verduin, At Hijwegen and Dick Fikkert.

April 1992

Jan van Katwijk
Programme Chairman

Table of Contents

Distributed Application Designed Using MASCOT and Implemented in Ada. 1
M.J.Looney, A. O'Brien

Real Time Ada in the International Space Station Freedom 9
Gary Raines

Managing Ada Object-Oriented Development 20
John A. Anderson, John D. Sheffler

Software Engineering, Ada and Metrics 35
Alison Wearing

Using Ada Source Code Generators in a Large Project 47
Rob Duell, Hugo J. Sebel, Franklin C.A. de Wit

Design and Code Metrics Through a DIANA-Based Tool 60
Wayne M. Zage, Dolores M. Zage, Manjari Bhargava, Dale J. Gaumer

Using Ada in Integrating ATC Systems 72
Miech Groeneveld

An Evaluation of Ada Source Code Reuse 80
W.M. Thomas, A. Delis, V.R. Basili

Porting Embedded Real-Time Ada Software 92
Fred A. Maymir-Ducharme

Reusable Executives for Hard Real-Time Systems in Ada 104
Juan A. de la Puente, Juan Zamorano, Alejandro Alonso, Jose L. Fernandez

Designing Hard Real-Time Systems 116
A. Burns, A.J. Wellings

Runtime System Support for Data-Oriented Synchronization in Ada-9X 128
M. Gobin, M. Timmerman, F.J.A. Gielen

Decimal Arithmetic in Ada 138
Benjamin M. Brosgol, Robert I. Eachus, David E. Emery

Task Dependence Net as a Representation for Concurrent Ada Programs 150
Jingde Cheng

Detection and Avoidance of Elaboration-Time Problems for Multi-Unit Real-Time Ada Applications 165
Leslie C. Lander, Sandeep Mitra

Simulation of Mosca Specifications in Ada 182
Arlet Ottens, Hans Toetenel

Considerations with Regard to Validation of Ada Debuggers 197
Steen Silberg

SWG APSE Test Support Toolset (Assessment of the CAIS-A Interface Set) 214
W. Treurniet

Compilation Integration: A Solution for the Challenge of Developing and Reusing Ada Software on Different Platforms 230
Thanh-Nu Do

Extending Working Environments for the Development of Reactive/Adaptive Systems with Intelligent Controls 242
Tzilla Elrad, Sungyoung Lee, Ufuk Verun

Predicting the Speedup of Parallel Ada Programs 257
Lars Lundberg

A Highley Parallel Ada Task Scheduler 275
Susan Flynn Hummel

STRAda - An Ada Transformation and Distribution System 287
G.Bazalgette, D. Bekele, C. Bernon, M. Filali, J.M. Rigaud, A. Sayah

AMPATS - A Multi-processor Ada Tool Set 300
Karlotto Mangold

A Pratical Use of the Ada Rendez-Vous Paradigm in Distributed Systems 312
M. Bayassi, H. Bitteur, J.-F. Jézéquel, P. Legrain

Distributed Application Designed using MASCOT and Implemented in Ada

M J Looney

DRA Maritime Division, ARE-PN, Portsmouth PO6 4AA, United Kingdom

A O'Brien

BAe Sema, 1 Atlantic Quay, Broomielaw, Glasgow, G2 8JE, United Kingdom

1 INTRODUCTION

The provision of effective and reliable software is becoming increasingly important with the rapid advance and spread of computer based technology. Costly project failures emphasise the need for soundly based disciplines for all aspects of software creation; these disciplines are, at present, still lacking.

The primary objective of this work was to assess the suitability of mating Mascot3 with Ada. The aim was to capitalise on the results of several earlier studies by implementing a realistic real-time Ada application of non-trivial size based on a Close in Weapon System (CIWS) design and, furthermore, demonstrate the distribution of an Ada-based system over heterogeneous processors.

2 BACKGROUND

A number of earlier pieces of work had led to this investigation into the use of Mascot3 with Ada for the design and implementation of real-time embedded systems (References 1,2,3,4,8,9,10&11). One such was the Alvey Mascot Design Support Environment, (MDSE), project (Ref 5). This produced a tool of the same name which provides a graphical, rule-based design aid for Mascot3 which also contains consistency checking facilities and interfaces to an Ada code generator (Ref 6).

These other studies identified the requirements and top level designed, in Ada and MASCOT, for parts of a naval Close In Weapons System, CIWS. For this project, the original CIWS design was split between host and target systems as many real applications are distributed. It was felt important to obtain information in this area since, as yet, little information is available about real Ada distribution or about the difficulties of using heterogeneous processors. The naval example chosen was thought to be sufficiently general to be able to provide information relevant to many application domains.

3 OVERVIEW

ARE supplied the infrastructure software, the demonstration scenario, and the target hardware. Yard Ltd provided the host processor, and made available the MDSE including the Ada code generator for the development of the CIWS application software. Several versions of the basic infrastructure were needed for various configurations. In the final arrangement the processing is distributed between a VAXstation II host using DEC's VAXAda and a Motorola target using Ready Systems' ARTX communicating via TCP/IP over an Ethernet.

The Mascot Organiser acts as a meta-scheduler which means that a full Ada rendezvous only occurs when there is actual resource contention. Although this leads to dramatic performance improvements this is only achieved with trade-offs elsewhere, notably in terms of responsiveness.

Small scale testing was done using non-Mascot harnesses since no concurrency was required at this level. The partly tested software was then incorporated into the MDSE for further design evaluation within a Mascot environment. The system uses two entirely separate copies of the Mascot Organiser: one each for the host and target.

Since the network could be used in loop-back mode and the display attached to the VAX, this configuration was used with VAXAda for the majority of the initial work. Standardised interfaces to the infrastructure assisted in minimizing the effort required when code was to be ported to the target system. Actual porting to the target processors was indeed greatly simplified by this approach and was achieved with the minimum of effort and with a high degree of confidence.

4 THE MDSE

The primary function of the MDSE as a CASE tool is to assist MASCOT designers in the production of high quality designs with diagrams checked for correctness, and in the diagnosis of some implementation problems at the design stage. The MDSE may be broken down into two main levels; the infrastructure, provided by the graphics interface and the data base, and the tools in the form of the modeller and the advisor and the auotmatic code generator.

5 INFRASTRUCTURE

The MASCOT3 Kernel was based on that used in the prior studies (References 3 & 4), however, a number of modifications were required to make it compatible with Ready Systems Ada.The Kernel has been written in "pure" Ada, which should make it portable to any Ada implementation. The drawback is that the Kernel makes use of the Ada tasking model, which means that the rather simple tasking operations required by MASCOT are implemented using more sophisticated Ada constructs.

The networking facilities for the Vax end were provided by Wollongong WIN TCP/IP from GEC-Marconi, while the target networking capablity was provided by RTAda-Net_E

An Ada interface to this suite was provided by ARE through a generic package STREAM_IO which is based closely on the standard Ada package SEQUENTIAL_IO. This allowed links to be established through the network for various data types, which were opened and accessed as though they were files. No underlying network details were apparent to the client packages. On the target processor the I/O requirement was meet by the use of RTAda-IO to provide high level file handling and to allow I/O to occur over more than one port on the target system at the same time.

The Ferranti VARS-H display was driven using a GKS interface provided by ARE which supports GKS level 1c implementations. During the preliminary phases of the project, some familiarity with GKS was obtained by writing programs using the DEC Ada GKS interface on the Host VAXstation to produce displays on the VAXstation console. Some consternation arose when the ARE interface was delivered, as it was found that ARE and DEC interfaces were almost totally incompatible. Whereas ARE had very properly implemented the GKS interface following the ISO standard, it appeared that DEC had produced their interface by closely re-mapping the FORTRAN GKS interface, making scarcely any use of the capabilities of Ada.

6 IMPLEMENTATION

The following are comments on the implementation process in general and indicating some of the problems found.

Ada

The project was developed on the VAXstation (Host) system running under VMS version 4.6 using the following Ada compilers :

(a) The DEC VAXAda compiler version 1.5-44, referred to below as the VAXAda compiler.

(b) The Telegen E68 (MC68030) cross-compiler version 3.22a supplied with Ready Systems Ada development system, referred to below as the RTAda E68.

Both compilers failed to compile valid Ada declarations of discriminated records with representation clauses, however minor "fudges" to the code were sufficient to overcome the problems.

No problems in writing portable Ada code were encountered, although the existing MASCOT Kernel needed modification. A bug in the compiler in its handling of unknown pragmas prevented the Kernel from being completely portable.

The VAXAda compiler and linker were substantially faster than the RTAda E68 compiler, binder and linker, and used considerably less disc space, which might be expected when comparing the performance of the DEC Compiler, hosted and targeted to a VAX and VMS , with the 68030 cross compiler targeted to the RTAda/OS which used ARTX.

The MASCOT3/Ada transformation used for the project maps every MASCOT component to an Ada generic package, which leads to extensive recompilation with either compiler after a minor change. This factor could also have a serious impact on development times for a large project. Consideration should be given to this point when selecting the compiler for a project, and when deciding whether this MASCOT3/Ada mapping should be used.

Discriminated record types were widely used in the implementation, particularly for event messages. The problem with these is that Ada forbids that the discriminant be assigned to or changed except as part of a complete assignment to the record. Such an assignment requires an aggregate specifying the value for every record field. If each variant of the record were completely different, this might be quite acceptable, but in this implementation it was the norm for most fields to be common to several variants, with only a few differences. Providing full aggregates for each case resulted in numerous replications of the same lines of code, expanding the size of the program and leading to extra work (and the possibility of errors) if changes were required.

A particular example of this problem occurred in the definition of LRR messages, which include 3 variants for New Contacts, Repeat Contacts and Dead-Reckoning positions. All 3 variants contain exactly the same information. Originally these were given separate discriminant values, however later the declaration was changed to use only one discriminant value UPDATE, and to distinguish the variants by a local field UPDATE_VARIANT. By doing this, 2 lengthy aggregate assignments could be removed from the network sender and receiver servers.

Many of the MASCOT3 components used in the Host program were identical except for the event data type. One possibility considered was to make the components common, operating on the portmanteau data type SENSOR_EVENTS of which the various event types are variants. This would have meant writing code to deal with nested discriminants, which would have compounded the problem described above, and this possibility was rejected.

The exception handlers were provided on all access procedures and in every activity root procedure, so that some clue could be gained as to where an exception originated. Even so, numerous bugs had to be found with no more guidance than an "others in procedure XXX" message. The inability of Ada to allow an "others" exception to be identified is a considerable omission, which appears to have been recognised by other developers, as several references to the problem have been made in submissions to the Ada 9X committee.

This problem was limited by including handlers for as many named exceptions as were thought probable at each point. These list were seldom exhaustive, and their presence expands and obfuscates the code.

Times recorded, to the nearest minute, were:

Compiler	Compile System Only	Compile All Multi-Files	Compile All Single Files	Bind	Link
VAXAda	16	70	41	N/A	5
RTAda E68	68	137	FAILED	11	23

(During these tests, the compilers, binder and linkers were run with default qualifiers except for the VAX Ada compiler which was run with /DEBUG).

The RTAda E68 compiler required substantially more disc space for the object code which it created than the VAXAda compiler. As a comparison, for the 3 variants of the Target program, the requirement in disc blocks is:

	VAXAda	RTAda E68
Object Library	10302	31747
Program files	3015	5589
Total	13317	37346

The MASCOT3 to Ada mappings used by the Code generation process create a generic package for every MASCOT3 component. If any change is made to the implementation of such a package, both compilers require that all enclosing packages are recompiled as well. The enclosing subsystems are no great problem, as they are entirely structural, so usually small, and compile quickly. Unfortunately the top-level system package must also be recompiled, which is not quick. This is an inherent drawback of the MASCOT3/Ada mapping used.

As a result, even a trivial change to a component leads to a major recompilation. From the above figures for compilation speed, the minimum cycle times to recompile the System package and to re-link the Target program, which represent the lower bound of the time to cure a trivial bug, would be:

- VAXAda compiler 21 minutes
- RTAda E68 compiler 102 minutes

It is understood from ARE that the most recent issue of VAXAda (version 2.1) no longer suffers from this recompilation problem, so that a change to a package implementation requires only a re-link, which will dramatically accelerate the debugging cycle.

Testing

Low level algorithms are most conveniently tested in non-MASCOT stand-alone harnesses, as these are much quicker and more flexible to develop. The harnesses should be treated as throw-away items, and the testing that they provide should be reproduced in later MASCOT test harnesses.

Groups of interacting components should be tested as complete subsystems, rather than as individual components. The component and subsystem design should take into consideration the need for testing in this way and should provide the necessary test interfaces.
Test harnesses should annotate the test log output to assist in output verification.

Debugging

The VAX debugger was generally useful but a bug prevented it from examining the global data in generic packages, which hampered debugging of MASCOT IDA's. The Telegen E68 debugger was unable to cope with Ada generics and could therefore not be used in debugging the MASCOT components in the system, which are all generic packages.

Exceptions

The MASCOT 3 to Ada mapping provides little help if an exception propagates back to the top level in an activity, as it is merely reported as an unknown exception. It is not possible to identify which exception it is, or where it was raised. To assist in debugging it was decided that exceptions should not be allowed to propagate more than could be avoided, so that the point where the exception was raised could be localised. An exception handler was therefore provided in every Access Procedure and in the Root procedure of each activity. Where appropriate, inner blocks with their own exception handlers are also used.
The action taken in the handlers is to call the MASCOT FATAL_ERROR procedure to report the exception. Specific handlers identifying the exception are provided for the standard Ada exceptions, such as CONSTRAINT_ERROR, and for any exception which is known to be likely at that point, such as the exceptions for the network interface package STREAM_IO in the Internet servers. An "others" handler is provided in every case.
Early testing caused this strategy to be modified slightly when it was realised that FATAL_ERROR itself raises SCHEDULER.FATAL. This could cause a cascade of further "others" exception errors to be generated in enclosing exception handlers. All handlers were therefore modified to re-raise FATAL without any error report. Exception SCHEDULER.END_ROOT is similarly re-raised to prevent spurious error reports for an activity which terminates itself.

Performance

The system was unable to cope with the message traffic generated by the ARE example scenario SCENARIO1_MAXI, but could cope with simpler scenarios generating a lower rate of message traffic. The problem seems to be in the communications between the Host and Target programs as event messages build up in the Host databases, during which time the Target processor was substantially idle. This problem will require further investigation. Some preliminary response times were measured. These times are taken from the Host program log, and are the time elapsing between a CIW Simulator "About to Attack" message, and a "Veto Attack" command from the CIW Display. They were well within the requires responce time.

Asynchronous I/O

As a consequence of the strategy in the MASCOT 3 Kernel used for the project, any MASCOT activity performing some activity which causes it to become I/O held prevents any other activity from running. This is because the Kernel maps each activity to an Ada task, and only allows one task to be runnable at any time (the underlying Ada Run Time Systems provided for both DEC Ada and Ready Systems Ada allow Ada tasks to run asynchronously, so this problem is specific to the MASCOT

Kernel implementation). In particular, calls to the Internet interface can become blocked for very long periods (minutes) if a communication link has not been established, which could paralyse the whole MASCOT system. To avoid this, it is necessary that activities performing such I/O calls be temporarily detached from the MASCOT scheduler, so that another activity can be scheduled while the first is "blocked". When the blocked task re-starts, it can re-attach itself to the MASCOT scheduler and will thereafter continue to be run under the control of the scheduler. The operations of detaching and re-attaching to the scheduler are simply performed using procedures DE_QUEUE and RE_QUEUE in the Kernel SCHEDULER package. (The Kernel itself uses the same technique to detach activities calling the MASCOT Delay primitive while the Ada task performs an Ada delay.)
It must be borne in mind that the MASCOT Kernel is written on the assumption that only one activity can be running at any one time, and it may not be secure if a detached activity is allowed to make further calls to Kernel primitives other than to RE_QUEUE itself. A possible source of error in this respect arises where the I/O operation can raise an exception. If this occurs, the RE_QUEUE procedure call may be by-passed which could lead to the activity running, and making calls to the Kernel, for example to FATAL_ERROR, whilst not under the control of the scheduler. This can have catastrophic consequences. The solution is to ensure that all DE_QUEUE/RE_QUEUE sequences occur in a block with exception handlers which contains a RE_QUEUE call for every possible exception by means of an un-named "raise".

GKS

The GKS model is modal, that is to say the action to a particular command may depend on the sequence of preceding commands. This may cause difficulties in a multi-tasking situation where more than one task attempts to interact with the display unit performing a succession of operations interleaved in an arbitrary manner. The solution is to protect access to the VARS display by a control queue in the VARS_GKS IDA, so that the various MASCOT activities which interact with the display only do so in a serial fashion.
This solution is effective, but may not be the most efficient as the granularity of interaction is quite large, ie once an activity had joined the control queue it may perform a fairly long sequence of interactions, during which time all other activities are locked out. Some further consideration should be given as to whether the queue could be held for smaller groups of operations, or whether the extra overhead of doing so would be counter-productive.
GKS does not provide any means to interrupt an activity when an operator interaction occurs, so it is necessary to poll for such events. As always, the polling interval must be chosen as a compromise between response time and polling overhead. One of the key measurements to be made using the system is the response time for a "Veto Attack" command, for which responses in the region of 2s are expected. In this context a polling interval of 200 ms seemed appropriate and this value was used.
GKS as provided on the VARS-H does not provide any text windowing model so that the textual displays on the screen have to be generated and maintained by the application software. This is inefficient and makes it difficult to maintain more than a minimal text window facility. As a result, the user interface is crude and unattractive. It seems unlikely that the GKS/VARS-H would be adequate in this respect for a real application.

7 EXPERIENCES

Not surprisingly, making a bare target system work can be significantly more difficult than for a self-hosted system on a full-function operating system. Standardised interfaces for infrastructure components, such as the Ada GKS binding used, make porting software much easier than interfacing directly to some proprietary package. It also allows target software to be developed on a more powerful host environment. Some Adas can handle asynchronous IO with tasking better than others. Ethernet with TCP/IP and RTAda-Net_E proved an acceptable means of distribution. Heterogeneous processor architectures and two completely different compilers technologies in one distributed system clearly needs care.

GKS is not an ideal graphics interface for a real-time system: ideally an interrupt driven input system is needed to enable an operator to respond immediately to an urgent situation; GKS's event driven input still requires polling from the driving system. The inherent use of implicit context prevents concurrent usage. The Mascot3 Organiser has some problems in that task-synchronous but system-asynchronous IO operations cause difficulties as it can only let one activity task run at a time so explicit IO decoupling is required. Because of the techniques used in the Organiser the Ada implementation must support tasks with comparatively large entry families.

Generics can cause difficulties unless bodies can be compiled without obsoleting their specifications. The Mascot3 mapping used here is particularly difficult in this respect as almost all the code is generic. Furthermore, systems with significant amounts of generic code can be hard to debug as some symbolic debuggers cannot handle their inherent complexity.

8 CONCLUSIONS

The prime objectives of the study are to demonstrate the feasibility or otherwise of the current MASCOT 3/Ada technology to produce a typical Command & Control System and to provide a benchmark facility for Ada compilers and run-time environments.

We have satisfied the requirement to assess the feasibility of the current MASCOT 3/Ada technology by producing a substantial body of Ada code and considering the problems in scaling up to a large system. It is our opinion, that with the minor modifications to MASCOT 3 and Ada as outlined below and with the automated support of a MASCOT 3 sensitive CASE tool, this technology will be applicable to the development of large, real-time systems.

There are still inadequacies in many Ada tools – especially debuggers. Limitations in tools can cause serious difficulties if there are direct conflicts of requirement versus capability. Problems encountered are often tool limitations rather than inadequacies of the Ada language itself. There will always be unsatisfactory ways of using particular language features and unfortunately tools often perform badly when these ways were originally unanticipated by the vendors.

The techniques and tools used on this project proved adequate, but for larger systems program generators must be able to produce incremental code changes: regeneration of the whole system is simply too much to do for every application-level change.

Overall, the project was able to draw together the various strands of earlier work and did succeed in its aims and demonstrated that:

1, Mascot3 *can* successfully map to Ada code for a project of non-trivial size,

2, Ada that is genuinely portable between different compilers *can* be written,

3, Heterogeneous processors *can* operate together even using different compilers.

REFERENCES

Ref 1: MASCOT3 with Ada Study, Ferranti FER-6798

Ref 2: A MASCOT3 Design Study, Foulkes, Coates, YARD YM5035A, Oct 1986

Ref 3: Ada in a MASCOT3 Design, Foulkes, MacLean, YARD YM5776 July 1987

Ref 4: Performance Implications of Ada in a MASCOT3 Design, MacLean, Murray, Hamilton, YARD YM5748, Feb 1988

Ref 5: MASCOT Design Support Environment - Final Report Chattam etc, Mar 1989, Alvey Project SE/044.

Ref 6: A Study in Automatic Code Generation, Hamilton, YARD YR3677 Jan 1989

Ref 7: Entry Limits Relieved, Elsom, ARE AXC4/CSA/1907/41/A, Dec 1989

Ref 8: The Implementation of a MASCOT3 Design in Ada - High-level Design,Hamilton, YARD YM 6707, Aug 1990

Ref 9: The Implementation of a MASCOT3 Design in Ada - Installation Guide Hamilton, YARD YM 6707, Aug 1990

Ref 10: The Implementation of a MASCOT3 Design in Ada - Experimenter's Guide, Hamilton,YARD YM 6707, Aug 1990

Ref 11: The Implementation of a MASCOT3 Design in Ada - Acceptance Tests O'Brien, YARD YM 6707, Aug 1990

Ref 12: Specification for Technical Publications for the Services MoD JSP188 Version 3.

Ref 13: The Official Handbook of MASCOT Version 3.1, Issue 1, Jun 1987

Ref 14: Scenario Generator Interface, Elsom, Oct 1989, ARE AX C4/CSA/1907/29/A.

Real Time Ada in the International Space Station Freedom

Gary Raines
NASA Johnson Space Center
Houston, TX 77058

Abstract: *This paper describes the Space Station Freedom, its Data Management System architecture, the on-board systems using this architecture, the design of the real time distributed Ada software, and methods of integration of the real time components. Problems encountered that are unique to the Ada programming language and their solutions will be addressed.*

1.0 Introduction

The Space Station Freedom Program is an international cooperative effort to achieve a permanent manned presence in space. The objectives are science and engineering research and a key step in the manned exploration of the solar system. International partners are the U.S. National Aeronautics and Space Administration (NASA), the European Space Agency (ESA), the Canadian Space Agency (CSA), and the National Space Development Agency of Japan (NASDA). Current schedules are for the launch of the first element in December 1995, achieving a manned tended capability in June 1996. Freedom will be permanently manned by November 1997, and a full international configuration will be achieved by September 1998. The assembly will continue through December 2000, at which time there will be sufficient resources to support a permanent crew of eight. Freedom is being designed for a life expectancy of 30 years.

The Freedom spacecraft is of a modular design which allows it to be constructed in space by repeated launches of its many components. These components include pressurized modules that will be used as crew living quarters, laboratories, equipment accommodations, and payload accommodations Data systems and software are updated with the launch of each of the modular components. Transition to the new software for each launch must be accomplished without compromising crew, vehicle, or mission safety or operations. This spacecraft assembly process has resulted in an incremental software development process to support it.

Ada was selected as the language for the flight systems before contract awards and before any work had begun. The cost of sustaining engineering of critical software for 30 years was a major factor in this decision. Many other factors influenced this decision including the incremental development process, requirements of critical real time systems, the difficulties caused by the geographic distribution of the many developers, and the desire to control development costs.

The Freedom program has recently undergone a design restructure, necessary to reduce resource utilization. These resources include launch weight, power consumption and cost. In spite of this restructure, the program has completed its preliminary design stage and has progressed into the detailed design phase. The system software development is leading application software development and the first release of the system software has been delivered for independent verification testing.

2.0 Data Management System Architecture

The Data Management System (DMS) is the first large scale distributed processing network designed for long term use in space. It provides a growth oriented base for automation to enhance the Station's operational capabilities. The DMS is physically distributed across the spacecraft to provide processor and networking resources as well as software services for use by the spacecraft's systems and payloads. The functional architecture of the DMS is shown in Figure-1.

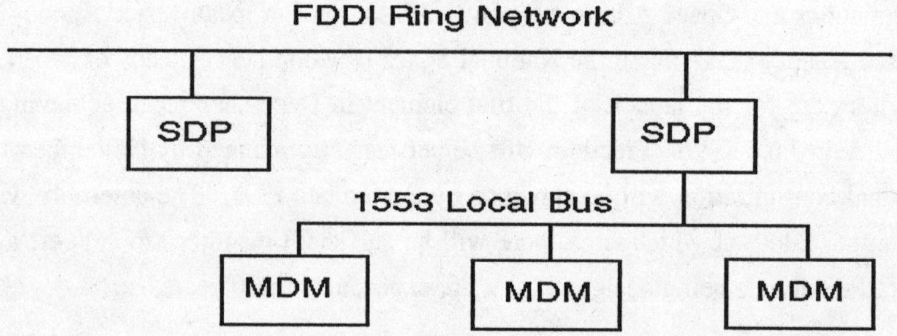

DMS Functional Architecture
Figure 1

The Freedom Data Management System Standard Data Processor (SDP) is based upon an Intel 80386 microprocessor utilizing the POSIX operating system. There are seven such standard processors on board, connected by a 100 megabit FDDI (Fiber Distributed Data Interchange) network. The processors also contain US_MIL-STD 1553 local busses for sensor and effector input/output. Real time data acquisition and distribution is achieved by Multiplexer-De-Multiplexers (MDM) on these local busses. These MDMs are also based upon the Intel 80386, but without the POSIX operating system. Mass storage units and crew displays and controls are also a part of the DMS.

The Freedom program chose to adhere to international data systems standards whenever possible, and to U.S. standards and industry standards. These standards were selected to insure interoperability and to allow for re-use of existing, proven software. Standards chosen include:

- Ada programming language,
- POSIX operating system (with Ada bindings),
- ISO/OSI family of network standards,
  (International Standards Organization / Open Systems Interconnect)
- X-Windows graphical user interface, and
- CCSDS telemetry standards
  (Consultive Committee for Spacecraft Data Systems).

The DMS software is physically distributed across the hardware items. The software is integrated into a consistent operational environment and command and control framework. The software architecture is modular and layered such that the details of interfaces and the physical location of shared or dedicated resources are transparent to the user.

The objectives of this DMS architecture are to allow operation during spacecraft assembly, interoperability with international partners, growth, technology update, non standard processors for payloads and experiments, and to control development costs.

3.0 The Spacecraft Systems

The DMS architecture is segregated into two parts: 1) the core systems necessary for the safe keeping of the crew and operations, and 2) payloads - which are its mission. This segregation was chosen to allow payload software to be developed independently of the core systems and not invalidate core systems testing every time payloads are changed. The U.S. core systems are:

- Communications and Tracking,
- Thermal Control,
- Environmental Control and Life Support,
- Guidance/Navigation/Control,
- Propulsion,
- Electrical Power,
- Mechanisms,
- Mobile Transporter,
- Extra Vehicular Activity/Air Lock, and

- Crew Health Care.

All of these systems utilize software as part of their design. As each system is developed by a separate contractor, the original design called for each system to have its own standard data processor. The power, weight, and volume burden of the associated DMS hardware was prohibitive, so after restructured design, two processors are shared by all core systems with two backup processors. The current estimate of the size of the core systems software is 736,000 source lines of new code, plus 490,000 of modified commercial off the shelf code, for a total of 1,226,000 lines of source code.

The U.S. payloads are separated from the core systems by means of a separate FDDI network with a high speed network bridge interconnecting them. Payloads may utilize a standard data processor or a processor of their choice. Interoperability is achieved through utilization of the above standards.

The Canadian design uses another standard data processor for the Mobile Servicing Centre. The European and Japanese modules have their own data processing systems, with interoperability achieved through utilization of the standards outlined above, and a network gateway.

4.0 Real Time Design

The execution efficiency of Ada generated code was an initial concern, but compiler maturity was expected to solve this problem, and it did. NASA selected a set of benchmarks of typical Freedom applications. These benchmark programs were compiled using the available compilers that targeted the Intel 80386. From this group, the two best were chosen, and more detailed tests were performed. Both compilers, Alsys Ada and DDC-I Ada, clearly demonstrated that current compiler designs have achieved sufficient efficiency of generated code execution to support real time requirements. Alsys Ada was selected, even though both compilers more than met requirements.

Raw execution speed alone, however, is not sufficient to insure correct operation of real time systems. Correctness depends upon the time at which outputs are available. Spacecraft systems require concurrent tasking with a scheduling mechanism to insure events occur at the correct time. This scheduler must assure that all tasks begin execution at the correct time and then perform their functions within the correct time period. Many of these time constraints are critical. The system also must be predictable enough that it can be analytically determined if the time constraints can be met. These tasks may be periodic tasks that must complete execution within a set clock period or aperiodic tasks that must complete within a set time from an event. One short coming of the Ada language is the lack of direct support of these requirements. Fortunately, methods to satisfy these requirements exist, such as Rate Monotonic Scheduling (RMS), Priority Ceiling Protocol, and the Catalogue of Interface Features and Options (CIFO).

4.1 Rate Monotonic Scheduling

C. Douglass Locke points out, in his case study of a Generic Avionics Platform [LOC90], that several currently held rules of thumb for the use of Ada in hard real time systems are violated when the system design is based upon "the Ada language *as it was designed to be used*, rather than continuing the practice of avoiding the very constructs Ada's designers created to meet real time requirements." By using a design methodology which results in complete predictability of real time response, he determined that the following methods could be used for design with tasks:

- Ada tasks can be used to protect shared data (not just for concurrency),
- Rendezvous can be used for system synchronization and for mutual exclusion,
- Periods and response times are not constrained to integral multiples of each other,
- Rather than severely limit the number of tasks, the tasking paradigm is used to separate functional concerns from each other as well as from timing constraints.

The technique used for real time design with "Ada as it was designed to be used" is the Rate Monotonic Scheduling (RMS) algorithm.

Rate Monotonic Scheduling was selected as the real time scheduling algorithm for Freedom software. RMS was first defined by C. L. Liu and J. W. Layland [LIU73]. It is a priority based preemptive schedule algorithm in which priorities are inversely proportional to the period for a set of periodic processes. Preemptive processes with bounded execution time can be assured of completing if total processing load never exceeds a predetermined percentage. This algorithm can be extended to aperiodic processes as well.

It is a natural tendency for systems designers to assign priorities to tasks so that the most critical tasks have the highest priorities. Although it seems intuitively correct, it is not the correct approach if predictable time constraints are required. The RMS methodology is to assign task priority based upon the cycle rate at which the task is to be scheduled. The highest priorities are assigned to the tasks that have the highest cycle rate.

L. Sha and J. Goodenough [SHA90] describe the use of RMS with Ada, and present a theorem showing that the upper limit of processor loading approaches 69% as the number of tasks increase. For a randomly chosen task set, the likely bound is 88%.

The DMS scheduler design implementation results in each task containing a loop that contains some kind of scheduling statement. This statement may be a periodic or on-update I/O command, or a scheduling event. When an event occurs or I/O is complete, the task performs the processing associated with the event and returns to the top of the loop to wait for the condition to be satisfied again.

For example, an application that must periodically compute a value from sensors and provide an output to another task would appear as follows:

```
Application Task one
     Open (Handle, ( Sensor A,
                             Sensor B,
                             Sensor C),
          Cyclic);
     loop
          Read (Handle);
          System_data:=function_of (A,B,C);
          Write (System_data);
     end loop;

Application Task two
     Open (Handle,
          System_data,
          On-Update);

     loop
          Read (Handle);
                    System_data now available for computation
     end loop;
```

In this example, each task requests DMS data service by the Open command which returns a handle for reference in the Read command. The cyclic control of the actual I/O command is maintained by DMS services.

Task one is synchronized by the Read statement to the cyclic data rate of Sensors A, B, and C. The task is held at the Read statement until the input cycle is complete. Task two is synchronized to Task one, but here the system is told to wait "On_Update" which makes it aperiodic. The actual cycle rates are contained in the table describing object attributes (described later).

4.2 Priority Ceiling Protocol

RMS assumes that high priority tasks can preempt lower priority tasks. This means that low priority tasks cannot block tasks with a higher priority for a significant period of time. The current Ada specification allows unbounded priority inversion.

Priority inversions are possible any time there is a contention for resources among tasks of different priorities. One such situation is when tasks hold access to a shared resource while executing in a critical section. System queues, such as message queues used in a client/server architecture, are another source of priority inversion. Ada's definition says that a Select statement can choose arbitrarily from several alternative tasks. If the Select is not based upon priority of the tasks in the queue, a priority inversion may occur. A server may be occupied with a low priority client, while a higher priority client is blocked.

Not only can the RMS scheduling not function with this problem present, but reliable execution cannot be assured due to the possibility of deadlocks. Deadlocks can occur when multiple tasks are competing for multiple resources and priority inversion occurs. A task may have already claimed one resource and be waiting for another resource, At the same time, a second task may have already claimed the resource the first task is waiting for and be waiting for the resource the first task has claimed. Neither task can proceed until the other task releases its resource.

The problem of unbounded priority inversion can be remedied by the Priority Ceiling Protocol [SHA90]. There are two components of this protocol. Priority Inheritance insures that when a task blocks the execution of higher priority tasks, the blocking task inherits the highest priority of all the tasks blocked. Second, no critical section must be allowed to start execution unless the section will always execute at a priority level higher than the level of any preempted critical section.

Priority Inheritance is implemented by modifications to the Run Time Environment. In addition, Ada tasks that share data must not call each other directly. Instead, they call a monitor task. Each monitor task contains an endless loop containing a single select statement with no guards. The ceiling protocol can be implemented as a modification to the Run Time Environment. However, for Freedom requirements it is sufficient to give these monitor tasks a priority that is just higher than the priority of any client task [SHA90]. The language specification is not violated with these modification, but the intended portability of the language may be sacrificed.

4.3 Run Time Environment Modifications

The Association for Computer Machines (ACM) Ada Run Time Environment Working Group (ARTWG) has addressed many of the problems related to using Ada in real time systems, and the Freedom community of professionals has been a leading participator in this activity. The ARTWG has produced a Catalogue of Interface Features and Options (CIFO) [ALL91]. This is a collection of features that can be added to the RTE that improve the language's ability to support real time operation. The extensions include some of these CIFO features along with other features:

- Non-preemptible sections
  (critical regions within code which can not be interrupted from execution),
- Special predictable delays,
- Pre-elaboration of program units,
- Task identifiers,
- Abortion by task identifier,
- Transmission of task identifiers between tasks,
- Dynamic priorities,
- Initialization and self test,
- Precision Time Service
- Message logging, and
- Task time slice with preemptive round-robin dispatching.

These modifications, along with RMS and Priority Inheritance, are to be a part of the commercially available compiler to insure product feedback from a large user base.

5.0 Integration of Real Time Components

Integration of Freedom software is complicated by the size of the software and the large number of participating organizations. The U.S. systems are being developed by three different prime contractors managed by three different NASA centers (Johnson, Marshall, and Lewis centers.) In addition, each prime contractor has numerous sub-contractors with the resulting organizations geographically distributed across the U.S. The long vehicle assembly process has the various pieces of software incrementally phased over several years. The necessity of sharing processors makes this integration more complicated.

The lack of Ada support of distributed processing across a network was another problem to be solved, and this turned out to be an integration problem more than a development problem. The Ada Language Reference Manual has nothing that directly supports cooperative process or programs running is separate machines, nor does it specifically support multiple programs in the same machine. However this does not preclude such an implementation.

Because of the very large number of software developers, a decision was made to design software around multiple Ada programs, even when these separate programs reside within the same machine. It was believed that this would reduce the interactions between systems. This would allow preliminary testing to proceed with missing software from other systems. Unfortunately, Ada provides no support for communications between programs or processors. To support these integration issues, NASA selected an object oriented table driven approach.

This approach is based upon a Run-time Object Data Base (RODB). This RODB is a resident table belonging to each program, specifying all of the objects and their attributes produced or consumed by that program. These objects include all:

- Sensor and effector data,
- Data that is shared among systems, or
- Data that must be available for display, telemetry, or check points.

A corresponding Master Objects Data Base Manager (MODBM) is the ground tool that manages the object data and builds the flight tables. In addition, it automatically produces all Ada Package Specifications for inclusion in the program to insure correct Ada definition of the data and attributes.

The normal interface control document that traditionally has been used to document the data that passes between programs or processors has been replaced in this system by the MODBM tool. Each system developer describes and enters into the data base all of the objects produced along with their attributes such as:

- Ada type,
- Valid modes,
- Data rates and limits,
- Logical name,
- Telemetry and Display details, and others.

Separate data bases are maintained for each stage of the spacecraft on-orbit assembly, and for special configurations for testing or training. The system developer also enters the objects required for consumption from other systems. The MODBM produces the Ada Package Specification for the consumer as entered by the data provider, thus insuring correct data specification. Some inheritance is provided, but the full object inheritance of traditional object oriented design is not.

Another feature of the RODB design was the placement of all common software functions normally performed by applications programs into the system software. Objects that are sensors and effectors are marked as such. The I/O operations is automatically performed by system software with the characteristics described by the object attributes. Limit sensing is performed automatically. Data required for consumption by outside processes is automatically transferred without action required by the sending or receiving application. Some object attributes, such as limit changes and physical addresses can be readily changed without modification of the application code of the producer or consumer.

One limitation of this design is that the Ada types of these objects is limited. Because the RODB represents the interface to the world outside of Ada, the data must obviously be exported from Ada. In order to do this all Ada types to be used must be known by the RODB and the MODBM and be pre-defined. This is not a serious limitation, but does limit some rich Ada type features such as discriminated record, variant record, and access types. It also requires that the exact physical construction of complex Ada types be fixed and understood. This limitation is really the result of multiple Ada programs across multiple processors, not the RODB design.

The software build process - that is the process of producing a mass memory image for a specific mission - is then the process of bringing together all of the identified programs specified for the mission, along with the related RODB tables. Then display formats. telemetry formats and other required data files are integrated. The correct version of each is verified by the MODBM tools. The definition of mission in this context goes beyond a physical launch, and means any time the mission of the spacecraft changes and requires a different software configuration. The new configuration is up-linked by telemetry to the mass memory, and the last version is archived on the mass memory as a back up in case of problems.

6.0 Conclusion

The support of real time multiple programs and processors by Ada is limited, and is a serious problem. Many features that are currently being proposed for Ada 9X would have been convenient, but the available features defined by Rate Monotonic Scheduling, Priority Ceiling Protocol, and the ACM ARTWG CIFO were considered essential to this real time application of Ada. More mature interfaces with other evolving standards would have aided this effort, such as standard interfaces with POSIX, OSI networks, and graphical user interfaces.

Regardless of these shortcomings, the best method of designing real time systems with Ada is to use the language as it was design to be used - that is by taking advantage of the Ada tasking model. The Run Time Environment extensions defined by the ARTWG, the Priority

Ceiling Protocol, and the Rate Monotonic Scheduling algorithm are the tools that allow the Ada tasking model to work in real time.

The decision to use Ada for Freedom flight software has undergone intense scrutiny, especially during the major design restructure and cost scrub exercises. The Ada decision has held since its characteristics and attributes compliment the management and technical problems that have been encountered. Some overhead, especially in the memory utilization area, has been a liability, but is probably no greater than could be expected with other high order languages. Lower order languages are considered unmanageable in such a large project. Performance issues are still yet to be proven. However current data indicates that it is in acceptable limits. The compiler author is still improving the performance figures. Ada compiler improvements such as RMS and CIFO have also been made and all of these improvements will be offered as part of their commercial product.

REFERENCES

[ALL91] D. Allen et al. Catalogue of Interface Features and Options for the Ada Runtime Environment, in Ada Letters, Vol XI, No 8, Fall 1991.

[LIU73] C. L. Liu and J. W. Layland. Scheduling Algorithms for Multi-programming in a Hard Real-Time Environment, in JACM Vol. 20, No. 1, pp 46-61, January, 1973.

[LOC90] C. Douglass Locke et al. Predictable Real-Time Avionics Design Using Ada Tasks and Rendezvous: A Case Study, in Ada Letters, Vol X, No. 9, Fall 1990.

[SHA90] Lui Sha and John B. Goodenough. Real-Time Scheduling Theory and Ada. IEEE Computer, Vol 23 No. 4, pp53-62, April 1990.

MANAGING ADA OBJECT-ORIENTED DEVELOPMENT

John A. Anderson
SYNETICS
8233 Old Courthouse Road
Vienna, Virginia 22182 USA
1 (703) 848-2550

John D. Sheffler*
The MITRE Corporation
7525 Colshire Drive
McLean, Virginia 22102 USA
1 (703) 883-6354
sheffler@mitre.org

ABSTRACT

Many object-oriented methods focus on the technical aspects of constructing Ada software but lack the management controls necessary for mitigating the cost, schedule, and technical risks of a project as a whole. The lack of management control is often attributed to object-oriented development's "iterative" nature. For object-oriented development to be practical on large-scale projects, it is essential that it reduce the risks of software development. This paper describes specific project management support built into an object-oriented life-cycle methodology that has been successfully used on several Ada efforts. The paper specifies how object-oriented modeling can control complexity and support management in requirements traceability, project planning and tracking, and configuration control.

1. INTRODUCTION

The introduction and adoption of the Ada language has helped push object-oriented technologies from the academic community into large-scale industrial software development. Many proponents of object-oriented concepts anticipated a rapid increase in software quality and productivity as a result of this introduction, but continue to be sadly disappointed. Developers of large-scale software systems desire to exploit the technology advances of object-orientation, but the software community has yet to agree upon a set of terminology, processes, and products that would effectively reduce the risk of applying these new technologies.

---

* This paper represents work done by the author before joining the MITRE Corporation.

The unanticipated schedule slips and cost overruns that have occurred on many large-scale Ada development efforts may actually be a natural result of the methods being applied (although some proportion can be attributed to the increased learning curve associated with the paradigm shift from earlier methods). These methods, while technically sound for constructing Ada software, consider object-oriented development an "incremental, iterative" process. One prominent author suggests that "round-trip Gestalt Design" is the foundation of the process of object-oriented design and that it is orthogonal to traditional waterfall life-cycle approaches [4]. The authors of this paper strongly oppose this position. The software *architecture* determines whether a system is object-oriented; a phased development process *can* be used to develop it; and it *is* possible to have such a process that does not impede creativity. Industry acceptance of object-oriented methodologies will be based not only on how well they address technical requirements, but on how well they address management's needs to plan, monitor, and deliver cost-effective software systems in a controlled environment.

This paper documents the management concepts behind an object-oriented life-cycle methodology developed and applied on projects delivered under DOD-STD-2167A guidelines. Various object-oriented methods were investigated, applied, and refined to establish a language-independent object-oriented development process that reduces risks across the entire life cycle. Many aspects of this methodology have been applied on several government Ada projects with a great deal of acceptance by developers and customers alike [1] [13]. To provide a context for the management approaches described later in the paper, Section 2 outlines some basic concepts and terminology that have resulted from this work. Sections 3, 4, and 5 discuss the models applied for object-oriented requirements analysis, preliminary design, and detailed design, focusing on the characteristics of the models that support project management. Section VI summarizes the benefits of this approach and the challenges ahead.

2. BASIC CONCEPTS

The difference between object-oriented and traditional, functionally-oriented approaches to software development is predominantly one of mind-set, which subsequently influences the software organization and development process. Functionally-oriented software is organized into functions that act upon data, and experience has demonstrated that such software is expensive to maintain. Object-oriented approaches, which organize the software into interacting objects, evolved from academic research in software engineering and from analysis of basic characteristics of good software construction to address common difficulties of earlier experiences in software development and maintenance.

An object is anything that can be perceived and is relatively stable in form; it must be denotable by name, have a well-defined context and interface, and exhibit a persistent internal state; finally, an object and its operations cannot be considered to be independent of one another. This intimate association of an object with its operations is the hallmark of object-oriented software. An object-oriented system development approach is one that models the requirements or solution based on the entities (i.e., objects) within the application problem domain, provides a balanced view of functional and data characteristics, and establishes or enforces rules that ensure the integrity of a system's characteristics throughout its life cycle. These definitions were established to be sufficiently general to address all phases of system and software development, and sufficiently specific to reflect the desired quality goals of effective software engineering. Reference [2] explains the fundamental concepts of abstraction, decomposition, and modeling in an object-oriented context and in terms of these definitions. The object-oriented methods and techniques within this methodology were designed to employ these concepts to reduce technical, schedule, and cost risks and to increase the manageability of complex system development.

Models constitute an essential component of structured development methods and have a central role in this methodology. This object-oriented methodology is "structured" in that it produces models of requirements and software via a well-defined step-by-step approach, and results in a software architecture that is understandable and maintainable. The methodology incorporates features of earlier traditional "structured" development approaches [7] [17], which apply modeling as a tool to document and communicate decisions before investing labor-intensive resources in software construction; however, the models used are object-oriented instead of functionally-oriented. Models of requirements, designs, and code endow these nebulous elements of software development with attributes that quantify their role within the system, their significance, their size, their complexity, etc.

Most importantly, the models establish tangible products that can be measured and placed under configuration management (CM). CM constitutes the backbone of software management because it facilitates control and monitoring of the development process in terms of concrete components. CM is concerned with identification of the system's components, status accounting of the development products, change control, and auditing to verify and validate the system [3]. The goal of CM is not to inhibit creativity but to ensure that development proceeds smoothly in spite of dynamic changes to requirements and design decisions. CM extends beyond organizational boundaries and formal deliverable documentation to the dynamic development process; therefore, developmental support for CM must be specifically defined for a methodology to be effective.

Although this methodology, like other object-oriented development approaches, closely associates software modules with corresponding problem domain entities, it recognizes a fundamental difference between problem and solution domain objects. Whether the objects are created in a phased development process, an iterative prototyping environment, or a reverse-engineering activity, different sets of models are recommended to represent information particular to a user's problem, the logical system solution, or the software modules used to implement that solution. The following sections briefly describe the models from this methodology and focus on the project management characteristics that were incorporated into them. Reference [2] discusses the technical content of the models and their development process, comparing and contrasting features with those of other published object-oriented approaches including Coad [6], Booch [4], HOOD [10], and Rumbaugh [12]. Refer to [13] for experiences using the methodology and how it improved Ada development on a NASA project.

3. REQUIREMENTS ANALYSIS

3.1. Object-Oriented Analysis Models

This methodology currently uses the object-oriented requirements analysis (OORA) method originated by Shlaer/Mellor [15] [16] because of its early availability and its innovative use of traditional modeling techniques. The authors' past four years of experience with the method has confirmed its technical effectiveness [1], but several refinements were required to support project management. The Shlaer/Mellor method integrates several traditional analysis models into a cohesive representation of the problem domain. As with several other OORA methods, the models document problem domain entities (i.e., objects), their behavior, and their functionality. Four interrelated models of requirements are constructed and refined to eliminate ambiguities, contradictions, and omissions based on a set of method rules: the Information Model, the State Model, the Process Model, and the Object Communication Model. Figure 1 illustrates the relationships among the requirements analysis models.

An Information Model illustrates the data and entities within a problem domain as object classes and their interrelationships. The Information Model is based upon the Entity-Relationship-Attribute (ERA) model [5]. The relationships represented are more than just the data dependencies often modeled in database analysis, but include constraint relationships similar to those discussed in [11]. For each object class in the Information Model, a State Model may be constructed. State Models apply the basic concepts of traditional state transition diagramming to model the behavior of the objects in the Information Model. Process Models use data flow diagrams to depict processing and data flow occurring within each state in the State Models. The data stores represented in the Process Models are the objects described in the Information Model.

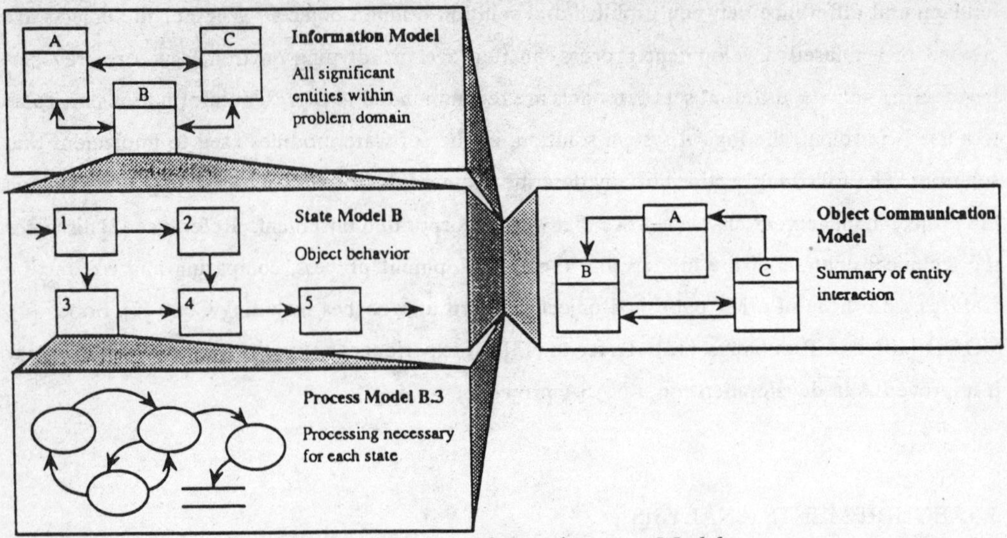

Figure 1. Integrated Requirements Models

An Object Communication Model (OCM) provides an overall view of behavior in the problem domain by illustrating the object classes with the significant events that cause state transitions.

3.2. Management Perspective

The Shlaer/Mellor OORA models have intrinsic characteristics that address some management concerns; other management "hooks" were incorporated into the models for methodology support. Whether intrinsic or augmented, these characteristics need to be explicitly defined in a Software Development Plan or their value may be overlooked. In many cases, industrial standards like DOD-STD-2167A [9] were used to identify the information needed to support management and acted as criteria for the initial selection of methods. Data Item Descriptions (DIDs) for deliverable documents were reviewed and tailored to correlate their requirements with the information represented in the methodology models. [18] describes the approach used on several U.S. government projects to document object-oriented requirements.

Technical Risk Management. The requirements for a system are the most critical aspect of an effort as all other activities are dependent upon their completeness, correctness, and consistency. The requirements must be unambiguously understandable by analysts, customers, designers, and testing staff. Most OORA methods extend beyond specifying functionality to model data as well; however, the models may be independently defined. Resolving inconsistencies among the Shlaer/Mellor models (identified by their specific rules) acts as a catalyst for analysts eliciting requirements and resolutions from users.

Most data and object-oriented methods suffer a common difficulty in reviewing an ERA model (on which the Information Model is based): the model is typically large and complex. Therefore, although the Information Model is the central unifying model for the Shlaer/Mellor method, the OCM was selected to guide the reviewers through the requirements. This methodology includes an OCM description to trace events that correspond with the higher-level (typically functionally-oriented) system requirements to be satisfied. The added description not only verifies the inclusion of all system requirements, but acts as a guide for readers who can trace processing from object to object.

Configuration Management and Progress Tracking. The Shlaer/Mellor method lends itself well to CM. Modifications were made to establish precise identification of individual requirements that preserve their context for better understanding. The Information, State, and Process Models can be collectively viewed as a hierarchical decomposition of the problem domain requirements with the Information Model at the top, the State Models at the next level, and the Process Models on the lowest leaves of the tree. Ward [18] organizes and numbers the requirements based on this hierarchy in a manner that permits unique identification and accounting of specific requirements. Each processing requirement is associated with an object in the problem domain (i.e., the entity in the Information Model) and the conditions under which the process must be invoked (i.e., a specific state from that object's State Model).

This hierarchical numbering of the models and requirement elements facilitates change control and impact analysis during development. The object orientation collects closely related requirements from the problem domain together, while the hierarchy reflecting their interdependencies limits the impact of changes on the overall requirements specification. For example, if a change is required to an object in the Information Model, that object's corresponding State Model is re-evaluated (along with other objects sharing relationships). Similarly, required changes in a State Model are localized to the Process Models associated with those changed states.

Similar to the system requirements verification process, software requirements must be allocated and accounted for throughout the life cycle. Decomposing requirements into these discrete models and elements allows management to more effectively track their satisfaction during design and implementation, especially when object-oriented development is applied.

Estimation and Projection. Decomposing requirements into these discrete, tangible models allows management to monitor progress during the analysis phase and helps project the scale of effort necessary for implementation. Earlier functional methods based projections on the number and complexity of processes specified during analysis; this object-oriented method captures, specifies, and accounts for all aspects of the requirements: information, behavior, and processing. With experience and historical data collection, better projections will become possible.

4. PRELIMINARY DESIGN

The aspect of this methodology that differentiates it from many other object-oriented development methodologies, is its focus on logical design. Other object-oriented development approaches progress from requirements directly to designing the actual software modules to be delivered, often relying on rapid prototyping and/or Program Description Language (PDL) construction very early in the design process. Our approach applies systematic problem solving to construct a language-independent, predominantly graphical, object-oriented solution that can be verified to satisfy the customer's requirements. This logical design identifies the objects that are *needed* in the solution and their required interaction with other objects. Developers are allowed to focus on creating the best physical software architecture to implement the objects in the target environment. The logical design models in this methodology have been proven detailed enough to support developers constructing a physical software architecture in Ada, and sufficiently understandable to facilitate technical and customer review before investing labor-intensive resources in software construction.

4.1. Object-Oriented Logical Design Models

A logical design is represented using a set of models that forms a comprehensive description of the system solution. Two kinds of primarily graphical models are used to document design decisions and illustrate the software architecture. An Object Structure Model (OSM) focuses on details about each of the object components in the design. A System Decomposition Model (SDM) illustrates the system as a whole by associating the objects into an overall software architecture and summarizing key information about those components.

Figure 2 illustrates that the logical design of the system is composed of layers of interacting objects that form a complete solution for a discrete portion of the problem. Each layer corresponds to a level of abstraction and each object is documented in its own OSM. Each OSM uniquely identifies and describes the object, specifies its interface, and documents its internal structure (i.e., lower-level objects with control and data flow) in user-oriented terminology. To assure a complete solution at each subsequent level of abstraction, every object is allocated a subset of the requirements and must satisfy or further allocate those requirements to lower-level objects. Figure 3 depicts an example OSM; the network of interacting objects (either subsystem or data) used to logically implement an object is graphically represented in an Object Structure Diagram, and details are textually documented in Object and Operation Descriptions.

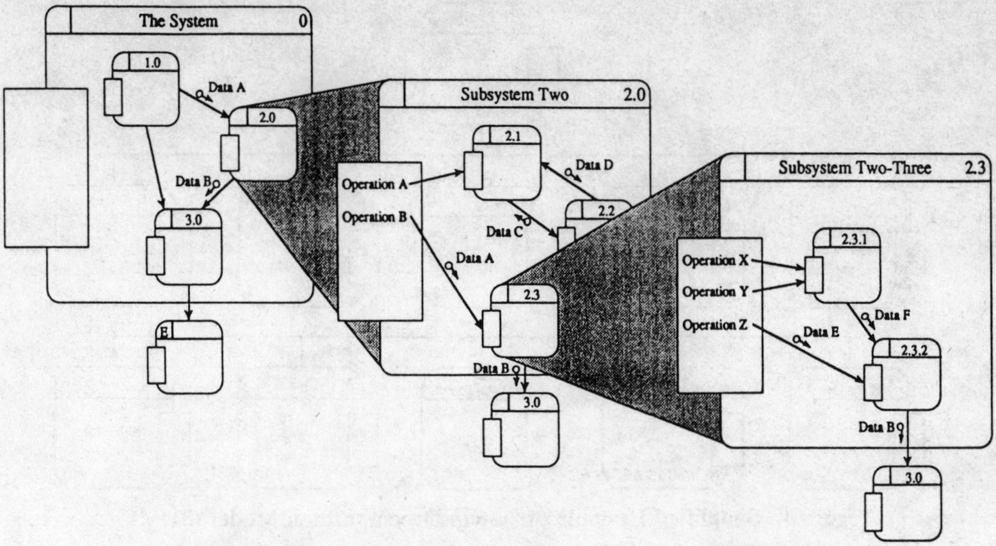

Figure 2. Object Decomposition Based on Levels of Abstraction

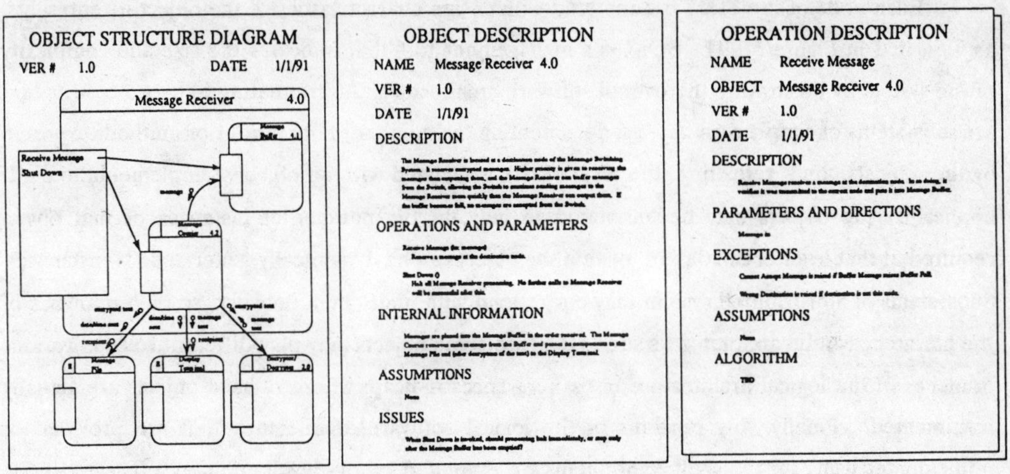

Figure 3. Example Object Structure Model (OSM)

While Object Structure Models focus on the component objects of the software solution, the overall design is summarized in a single SDM. This model provides a global hierarchical view of the layers of objects by illustrating how the Object Structure Models fit together to form a complete system. An example portion of a simplified SDM is illustrated in Figure 4. This hierarchy preserves the layered abstractions and object orientation of the design, while facilitating documentation production and project planning.

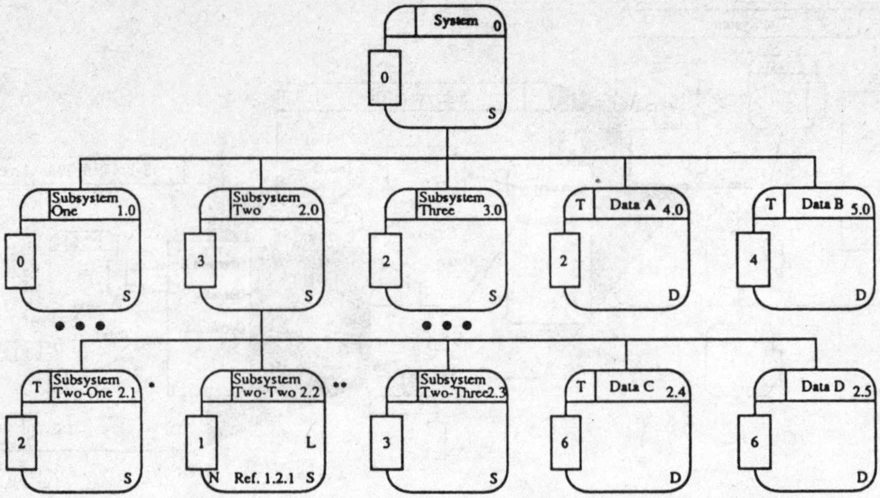

Figure 4. Simplified Example of System Decomposition Model (SDM)

Each node of the SDM is annotated with design characteristics of the object it represents, as indicated in Figure 5. The SDM is a management tool that indicates the size and complexity of the system by illustrating the overall software architecture, differentiating between objects that are subsystems or simply data objects, documenting the number of operations or methods exported by the objects, and reflecting the level of risk associated with an object's implementation. If applicable, the objects may be annotated to indicate the number of instances of that object required at that level of the design, or that the object can be dynamically generated (N instances). Subsystems in a distributed system may correspond with nodes on a network, so such branches of the hierarchy can be annotated as such. Because some objects may play different roles in various branches of the logical architecture, cross references indicate where re-used objects are actually documented. Finally, any portions of the logical software architecture that are provided or implemented using off-the-shelf components are annotated as non-developmental software (NDS).

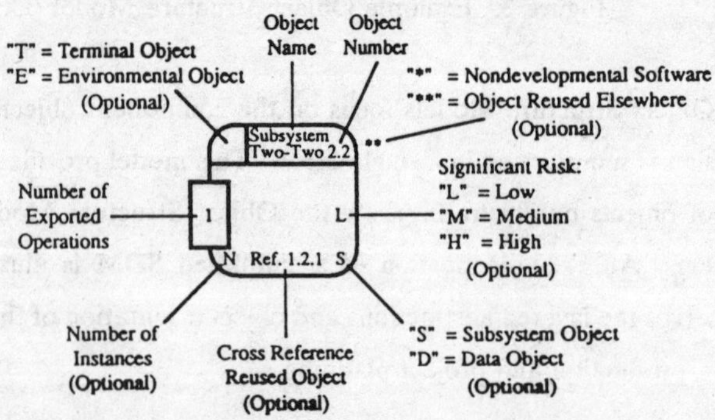

Figure 5. System Decomposition Model Node Key

4.2. Management Perspective

Technical Risk Management. An important feature of the OSM is that Object Descriptions contain sections to capture assumptions and/or issues identified as the system design evolves (see Figure 3). This information is critical to the manager's ability to monitor and quantify the overall technical risk of the project. Designers are encouraged to use these sections to immediately document and communicate their concerns as they arise. A complete SDM reflects these risks and associates them with individual objects in the hierarchy. Managers evaluate the SDM to determine how many of the objects in the design have risks associated with them, how well the risks are localized, and their degree of difficulty. The issues identified, localized, and quantified in the logical design are then worked into an effective risk mitigation plan for the detailed design and implementation phases.

Configuration Management and Progress Tracking. Objects and their corresponding models lend themselves especially well to configuration management. As utilized in Figures 2 and 3, the hierarchical organization based on their decomposition supports unique identification and numbering of design components. As a system is designed, the objects within the system decomposition proceed through several discrete states that are monitored to track development progress. Collectively examining the state of the objects within an evolving design provides insight into its stability and the overall project status. The states that an object progresses through during preliminary design are:

- **Identified**--An object becomes officially "identified" as a subsystem or data object when it appears on a higher-level (sub)system Object Structure Diagram, and its description and interface have been documented in an Object Description.
- **Defined**--An object is considered "Defined" when all internal objects at the next lower level of abstraction have been "Identified" and their interaction documented in a complete Object Structure Diagram.
- **Completed**--An object's design is considered "Completed" when its internal objects at *all* lower levels of abstraction are "Defined."
- **Finalized**--An object is "Finalized" when the complete system decomposition has been reviewed, required changes incorporated, and the final design approved.

Transition from one state to another occurs when the design, or parts thereof, are placed under baseline control after review and approval.

The object orientation built into the logical design models also limits the impact of change to localized portions of the software. Changes may occur in either an object's internal structure or its interface. When information hiding is used effectively, changes to an object's internal structure are localized to the object and its lower-level (logically internal) objects. When an object that is passed among other subsystem objects changes, those objects must also be re-evaluated. Finally, if an object's interface changes at a given level of the system, all other objects at that level must be re-evaluated to determine if the change has an impact on them. When an object appears in multiple places in the SDM, each occurrence must be re-evaluated at its particular location in the design. In some cases, a reused object may have to be specialized into distinct objects to address unique context-specific requirements. The status of the object components during development, the urgency of a proposed change, and the cost/benefit of making the change now versus later can be assessed, and an action plan established.

Estimation and Projection. The establishment of the logical architecture provides the first concrete information that can be used to project the size of the system and the effort necessary for its implementation. Prior to the construction of a logical architecture, the system's size, cost, and schedule can only be *estimated* based on historical data from previous projects, data collected from requirements analysis, customer cost limitation, etc. Until a solution is constructed, there are simply too many unknowns to establish reliable projections. The logical architecture, which represents a *complete* solution, can be used to quantify the size of the project in terms of the number of modules and units of code to be implemented, the number of lines of code to be produced, and the amount of documentation to be written. Because the models reflect the developers' assessment of technical risk at the object level, the relative technical risk associated with implementation of the system as a whole can also be quantified and documented.

Software size and cost are projected by associating a number of work and/or software units with each object in the SDM. (Work units may correspond directly with computer software units (CSUs) in some strategies.) Each object corresponds with a module in the final design. A subsystem object will generally require one CSU for each operation it exports, plus two units for the object structure itself (corresponding with the encapsulating module and its interface). Each data object may be considered a CSU in itself; however, in Ada, it may actually be implemented with several separately compiled subunits that encapsulate its data structure and operations. Using historical data from past projects that indicate the average number of lines of design language, code, or documentation associated with a CSU, the size of the overall system can be reasonably projected. Historical productivity rates can also be applied to the size projections to quantify and anticipate schedule and/or cost risks.

5. DETAILED DESIGN

Because the logical design constitutes a complete solution for the customer's problem, physical software architectural design and implementation can continue with substantially less technical risk. The developers use the logical design models to create a physical software architecture for the system that satisfies its intent. In a rapid prototyping environment, this next stage may actually result in final coding of various parts of the system. In a more phased development environment, a physical model of the software system would be created and reviewed before the final code is created. The models used to represent the physical software design depend on the implementation environment to be used for the final system. If a procedural language is to be used, the Ada programming language [8] is recommended as a PDL so that the physical architectural design can be analyzed and issues resolved early. If an object-oriented programming language is to be used, a class hierarchy is constructed.

5.1. Physical Software Design Models

Physical software architectural models may take several forms, but should represent sufficient information to allow coding to proceed with reasonable risk control. Ada-PDL can expressively represent detailed decisions regarding algorithmic logic and the language structures to be used. The logical design models have proven to be sufficient to support effective decisions with regard to implementation of objects in Ada-PDL using packages, generics, and/or abstract data types [13]. In addition to just constructing a physical software architecture, this life-cycle approach requires maintenance of the connections among requirements, logical design, and code. Thus, the correlation among logical design objects and the software modules used to implement them (usually represented by a matrix) is also an essential model of the physical software architecture. Since the logical design objects are explicitly allocated specific requirements, a clear connection between requirements and design is established. A fabric of understanding is woven throughout the system definition represented by requirements, logical design, and code.

5.2. Management Perspective

<u>Technical Risk Management</u>. In spite of the expressive power of the Ada language, systems built in Ada are quite difficult to understand from a system architecture viewpoint. Instead of relying on PDL, developers continue to use the logical design to discuss and illustrate the design in later reviews (although associated PDL or code can be provided whenever necessary). Customers and application experts can review changes to the logical design as detailed engineering activities progress. When additional detail is necessary, the logical architecture can be used to pinpoint a particular area of code to be investigated.

During physical software architectural design, the logical design can also be used to assess the technical risks of various constraints in the target environment. The SDM indicates the potential size and organization of the software modules, which can be compared to the hardware configuration and memory budgets associated with the target environment (e.g., virtual memory, distributed architecture, etc.). The Object Structure Models illustrate critical interfaces that must be implemented between modules, between processors, and across networks. Alternate strategies (e.g., specialized optimization, code overlays, and/or code swapping) can be identified to handle problems identified before the software is completed, thus reducing rework and surprises.

Configuration Management and Progress Tracking. Because the logical design preserves the user's viewpoint and organization of the solution, the logical models are critical in identifying and localizing requirements changes and/or associating issues with specific Ada modules within the physical software architecture [13]. Without a logical design as a guide, there is little indication of which modules should be examined when a problem occurs during integration, testing, and maintenance. The association between the logical and physical software architectures also improves insight into the development progress of the project. As the detailed design (or implementation) of each object is completed, its status is noted or updated on the SDM. Management gains a clear understanding of how much of the detailed design or code is completed, and which risks have been resolved or deferred. Frequent changes to Ada-PDL modules or code associated with a portion of the logical design may indicate a problem with those requirements or with the understanding of the logical design itself.

Estimation and Projection. Throughout the detailed design and implementation process, the effort and number of lines of PDL and code used to implement the objects in the logical architecture should be monitored. Productivity can be measured on a component by component basis as the physical designs are completed and/or code is produced. Many methods measure progress against an estimated number of the lines of code established at proposal time. Besides updating those estimates with a projection based on the initial logical design, the projections are adjusted as groups of objects are implemented. Variances on an object-by-object basis can be tracked, and updated projections for the overall project can be extrapolated [14] in an ongoing basis. Management acquires a capability to monitor and mitigate size, cost, schedule, and productivity risks on the project.

VI. CONCLUSIONS AND STATUS

The object-oriented approach and models described in this paper cannot be expected to solve all of the problems of software development, but do provide rigor required to plan, monitor, and control many aspects of large-scale object-oriented software projects. Object-oriented development is not "the antithesis of cookbook approaches," as Booch asserts [4], and need not be a "terribly unconstrained and fuzzy process." Well-planned, pragmatic application of these modeling techniques can achieve early and better understanding of the problem and solution, improve insight into the resources needed to completely deliver the system and its documentation, and reduce maintenance costs.

Object-oriented development must be manageable to be accepted in the mainstream of large-scale development. Management indicators and techniques must be explicitly incorporated into the software development plans and the development organization's operational environment to be effective. The technical practitioner is the primary agent for evolving object-oriented processes and products from state-of-the-art to practicality. Managers can increase the speed of that evolution by expecting proposed methods to support their planning, monitoring, and control activities, and by supporting their developers in identifying novel solutions to these challenges. With management and technical personnel working together, software production can eventually progress to software engineering.

VII. REFERENCES

[1] Anderson, John A. & Ward, Elaine S., "Technology Transfer: Experiences In Introducing Object-Oriented Methods to Government Projects," *Proceedings of the Eighth Washington Ada Symposium/Summer SIGAda Meeting, June 17-21, 1991*. ACM, Inc., 1991.

[2] Anderson, John A., Sheffler, John D., & Ward, Elaine S., "Manageable Object-Oriented Development: Abstraction, Decomposition, and Modeling," *Proceedings of Tri-Ada '91, October 21-25, 1991*. ACM, Inc., 1991.

[3] Bersoff, Edward H., et al., Software Configuration Management, An Investment in Product Integrity. Englewood Cliffs, NJ: Prentice-Hall, Inc., 1980.

[4] Booch, Grady, Object-Oriented Design with Applications. Menlo Park, CA: Benjamin/Cummings, Inc., 1991.

[5] Chen, Peter, The Entity-Relationship Approach to Logical Data Base Design. Wellsley, Massachusetts: Q.E.D. Information Sciences, 1977.

[6] Coad, Peter, & Yourdon, Edward, Object-Oriented Analysis, 2nd Edition. Englewood Cliffs, NJ: Object International, Inc., 1991.

[7] DeMarco, Tom, Structured Analysis and System Specification. Englewood Cliffs, NJ: Prentice-Hall, Inc., 1979.

[8] U.S. Department of Defense, Reference Manual for the Ada Programming Language, ANSI-MIL-STD-1815A-1983. Washington, D.C.: GPO, 17 February 1983.

[9] U.S. Department of Defense, Defense System Software Development, DOD-STD-2167A. Washington, D.C.: GPO, 29 February 1988.

[10] European Space Agency, HOOD Reference Manual, Issue 3.0. WME/89-173/JB. HOOD Working Group. The Netherlands: European Space Research and Technology Center, 1989.

[11] Mili, Hafedh, et al., "An Object-Oriented Model Based On Relations," *Journal of Systems Software*, 1990:12. Elsevier Science Publishing Co., Inc., 1990.

[12] Rumbaugh, James, et al., Object-Oriented Modeling and Design. Englewood Cliffs, NJ: Prentice-Hall, 1991.

[13] Schuler, M. P., "Evolving Object-Oriented Design, A Case Study," *Proceedings of the Eight Washington Ada Symposium/Summer SIGAda Meeting, June 17-21, 1991*. ACM, 1991.

[14] Schultz, Herman P., *Software Management Metrics*, ESD-TR-88-001. Bedford, MA: The MITRE Corporation, May 1988.

[15] Shlaer, Sally & Mellor, Stephen, Object-Oriented Systems Analysis, Modeling the World in Data. Englewood Cliffs, NJ: Yourdon Press, 1988.

[16] Shlaer, Sally & Mellor, Stephen, Object Life Cycles: Modeling the World in States. Englewood Cliffs, NJ: Yourdon Press, 1991.

[17] Yourdon, Edward, Techniques of Program Structure and Design. Englewood Cliffs, NJ: Prentice-Hall, Inc., 1975.

[18] Ward, Elaine S., & Anderson, John A., "Documenting Object-Oriented Requirements Analysis Understandably for DOD-STD-2167A," *Proceedings of the Structured Development Forum XI, April 30-May 3, 1990*. CSC, 1990.

Software Engineering, Ada and Metrics

Alison Wearing
Evisa Systems, 17 Orford Avenue
Disley, Cheshire, SK12 2BH, UK

1 Introduction

In the late 1970s and early 1980s there was a belief that if software could be developed using engineering practices then the software crisis could be overcome. The development of the software language Ada was seen as one solution and has done much to advance software development. However, there is still a software crisis despite all the new software engineering concepts, for example Object Oriented Design and Reuse, that have been encouraged by Ada.

Perhaps because there was little measurement of the software development process, we did not know the size of the problem in the first place. Measurement began, in earnest, when cost estimation models required information about the size of the proposed software system, and other cost driver information. Although many cost estimation models, for example Boehm's COCOMO [1], were based on data collected from projects, it quickly became obvious that in order for models to provide "accurate" estimates it was necessary to calibrate the models to a company's own software development environment. This demonstrated the need to collect software metrics.

Despite the need for calibrating cost estimation models and the desire to build software products according to engineering practices, the use of software development metrics has not been widely adopted. The improved visibility obtained by measurement allows an understanding of the software engineering process to be achieved and once this understanding has been gained then the process can be more successfully controlled. If necessary, changes can then be made to the process, as a result of the measurements made, which can be monitored by the continued measurement of the process.

This paper considers different aspects of metrics with respect to software systems, especially those built using the language Ada. It particularly focuses on how metrics can help software engineering, provides definitions for collecting metrics from software systems built in Ada and discusses the problems associated with data collection.

2 How metrics can help software engineering practices

There are many ways in which measuring the software development process can assist an individual organisation. The analysis can contribute to:

- the management of the project, for both the developer and the customer, in that greater visibility of the process is achieved;
- the training of project staff as trends, in the phases that errors are introduced, can be observed and hence training needs identified;
- improved cost estimation for future projects if costs, and associated information, are retained from past projects, leading to organisation–specific prediction models of cost and schedule;
- measurement of reliability and integrity, which provide further objective evidence to the customer of product quality;
- measurement of productivity (this is especially useful when evaluating the impact of a new method/tool; if the productivity is known when the method/tool is not used then the improvement/degradation from using the method/tool can be determined);
- setting goals for the project so that success in meeting these goals can be measured.

The measurement of the software development process will not improve it. Actions have to be taken based upon the results of analyses. There is little to be gained from the measurements if no actions are to result. However, actions can only be initiated if the results of the analyses are presented in such a form as to enable the necessary actions to be seen clearly. The level of detail provided in the results must be meaningful to the management who will authorise any necessary actions. It is also important that the measurement programme is supported throughout the organisation so that management are willing to authorise any actions based on the analysis results.

Once the metrics have been chosen it is necessary to provide definitions and counting rules so that the data collected is comparable. There are many definitions of metrics which can be provided irrespective of the application domain, for example effort used, faults found, type of fault. However, there are also definitions which are application domain specific. These are closely associated with the product and the process that developed it, for example size of design, size of code, structure of design (and hence complexity).

There are now cost estimation models, for example Boehm [2] and Reifer [3], which have been specifically designed for Ada applications and hence contain metric definitions applicable to Ada software. However, the terminology used by these models can seem inappropriate. As an example, the Asset R tools (developed by Reifer) use the term rendezvous as a measurement of size of requirement documents. To many engineers developing Ada software systems the term rendezvous is synonymous with the rendezvous defined by the Ada language. It would not be possible to measure the number of Ada rendezvous at the requirements analysis phase. However, the Asset R tool uses the term rendezvous to be a measure of concurrency. For example 'each handshake between processes or tasks' is counted as 1 rendezvous.

The use of more tailored definitions and counting rules should enable metrics collection to be more practical and the results obtained more accurate. Therefore modified definitions for measuring size and structure of the various products of the software engineering process for Ada software systems have been developed and are presented below. They are based on the work of Boehm, De Marco and Reifer and an in-depth knowledge of developing real-time systems.

3 Size Metrics

Before the proposed definitions for size metrics are given it is useful to examine why size metrics are useful. The size metric is used extensively to "normalise" other metrics. For example error rates are frequently given with respect to the size of the product, 10 errors per 1000 lines of code. The other most common use of size metrics is as an input to a cost estimation model. Generally, cost estimation models have required estimates of the size of the system to be built in terms of an estimate of the code to be produced, e.g. Boehm's COCOMO model.

Whether size is being used to normalise other metrics or as an input to a cost estimation model it is important that a measure of size is obtained for all products of the software development process and not just for the code. Once a size measure is available for all products then, for example, cost estimation can be repeated throughout the development lifecycle and hence more accurate estimates can be obtained for the later phases.

3.1 Requirements Analysis

During requirements analysis the calculation of "Function Points" [4] as a measure of product size has become very popular within the data processing community. The Function Point measure is a synthetic metric derived from base counts that can be extracted from a requirements document. Function Points are meant to reflect the user-view of the system and as such may be regarded as a measure of the size of the problem the software is intended to solve.

The following is a proposal for a size measurement, which is analogous to the Function Point base measurements, for the typical requirements of a real-time system. This size measure can be used during the initial cost estimation, perhaps at bid phase, for the system to be built because it is important to know the estimated cost of a piece of software whether it is being built for a particular customer (either internal or external) or as a package for "off-the-shelf" sales. Unless a good estimate of cost is known then it is not possible to accurately plan a project.

No of external input streams - this will include the number of sensors which provide input to the software system, probably using a hardware interrupt mechanism.

No of external output streams - this will include the number of devices driven by the software system, probably using a hardware interrupt mechanism.

Interrupt rates - for each external input stream and output stream the data rates, that is the number of interrupts per chosen interval of time, that can be expected. Values should be given for average and maximum rates.

No of concurrent activities - this is the number of different functions that need to be carried out at any time.

No of processors - this is the number of interacting processors on which the software system will be loaded.

No of operands or operators or algorithms - a measure of the size consumed by mathematical equations specified for the system.

3.2 Software Specification

De Marco's Bang metrics [5] were the first metrics proposed to provide a measurement of the size of the software system that could be made at the specification phase. They are synthetic metrics based on counts derived from data flow diagrams (DFDs) and entity-relationship (E-R) models. These notations are used to record the specification of a system when De Marco's Structured Analysis and Design method is being used [6]. Bang metrics measure attributes of the most abstract system definition. They reflect the information processing aspects of the solution to the users problem.

There are two synthetic Bang metrics. One synthetic metric is intended to measure the size of "function strong" systems (i.e. systems where the majority of the development work is oriented towards developing procedures), which is based on counts obtained from DFDs. The other synthetic metric is intended to measure the size of "data strong" systems (i.e. systems where the majority of the development work is oriented towards developing a database), which is based on counts obtained from the E–R model. (It should be noted that De Marco does not distinguish between metrics which relate to structure and metrics which relate to size.)

The choice of size measure for software specifications depends on the design methodology being used. In many cases the use of De Marco's Structured Analysis and Design will not be appropriate to Ada applications, Mascot or Hood (Hierarchical Object Oriented Design) are probably more appropriate. Designs using Hood are beginning to become more widespread as the methodology is maturing and being supported by tools. Designs built following the Hood methodology describe the system as a set of objects, the objects can be of different types, for example environment object and class object.

The following description gives definitions for the base counts which can be made for Hood designs that are comparable to the base counts for the Bang metrics. The base counts can be combined to form a "Bang" metric and used to derive other metrics, for example productivity and error rates, and to refine cost estimates.

No of Objects – the number of child objects contained in the Object Definition Skeleton (ODS) of a non–terminal parent object.

No of Instance Objects – the number of instance objects (instances of class objects) contained in the ODS of a non–terminal parent object.

No of Operations – the number of operations identified in the "Provided Interface" section of the ODS of a non–terminal parent object.

No of Child Operations – the sum of the operations defined for each of the child objects as declared by the ODS of each of the child objects.

Size of Data Flow – the number of bytes of each data flow defined in the ODS of the non–terminal parent object.

3.3 Design

At the low level design stage, Ada specifications for packages and tasks are often defined in Ada pseudo code.

The following size measurements can be made from the Ada pseudo code using the information provided in the specifications for packages and tasks. These size measurements can be used to calculate size–related rates relevant to the design phase and to further refine cost estimates.

No of Packages
No of Tasks
No of lines of pseudo code

3.4 Code

Following the implementation of the Ada pseudo code, new measures of size can be obtained from the code itself. Apart from the calculation of size–related rates for the coding phase the size measures can be used to assess the relationship between earlier size measurements and the size of the code. This can be particularly useful for predicting the hardware memory and/or storage requirements size for future software systems. These measures are similar to those that would be made for any system independent of the implementation language or application area, for example Lines of Code.

For Ada (as for other languages), there are several alternative definitions of a "line of code". An IIT study sponsored by the DoD [7] identified five different definitions in current use. The study itself used one of the definitions based on terminal semicolons which defined a line of code as:

A statement terminated by a semicolon including data declarations, code used to instantiate a reusable component, and the reusable component itself for the first time it is instantiated. Comments, blank lines, and non-delivered code are ignored.

4 Structure Metrics

As for size metrics, it is useful to examine how structure metrics can be used during the software development process. Structure metrics describe the links between software components. At the code level, they usually describe the control flow to and from program fragments. Control flow metrics are used to identify procedures which are potentially difficult to test.

At the specification and design levels, structure metrics attempt to measure coupling which is the extent to which components interact with one another. It is generally accepted to be good design practice to aim at low-levels of coupling. High levels of coupling, therefore reduce confidence in the integrity of components.

Coupling metrics are usually derived from fan-in and fan-out counts, where fan-in is the number of "links" going into a component and fan-out is the number of "links" coming out of a component. The "links" may be based on a number of different features, e.g. calling links which indicates that a procedure calls another procedure, information links which indicates that a component passes some information from or to another component, etc.

Measurements can be made throughout the software development process to monitor the risk that the software is becoming too complex in structure and hence cause remedial action to be taken. It is obviously not appropriate to measure the structure at the requirements analysis phase.

4.1 Specification

Some of the metrics related to size can be viewed as structure measures when they indicate the extent to which a component is linked to other components. As for size metrics, the definitions of structure metrics for the specification phase depends on the design method used. The following definitions for structure metrics are proposed for Hood designs:

No of Used Objects – the number of used objects defined in the "Required Interface" of the ODS of a non–terminal parent object.

No of Environment Objects – the number of environment objects defined in the "Required Interface" of the ODS of a root parent object.

No of Op–Control Objects – the number of op–control objects (op–control objects handle the object control structure of an active parent object) identified in the "Object Control Structure" section of the ODS of a non–terminal parent object.

No of Data Flows for each Child Object – the number of data flows that interface between one child object and another child object as described in the ODS of each child object.

4.2 Design

Certain structure metrics can be extracted from the specifications written in Ada Pseudo Code as follows:

No of With Clauses per package – for each package the number of 'with' clauses contained in the package specification. This gives an indication of the extent to which a particular package depends on other packages.

No of Visible Procedures per package – for each package the number of procedures that are identified in the package specification. This gives a measure of the number of procedures that can be called by other packages.

No of With Clauses referencing a particular package – for each package the number of other packages which use its visible procedures. (Note This cannot be obtained directly from the package information for a particular package.)

No of Entry Statements per task – for each task the number of entry statements that are identified in the task specification. This gives a measure of how many potential rendezvous points exist within the task, and hence an indication of the interaction between tasks.

4.3 Code

Code–based structure metrics can be based on counts related to the control flow within procedures, but there are additional measures which are available when the code is implemented in Ada:

Fan–in and Fan–out within a package – the standard fan–in fan–out measurements restricted to those calls made within a package. That is calls to procedures from procedures in another package and calls from a procedure to procedures in another package are not included. Rendezvous between tasks in the same package are included.

Fan–in and Fan–out between packages – the standard fan–in fan–out measurement except that only those calls to or from procedures in other packages are considered. Rendezvous between tasks in different packages are included.

5 Data Collection Facilities

One of the difficulties of using software metrics is their collection. This is often thought to be a time–consuming exercise of little benefit. It is no longer practical to consider that data collection can take place using a paper–driven system because all engineers and managers are completely PC–literate and will demand an automated data collection process. Tools are now becoming available which can be tailored to meet an organisation's needs for the metrics to be collected and hence reduce the time involved.

The National Computing Centre has developed a Data Collection and Storage System as part of the Mermaid Esprit project [8]. This system allows the user to define the data model and data definitions (although data definitions are provided) for their own purposes. At the time of writing, a number of organisations have viewed the system and some are Beta Testing the suite. Some of the Cost Estimation Tools, for example Checkmark [9], have included a metrics collection facility which can be partially adapted to meet a user's needs.

A data collection facility must be integrated with any existing data collection activities operating in an organisation so that data is only collected once. It is therefore essential that there is a mechanism to import and export any shared data.

There is, however, a difference between collecting the data and measuring the data and this is especially so for size and structure metrics. Assistance in measurement implies that all tools used during the project should have a measurement facility of the products they manipulate. Providing the definitions and counting rules for metrics is of little practical use unless there are automatic facilities to perform the measurement. At the current time there are few tools which automate the process and this is a problem which needs to be addressed. If customers of tools, for example Ada Compilation Systems, do not specify in their requirements the ability to measure attributes of the software system being developed, then the suppliers of these tools will not provide the necessary facilities. A major difficulty in the past has been the lack of clear definitions for tool suppliers to use. The definitions described above address this difficulty and thus clear the way for enhanced tools to be built which include a measurement capability.

Summary

This paper has described, briefly, how measurement of the software development process can improve the probability that software will be built such that it meets its requirements, is on time, within budget and of the required quality. It is widely believed that the use of Ada has helped these criteria be met, although there are few figures available in the public domain that demonstrate this. It is only when the software development process is measured that we can identify the advantages, and disadvantages, of certain methods and initiate actions to ensure the software crisis becomes a thing of the past. For measurement to be successful it needs to be automated and hence standard definitions are required. The presentation of definitions for size and structure metrics in this paper is a beginning and hopefully will encourage suppliers to incorporate a measurement capability within their software tools.

References

1. Boehm, B. W. (1981) *Software Engineering Economics*, Prentice–Hall.
2. Boehm, B. W. and Walker, R. (1987) Ada COCOMO: TRW IOC version, in *Proceedings of the Third COCOMO Users Group Meeting*, Software Engineering Institute.
3. Reifer Consultants Inc (1988) *Softcost – Ada Users Manual Version 1.3*, available from Bakst International (UK) Ltd, Slough.
4. Albrecht, A. A. and Gaffney, Jnr, J. E. (1983) Software function, source line of code, and development effort prediction: a software science validation, *IEEE Transactions in Software Engineering*, SE–9.
5. DeMarco, T. (1982) *Controlling Software Projects*, Prentice–Hall.
6. DeMarco, T. (1978) *Structured Analysis and Design*, Prentice–Hall.
7. IIT Research Institute (1989) Test–case study: estimating the cost of Ada software development, IIT Research Institute, Lanham, Maryland.
8. Mermaid Project DCSS, (1991) NCC Ltd, Oxford Road, Manchester M1 7ED, UK.
9. Checkmark, (1990) Macleod Group Solutions, 11–15 High Street, MArlow, Bucks SL7 1AU UK.

USING ADA SOURCE CODE GENERATORS IN A LARGE PROJECT

Rob Duell, Hugo J. Sebel, Franklin C. A. de Wit

Royal Netherlands Navy
Center for Automation of
Weapon and Command Systems

Abstract

In large software projects, especially for heterogeneous systems, good support for parallel Application Function development is essential. For this reason the RNLN/CAWCS has developed a concept in which there is a clear split in system-wide software infrastructure (related to ISO layers 2-6) and multiple, domain specific Application Functions.

The approach taken comprises building information models for the complete hardware architecture, the software architecture, and the system level information (emanating from the Application Function Information Modeling activities). Major standards such as the OSI stack have been adopted. The second step in the process was to build one large database application from these models. Code generators then were produced for the different end products, such as ADA source code and LaTeX source files for documentation.

The adopted strategy has already proven itself for CAWCS-built systems, especially in the areas of a rapidly maturing process for the code generator, high quality code and superior flexibility in a System Integration phase. The produced software components are specific in the sense that only the required infrastructure is generated for each Application Function in each computer, instead of one generic general purpose package.

1 Introduction

The area of Naval Combat Systems is no exception to the phenomenon of the ever increasing demand for a higher level of automation. Taking into account the decreasing personnel and equipment budgets, it is obvious that this calls for new strategies and software engineering concepts.

The production of more lines of source code (SLOCs), reflecting the increase in demand for such a higher level of automation, with the same or even smaller staff necessitates the use of previously developed and tested parts of software (reuse) and a considerable increase of the overall quality of newly produced parts. The same fault density, expressed in undiscovered bugs per SLOC, will lead to a larger absolute number of undiscovered bugs when more SLOCs are produced. This problem can be alleviated by introducing new system approaches and software production techniques.

In this paper we present the approach taken by the development team of the software for the Royal Netherlands Navy M-Frigate and focus on the use of Ada source code generators as a means of both increasing the productivity per capita and the overall quality of the produced code.

2 M-Frigate Software Architecture

2.1 Overview

Figure 1 depicts the M-Frigate Software Architecture as a three dimensional model consisting of layers.

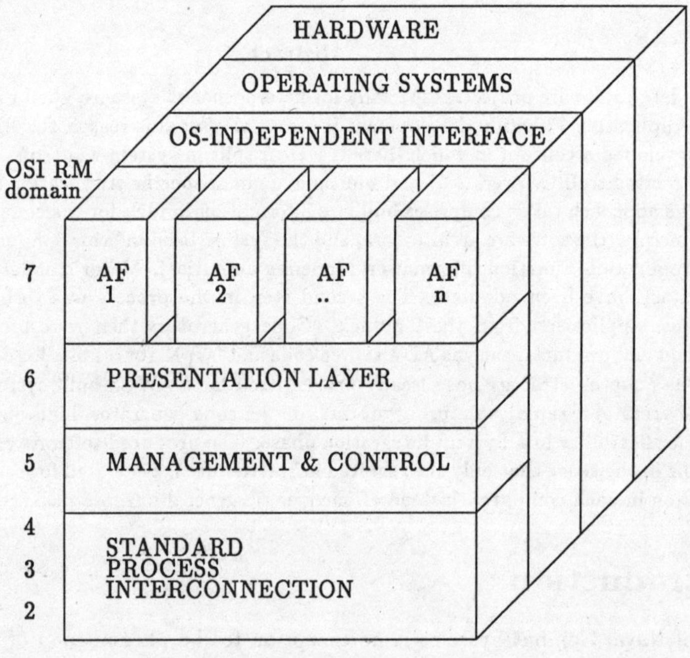

Figure 1

The basic layer encompasses the hardware units used, e.g. computers, processor boards and networks. On top of this layer we find the software units such as operating systems and the M-Frigate software. The software in itself is layered. There exists a layering from application or system component (slice in front), through the operating system independent interface to the operating system itself. The front slice is also layered and relates to the ISO/OSI Reference Model.

2.2 Hardware

The main computing platform of the M-Frigate is a heterogeneous system comprising a range of computers, workstations, peripherals and interconnecting elements.
The computers come in many varieties, both in memory architecture as in processor architecture. Workstations enable the user to communicate with the system using several input devices (trackball, lightpen, keyboard, programmable keys) and output devices (multicolor, multiplane 19" and monochrome 12" displays). Peripherals are sensors (radars, etc.), weapons (missiles, guns, etc.) and internal and external communication equipment. All these elements are interconnected using networks (Ethernet, Token Ring, etc.) and buses (VMEbus, etc.). Most of the computing equipment and networks are duplicated or even triplicated to provide redundancy and survivability.

The rationale for such a heterogeneous system is that in our line of work computers must meet specific requirements. In the real-time domain the need arises for fast, special purpose computers with specialized interfaces and programming languages. Typical demanding applications can be found in the area of sensor and weapon control. Typically, these real-time computers are not well suited for non real-time applications making demands of a different nature such as the availability of large amounts of disk or memory. Among these non real-time applications we find message and information handling systems, geography-, mission planning- and training facilities. Porting and maintaining the products, tools and languages often found on commercially available equipment is not cost effective because of the small customer base. Companies specialized in specific areas as compilers, databases and general purpose computing equipment are far more able to develop and maintain their products because of the economy of scale. The commercially available hardware and software greatly reduces the effort needed to produce a large product like the M-Frigate Software. This results in a shift of funds from the development of specialized software and hardware to the acquisition of commercially of the shelf (COTS) products.

2.3 Operating Systems

The operating systems running in the different types of computers are as varied as the computers themselves. We can discern VMS, MARS-E, SME/2, OS-9, several Ada Run-Time Executives and other kernels.

Ideally, an Application Function must not be bothered with the specifics of the operating system it is running on. Therefore we have developed an operating system independent interface to the likes of POSIX. It facilitates Application Functions to call system services of the underlying operating system (e.g. to reference the local clock) without knowing which system it actually is and thus greatly enhances portability.

2.4 Software Infrastructure And Application Functions

The front slice in figure 1 depicts the layer of software produced by our Center. To create possiblities for reuse and portability this layer is produced using the OSI Reference Model.

The layer contains parts that are present system wide (i.e. layers 2 through 6 of the OSI stack) and parts that are specific to a computer or a set of computers (layer 7). We thus have created a division between an, as large as possible, hardware independent part and a part directly releated to the run-time environment. The hardware independent software — the Application Functions — or parts thereof, are candidates for reuse in other systems and should be made portable to facilitate a remapping of these functions within the system. The hardware dependent part or Software Infrastructure (layers 2 through 6) must therefore hide all the details of the run-time environment for the Application Functions.

How is this achieved ? The mere existence of an Application Function lies in its ability to add information to the system. Exchange of the added information and the information it needs from the system is performed using (system level) messages. The Presentation Layer of the OSI stack (layer 6) provides the Application Function with a uniform, syntax independent, high-level interface. To enhance portability and reuse the Application Function does not assemble the messages itself, but uses procedure calls to the Presentation Layer. The procedure call bears the name of the message and the attributes of the information to be conveyed, are the procedure's parameters.

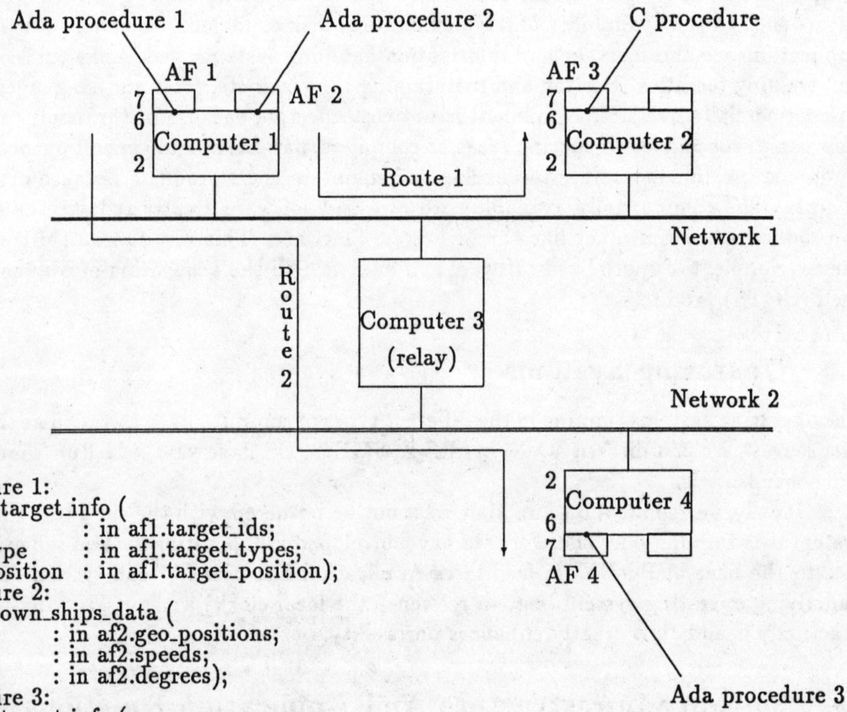


```
Ada procedure 1:
  procedure target_info (
    target_id        : in af1.target_ids;
    target_type      : in af1.target_types;
    target_position  : in af1.target_position);
Ada procedure 2:
  procedure own_ships_data (
    position     : in af2.geo_positions;
    speed        : in af2.speeds;
    course       : in af2.degrees);
Ada procedure 3:
  procedure target_info (
    target_id        : out af4.target_ids;
    target_type      : out af4.target_types;
    target_position  : out af4.target_position);
C procedure:
  void own_ships_data (
    geo_positions        position;
    speeds               speed;
    degrees              course);
```

Figure 2

As a result the Application Function does not need to have knowledge of the format of the message (in bitpositions) nor does it have to add or have knowledge of any headers needed for routing the message to its recipient. The Application Function is allowed to determine the type of the parameters passed to the procedure and thus becomes syntax independent from the system. Figure 2 depicts a configuration where Application Function 1 in computer 1 adds information (containing info on a target) to the system. This information is wanted by an another Application Function (4) located in computer 4. The message is inserted into the system by calling the procedure *Target_Info* with its parameters. The Software Infrastructure is then responsible for routing the message through the system to the receiving Application Function. This way, the Application Function does not need to concern itself with the characteristics or the whereabouts of the recipient(s) of the information. The receiver may be programmed in a different language or may even run on a different type of computer. This is the case for the exchange of a message between Application Function 2 programmed in Ada located in computer 1 and Application Function 3 programmed in C located in computer 2, as shown in figure 2.

The Software Infrastructure is responsible for the delivery of the information to any other Application Function requesting this information, independent of the location of this recipient. This could be the same computer, but also a different computer on the same network or even a computer on a different network.

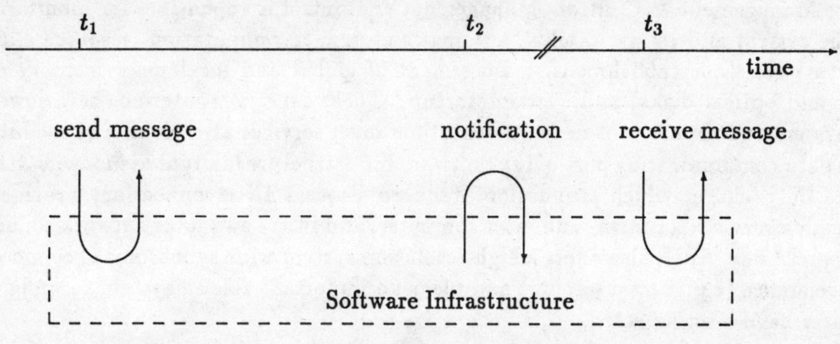

Figure 3

On receipt of the information in the destination computer, the Application Function requesting the information is notified of the arrival of the information. The receiver then retrieves the information from the system, by calling the proper interface procedure. Note that this done at a time that is convenient to the Application Function (see figure 3).

The specification of the type of the procedure parameters is up to the receiving Application Function and could be of a different type than that specified by the sending entity, even within the same computer and using the same language — as depicted in figure 4.

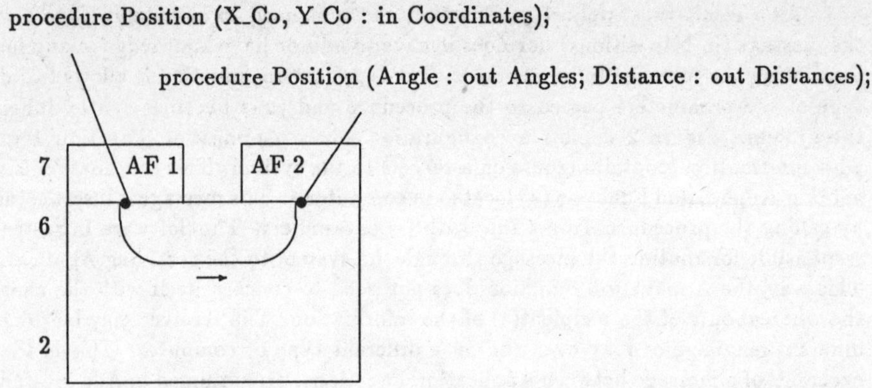

Figure 4

To facilitate this, the Presentation Layer converts the local syntax defined by the Application Function into a common syntax defined at datalink level (layer 2 of the OSI stack).

Below the Presentation Layer we find an implementation of the Session Layer of the OSI stack: Management & Control. Management & Control is reponsible for monitoring the state of the system and its availability, automatic system reconfiguration, resource allocation on (operator) session establishment, management of global and local mass memory devices (magnetic and optical disks) and system startup. These functions interface at a lower level with the system and thus do not need Presentation Layer services at their side of the interface.

The data communicating part of the Software Infrastructure is situated in layers 2 through 4. The SPIN package, which stands for Standard Process INterconnection, provides data communication services for intra- and inter computer, and intra- and inter network connections in a transparent way. SPIN also offers a high-resolution system-wide synchronized common time frame for reference (e.g. timestamping) and plays an important role in system reconfiguration when failures have been detected.
It also takes care of automatic rerouting upon failure and load balancing in case of multiple physical paths (e.g. the triplicated backbone Ethernets). For example: When a physical path between two computers is failing, SPIN will automatically reroute the traffic through another link and establish a test protocol in order to detect the repair of the affected path. If the test protocol eventually reports the availability of the previously failing link, SPIN resumes the communication scheme to the one used before the failure arose.

Application Functions are domain specific (Message Handling, Information Handling, Tactical Datahandling, etc.) and are portable, reusable pieces of software having one and only one interface to the system (i.e. through the Software Infrastructure).
Note the total absence of direct links between Application Functions in figure 1, denoted by

the small gaps between the blocks in layer 7. This way, it is possible to agree upon the characteristics of the interface of the Application Functions in the early stages of the development phase, allowing for parallel development — in time — of those Application Functions.
Traditional approaches would have resulted in the production of non-portable (and therefore limited-reusable or even non-reusable) Application Functions with their own Software Infrastructure tied into the design/code also resulting in redundant work to be done in both the design and implementation phase. Because of the differences in implementations to obtain the same functionality, traditionally produced code would have needed more testing and would have been less efficient and maintainable. There are also differences in the interpretation of the interface agreements accross all levels, leading to an increase in the effort needed to successfully integrate an Application Function into the system.

The Software Infrastructure is produced by one team, responsible for all the system interfaces, both to Software Configuration Items like Application Functions and Operating System Independent Interface and to Hardware Configuration Items like subsystems and peripherals. Therefore it is important to isolate the developers of Application Functions from the idiosyncrasies of the (sub)system and offer them one portable, system independent interface as depicted in figure 5.

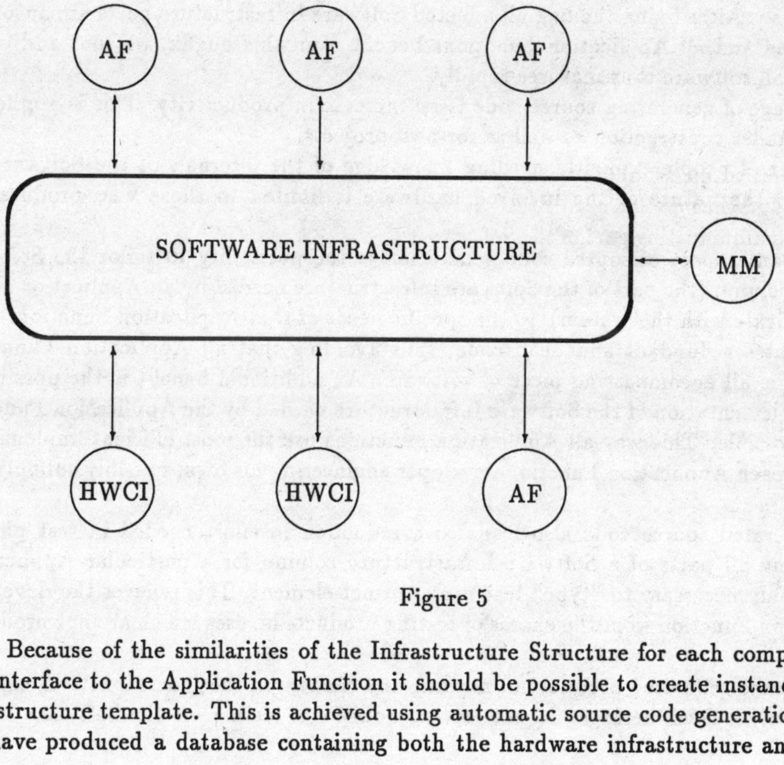

Figure 5

Because of the similarities of the Infrastructure Structure for each computer, language and interface to the Application Function it should be possible to create instances of a generic Infrastructure template. This is achieved using automatic source code generation.
We have produced a database containing both the hardware infrastructure and the software

structure, augmented with system level messages emanating from the information modeling phase for the Application Functions. This database is called the Infrastructure Database and is the starting point for a host of activities among which are the source code generators.

3 Rationales For Using Automatic Source Code Generators

One of the means to increase the productivity of a software developer while at the same time increasing the quality of the produced code is the use of automatic source code generation. Building source code generators calls for a different software engineering approach than for source code produced manually. The internals of a source code generator describes in a formal manner how a particular piece of software should be constructed.

Because all Application Functions use the same method of interfacing to the system, it is possible to reuse large parts of the Software Infrastructure and have the generator tailor these parts to the requirements of the Application Function.

There are several advantages in this approach. A bug discovered in the Software Infrastructure in the test or maintenance phase, only affects the generators or the generic templates the generators use. After fixing the bug all affected Software Infrastructure parts are automatically regenerated and all Application Functions benefit from this bugfix, without additional effort. The overall software thus matures rapidly.

Another advantage of generating source code is an increase in productivity. This is applicable for the system under construction as well as for new projects.

Also the number of people explicitly needing knowledge of the internals of the Software Infrastructure and the nature of the involved hardware is limited to those who produce the generators.

Another important aspect of source code generation is the possibility to tailor the Software Infrastructure Column (the part of the Software Infrastructure needed by an Application Function to communicate with the system), to the specific needs of that Application Function. This tailoring eliminates redundant and dead code, thus avoiding that all Application Functions must use a single, all encompassing piece of software. An additional benefit is the possibility to make the implementation of the Software Infrastructure needed by the Application Function as efficient as possible. This way all Application Functions use the most efficient implementation, instead of each Application Function developer engineering his own, possibly suboptimal, solution.

The use of generated source code also leads to a reduction in effort needed in test phases. Instead of testing all parts of a Software Infrastructure column for a particular Application Function, it is only necessary to "type" test each distinct element. This relieves the developer of the Application Function from the chores of testing products he uses which are not produced by himself.

Also, changes in the generated product not needing any changes in the generator itself, e.g. the addition of a system level message, do not lead to additional testing for the Software Infras-

tructure but is limited to the Application Function's domain.
Together with the generation of source code the applicable documents describing the contents of the Software Infrastructure and the Application Function's interface with it, are generated. This ensures that all documentation is always in synch with the software, which is very important.

4 Infrastructure Database

We have modelled the information available on hardware configuration, software configuration and system level messages, and created a database application to store this information for future reference. This database is called the Infrastructure Database.

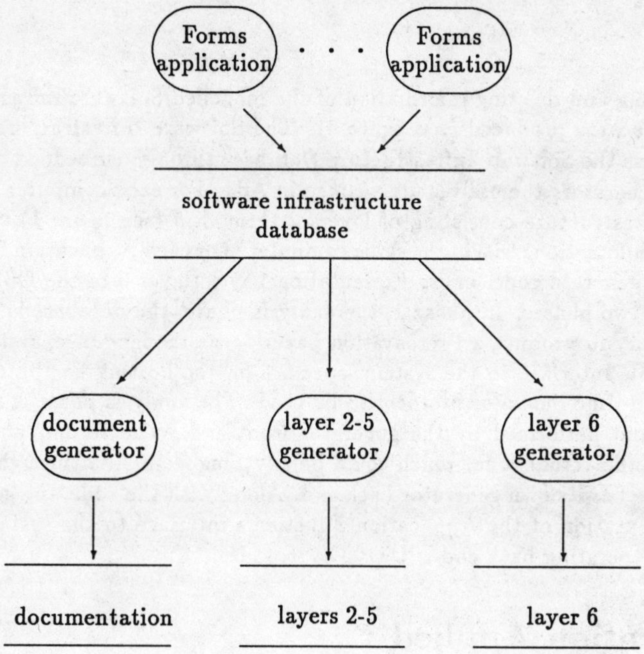

Figure 6

Within this database we find items representing Software Infrastructure elements. These elements include, among others:

- computers
- networks
- application functions
- system level messages

Also stored are relationships between:

- computers and networks
- application functions and computers
- application functions
- etc.

For entering, changing and deleting information of the modelled Software Infrastructure several Forms applications were produced (see figure 6). The Software Infrastructure Source Code Generators can access the Software Infrastructure Database through embedded database access statements. The generators themselves are written in Ada. For each computer we then generate the Software Infrastructure consisting of layers 2 through 5 (see figure 1), which is common for all Application Functions within the same computer. For each Application Function within that computer we generate code for its Presentation Layer (layer 6 of the OSI stack). This code is generated in two phases. In phase 1, the analysis phase, the database is scanned for all information necessary to produce a Presentation Layer — source language, system, etc. — level messages within its interface to the system, specifics on the hosting computer (word size, word format) and run-time model or protocol to be used. The analysis phase is common for all target languages and performed by the generator front end. The second phase, the synthesis phase, produces the actual code, which could be anything from Ada through RTL/2 to C. Each target language has its own generator back end. Along with the code, the generator also produces the documentation of the Application Function's interface to the system. The output of the document generating back end is LaTeX source files.

5 Code Generation Applied

Figure 7 shows the general layout of a Presentation Layer specification. The main package is *Presentation_Layer* which contains two other packages: *Output* and *Input*. The package *Output* contains the messages that can be used within this Presentation Layer to send information to the system. The package *Input* contains the messages that can be used within this Presentation Layer to receive information from the system. The above packages reference the package *Presentation_Layer_Types*, containing definitions for this specific Presentation Layer.

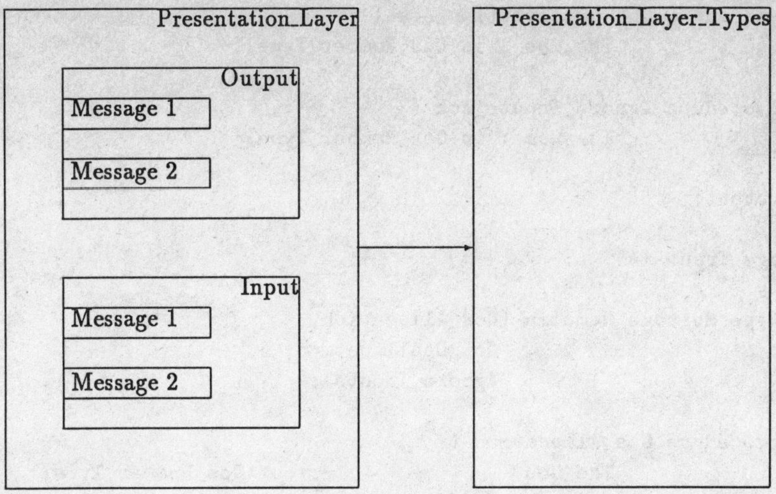

Figure 7

An example of the Presentation Layer code generated for a specific Application Function is shown in figure 8.

```
with Application_Function_X_Types;
  use Application_Function_X_Types;

package Application_Function_X_Presentation_Layer is

    package Output is

        type Message_Name is (Gos_Allocation_Ack,
                              Gos_Deallocation_Ack,
                              Ignore_Inputs_Ack);

        procedure Gos_Allocation_Ack (
                     The_Gos : in Gos_Number_Type);
```

```
    procedure Gos_Deallocation_Ack (
                 The_Gos : in Gos_Number_Type);

    procedure Ignore_Inputs_Ack (
                 The_Gos : in Gos_Number_Type);

  end Output;

  package Input is

    type Message_Name is (Gos_Allocation,
                          Gos_Deallocation,
                          Ignore_Inputs);

    procedure Gos_Allocation (
                 The_Gos                  : out Gos_Number_Type;
                 The_Operator             : out Operator_Id_Type;
                 The_Functionary_Number   : out Functionary_Number_Type;
                 The_Extension            : out Extension_Number_Type;
                 The_Functionary_Type     : out Functionary_Type_Type;
                 The_Menu_Item            : out Menu_Item_Type);

    procedure Gos_Deallocation (
                 The_Gos : out Gos_Number_Type);

    procedure Ignore_Inputs (
                 The_Gos              : out Gos_Number_Type;
                 The_Functionary_Type : out Functionary_Type_Type);

  end Input;

end Application_Function_X_Presentation_Layer;
```

Figure 8

To illustrate the benefits that come with generated source code, figure 9 shows the effort needed to add a message to the sets of messages within an Application Function's interface to the system.

Phase	Hand coded	Generated
Implementing	4 hours	10 minutes
Testing	8 hours	built-in
Documenting	2 hours	built-in

Figure 9

6 Conclusions

In resumé we conclude that, based on experiences from several large projects, the approach taken in the M-Frigate project does have the expected benefits. We have succeeded in increasing both the productivity and the overall quality of the product by generating source code from the Software Infrastructure Database. It is estimated that hand coding the same products would have cost three times as much (including testing and documenting). At the same time we have succeeded in producing a robust, but flexible overall product which is very maintainable. This has already proven itself when new Application Functions have been added the M-Frigate software recently. Furthermore, the Application Function's portability and reusability facilitate the use of these Application Functions in new projects, thus capitalizing on investments made earlier.

DESIGN AND CODE METRICS THROUGH A DIANA-BASED TOOL

Wayne M. Zage and Dolores M. Zage
Computer Science Department, Ball State University
Muncie, IN 47306, USA

Manjari Bhargava and Dale J. Gaumer
Magnavox Electronic Systems Co.
Fort Wayne, IN 46808, USA

Key Words - Design metrics, code metrics, quality assessment, DIANA.

Abstract - This paper discusses a metrics approach for analyzing software designs which helps designers engineer quality into the design product. These metrics gauge project quality as well as design complexity at all times during the design phase. The metrics are developed from primitive design metrics which are predictive, objective and automatable. The architectural design metrics used are comprised of terms related to the amount of data flowing through the module and the number of paths through the module. A detailed design metrics component takes into account the structure and complexity of a module. To automate the calculation of the design metrics in the Rational environment, DIANA (Descriptive Intermediate Attributed Notation for Ada) was utilized. Provided in the environment are packages allowing for the traversal and retrieval of the DIANA structure. By combining the defined packages with customized packages, an Ada design metrics analysis tool was developed. This paper will discuss our design metrics and their automation at Magnavox. Empirical results will illustrate the metrics' success in identifying stress points in a software design and demonstrate their relationship to the quality of the resulting software.

Background

Meaningful measurements of software complexity and quality are desirable to help ensure system dependability, to evaluate development methods, to contribute to process control, and to verify that the product meets a set of quality goals. Further, on large and/or complex systems, it is important to make measurements during development so that potentially troublesome designs or code can be detected early enough to perform corrections with minimum additional effort.

It has been recognized that most of the important structural decisions have been made irreversibly by the end of architectural design [ROMB90]. Thus researchers are striving to measure many aspects of design products. Information flow metrics, some software science metrics and McCabe's cyclomatic complexity have been used to predict code quality early in the life cycle [HENR90]. A software complexity metric based on module interaction has been developed which helps analyze a software system during development in order to provide a guide to system decomposition, and ultimately lead to more reliable software [LEW88]. Gibson and Senn have found that system structural differences impact software maintenance performance [GIBS89]. Li and Cheung have suggested hybrid metrics to remedy the lack of completeness of most single factor measures of program volume, complexity and control [LI87]. Methods to monitor software development by calculating a variety of metrics during the entire software development process have also been proposed [KITC89].

Researchers have sought a metric which would identify problematic components early in the life cycle. Studies have shown that approximately 20% of a software system is responsible for 80% of the errors [BOEH88]. It is possible that such error-prone modules exhibit some measurable attribute to identify them as design stress points. In Basili's study, the measures V(G), calls, LOC, executable statements, revisions and Halstead's effort metric E were correlated with errors. The metric with the highest correlation with errors was the number of revisions at .67 [BASI81]. Obviously, a revision metric does not occur early enough in the life cycle to help the software developer take corrective measures in design. In the Distos/Incas experiment, information flow measures had only average predictive capabilities [ROMB90]. Some researchers have used a non-integrated approach to identify high-risk components of a system, such as a classification tree method which extracts data from previous projects to identify high-risk components in new projects [PORT90].

Metrics play an important pivotal role in the evaluation of software products. There is a deep need for the measurement of software product quality. In 1989, the Software Engineering Institute (SEI) initiated an effort to promote the use of objective measures. Measurement and its evaluation will be important factors in the SEI software maturity level framework for organizations.

The Software Engineering Research Center (SERC) design metrics research team at Ball State University has developed a metrics approach for analyzing software designs which helps designers engineer quality into the design product. These metrics gauge project quality as well as design complexity at all times during the design phase. Having quantifiable measurements can help managers and software developers determine the better design when alternative choices exist, as well as identify stress points which may lead to difficulty during coding and maintenance.

The HW*WD Scenarios

There are many aspects to measuring the quality of a software system, and different approaches are used for different sets of aspects. One way to group current approaches is as follows, where the order is roughly from least mature to the most mature.

HWCWD (How Well Can We Do?) are approaches which may be applied before much of the system is developed, and are especially valuable if usable before detailed design is begun. Ideally, measurements of the architecture should indicate where problems are likely to occur. Such an approach would be a reliable predictor of quality and also contribute directly to the design process.

HWAWD (How Well Are We Doing?) are approaches which may be applied during further development of the system. It may be helpful to also have a measure of algorithmic complexity, or even to combine the measures of complexity external to, and internal to, all modules.

HWDWD (How Well Did We Do?) approaches are applied on a software system that is essentially complete. This has the major disadvantage that correcting a deficiency may involve much rework. However, such approaches may be helpful in the maintenance of software.

After a presentation of our design metrics, we'll see how these metrics can be applied in each of the above scenarios.

Our Architectural and Detailed Design Metrics

The metrics research team at Ball State University has developed for a design G, a design quality metric D(G) of the form

$$D(G) = k_1 D_e + k_2 D_i$$

In this equation, k_1 and k_2 are constants and D_e and D_i are, respectively, an external and internal design quality component. In D_e, a module's *external* relationships to other modules in the software system are considered, whereas in D_i factors related to a module's *internal* structure are incorporated.

The metrics D_e and D_i are developed from primitive design metrics which are predictive, objective and automatable. D_e is calculated for each module in a system and is comprised of two terms: one product related to the amount of data flowing through the module and another product giving the number of paths through the module. More precisely,

$$D_e = (weighted\text{-}inflows * weighted\text{-}outflows) + (fan\text{-}in * fan\text{-}out)$$

where

weighted-inflows is the number of data-items (simple variables, records, etc.) passed to the module from superordinate or subordinate modules,
weighted-outflows is the number of data-items passed from the module to superordinate or subordinate modules,
fan-in is the number of superordinate modules directly connected to the given module, and

fan-out is the number of subordinate modules directly connected to the given module.

The internal design metric component D_i takes into account the structure and complexity of a module and has the following form:

$$D_i = w_1(CC) + w_2(DSM) + w_3(I/O)$$

where

CC (Central Calls) is the number of procedure or function invocations (calls to non-library modules),

DSM (Data Structure Manipulations) is the number of references to complex data types, which are data types that use indirect addressing (e.g., pointer, array, record, type definition, ...),

I/O (Input/Output) is the number of external device accesses, (such as read file, port, device, ...)

and w_1, w_2 and w_3 are weighting factors.

The metrics D_e and D_i are designed to offer useful information during two different stages of software design. The calculation of D_e is based on information available during architectural design, whereas D_i is calculated during the detailed design phase of software development.

The practical method of application of these metrics is displayed in Figure 1 below. After a portion of the architectural design is completed, D_e values are calculated for each module (package, etc.) in the developing system. Based on these values, stress points are identified, and the software designer may then modify the architectural design (as depicted by the right-to-left flow in Figure 1). Once the D_e values appear satisfactory to the designer, he can further develop the architectural design or begin detailed design. After detailed design is completed, D_i values are calculated, stress points are identified and the system is again reviewed by the software designer. The designer can either choose to revise the detailed design (or in drastic cases, even the architectural design) or proceed to the coding phase of the life cycle.

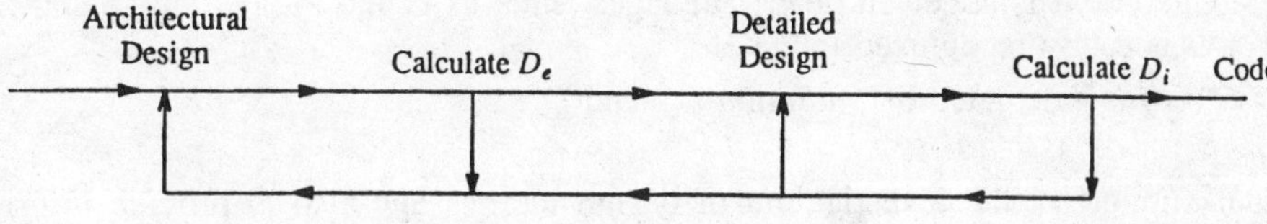

Figure 1: The Calculation of Design Metrics in the Life Cycle

Tool and Software Analyzer Development

Tools must be available to successfully integrate the use of software metrics into the software development process. Tools insure consistent measurements and minimize the interference with the existing work load.

Many large projects which resided or could be ported to the Rational environment were offered as data for this research. To make this analysis more efficient and complete, a Design Metric Analyzer was created. To automate the calculation of design metrics in the Rational environment, DIANA (Descriptive Intermediate Attributed Notation for Ada) was utilized. DIANA is the standard intermediate representation of Ada programs. DIANA was developed to provide a common interface between different phases of the Ada compiler. The DIANA structure stores the syntactic and semantic aspects of Ada designs and programs in the Rational environment.

The DIANA structure and the interface packages were used as a basis for the analysis of Ada programs. By combining the defined packages with customized packages, an Ada design metrics analysis tool was developed. The Design Metric Analyzer, or DMA, exploits Rational's DIANA interface package to determine several metrics which are fundamental to the design metrics calculations, including:

- Number of calls to and from superordinate or subordinate subprograms
- Number of parameters passed to and from a subprogram
- Number of external variables referenced and modified by a subprogram
- Number of calls to task entry points
- Number of complex data types (records, arrays, access types) accessed
- Number of central calls (subprogram and task entry calls)

Finally, the DMA calculates and reports the design metrics for each subprogram and for the system:

- D_e is calculated for each module from the data flow and fan-in and fan-out metrics.
- D_i is calculated for each module from the central call and complex data structure counts. Currently, input and output metrics are not included in the calculation due to the difficulty in identifying non-standard Ada I/O operations. (This count is added in other languages, such as C and Pascal, where standard I/O is easily recognized.)
- $D(G)$ is calculated by summing D_e and D_i.

To further support in the investigation of design metrics and also to provide information about the code itself, DMA also performs an analysis of the types of statements, declarations, other size measurements such as LOC, number of logical statements, number of comments, number of embedded comments, and many other primitive metrics.

Design Metrics and the HW*WD Scenarios

The HW*WD scenarios provide a framework in which we can review the value and utility of our design metrics. By calculating the design metrics at various times during the development of design, project personnel can identify favorable and unfavorable design trends in an effort to determine HWCWD. This information could help managers and software developers determine the better design when alternative choices exist, as well as identify stress points which may lead to difficulty during coding and maintenance. Locating these stress points early will reduce the cost of development and ultimately lead to more reliable software.

To review the HWAWD scenario using design metrics, consider the DMA, which is a tool that can be used to make early and periodic measurements of complexity and interactions in a developing system. It is able to identify where difficulties may arise in the future in further development and later operation. Since the indications from DMA are localized in that both internal and external complexity are reported for each module, changing the program to improve a metric value may necessitate redesign of a module or, because the module interface is factored in, the group of modules with which it interacts. The amount of redesign is limited if the tool is applied frequently during development.

An earlier experimental version of the DMA tool was applied during design by performing static analysis on architectural information extracted from the repository of a CASE tool, in particular Teamwork from Cadre Technologies, Inc [ZAGE91a]. This approach was not used with the current Ada version because it was not applicable to the way the software would be developed on the first large system intended for use (the Advanced Field Artillery Tactical Data System, AFATDS, of the U.S. Army). Direct use of a CASE repository gives information earlier in development and is therefore desirable. If repositories with standardized interfaces become common, the use of CASE repositories will be much more practical.

The proof of the validity of the design metrics is of course in the HWDWD scenario. This issue is addressed in the next section.

Empirical Results on Design Metrics as Indicators of Software Quality

The goal of the design metrics calculations is to identify error-prone modules during the design phase of software development. The method employed is to calculate the particular design metric for each module under consideration. Then outliers (or stress points) are identified as those modules whose metric value is more than one standard deviation above the mean for that metric over all of the modules considered. Later, when error reports are available, we determine to what extent modules identified as stress points are error-prone.

Metrics Applied to University-Based Projects

Our metrics were first tested on projects developed at Ball State University in a software engineering sequence. These projects varied in length from 2,000 to 30,000 SLOC and also in the application language. The metric D(G) gave excellent results as a predictor of error-prone modules on the software projects developed at BSU for client-partners in industry. More specifically, the 12% of the modules highlighted as stress points by D(G) contained 97% of the known errors [ZAGE90].

Our research team also has obtained excellent results on finding error-prone modules in relatively small projects by simply calculating the D_e values. The 12% of the modules identified as stress points by D_e contained 53% of the known errors over all the systems in our database [ZAGE90].

Metrics Applied to Large-Scale Industrial Projects

The external design metric D_e has also been evaluated on a subset of a large-scale standard financial software system developed in industry. In that study, D_e performed even better than on the university database by targeting 67% of the known errors while identifying only 12% of the modules as stress points [ZAGE91b].

We have also found that extreme outlier modules (with respect to D_e and D_i) exist in large-scale software. These modules, with their extreme metric values, adversely affect our stress point cut-off values. This led to our *X-less design metric algorithm* in which we remove X such modules from the calculation of cut-off values to dramatically improve our results. We found that if enough extreme outliers are taken into account when calculating D_e so that 32% of the modules are identified as stress points, then 97% of the errors in a large-scale software system were found [ZAGE91b].

D_i also performed well when applied to this large-scale software project. In this study, D_i alone identified 54% of the errors while only highlighting 10% of the modules. And if 20% of the modules are identified as stress points (using the X-less algorithm), then 74% of the errors were found. Moreover, for these data, we found that 27% of the variance in errors was due to the DSM count.

The $D(G)$ metric was very successful in detecting the modules with errors, with false detection of very few error-free modules. On this test bed, 74% of the errors were detected for modules with 10 or fewer errors, 82% of the errors were detected for modules with 11 to 20 errors, and 100% of the errors were detected for modules with 21 or more errors [ZAGE91b]. In other words, modules with high concentrations of errors were always identified as stress-points by $D(G)$. These results are summarized in the graph shown in Figure 2.

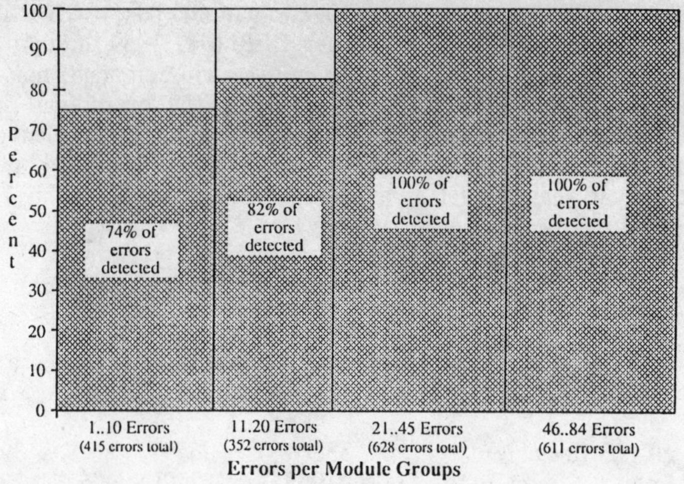

Figure 2: The Performance of D(G) on the Industrial Test Bed

We also compared the error versus errorless modules with respect to their D_e values in this study. The results are contained in Table 1. Note that the D_e mean for error-prone modules was more than six times the mean for errorless modules!

Table 1: Error vs. Errorless Modules

	Error Modules	Errorless Modules
Number of Mods	314	2070
D_e Mean	355	54
D_e Std Dev	666	375

An Architectural Design Metrics Study

Our D_e results had been based on the calculation of D_e only at the end of architectural design. However, the design of software is an incremental process as the designer adds new information or explores alternative designs. The notion of a time-based approach to monitor certain attributes previously has been applied to measure and manage software maintenance [GRAD87]. In this study, we focused on the integration of the construction of architectural design and the measurement of this process by a sequence of D_e calculations. By evaluating D_e over time, we hoped to gain an understanding of design dynamics in order to highlight favorable trends and avoid unfavorable ones in software design.

The target software in this study was the Advanced Field Artillery Tactical Data System (AFATDS) Project. Our goal was to identify trends and determine the relationship of the design metrics to the complexity and quality of a maturing system. This is a multiphase project with the initial Concept Evaluation Phase (CEP) followed by the Full Scale Development (FSD) Phase. During CEP, May 1984 through April 1989, the AFATDS program generated more than 1.2 million non-comment, non-blank (NCNB) lines of Ada which were delivered in 4 releases. The operational software of the AFATDS CEP consisted of nine major components that were further partitioned into minor components. Code from releases 2, 3 and 4 (R2, R3 and R4) of a minor component called Human Interface (HI) was selected for this study. Table 2 presents some of the metrics that were collected through the DMA.

Table 2: Data on the Releases of the HI Component

	Release 2	Release 3	Release 4
Ada Units	495	586	620
NCNB lines	53301	67997	84322
Logical Source Stmts	21968	27208	34222
Total Modules	1511	1807	2275
D_e Mean	96.4	90.8	103.9
D_e Std Dev	533.1	468.4	596.4
D_i Mean	14.1	15.0	14.1

As shown in Table 2, the standard deviation and mean for D_e is higher in R2, relatively lower in R3 and highest in R4. Studies completed on other large-scale industrial software to evaluate the performance of D_e have found that modules with higher D_e values in relation to the other system modules have a higher probability of being error-prone [ZAGE91b]. A large standard deviation represents a system that contains modules with extremely high D_e values, viewed as pockets of complexity in the design which tend to be error-prone. Assuming that D_e is an effective indicator of software quality, numbers obtained in this study can be interpreted to mean that there was a decrease in complexity and an improvement in quality of the software from R2 to R3, and an increase in complexity in R4. Dialog with project personnel regarding this observation correlated with the metrics results. Proceeding from R3 to R4, there is an increase in architectural complexity. Project personnel suggested that the increase was due to an overall increase in the functionality of the system [BHAR91].

To further analyze the transformations of the architectural design metric D_e, a distribution of the modules in the releases and the subsequent changes in the D_e values of these modules were examined. During this analysis, overloaded subprograms that could not be uniquely identified were averaged. (The use of multiple subprograms with the same name is called overloading.) There were 56 overloaded modules in R2, 55 in R3, and 134 in R4, giving a total of 167, 149 and 347 modules in releases 2, 3 and 4 respectively. Figure 3 presents the distribution of modules and the D_e results for all releases. The D_e values for the 957 modules that were present in all three releases gradually increased, which may be a good indicator of overall system growth and increasing functionality [BHAR91]. The same trend can also be observed in the 327 modules that were present in R2 and R3 (and not in R4), and in the 319 modules in R3 and R4 (and not in R2).

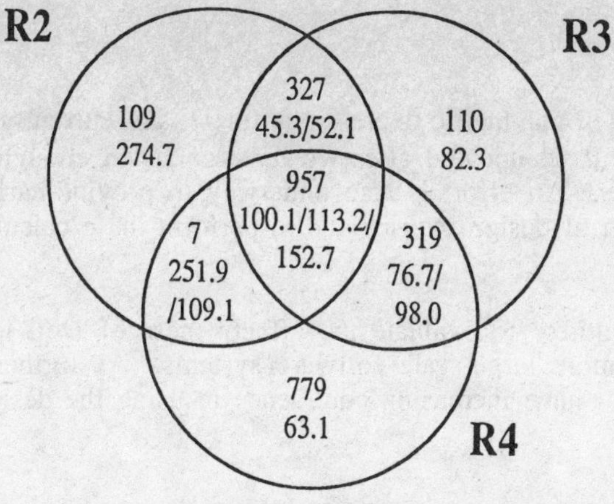

Figure 3: D_e Averages for Modules in Release 2, 3 and/or 4

Note from Figure 3 that the 109 modules in R2 with a relatively high D_e average of 274.7 were not included in R3, indicating the redesign of complex modules. Also shown in the figure is the fact that 110 modules in R3 with a relatively low D_e average of 82.3 were excluded from R4. It turns out that these modules were temporary stubs [BHAR91]. In general, when designers enhance a system, the new modules which are added have a lower average D_e value than those present from the previous version. Also, the average D_e value for the modules from a previous version increases as they are incorporated into a new version.

Table 3 shows how the values of D_e changed from one release to the next. As one can observe from the table, the majority of the modules in all of the categories retain their D_e values. Out of the remaining modules, more have a reduced D_e value, rather than increased D_e, when going from one version to the next. This indicates that most of the changes have resulted in less complex modules, giving a better system. Modules with higher D_e values when going from one version to the next were found to have increased functionality in the later release.

Table 3: How D_e Changed Over the Releases

Release	Modules	Same D_e	Lower D_e	Higher D_e
R2 to R3	327	277	40	10
R2 to R4	7	5	1	1
R3 to R4	319	115	153	51
R2 to R3, also in R4	957	645	174	138
R3 to R4, also in R2	957	506	310	141

Future Research

All weighting factors in our metric expressions for D_e are currently set to one. In our future work, these will be updated after we have collected enough data to determine the appropriate values. An effort is also underway to provide earlier automated support in the calculation of design metrics and to perform these calculations on a variety of platforms.

At this point, we continue to evaluate the effectiveness of $D(G)$ as an indicator of software quality on more large-scale software systems. As further evidence is gathered, practitioners will have increasing confidence in using the design metric $D(G)$ in systems development.

References

[BASI81] Basili, V., "Evaluating Software Development Characteristics: Assessment of Software Measures in the Software Engineering Laboratory", *Proceedings of the Sixth Annual Software Engineering Workshop*, SEL-81-013, December 1981.

[BHAR91] Bhargava, M., *Analysis of Multiple Software Releases of AFATDS Using Design Metrics*, Master of Science Degree Thesis, Ball State University, December 1991.

[BOEH88] Boehm, B. and P. Papaccio, "Understanding and Controlling Software Costs", *IEEE Transactions on Software Engineering*, Vol. SE-14, No. 10, pp. 1462-- 1477, October 1988.

[GIBS89] Gibson, V.R. and J.A. Senn, "System Structure and Software Maintenance Performance", *Communications of the ACM*, Vol. 32, No. 3, pp.347-357, March 1989.

[GRAD87] Grady, R., "Measuring and Managing Software Maintenance", *IEEE Software*, Vol. 4, No. 5, pp.35-45, September 1987.

[HENR90] Henry, S. and C. Selig, "Predicting Source Code Complexity at the Design Stage", *IEEE Software*, Vol. 7, No. 2, pp.36--43, March 1990.

[KITC89] Kitchenham, B.A. and J.G. Walker, "A Quantitative Approach to Monitoring Software Development", *Software Engineering Journal*, pp.2-13, January 1989.

[LEW88] Lew, K., T.S. Dillon and K.E. Forward, "Software Complexity and Its Impact on Software Reliability", *IEEE Transactions on Software Engineering*, Vol. 14, No. 11, pp.1645--1655, November 1988.

[LI87] Li, H.F. and W.K. Cheung, "An Empirical Study of Software Metrics", *IEEE Transactions on Software Engineering*, Vol. SE-13, No. 6, pp.697-708, June 1987.

[PORT90] Porter, A. and R. Selby, "Empirically Guided Software Development Using Metric-Based Classification Trees", *IEEE Software*, Vol. 7, No. 2, pp.46--54, March 1990.

[ROMB90] Rombach, H.D., "Design Measurement: Some Lessons Learned", *IEEE Software*, Vol. 7, No. 2, pp.17--25, March 1990.

[ZAGE90] Zage, W.M. and D.M. Zage, "Relating Design Metrics to Software Quality: Some Empirical Results", SERC-TR-74-P, May 1990.

[ZAGE91a] Zage, W.M., D.M. Zage, S. Wagner, "The Design Metric Software Design Analyzer", SERC-TR-97-P, March 1991.

[ZAGE91b] Zage, W.M., D.M. Zage, P. McDaniel and I. Khan, "Evaluating Design Metrics on Large-Scale Software", SERC-TR-106-P, September 1991.

USING ADA IN INTEGRATING ATC SYSTEMS

Ir. Miech Groeneveld
Systems Designer ATC systems and ATC Simulators

THOMSON-CSF
Domain Air Traffic Control / SIGNAAL
P.O. Box 245
7300 AE Apeldoorn
The Netherlands

Phone number: 31.55.432119
FAX number: 31.55.432553

Abstract

To be able to integrate systems as complex as ATC systems a number of aspects has to be taken into account during the design of those systems. THOMSON-CSF/SIGNAAL takes these aspects into account during the design of their family of ATC systems EUROCAT 2000. Besides a controlled way of software design ADA is used as highly structured programming language supporting modularity, extendability and maintainability. This paper describes the way of software design and integration of the EUROCAT 2000 systems and the use of ADA therein.

1. INTRODUCTION

After the merge of the Air Traffic Control (ATC) division of Hollandse Signaalapparaten (SIGNAAL) in The Netherlands with the ATC department of THOMSON-CSF in France the strengths of both companies are combined into a new system concept of ATC systems.

In this paper a description is given of the development of a new family of ATC systems, called EUROCAT 2000, using this new system concept. During this development the fact that the components of the system have to be integrated into a complete working system is constantly taken into account.

Because there is a direct relation between the number and complexity of the interfaces in a system and its integration the first part of the paper gives a short description of a EUROCAT 2000 system.

The second part of the paper gives a description of the way system level software interfaces are defined during the design of the system. The third part of the paper describes the definition of lower level software interfaces.

The fourth part focusses on the preparations that are done before the integration and the activities that are done during the integration. Especially the preparations before the integration are very important to control the interrelated integration activities.

The fifth part describes how the components of a THOMSON-CSF EUROCAT 2000 system can be integrated into other systems (e.g. in ATC simulators).

The paper concludes with the list of references.

In the paper use is made of an example to illustrate the text. This example shows extracts of the definition of the system track interface between the radar data processing part and the display data processing part of a EUROCAT 2000 system. A system track is the logical representation of an aircraft that is detected by a number of radars.

2. EUROCAT 2000 SYSTEM DESCRIPTION

To be able to handle the currently increasing air traffic density and the increasing aircraft performance THOMSON-CSF/SIGNAAL has developed a new family of ATC systems, EUROCAT 2000.

The figure below shows the context in which such an ATC system operates.

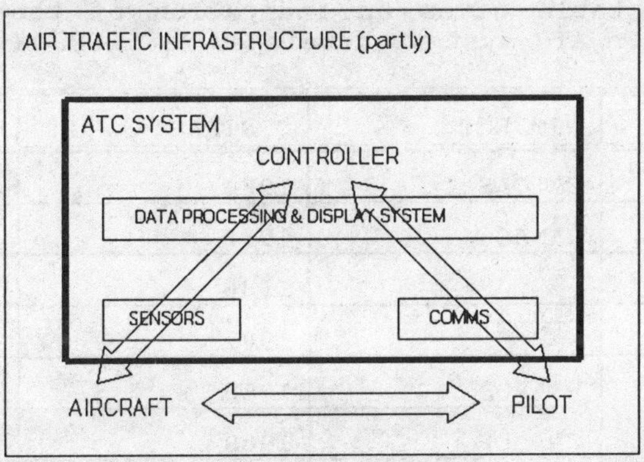

Figure 1 ATC systems context

Systems of the EUROCAT 2000 family are distributed real-time systems that are characterized by their use of standards and their system modularity.

The real-time character of the systems is shown by the strict performance requirements (it does not make sense to present an aircraft on a display a number of minutes after it has been detected by a radar) and the degree of availability (both hardware redundancy and graceful degradation are supported).

The architecture of the systems is distributed in two ways:

(1) the total system functionality is distributed over multiple processors,

(2) the controllers using the system all have their own

dedicated processor that provides a number of locally available functions.

Standards (both formal and de-facto standards) are used throughout the system: VME, Ethernet, UNIX, TCP/IP, X, ADA.

The modularity of the system is achieved by a clear system design in which mainly off-the-shelf products are used having clearly defined interfaces.

These clearly defined interfaces apply to interfaces on system level, on software level and to the interfaces between application software and underlying software platform (operating system and operating system supporting software).

Due to this approach the extension of the system with either a system level component (e.g. a processor) or a software level component (e.g. extra functionality implemented in software) is relatively simple.

Although ATC systems consist of both hardware and software components this paper focusses on the software components and on the integration of those software components.

The next table gives an indication of the amount of ADA software in ATC systems developed by THOMSON-CSF.

COUNTRY	PROJECT	CONTRACT AWARD	LINES OF CODE
DENMARK	CATCAS	1984	300,000
BELGIUM	CANAC	1986	370,000
KENYA		1986	150,000
PAKISTAN		1987	170,000
NETHERLANDS	PHAROS	1988	550,000
IRELAND	CAIRDE	1988	190,000
NEW ZEALAND	AMP	1989	250,000
CLASSIFIED	CLASSIFIED	1990	500,000 (estimate)

3. SYSTEM LEVEL SOFTWARE INTERFACES

For the definition of the interfaces on system level use is made of the real-time structured analysis method as described by Hatley and Pirbhai [1].

According to this method a number of main system functions are identified and are decomposed in sub functions to obtain insight into the complexity of the system. The interfaces between the main functions and between the sub functions are described in a functional way (indicating what data is on the interface) in a Data Dictionary.

The following is an extract of the definition of the system

track interface between the main system functions 'Handle multiple radars' and 'Display air traffic':

```
system_track (dataflow)
track_identification + track_position + track_type +
update_time + speed + heading + (mode_C)
```

The main system functions are allocated to components on system level. These can be system level hardware components (e.g. processors) or system level software components (e.g. radar data processing software, flight plan processing software). The interfaces between those components are described in a more detailed way using the previously developed Data Dictionary as basis.

For each interface between two software components the means of communication (e.g. point-to-point interface, broadcasting interface) is defined. This does not have any software impact because in the EUROCAT 2000 systems a number of communication means on system level are supported by the platform on which the application software is running.

The main system functions 'Handle multiple radars' and 'Display air traffic' are allocated respectively to the system level software components 'Radar Data Processing' and 'Display Data Processing'. An extract of the detailed interface definition between these components regarding system tracks is given below:

system_tracks: broadcasting interface via MRT store.

MRT store		
Field name	Values	Units
track_identification	1..550	
Track_x_position	-300..+300	NM
Track_y_position	-300..+300	NM
Track_type	PSR¦SSR¦CMB	
Update_time		ms
Speed	0..+5000	NM/h
Heading	0..359.9	degrees
Mode_C_present	True¦False	
Mode_C	-12..+1270	FL

Using the detailed interface definition ADA interface packages are produced for each interface between two software components. These interface packages are the physical representation of the data that is sent on the interface. ADA types used in the interface packages are defined in so-called common packages. These common packages form the collection of standard ADA types that developers use when producing their software. In this way reuse of existing type definitions is enforced and a first check on the interfaces between the software components can be performed.

The collection of interface packages and common packages is considered as a system level software component with which all the other system level software components interface.

An extract of the interface package for system tracks and an extract of one of the used common packages is given below:

```
type SYSTEM_TRACK_T is record
     TRACK_NUMBER          :
          IAC_SYSTEM_TR_PROP_TYPES.SYSTEM_TRACK_NUMBER
          _INDEX_T;
     POSITION              :
          KINEMATICS.STEREOGRAPHIC_POSITION_T;
     POSITION_UPDATE_TIME:
          ARTTS_TIME.TC_TIME_UNIVERSAL;
     DETECTION_STATUS      :
          IAC_SYSTEM_TR_PROP_TYPES.DETECTION_STATUS_T;
     SPEED                 :
          KINEMATICS.SPEED_T
     HEADING               :
          KINEMATICS.ANGLE_T;
     MODE_C_CODE_DESCRIPTOR     :
          IAC_MODE_C_CODE_TYPES.MODE_DESCRIPTOR_T;
     MODE_C                :
          KINEMATICS.MODE_C_T;
end record;
```

Extract of common package IAC_SYSTEM_TR_PROP_TYPES:

```
subtype SYSTEM_TRACK_NUMBER_INDEX_T is
      STANDARD_TYPES.INTEGER_16 range
          SYSTEM_CONF.MIN_SYSTEM_TRACK_NUMBER    ..
          SYSTEM_CONF.MAX_SYSTEM_TRACK_NUMBER;

type DETECTION_STATUS_T is (PSR, SSR, COMB);

for DETECTION_STATUS_T
      use (PSR => 0, SSR => 1, COMB => 2);
```

Next to the interface definition made so far, being the static interface definition, the dynamics of the interface are defined. For each interface a description is made when (i.e. on what stimulus) the data is sent on the interface and how the receiver has to act after receiving the data.

4. LOWER LEVEL SOFTWARE INTERFACES

Sub functions derived from a main function allocated to a system level software component are allocated to software components inside that system level software component.

For the definition of the lower level software components use is made of so-called ADA module libraries. These module libraries are developed because the system level software components are very similar over a range of systems (e.g. all EUROCAT 2000 systems perform radar data processing and display data processing, all extended EUROCAT 2000 systems perform flight plan processing). The modules in the libraries contain the ADA implementation of a number of standardized sub functions (sub functions used in more systems) and so standardized interfaces to access these functions. An ADA module can either be implemented by an ADA package or a number of grouped ADA packages.

The main system function 'Handle multiple radars' is built from a number of ADA modules like 'Multi-radar tracking' (which in fact generates the system tracks), 'Altitude tracking' and 'Automatic radars alignment'.

The interfaces between the ADA modules and newly developed (project specific) packages are defined by means of a Data Dictionary in combination with Buhr diagrams [2]. Using this notation a direct insight is given how the modules (and thus the ADA packages implementing the modules) interact. For interfaces that are already defined on system level (like system tracks) in the lower level Data Dictionary reference is made to the Data Dictionary on system level.

5. SOFTWARE INTEGRATION

During the development of the software a large number of system level interface packages, ADA packages and ADA modules become available. All these parts of the system have to be integrated to obtain a complete working system. This integration can only be performed successfully if it is done in a controlled step-by-step way.

To support the development and integration of the software use is made of the configuration management tool SPMS+ (Software Project Management System) [3]. In this tool a structure is built related to the interfaces on the different levels of the system to store all ADA packages produced. The following picture shows the SPMS+ structure for integration.

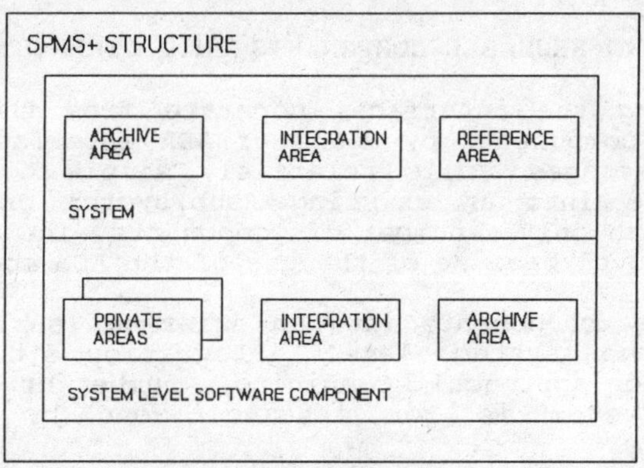

Figure 2 SPMS+ structure

Each system level software component has its own Private Areas, Integration Area and Archive Area. In the Private Areas the lower level software components that form the system level software component are produced. The lower level software components are integrated in the Integration Area of the system level software component. The static consistency of the interfaces between the lower level software components is checked during compilation. The dynamic behaviour of the interfaces is tested by activating the interfaces by giving the component external stimuli (using for instance a message feeder).

After a system level software component is completely integrated it is placed in its Archive Area. The Archive Area is used to store subsequent versions of the system level software component.

After the interface packages and common packages have been produced (see 3) they are stored in the Reference Area on system level. This area has to be used by all producers of the system level software components to test the external interfaces of these components (the interface packages represent the input and output data for all system level software components).

All system level software components that have to be integrated into a complete system are copied from their Archive Area to the Reference Area on system level.

The integration itself is done in the Integration Area on system level. During this integration a number of system level software components are combined via the interface packages and they are tested for their combined dynamical behaviour. This is an incremental process, adding one system level software component at the time.

Subsystems of the complete system that are worth it to save for subsequent integrations are stored in the Archive Area on system level. In this area also the complete system is stored after the final integration.

6. INTEGRATING REUSABLE COMPONENTS INTO OTHER SYSTEMS

By keeping the interfaces separate from the system level software components by means of ADA interface packages and common packages it is relatively simple to integrate new components into an existing (sub)system or to compose a system with only a number of components. The same applies on a lower level because of the use of the ADA module libraries.

Adding new components into an existing (sub)system is done during the system level integration (the incremental integration approach). Combining a number of components into a new system is for instance done by producing ATC Simulators.

The system level software architecture of ATC Simulators normally is different from that of operational ATC systems but a number of system level software components are common to both types of systems (e.g. there is no direct connection to a radar head in an ATC Simulator but radar data processing and display data processing is done).

In the EUROCAT 2000 development the interfaces between the Simulator specific system level software component(s) and the already existing component(s) are defined and implemented as interface packages. These interface packages are stored in the SPMS+ Reference Area on system level.

The Simulator specific system level software components are further decomposed and produced as described in 4. After production the components are integrated with the existing components using the interface packages in the SPMS+ Integration Area.

Working this way a high degree of reusability for future systems can be obtained because large parts of those systems and their interfaces already exist and can be used directly from the EUROCAT 2000 development environment (this applies to both components on system level and on lower level).

7. REFERENCES

[1] Strategies for Real-Time System Specification
Derek J. Hatley, Imtiaz A. Pirbhai
1987, Dorset House Publishing Co. Inc. - New York

[2] System Design with Ada
R.J.A. Buhr
1984, Prentice Hall Inc. - New Jersey

[3] SPMS+ Reference Manual
1991, SYSECA Logiciel - France

AN EVALUATION OF ADA SOURCE CODE REUSE*

W. M. Thomas, A. Delis & V. R. Basili

Department of Computer Science
University of Maryland
College Park, MD 20742

Abstract

This paper presents the results of a metric–based investigation into the nature and benefits of reuse in an Ada development environment. Four medium scale Ada projects developed in one organization over a three year period were analyzed. The study indicates benefits of reuse in terms of reduced error density and increased productivity. The Ada generic features are observed as an enabler of reuse at higher levels of abstraction. Finally, using several metrics, we identify trends indicating an improving reuse process.

1 Introduction

Reuse has long been cited as essential for obtaining significant improvement in software development productivity. Jones [16] indicates that only 15 percent of the developed software is unique to the applications for which it was developed. As development effort is often considered to be an exponential function of software size, a reduction in the amount of software to be created can provide a dramatic savings in development cost [8]. Reduced development cost is not the only benefit of reuse. Reused software has a track record—it has been well tested and exercised and thus may be more reliable and defect–free than newly developed software. The effect of the improved quality will not stop at the completion of development–rather the most significant benefit of reuse may be its effect on maintenance [18, 23].

To realize such benefits, techniques to achieve effective reuse have been the focus of extensive research effort over the past twenty years [24]. Generational approaches such as those described in [4, 5] attempt to achieve reuse through the generation of source code from other forms. Boyle and Muralidaharan [12] view the automatic translation as a successful mechanism to transfer programs into new programming environment. Repository based techniques strive for reuse by collecting reusable entities and providing efficient means to locate the appropriate object for a particular task. Techniques for storing objects to allow for effective automated retrieval are outlined in [2, 22]. Lanergan and Grasso [18] were able to provide for their organization a classification of functional modules in the context of the COBOL language and obtain a leverage of 60% of the regularly used code. Cheatham [25] outlines a methodology of abstract programs that can be *instantiated* to a family of concrete programs using very high level languages. Some other attempts geared predominantly towards source code reuse are found in [19, 20]. The common element in these efforts is that they all

*This was supported in part by the National Aeronautics and Space Administration grant NSG–5123 and a TRW Graduate Fellowship.

strive for the reuse of products or by-products of the software life cycle. Basili et al. [6, 7] indicate that the reuse of processes in addition to software products may result in even greater benefits.

Caldiera and Basili [13] identify four fundamental steps in a reuse process cycle and introduce the idea of metric use for the identification and extraction of reusable code. An validation study was performed focusing on the identification of reusable components in a C/Unix environment.

In this paper we discuss the use of measurement to better understand and evaluate an Ada reuse process. Using various metrics, we analyzed the effect of reuse in Ada developments in a single organization over a 3 year period. This paper extends the work presented in [13] in the Ada environment and generalizes the approach of using software metrics to determine the effectiveness of reuse. We argue that metrics, in addition to facilitating the extraction of software components, can aid in the evaluation of reused code and reuse processes. We have performed an investigation into the nature and relative benefits of reuse in the Software Engineering Laboratory (SEL). The SEL is a joint effort of the NASA/Goddard Space Flight Center, the University of Maryland, and the Computer Sciences Corporation to study software engineering issues and promote modern development techniques.

The paper is organized as follows. Section 2 describes the use of metrics for the assessment of a reuse process. Section 3 describes the environment that was analyzed. Section 4 presents the results of the analysis in three areas: the resulting effect of reuse in the development environment, how well the Ada generic constructs support reuse, and what trends can be seen as the organization gains reuse experience. Section 5 summarizes and identifies major conclusions.

2 A Measurement Guided Reuse Process

Basili and Rombach [7] outline a framework for the support of a reuse oriented development environment. The framework consists of a reuse model, describing how objects are taken from a repository to their new context, a characterization schemes for the model, allowing for effective use of the model, and an environment model supporting the integration of reuse into the development environment.

A project organization can be tailored toward reuse by separating project concerns from software component development concerns. Such an organization is described in detail in [13]. The distinction with traditional development is that in this reuse oriented organization, the project organization provides specifications to the factory organization, which retrieves the appropriate components, and provides them to the project organization for integration. As shown in figure 1, the project side of the development is relieved of the of the work in developing components, rather, it must specify, design, and integrate components into a working system. The item of concern in this organization is the system, not the components. Component release takes place in the factory side of the organization. Components requested by the project organization can be created new, or reused from a component repository. Thus activities involved in the factory side include searching for components, adapting and creating components, qualifying and storing the components. This side is focused on the component rather than the system into which the component must be integrated. It is not expected that the factory side is driven solely by project requests; rather domain analyses will sustain continuing development in the factory.

The work of Caldiera and Basili [13] deals with the factory side of the organization. The major goal of that work is the ability to locate potentially reusable components in existing software using tuples of software metrics for the qualification of the candidates. Once identified as a candidate, the component is re-engineered in to an object suitable for the repository. This re-engineering may be in making the component more general, removing certain domain dependencies, or in adding a detailed specification.

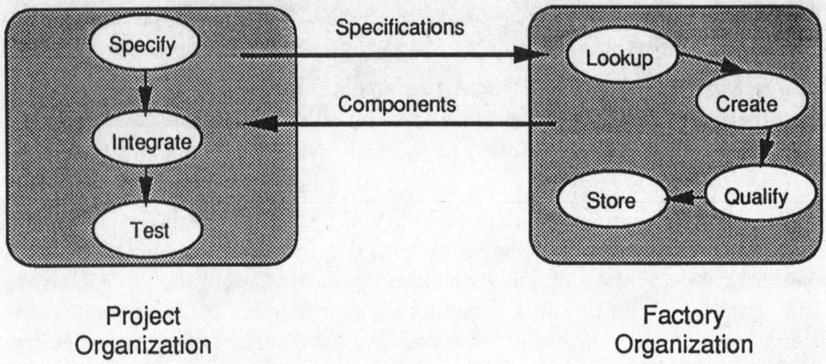

Figure 1: A Reuse-Oriented Software Development Organization

Ada provides support for reuse in several ways. Separation of specifications from bodies allows the developer to separate the concerns of the interface from the implementation. Packages provide for the encapsulation of related entities, and facilitate the creation of abstract data types. Generic program units provide parameterized program templates that enable the adaptation of an abstraction to a variety of contexts.

Even with such language features, the transition to a reuse–oriented organization will be a gradual one. As more and more experience is captured and packaged, we expect a decrease in effort spent in the product life cycle, an increase in effort spent in the factory cycle. Throughout the transition the effectiveness of reuse can be monitored. Measurement can help us to better understand, evaluate and improve the quality of the reuse processes. A general architecture supporting the integration of measurement with software development processes is outlined in [7]. The reuse-oriented organization can only be effective if it shows an overall improvement over a traditional organization. By monitoring the resulting effect on the cost and quality of the final product, we can better understand the reuse process and evaluate its effectiveness.

Our goal is to examine, through the use of various metrics, the development side of the cycle to understand how reuse facilitates Ada development. In particular, we wanted to learn what benefits can be achieved relative to reuse in terms of quality and cost. A second goal was to examine the use of the Ada generic features to determine how well they support the reuse process. Finally, we try to identify trends that can be observed as the organization gains reuse experience. To determine the effectiveness of reuse in the environment, we examined error density, program complexity, and productivity relative to reuse rates. We examined the use of generics relative to error density and complexity to better determine how the Ada language features were being used in the context of reuse.

3 Description of the Experiment

We analyzed a collection of four medium-scale Ada projects developed at the NASA/Goddard Space Flight Center. The projects ranged in size from 35 to 75 thousand non-comment non-blank source lines of code (KSLOC), and required development effort of 30 to 175 technical staff months. We analyzed reuse from two perspectives, the first, off-the-shelf code reuse of previously developed compilation units, and the second, reuse of functionality achieved with generic instantiations. Another direction that was taken was to investigate the project development over time, and assess how experience acquired to date has contributed to greater reuse achievements in the SEL environment.

The percentage of reused code on these projects ranged from 9 to 87 percent (verbatim), and 29 to 94 percent (verbatim and with modification) [17].

The purpose of this experiment was to quantify reuse with objective metrics, assess the impact of reuse on complexity, and to investigate the viability of a metrics based approach to reuse in an Ada development environment. The NASA/GSFC SEL has collected a wealth of data on software development over the past fifteen years. We used several types of data in our analyses. The first type of data has to do with the origin of a component—whether it was newly created or reused. For each component in the system a component origination form is filled out by the developer, identifying the origin as one of four classes: newly created, reused with extensive modification (greater than 25% of the SLOC modified), reused with slight modification (less than 25% of SLOC modified), and reused verbatim. For Ada systems, a compilation unit is viewed as a component. Thus our analysis focuses on looking at the different classes of compilation units.

Our second notion of reuse is the reuse achieved via the instantiation of generic units. For this analysis, we split our system into two parts, the generic part, consisting of units associated with generic library units and instantiated library units, and the non-generic part, consisting of units associated with all other library units. As with custom versus reused code, we believed we would see differences between the two classes.

We analyzed the systems with a source code static analysis tool, ASAP [14], which provided us with a static profile of each compilation unit, including, for example, basic complexity measures such as McCabe's Cyclomatic Complexity and Halstead's Software Science, as well as counts of various types of declarations. ASAP also identifies all **WITH** statements, so we were able to develop a measure of the externals visible to each unit.

Two measures of development productivity were analyzed, namely, the productivity associated with the code/unit test phase, and the productivity in the system and acceptance test phases. We also use, as a measure of quality, counts of development error reports for each compilation unit.

4 Results

In this section we discuss results of our analysis in three areas. The first compares reused with newly created code from the perspective of the resulting effect on product quality and development effort. We then analyze how well the Ada Generic features facilitate reuse. Finally, we discuss how measurement can be used to identify trends in reuse over several projects.

4.1 Effect of Code Reuse on Product Development

Reuse has been advocated as a means for reducing development cost and improving reliability. Boehm and Papaccio [9] identify the reuse of software components as one of the most attractive strategies for improving productivity.

The following sections describe what we have seen relative to reuse across four recent projects in three areas: error density, product complexity, and productivity.

4.1.1 Error Density

Rework has been identified as a major cost factor in software development. Jones [15] indicates that it typically accounts for over 50% of the effort for large projects. Reuse of previously developed,

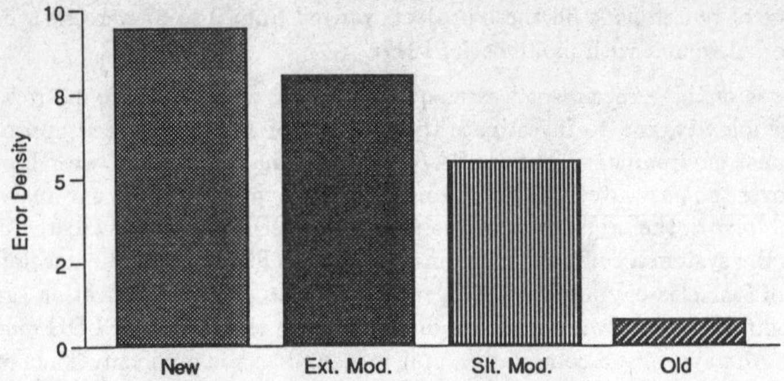

Figure 2: Error Density by Class of Reuse

tested, and qualified components can reduce the number of errors in development, thus reducing rework effort.

Figure 2 shows the error density found in each of our four reuse classes over the four projects analyzed. The bar labeled "New" indicates error density in newly created components. "Ext. Mod.", "Slt. Mod." and "Old" refer to error densities found in the components in the classes of Extensively Modified, Slightly Modified, Reused Verbatim, respectively. As expected, fewer errors were found associated with reused code vs. new code. Error density (Errors/KSLOC) was found to be 0.9 in the code reused verbatim, 5.6 in the slightly modified code, 8.1 in the extensively modified code, and 9.5 in the newly developed code. The lower density in the reused components implies an easier time in integrating the reused components into a new system than in developing code from scratch. However, it also appears that there is a significant difference in error densities of the modified code compared to the verbatim code. In fact, there seems to be no difference in error density between components that were developed new and those reused with extensive modification. The slightly modified code shows a 40% improvement in error density relative to newly developed code; however the most significant benefit comes with the unchanged components, as they show a 90% reduction relative to the new components. Clearly, the greatest benefit comes from reusing the code without modification.

4.1.2 Product Complexity

A software system can be viewed as an inter-related collection of components. The quality of the system thus is a function of the quality of both the components and the component relations. Cyclomatic complexity [21] is a graph–theoretic measure of the control organization of a component. Highly complex components may be more error-prone and difficult to understand. In the context of reuse, excess complexity is seen as an inhibitor of effective reuse, as it can make the integration and rework costs outweigh the cost of developing a component from scratch [13]. The complexity of the component interface is also an important factor. Limiting program dependencies is suggested as a means for improving reusability, and techniques for transforming existing software to limit dependencies is discussed in [3]. Agresti et al. [1] have developed multivariate models of software qualities using characteristics of the software architecture. Increasing dependencies in the system is shown to reduce the reliability of the system. There is a trade–off between these two complexities. One can achieve a simple interface complexity at the expense of increased internal complexity, and vice versa. Developers strive for the proper balance of these complexities.

To assess the internal complexity of the components in the systems, we examined the cyclomatic

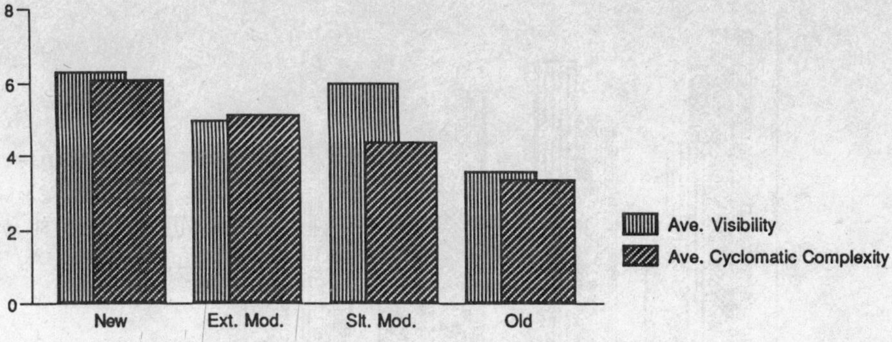

Figure 3: Relationship of Reuse and Program Complexity

complexity of the executable program units. As a rough measure of the interface complexity of the compilation unit we observed the number of library units that are made visible to the compilation unit. Figure 3 shows the relationship between reuse, cyclomatic complexity, and visibility. Among the executable program units, the mean program unit cyclomatic complexity was lower for reused components than for the new components. New components had an average complexity of 6.4, extensively modified 5.1, slightly modified 4.4, and unchanged 3.6. A nonparametric test of the significance of the difference in the class medians indicates the difference to be statistically significant at for all pairs of classes except in distinguishing between new and extensively modified components. The overall relation ship of reuse with project complexity is not so clear. While there seems to be a significant drop in average complexity (over the entire system) from the first project to the second, there is only a slight decrease in each of the subsequent projects.

In terms of the visibility to the compilation units, we observed a lower average number of visible library units in the verbatim reused components. This average visibility was found to be 6.3 in the class of new components, 5.0 in the extensively modified, 6.0 in the slightly modified, and 3.6 in the reused verbatim. While there was a significant difference (at .0001 level) between the visibility in the reused verbatim class and each of the other classes, no such distinction was found when comparing the classes of new, slightly modified and extensively modified components. This supports the view presented in [3] that reducing dependencies may make a module more reusable.

One possible explanation for the lower complexity observed in the reused code is that the reused components comprise only simple, straightforward functions (e.g. general utilities), and as such, should have lower complexity and fewer dependencies. However, in this environment we saw an increasing level of reuse from project to project, and a decreasing complexity over the entire system. Figure 4 shows the relationship between reuse and complexity from the four observed projects. We see reuse of increasingly complex objects, both in terms of their internals and their interfaces, but at the same time see an overall reduction in the complexity of the entire system. While it certainly is true that general utilities are being reused, it also is evident that there is a trend toward the reuse of more complex functionality.

4.1.3 Productivity

We also analyzed productivity across the projects from the perspective of reuse. In particular, we wanted to see if reuse would provide a significant reduction in effort in the testing phases, as well as in the coding phase. We defined implementation productivity as thousands of non–comment, non–blank source lines of code divided by staff-months (KSLOC/SM) charged during the code/unit

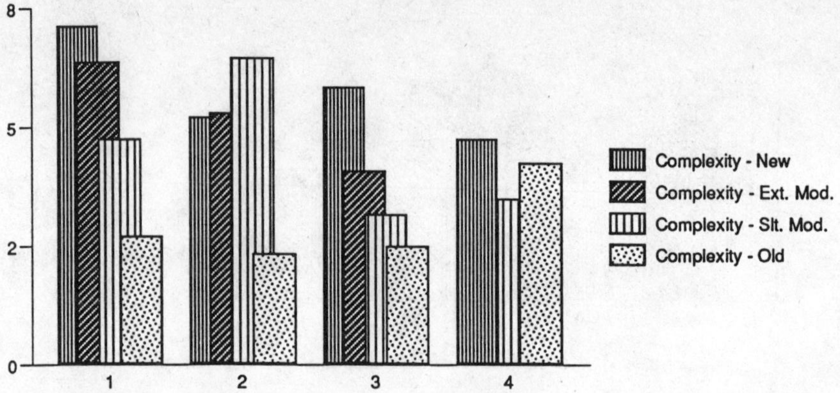

Figure 4: Complexity of Reused Objects Over Time

test phase, and test productivity as KSLOC divided by staff-months charged during the system and acceptance test phases.

Figure 5 shows that as reuse increases, productivity increases both in the implementation phase and the test phase. The lines indicate the (log of the) percentage of reuse, both verbatim reuse and total reuse, and the bars indicate implementation and test productivities. Implementation productivity ranged from 2.5 KSLOC/SM on the project with the least reuse (26%) to 5.8 KSLOC/SM for the project with the most reuse (94%). It was expected that reuse would have a significant positive impact on effort expended in the implementation phase. We observed a similar result with respect to productivity in the system and acceptance test phases, as we saw a productivity range from 2.5 to 6.5 KSLOC/SM. While this data is not sufficient to build an accurate model relating reuse and cost, it does provide an indication that the effect of reuse is widespread—in addition to the savings in the implementation phase we see an indication of savings in integration and test phase.

Figure 5: Effect of Reuse on Productivity

4.2 Generics vs. Non–Generics

Booch [10] identifies the primary use of generic units as reusable software components. The or increased complexity. To investigate this, we divided the components in two classes - generics,

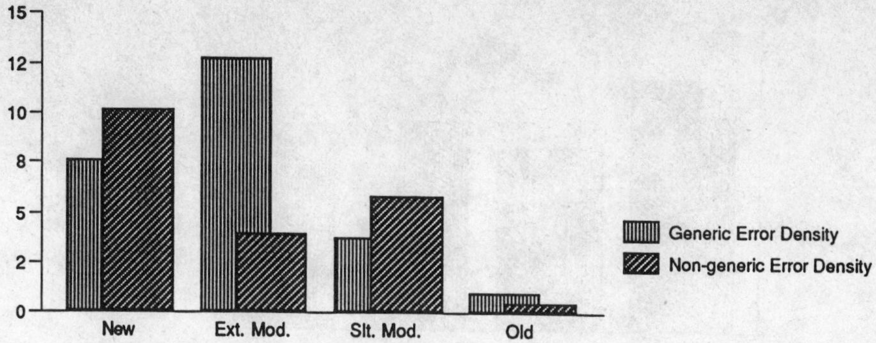

Figure 6: Error Density Profile in Generic and Non–Generic Components

consisting those compilation units related to generic library units either by instantiation or as a secondary unit, and non-generics, consisting of the others. Ignoring the origin of the components, we see a lower error density in the generics, relative to the non-generics, as the error density was 4.6 errors/KSLOC in the generic part, and 7.7 in the non generic part. We expected a significantly lower error density in the generic part, since it may contain a greater proportion of reused software. When we further distinguish between classes of component origins, as described previously, we see more interesting patterns. Figure 6 shows the error density profile in each class of component origin for both the generic units and the non-generic units. Overall, among the newly developed units, we found a significantly lower error density in the generic components (8.0 errors/KSLOC) than in the non-generic components (10.1). Among the components reused with modification, the overall error density is 6.6. For the generics, we found a slightly higher error density, 7.5 errors/KSLOC, vs. 5.7 for the non-generic part. Among the reused verbatim components, overall error density is very low (0.7 errors/KSLOC), and there was little difference in the error densities associated with the reused generics versus reused non-generics.

These results may be interpreted as follows: either that the developers of the generic units took more care in their creation, and thus made fewer mistakes, or that the generic components were simple units to develop, and should have fewer errors associated with them. Further analysis of the complexity of the newly created generics over time show that more and more complex objects are being created generically, and simpler objects being created as non-generics. Figure 7 depicts this trend. As the generic proportion of the software increases, we see little change in the complexity of the generic part, while observing a significant reduction in the complexity in the non-generic part.

There is a different pattern in the generic components when comparing error density by origin. Among the modified components, there is a lower error density than in the new components. However, in the class of modified components we see a higher error density in the generics than in non-generics. This suggests a greater difficulty in modifying generic components than in non–generic.

4.3 Reuse Trends

Our final purpose was to examine the effect of reuse over time using a metric–based approach. The change to a more generic architecture is evident from the percentage of the generic portion of the system. This change provided significant benefits—a reduction in development cost, duration, and error density [11]. Looking across all projects, we see few differences among the classes in terms of the complexity metrics. However, when we look at each project individually, we see a changing

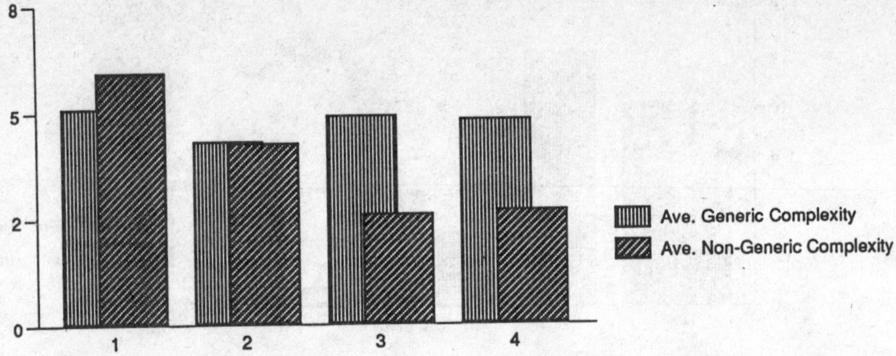

Figure 7: Cyclomatic Complexity in Generic and Non-Generic Components

pattern of reuse. Figures 8 and 9 show the changing profile of reuse over time. The class of custom components includes both the newly created and extensively modified components, while the reused class includes slightly modified and verbatim reused components.

Across the four projects we see a slight trend of increasing complexity in the reused components, and decreasing complexity in the custom components, both in terms of internal (cyclomatic) and external (visibility) complexities. This suggests that as an organization packages more and more domain experience, the complex objects will be reused, and relatively simple objects will be newly created to join them together. This is supported by the falling complexity in the custom, non-generic components (i.e. the most application specific components). We do not see such a clear pattern in the visibility of the custom non generic components. This may simply be evidence that these components are still being created at a relatively high level in the application hierarchy. When we examine the complexities of the reused components, we see a trend of increasing complexity in the reused generics, both in terms of cyclomatic complexity and visibility. This may indicate that more complex objects (including those at higher levels in the application hierarchy) are being reused.

Analysis of the complexities of the objects over time illustrates the improvement of the reuse process. Object-Oriented design and the Ada language features may be a primary reason for the improving reuse process in this organization. The increased complexity of the reused objects suggests that reuse is occurring at higher levels of abstraction. This supports the notion that a model of reusability must be evolved over time to keep pace with a changing environment [13]. While the

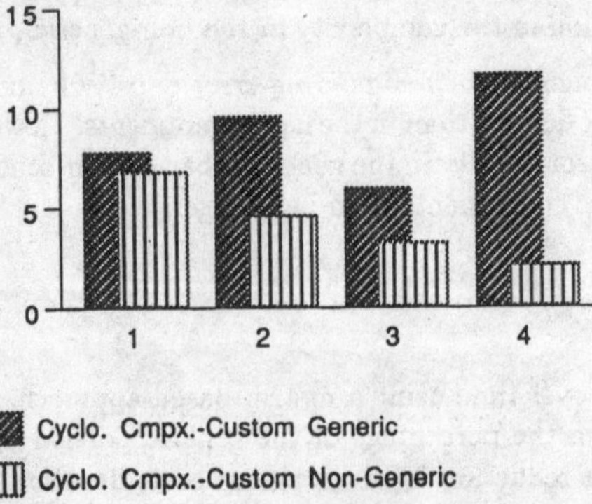

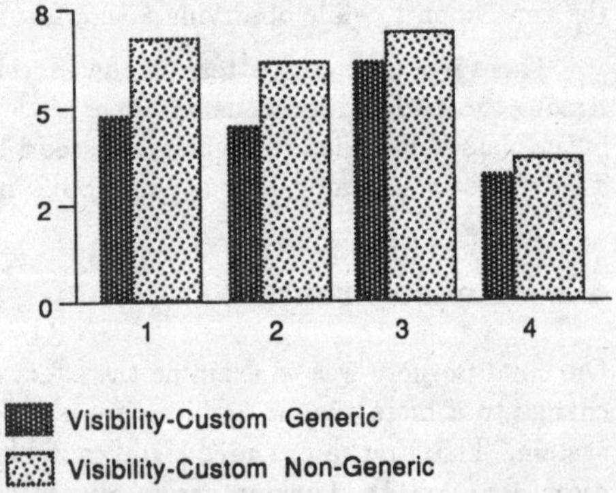

Figure 8: Complexity Trends in Custom Components

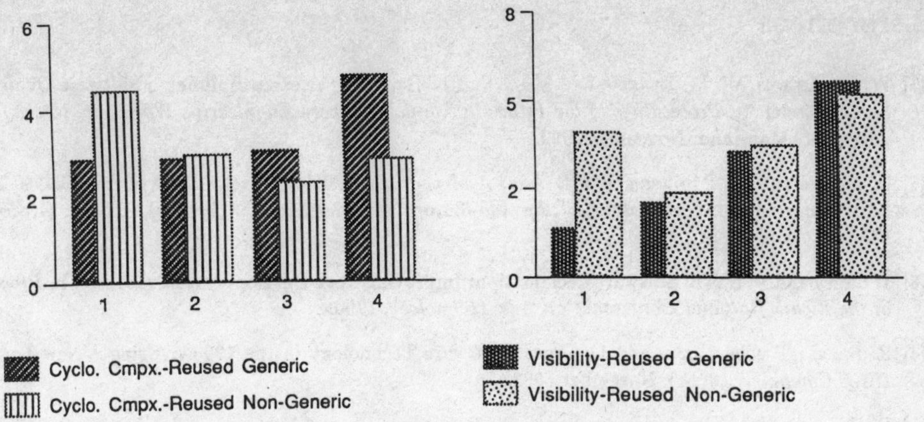

Figure 9: Complexity Trends in Reused Components

lower cyclomatic complexity and visibility associated with the reused components indicates that such measures may work well in the initial assessment of reuse candidates. Clearly, however, reuse with Ada is not limited to these types of candidates.

5 Conclusions

In this paper we present a metrics-based process to assess Ada reuse. We analyzed an Ada development environment from a reuse perspective and found significant benefits of increasing reuse. Productivity increased and error density was reduced. As expected, we observed that while reduced error densities (compared to newly created components) can be achieved both in verbatim reuse and in reuse with modification, a much more substantial reduction occurred with the verbatim reuse. This supports the view that the most benefit from reuse comes from direct reuse without modification.

The Ada package and generic constructs enable effective reuse within an application domain. The marked improvement in verbatim reuse has shown substantially lower error rates and development effort. The adoption of a generic architecture in the SEL [11] clearly has resulted in an improved, reuse-oriented development. We see no indication that generics are significantly more difficult to develop than non-generics, in fact we have seen lower error densities in newly developed generic components than in newly developed non-generic components. In terms of reuse of the generics, we observed little difference between error rates associated with verbatim reuse of generics and non-generics. However, when looking at the modified components, extensive modification of the generics was seen to be significantly more error prone than extensive modification of non-generic components.

Finally, we have indications that metrics can be used to show trends of an improving reuse process. The increased use of generics has resulted in the creation of simpler custom components, and allowed the reuse of more complex components.

6 Acknowledgment

We would like to thank Frank McGarry of NASA/GSFC and William Agresti of the Mitre Corporation for their help in the realization of this study.

References

[1] W. W. Agresti, W. M. Evanco, and M. C. Smith. Early Experiences Building a Software Quality Prediction Model. In *Proceedings of the Fifteenth Annual Software Engineering Workshop*, NASA/GSFC, Greenbelt, Maryland, November 1990.

[2] N. Badaro and Th. Moineau. ROSE–Ada: A Method and a Tool to Help Reuse of Ada Codes. In *Ada: The Choice for '92 (Proceedings of the Ada–Europe International Conference)*, Athens, Greece, May 1991.

[3] J. Bailey and V. Basili. Software Reclamation: Improving Post-Development Reusability. In *Proceedings of the Eighth National Conference on Ada Technology*, 1990.

[4] R. Balzer, T. Cheatham, and C. Green. Software Technology in the 1990's: Using a New Paradigm. *IEEE Computer*, 16(11), November 1983.

[5] D. Barstow. Rapid Prototyping, Automatic Programming, and Experimental Sciences. *Software Engineering Notes*, 7(5), December 1982.

[6] V. Basili, D. Rombach, J. Bailey, and A. Delis. Ada Reusability Analysis and Measurement. In *Proceedings of the 6th Symposium on Empirical Foundations of Information and Software Sciences*, Atlanta, Georgia, October 1988.

[7] V. R. Basili and H. D. Rombach. Support for Comprehensive Reuse. *Software Engineering Journal*, 6(5), September 1991.

[8] B. W. Boehm. Software Engineering Economics. *IEEE Transactions on Software Engineering*, SE–10(1), January 1984.

[9] B. W. Boehm and P. N. Papaccio. Understanding and Controlling Software Costs. *IEEE Transactions on Software Engineering*, 14(10), October 1988.

[10] G. Booch. *Software Engineering using Ada.* Benjamin–Cummings, second edition, 1987.

[11] E. W. Booth and M.E. Stark. Designing Configurable Software: COMPASS Implementation Concepts. In *Proceedings of Tri-Ada 1991*, October 1991.

[12] J. Boyle and M. Muralidaran. Program Reusability through Program Transformation. *IEEE Transactions on Software Engineering*, SE–10(5), September 1984.

[13] G. Caldiera and V. R. Basili. Identifying and Qualifying Reusable Software Components. *IEEE Computer*, 24(2), February 1991.

[14] D. Doubleday. ASAP: Ada Static Analyzer Program. Technical report, University of Maryland, May 1987. CR–TR–1897.

[15] C. Jones. *Programming Productivity.* McGraw–Hill, 1986.

[16] T.C. Jones. Reusability in Programming: A Survey of the State of the Art. *IEEE Transactions on Software Engineering*, SE–10(5), September 1984.

[17] R. Kester. SEL Ada Reuse Analysis and Representations. In *Proceedings of the 15th Annual GSFC Software Engineering Workshop.* NASA/GSFC, November 1990.

[18] R. Lanergan and C. Grasso. Software Engineering with Reusable Designs and Code. *IEEE Transactions on Software Engineering*, SE–10(5), September 1984.

[19] S. Litvintchouk and A. Matsumoto. Design of Ada Systems Yielding Reusable Components: An Approach Using Structured Algebraic Specification. *IEEE Transactions on Software Engineering*, SE–10(5), September 1984.

[20] Y. Matsumoto. Some Experiences in Promoting Reusable Software: Presentation in Higher Abstract Levels. *IEEE Transactions on Software Engineering*, SE–10(5), September 1984.

[21] T. McCabe. A Complexity Measure. *IEEE Transactions on Software Engineering*, SE-2(4), December 1976.

[22] R. Prieto-Diaz and P. Freeman. Classyfying Software for Reusability. *IEEE Software*, 4(1), January 1987.

[23] H. D. Rombach. Software Reuse: A Key to the Maintenance Problem. *Information and Software Technology*, 33(1), January/February 1991.

[24] T. Standish. An Essay on Software Reuse. *IEEE Transactions on Software Engineering*, 10(5), September 1984.

[25] Jr. T. Cheatham. Reusability Through Program Transformations. *IEEE Transactions on Software Engineering*, SE–10(5), September 1984.

PORTING EMBEDDED REAL-TIME ADA SOFTWARE

Fred A. Maymir-Ducharme, PhD - *Grumman Data Systems*
1000 Woodbury Road (D12/237), Woodbury, NY 11797 USA

1. INTRODUCTION

Ada, developed in response to the software problems being faced by US Department of Defense (DoD) in the 1970s, is a single high-order programming language designed to, amongst other things, facilitate the development of portable software. One requirement for the development of Ada was that the language be portable. Standardization of the language has gone a long way toward achieving that goal. For real-time systems, however, that goal is still far from being achieved. Besides the use of machine-dependent assembly language, part of the problem is caused by the differences in timing between Runtime Environments (RTEs.) Timing requirements for a system may be met using one RTE and not met on another. In this case, although the code may compile and execute on both RTEs, the system does not meet its (timing) requirements on the latter; therefore, the system is not portable. Another deterrent to portability is the set of implementation-dependent features permitted by the Reference Manual (RM) [1]. Low-level access to machine capabilities, for example, require exploiting the specific machine architecture. Therefore, the RM does not constrain compiler vendors on the implementation of these features. Since embedded, real-time systems frequently utilize and depend on these low-level access capabilities, they do not port well, due to differences in the implementations of these features.

Experiences during a recent research project involving the porting of Ada software are discussed and analyzed. The port entailed going from an Intel processor to a Motorola processor. The port also entailed using different compilers, architectures and periphery. This paper describes the process used to port embedded, real-time Ada software. Deterrents experienced are identified, alongside the solutions implemented to successfully transport the Ada software. A summary of "Lessons Learned" and critical issues to consider when porting from dissimilar systems are included in the conclusion. Future industry needs and directions in the area of Ada transportability are also identified and discussed.

A primary benefit of the Ada language is the potential portability of software written in Ada [1]. Since the inception of the language, a strong emphasis of the Ada Joint Program Office (AJPO) has been the maintenance of a single Ada standard. Part of the rationale for this focus is to assure the portability of Ada through the standardization of the language. The standardization has been successful to the extent that the efforts of the Department of Defense (DoD), American National Standards Institute (ANSI), International Standards Organization (ISO) and other standards organizations have resulted in a single Ada standard. In addition, the process of validating Ada compilers is widely accepted to ensure that the language is not prey to multiple dialects. However, the standardization process does not cover the area of direct hardware control or performance and response time. These areas are of particular interest to developers of embedded real-time systems.

Embedded real-time systems are highly interactive within their environments. The result of this is the need to directly control various hardware devices. In addition to controlling the hardware, there are stringent timing constraints on these systems, which necessitate that the controlling software be extremely efficient. When software directly controls hardware, the level of portability is diminished.

Sound software engineering principles [2] are essential to facilitate the portability of Ada software. Transportability requires that the development phase must minimize the dependencies on hardware control outside the control of the language. Guidelines for the development of embedded real-time systems have been developed to maximize transportability [3,4,6]. A basic tenet of these guidelines is that portability is not a yes or no attribute; that is, software is not either portable or nonportable, but rather portable to varying degrees. The guidelines provide a baseline for increasing the degree of portability of embedded real-time software.

One of the objectives of this project was to validate these transportability guidelines [6]. These guidelines were validated by comparing them to the experiences of an actual porting effort, transporting existing real-time software to a different target configuration, using a different Ada compiler. The second objective of this project was to derive an updated and validated set of transportability guidelines specifically tuned to embedded real-time systems, including a detailed report on the procedures followed and the lessons learned.

2. ADA SOFTWARE PORTED AND THE TRANSPORT GUIDELINES

2.1 The Automated Missile Defense System

The software system transported, the Automated Missile Defense System (AMDS), is a missile control system designed to acquire positional information on mechanized targets through radar, fire missiles to intercept the targets and to control the missiles during their flight. The AMDS operates in two modes, manual and automatic. In automatic mode the targeting and firing of the missiles is controlled by the computer, and in manual mode the targeting and firing of the missiles is controlled by the human operator with a mouse. Both the mechanized targets and the launched missiles are displayed in color on a two-dimensional battlefield.

The AMDS utilizes two separate types of timing constraints: a strict timing budget, which details the average execution times allowed for the majority of the system, and a set of timing thresholds for individual functions within the system. The timing budget reflects the timing model developed in the original design and sets timing standards which allow for each program activity to be serviced by the cpu. The budget reflects average timing standards a allows for program activities to exceed their allotted time in any given cycle without adversely effecting the long-term functionality of the system. The timing thresholds are hard real- time constraints which result in a mission failure if they are not met.

The timing budget handles 205 interrupts per second and accounts for 2040 total activities per second. A partial list of the timing budget is shown in the table below:

Function	Average Iterations per sec	Time/ Iter'n (ms)	Required Time (ms)
Decode Missile Report	200	800	160000
Compute Missile Altitude	200	2000	400000
Transmit Missile Update	10	200	2000
Display Missile Position	200	725	145000

Some of the timing thresholds required for the AMDS are shown in the table below:

Function Description	Timing Constraint
Target Reticle(Mouse Cursor)	- Current w/in 50ms
Missile Guidance Messages	- < 100ms between messages
Target Reports	- 1000 reports/second

The AMDS was developed in Ada. The completed system contains over 3000 Lines of Code (LOC), and eleven concurrent Ada tasks that communicate through the Ada rendezvous. Two benchmarks are required for the operation to be considered successful. One is that the AMDS can be successfully re-compiled and maintain equivalent functionality. The other requirement is that it also meet its timing constraints.

The original AMDS was targeted on an Intel 80386-16MHz. The man-machine interface consisted of a Logitech Mouse and EGA graphics. The system was developed on a MicroVAX II (VMS) using a DDC- I compiler.

The re-hosted AMDS is targeted onto a gpc68020 microprocessor with a m68881 math co-processor also running at 16MHz. A Sun 3/80 workstation running with the Verdix Ada Development System (Verdix/VADS 5.41) cross compiler serving as the host, including the Sun graphics terminal for the man-machine interface; the display is on the 19" color monitor and the mouse is the Sun's two button mouse.

2.2 Transport Guidelines

The following is a condensed version of the transport guidelines [6] used by this transport project and critiqued in this paper. The guidelines were broken up into the following sections by the original guideline author. The list of guidelines are included in this section solely for quick references; please refer to the original document [6] for additional information and elaboration of the guidelines cited below.

ERRONEOUS PROGRAMS AND INCORRECT ORDER DEPENDENCIES:

Guide(01): Programmers should be aware of specific mechanisms that produce erroneous programs. Care must be taken to avoid these mechanisms.

Guide(02): Incorrect order dependencies should not exist in well designed programs.

STORAGE ISSUES:

Guide(03): If memory space is limited, determine how specific the linker (binder) is when selecting data and code for inclusion into the executable image.

Guide(04): For array types which must have exact storage layout requirements, use a length clause for the entire object and insure that the number of elements multiplied by the bits specified for all possible values of the element type is exactly equal to the number of bits specified by the length clause.

Guide(05): If access types are used, verify that sufficient space is made available for each access collection.

Guide(06): If tasks are used, verify that sufficient space is made available for task activation.

Guide(07): If pragma PACK is used, verify that it is supported in the same way in both implementations.

Guide(08): Dependence on the STORAGE_ERROR exception is not advised.

PERFORMANCE ISSUES:

Guide(09): If pragma suppress is used, verify that it has an effect and that performance improves.

Guide(10): Use of package MACHINE_CODE should be strictly controlled and delineated by configuration management.

Guide(11): If pragma INLINE is used, insure that the compiler generates a warning if the desired effect is not achieved.

Guide(12): Be aware that some implementations have substantial overhead associated with the elaboration of block statements.

Guide(13): Exception propagation overhead varies considerably, among implementations. Document any expected fast exception propagation.

Guide(14): Do not use implementation-defined exceptions. Be aware of compiler inconsistencies.

Guide(15): Aggregate assignments both in elaboration and execution code vary widely between implementations.
Guide(16): Be aware that exception handling overhead can vary greatly as a function of compiler and/or linker switches.
Guide(17): Measurements should be done on the execution time of every procedure as well as each rendezvous.

TASKING ISSUES:

Guide(18): There is no standard scheduling algorithm. Use a configuration file to define all of the priority constraints, specifying priorities in terms of PRIORITY'LAST and PRIORITY'PRED.
Guide(19): Do not depend on task activation to occur at the priority of the activator or the task being activated.
Guide(20): It is advised that each task have a "Synchronize" entry that is signaled as a consequence of the main program execution.
Guide(21): If the main program terminates via an exception handler, it should abort any library-level tasks.
Guide(22): Task abortion may or may not take place immediately.
Guide(23): Only specify one task per abort statement.
Guide(24): The use of implementation defined pragmas to indicate specific optimizations should be allowed only when absolutely necessary.
Guide(25): Do not depend on "Delay 0.0" to result in a scheduling event.
Guide(26): Do not expect delay resolutions of less than 5ms.
Guide(27): If more than one delay alternative is specified in a selective wait, do not depend on a certain one being taken.
Guide(28): Use pragma SHARED for any scalar variables accessed by more than one task.
Guide(29): Do not allow a task that contains interrupt entries to terminate prior to disabling the interrupt source.
Guide(30): Tasks with interrupt entries should have the highest priority.
Guide(31): Do not perform an unconditional rendezvous within an accept statement for an interrupt entry.

NUMERIC ISSUES:

Guide(32): Do not depend on NUMERIC_ERROR, as some implementations do not support it.
Guide(33): Make sure that each calculation is performed within the range of the base type of the operands.
Guide(34): Do not depend on overflow detection, as some implementations do not support it.
Guide(35): Do not use equality comparisons for floating points.
Guide(36): Avoid dependence on a particular rounding convention.
Guide(37): If errors are possible due to the rounding algorithm used for the REAL predefined operator types, the type should be defined with additional digits of accuracy, or additional code is necessary to compensate for accumulated error.
Guide(38): Do not use predefined numeric types.
Guide(39): Do not depend on fixed point type length clauses that are not a power of two as some implementations do not support it.
Guide(40): It must not be assumed that a static expression is evaluated with the same accuracy as that of the model numbers of a particular real type.

SUBPROGRAM ISSUES:

Guide(41): Since parameters of composite types may be passed by reference, it is possible to have multiple access paths for these objects.
Guide(42): Verify that any storage created for function returns is deallocated after the call.
Guide(43): Always assign a value to an OUT mode parameter.

Guide(44): If command line (invocation) parameters are used for the main program (to invoke an Ada program), application access to them should be strictly hidden by an application defined subprogram.
Guide(45): Functions should not have side-effects. Any necessary function side-effects should be clearly documented.

INPUT/OUTPUT ISSUES:

Guide(46): Assume as little as possible about the I/O support available.
Guide(47): Handling of temporary files should not use a null string to name the file.
Guide(48): Requiring interchange of any files between two separate environments has a high probability of making a program nonportable.
Guide(49): Be cautious while porting I/O with access types or unconstrained types.
Guide(50): If concurrent sharing of external files (this is implementation dependent) is required, document and provide details.
Guide(51): Avoid use of the FORM parameter.
Guide(52): Do not depend on DATA_ERROR.
Guide(53): Always close files prior to termination.
Guide(54): Do not depend on a specific representation for LINE, PAGE, and FILE terminators.
Guide(55): Do not depend on a specific representation for GET_LINE or GET.
Guide(56): Many systems buffer I/O. This effects the system timing.

OTHER ISSUES:

Guide(57): Avoid use of implementation defined attributes, types, and exceptions.
Guide(58): Use only ISO seven-bit characters in comment fields.
Guide(59): Restrict representation clauses for enumeration literals to unsigned integers.
Guide(60): Always initialize a variable prior to using it.
Guide(61): Document the bit ordering used for all record representation clauses.
Guide(62): Do not reference generated names for implementation dependent record components.
Guide(63): Isolate implementation dependencies within separate compilation units.
Guide(64): Provide fully expanded names for all objects not defined in the immediate compilation unit.
Guide(65): Avoid use of languages other than Ada.
Guide(66): Unchecked Conversion should only be used for statistically constrained types of the same size.
Guide(67): Do not reference SYSTEM.MEMORY_SIZE.
Guide(68): Modifications to vendor supplied runtime must be clearly documented and categorized as application related or target processor related.
Guide(69): Add a field in the documentation template, for every program unit, indicating if any nonportable features are present.

3. PORTING ADA SOFTWARE

3.1 The Transport Process

The task of validating the transportability guidelines was broken down into a three-step process. During the first step, transport team became familiar with the existing documentation. This step consisted of a comprehensive review of the AMDS source code and of the "Transportability Guideline for Ada Real-Time Software," as well as the other literature cited in the bibliography. The porting team then used the insights gained from these papers to formulate the remainder of the approach.

During the second step, the AMDS was ported to the Microbar gpc68020_68881 board utilizing the VADS 5.41 compiler, running on a Unix based Sun 3/80 as a host. Both the approach taken to perform the port and the actual performing of the port were geared toward gaining insights into the porting process. These insights were used to further validate and extend the transportability guidelines.

The first task of porting the Automated Missile Defense System was to customize the environment to enhance the portability of the application program. This consisted of choosing the exact configurations of the hardware and software of the system, as well as choosing the Ada compilation system and library packages to be used. This can only be done after an analysis of the application has been made. The environment chosen should minimize the required source modifications, increase the reliability of the ported application, and decrease the number of errors which become evident after compilation time.

After customizing the environment, a test bed was developed to assess whether the porting of the application is successful. Tests were developed for the final application for the modules that comprised the application. The modified modules were the most crucial for test development, which required testing for functional equivalence and performance analysis.

In parallel with the development of the test bed, the code modification of the Automated Missile Defense System was performed. This included removing and/or replacing machine-dependent assembly code, varying compiler Ada functions, and implementation-dependent features (e.g., pragmas) that differed in implementation or support. The code modification first required the identification of the differences and the code to be modified. After modifications were made, the test procedures were used to determine performance problems.

After the Automated Missile Defense System was ported, the final step in the validation process was to analyze the findings of the port, compare these to the findings found in the initial review and prepare a comprehensive list of recommended changes and extensions to the guidelines. The guidelines where thereby validated and extended appropriately.

3.2 Critique of the Guidelines

The existing guidelines contain a thorough analysis of the coding issues that are most likely to impact portability. Because of this, the existing guidelines may be utilized as a highly effective tool by the programmer to develop more portable code. However, a stronger emphasis on the issues of form and style for the entire software product is needed. This should include additional coverage of coding style, in-line comments and documentation. While these things will not necessarily make the code any more portable they will aid in the task of understanding the software design and code, facilitating the port effort.

The code must be testable. In order to adequately test the software, the transporter must know the functionality of the system and of each module within it. It is particularly important that those modules which are to be modified are accurately described with regards to their functionality. A test suite with the associated input and test results expected should be included with the code submitted for porting. This is necessary to validate and verify the functional and temporal equivalence of the software after the transport is complete.

Source and object code of all test programs should be provided by the developer. This makes it easier for the transporter to test the system after it has been ported. Admittedly, this suggestion does raise the rather unfortunate problem of portability for the test programs. The design of the test programs is reusable without these hindrances.

Vendor-supplied library units that were used in the original development of the application should be identified. This information is important to the transporter because the same library units will probably not be available on the target system. This presents a particular problem when dealing with real-time systems, because few library units are supplied with most compilation systems targeted to a bare board. For example, VADS does not supply a text_io package due to the fact that there is not a standard monitor interface to develop one around.

3.3 New Guidelines Developed

Guide 70) Remove pragma inline during the debugging stage of the port and replace it after the port has been functionally tested. Code that is inlined using pragma inline is not mapped to source for debugger. Pragma inline caused problems debugging; these were not runtime problems. Source lines were not available to be mapped onto the debugger. This prevented tracing of the code. This is more of an inconvenience that a restriction.

Guide 71) Inlined code should be of the highest quality (error free). Exceptions were not trapped in inlined code and caused the program to crash. The exceptions should have been raised to the parent procedure/package/function and handled there, unfortunately they were not and the system crashed in an untraceable manner. This primarily happened in a function which converted battlefield coordinates to screen coordinates. Numeric errors were raised which coincides with the numeric nature of the procedure. In this case, use of formal verification techniques would have been very effective for quality assurance.

Guide 72) All dynamic variables should be defined in either package or task bodies. Variables were declared in the specification of a package. This allowed them to be modified by other packages. Some variables were even modified by other tasks. Allowing external modifications like this makes the code cryptic and difficult to understand. The benefits of information hiding are well documented. Modifications should be performed either through functions, procedures or task entries. If a task needs to modify a variable defined in another task it should always be through an entry.

Guide 73) Don't use the "Use" clause. The Ada statement "use" should be avoided and the with'ed packages explicitly named. Justification for this tenet is well documented in literature today. Even after "use" was used, the VADS compiler required the explicit conversion of some operations; essentially, the "use" statement was unreliable. Use was used primarily to allow implicit access to types and operators. The use of "use" is more applicable to packages overloading operators to make code more readable; the scoping complexities can be minimized by minimizing the number of packages with'ed.

Guide 74) Operations which have a low probability of porting successfully should be isolated. I/O and vendor supplied utility packages are different on different systems and I/O intensive code is more likely to . All code which was heavily laced with I/O (including protocols and predefined text_io) required extensive redesign. Code involving I/O was spread throughout the system making it difficult to trace and hence modify. All I/O should be isolated into a small number of packages which contain system independent specifications. A port to a radically different system should only require the rewriting of the bodies of these packages. Avoid the use of vendor supplied support packages. If these packages are used then references and calls to them should not be inlined but used indirectly through another more general package as described in the solution to Problem 9. The use of representation clauses to map task entries to hardware interrupts is not standard and requires code modifications, it is therefor considered high risk.

Guide 75) Code must be written to accept the full spectrum of non-deterministic task interactions. Tasks, by their very nature, are non-deterministic. Code which assumes an implied order of task interaction which is not forced though standard task sequencing mechanisms (accept statements) is likely execute differently on different systems. Delay statements are not acceptable sequencing mechanisms. To assume that a context switch is going, or not going to occur due to an operation such as a delay statement or I/O operation is erroneous. One task in the AMDS updated a variable accessible to another task. The other task did not access the variable until the first task had accessed the variable again and overwritten the data. Critical information was lost, due to this design flaw, which caused a system failure. This problem would not have occurred had problem 7 occurred. Information which a task accesses outside it's own scope should never be assumed to be in any state. States which are erroneous (the other task should not be in) should be handled through some sort of exception mechanism.

Guide 76) Storage errors must be handled for all dynamic data structures. Queues, Stacks and other data structures occasionally overflow/underflow in multitasking environments (and often in uni-tasking environments). The data structures which are effected include all dynamic data structures: those which use access types, those which are defined using dynamic data, and those which are defined after elaboration. The queue which contains the graphics to be displayed overflowed and an exception was explicitly raised which was not handled. The system failed. Exception handlers which restore the integrity of the data structure (often at the unfortunate loss of data) should be developed surrounding all calls and actions which modify the data structure.

Guide 77) Exceptions which are explicitly raised by the Ada code must be handled. Exceptions which are explicitly raised will cause the system to fail if they are not handled. If a named exception exists in a unit then it should be handled by all units which utilize it. In the AMDS, a user defined exception was raised when a queue overflowed. This exception was not handled at a higher level and caused a system failure.

Guide 78) Capabilities which exceed the Ada standard must be identified and isolated. The following paragraphs describe some examples of non-standard Ada which we encountered: An assertion error was raised when attempting to perform a division of a fixed point type by a universal real and was unsuccessful. This operation is not supported according to the Ada RM 4.5.5 yet was supported and used in the original system. The operation Universal_real / Universal_real was not supported on one compiler yet was supported on another. According to the Ada RM this is not a supported operation although is supported by the many Ada compilers. This occurs when a constant is divided by another constant. The integer value 0 was used to used as a comparison operator when the other operator was of predefined type Calendar.Duration which is a real type not an integer type. The attribute 'Range cannot be used on a discrete type. The attribute 'Range was used on a subtype of type integer to define the index to an array. The 'Range attribute was later used to define a loop counter. This was "bad Ada" and should never have worked in the original system. A discrete type should have been used to define an index to an array. The compiler prevented an infinite loop from being coded even though it was intentional. The loop was a simple loop with no exits and ran as the main process of a system designed to run forever. The infinite loop is a reasonable construct for an embedded real-time system. We placed an exit which is never called in the loop to fool the compiler. Placing such exits as a precautionary measure seems an extreme measure for a compiler disfunction. While the ACEC detects deficiencies in compilers it does not detect to see if the compiler supports capabilities which are beyond the scope of standard Ada. This appears to be a pitfall of portability which is difficult to prevent. Any problems of this type which are known to the developer should be treated as compiler provided utilities. In this case the values were converted to float and then the division was performed, this is admittedly a poor solution.

Guide 79) Unless a constraint or numeric error has been proven impossible by formal methods exception handlers should be used whenever mathematical calculations exist. In the original AMDS the task creating missile positions and the task receiving missile positions were relatively synchronized (sequences of reads were always close together). The ported AMDS caused lapses where missile positions could be far apart. The change in missile position was calculated and a constraint error was raised, which would not have occurred had the lapse in positions not occurred and had the positions been closer together.

Guide 80) Avoid the explicit use of a task's memory, (e.g., 'STORAGE_SIZE) since these are inconsistent from one architecture to another; or one must resize each task for the port. The amount of memory a task uses is not constant from machine to machine. Explicit memory allocation for individual tasks as defined by the attribute 'STORAGE_SIZE is not portable as data structures which are identical differ in memory required from machine to machine. A simple example is the boolean construct, some machines allocate a single bit, some a nibble (4 bits), and some a byte (8 bits). Tasks also require memory allocation to map to the task control block which is not of a standard size.

Guide 81) Always include the alignment clause if a record representation clause is to be used. The record representation clause defined in 13.4 of the Ada RM may use the default storage size for the alignment clause if no alignment clause is given. If the actual size defined by the component clauses does not equal the default storage size then a storage error may occur. A segmentation error may be raised as only 2 of 8 bits are used.

```
(e.g.,) type X is
         record
           A : boolean;
           B : boolean;
         end record;
       for X use
         record
           A at 0 range 0..0;
           B at 0 range 1..1;
         end record;
```

To prevent the segmentation error, the previous declaration should become:

```
type X is
   record
     A : boolean;
     B : boolean;
   end record;
 for X use
   record at mod 2;
     A at 0 range 0..0;
     B at 0 range 1..1;
 end record;
```

Guide 82) Limit the number of tasks and the number of rendezvous, because the RTE often has limited concurrent resources to model them after. The underlying architecture of the Ada rendezvous mechanism varies depending upon the compiler and the hardware. Often some form of a software interrupt or asynchronous system trap is used to implement the rendezvous at the RTE level. The number of these interrupts/traps which are available to be used is often limited; this, in turn, limits the number of tasks and/or entries which may be used. The number of interrupts may be exceeded by an acceptable number of tasks. The level of multitasking and number of rendezvous can adversely and directly affect real-time.

Guide 83) Static information should not be kept in duplicate forms. Inevitably this information may be inconsistently changed at some time during the port. The porter may not realize the existence of the duplicate. Redundant static information should be avoided. If two packages which do not have visibility to each other require the same static information, then that information should be derived from a common source and passed into one or more of the packages via a generic formal parameter or just withing the package which contains the constant.

Guide 84) Don't use operations passed in as generic formal parameters during elaboration. Functions or procedures which have been passed into a compilation unit as generic formal parameters may not be elaborated prior to the elaboration of the generic unit which receives them. If used during elaboration these functions or procedures will cause an elaboration error.

3.4 Additional Lessons Learned

1) Use of a common data stack, and therefore common procedures and or functions, by multiple Ada tasks caused a corruption of data local to the common code if a context switch occurred while one task was in a procedure and another task called that procedure before the first task was done with it. This problem is created by erroneous compilers (e.g. it shouldn't happen). Two alternative solutions were suggested. One is the use semaphores to keep tasks out of critical portions of the code. Unfortunately this forces synchronization of tasks and causes additional scheduling problems (e.g., priority inheritance related problems and priority inversion anomalies). The second alternative involves the selection of a compiler which uses separate stacks for each task.
2) The RTE allocated a predefined fraction of the code for each individual task in both stack and heap memory. While the sum storage of the system did not exceed either the stack or heap limits some tasks did and this caused the system to fail during elaboration. Providing a memory map for the entire system is not always enough to prevent memory allocation problems. Often the memory allocated per task is a configurable parameter and this may be solved be reconfiguring the system. Sometimes the space allocated per task may be allocated in the system on a task by task basis.
3) Dynamically allocated tasks were not given a stack of their own by the compiler and used the stack allocated to the parent task. This caused both stack overflows and corrupted data when both tasks attempted to use the stack at the same time. To prevent this tasks should not be dynamically allocated.
4) A new graphics device which contained higher resolution than the original was used in the port. The system contained pixel mapping rather than coordinate mapping and the objects created by the ported system were so small as to hinder the use of the ported system. The specifications for the AMDS contained a minimum array of pixels and a minimum number of colors to be available. These specifications were exceeded by the Sun graphic capabilities. Specify the minimum and maximum size of pixels for a useful graphical interpretation of the output. Perform graphics based on coordinates rather than pixel mapping.
5) Intermediate values of calculations may cause constraint errors. This error was not handled and caused the system to fail. The following equation was used to calculate distance:

((A - B)2 + (C - D)**2)**0.5**

Assume all variable are of a type ranged 0.0 .. 100.0 and the values used are A := 30; B := 19; C := 10; D := 10; The end result, 11.0 is within the range of the type but the intermediate result of (A - B)**2 which is 121.0 is not. This caused an error, since the intermediate result was checked. This error is contrary to standard Ada; intermediate values should not be checked according to the Ada RM. For numeric calculations which contain multiple operations convert the inputs to a more comprehensive type and then convert to the desired type after the calculations are complete. Again, this error is contrary to standard Ada.
6) A Random Number Generator utility was not available on the new system; although one was supported and used for the original code. The creation of such additional feature packages is necessary to compensate for the variance in implementation dependent feature support across compilers.
7) Erroneous programming may function correctly by chance on one machine yet not on another. Particularly when tasks introduce non-determinism into the system.
8) A loop parameter specification overloaded a variable previously declared in the same package. This created an ambiguous homograph which was undecipherable. Although it is not required by the Ada RM, unique variable names within packages or within any single declaration unit are recommended.

4. SUMMARY AND CONCLUSION

The problems encountered during the transporting of the AMDS manifested themselves in several categories. Most of the problems encountered were directly related to the low level I/O interfaces, in particular the graphical and mouse interfaces. Some of the problems occurred due to different compiler interpretations of the language Ada. The most difficult problems to find were those which resulted from subtle differences between the two runtime environments (RTE). On a larger scale, detection of problems and the actual porting were hindered by limitations imposed by the methodologies used to develop the original system and to port the system.

Low level I/O is generally very machine dependent and requires the development of custom code for each low level functionality. In addition, different requirements arise with new hardware (e.g. a new mouse may require the software to initialize it where an old mouse did not). The modifications in the code which result from changes in low level I/O are, in general easily found and modified throughout a properly designed system. I/O is usually limited to a small portion of the code and tends to very modular in nature, this allows for new components to be plugged in to replace the old ones.

Compiler problems may be divided into two different types; those problems which manifest themselves during compile time and those that do not. Most of the problems which occur during compile time are easily detected and easily solved. One example of a problem of this type is a task priority that is out of bounds on the new compiler which was within range on the old compiler. Most of these problems are easily addressed, although occasionally a functionality of the old compiler is not available in the new compiler. These problems occasionally require a great deal of effort to overcome frequently requiring the functionality be added either in the RTE or the application layer. Those problems which do not manifest themselves during compile time are much more insidious in that they are difficult to detect and may require extensive reworking of either the code or the RTE. Two of these problems are: numerical calculations, especially floating point calculations; and the specification of the parameter passing mechanism. Neither of these are specified in Mil-Std Ada (1815A). For example, the method of parameter passing may be pass by reference, or pass by value; this is not controlled in the Ada standard and hence compilers vary. The different parameter passing mechanisms create both functional and timing discrepancies, and necessitate complex analyses of possible side effects and other fault tolerance issues (e.g., exception propagation.)

Different compilers handle numbers and operations which push the system limits of the number representation. This can result in discrepancies in the least significant bits of numbers which represent an irrational result. This is particularly true if the numerical spaces between X'SAFE_LARGE, X'SAFE_SMALL, X'LARGE, and X'SMALL are involved.

The most pervasive problems in real-time systems are invariably timing problems. Often code is optimized on the original system to accommodate the underlying environment. When a transportation is made the new system rarely has the same timing characteristics as the original environment. Functionally equivalent code may totally fail its mission on the new environment if it does not run fast enough. At times the new system may just not be up to the task at hand. For example: a high speed simulation developed on a Cray II just isn't going to work on an IBM PC. Often the code may be brought up to speed with some customizing to take advantage of the new system's traits. An example of this from the AMDS port is as follows: the graphical images of tanks were produced on the original system by using high speed BIOS calls; this could not be emulated in a time effective way on the new system as all communications were being handled over a serial port rather than an internal bus and a graphics cable. The information being passed over the serial port was sent at a more abstract "object" level and the capability of moving graphical objects inherent in the Sun's graphics were used.

Of course transporting code is only cost effective if the combined effort required to transport the code (including maintenance) is less than the effort that would have been required to develop a new system on the new hardware. A comprehensive study of the level of effort and the error rate of completed code were tracked and analyzed for this project. These results are compared to the level of effort required to develop the code originally. The guidelines document defined the transportability in relation to the percentage of the time spent developing the original software and the time spent porting it. The original AMDS project is estimated to have taken 2200 man-hours; whereas the port is estimated to have entailed approximately 1200 man-hours. The portability index is thereby 45%, using the portability formula cited earlier. It must be noted that a majority of the porting effort went into the re-design necessary to handle different I/O and the creation of new graphics and mouse software on the Sun. These changes were necessary because of the different architecture selected for the port. Had the port only entailed transporting to a different CPU board, the effort may have only taken 500 - 600 man hours, making the code 75% portable. Obviously, this metric must take into consideration the level of the transport, which must include the variance in changes necessary. Future studies are needed (and currently in the planning stages) to better define the necessary evaluation criteria for portability metrics and evaluate several different level ports to validate the results.

Another related study may be the extension and tailoring of these guidelines from the Reuse perspective. Clearly, developing portable code and reusable code share many commonalities and are in the interest of developing sound software.

5. ACKNOWLEDGEMENTS

Special thanks to David Scheidt for his technical help and participation on this project, as well as for his contributions to earlier draft versions. Additional thanks are also due Mary Bender for her review and comments on earlier draft versions. And many thanks to the various other referees and reviewers for their comments and suggestions.

REFERENCES

[1] Reference Manual for the Ada Programming Language, ANSI-MIL-STD-1815A-1983, American National Standards Institute, Inc., 1983.

[2] Booch, G. Software Engineering with Ada, Benjamin/Cummings Publishing Co., Menlo Park, CA, 1983.

[3] Griest, T. and Bender, M. "Limitations on the Portability of Real Time Ada Programs," Proceedings of the TRI-Ada '89 Conference, Pittsburgh, PA, October 23 - 26, 1989.

[4] Matthews, E. "Observations on the Portability of Ada I/O," ACM Ada Letters VII(5), Sept./Oct. 1987.

[5] Nissen, J. and Wallis, P. Portability and Style in Ada, Cambridge University Press, Great Britain, 1984.

[6] "Transportability Guideline for Ada Real-Time Software," January, 1989, Center for Software Engineering, CECOM, Ft. Monmouth, NJ; prepared by LabTek Corporation, Woodbridge, CT.

Reusable Executives for Hard Real-Time Systems in Ada *

Juan A. de la Puente † Juan Zamorano ‡ Alejandro Alonso §
Jose L. Fernández ¶

1 Introduction

At the end of 1989 the *Subdirección General de Tecnología e Investigación* provided funds for an eighteen month research project to investigate the viability of Ada in the development of reusable software components for their use in future projects by the Spanish aerospace industry. A description of the overall project can be found in [6].

The project participants were ISDEFE as the prime contractor, CASA and the Universidad Politécnica of Madrid (UPM) as subcontractors.

The first task of the project was a domain analysis to identify those reusable components that could be used for the development of real-time systems, emphasizing those applied to avionic systems. A main group of the selected components were those related to reusable avionics executive software [4]. This concept can be adapted to the conditions imposed by the Ada programming language and it can be applied to other hard real-time systems. The domain analysis identifies two kinds of executives of interest, that are complementary, in the sense that the special advantages of one of them are the disadvantages of the other one, and vice versa:

- In most avionic applications, the embedded hard real-time software is developed following a cyclic execution model. The advantages of this approach are its deterministic execution scheme, a simple structure, low system overloading and the large experience available. The *cyclic executive* has been developed following this approach.

- A new approach to avionics software development [11] is based on the rate monotonic scheduling method. Its specific advantages are a higher abstraction level, flexibility and an easier maintenance. The *tasking executive* is based on this scheduling method.

---

*This research was funded by contract No. 508/24/90 from the ***Subdirección General de Tecnología e Investigación, Ministerio de Defensa de España***

†E.T.S.I. de Telecomunicación, Politécnica de Madrid
‡Facultad de Informática, Universidad Politécnica de Madrid
§E.T.S.I. de Telecomunicación, Politécnica de Madrid
¶ISDEFE, Madrid

Those executives are reusable subsystems that allow users to develop hard real-time systems in Ada. A subsystem, in reusable terminology, is a reusable software component, composed of a set of cooperative (sub)components [3]. Subsystems are needed when the abstraction to be modelized is too complex to be designed with only one component.

It is important to note that these executives are not complete systems on their own, but rather consist of a set of building blocks that allow users to develop hard real-time systems. They rely on Ada features and run-time system. Both executive subsystems are designed in such a way that hard real-time deadlines can be guaranteed for real-time processes. The executives also support aperiodic tasks, mode changes and failure recovery.

2 Cyclic Executive

This executive is intended to be used in safety-critical applications. Since compliance with *safe Ada* [7] was required, tasks and some other Ada features could not be used.

The executive design is based on the *cyclic executive* model [2].

It is an iterative procedure which activates, in a sequential way, the application processes in turn. So process execution is fully deterministic and real-time restrictions can be met.

With the *cyclic executive* approach, all the application processes are periodic. Sporadic processes are implemented by polling servers. Each process's deadline is at the end of its period. Furthermore, process periods are usually adjusted so that they are harmonic, in order to simplify scheduling.

An application process is defined by:

- The parameterless procedure which is the code it executes.
- Its maximum computation time.
- Its maximum dynamic data space size.

An application execution mode corresponds to an operation mode in the controlled real-time system. Every application execution mode is defined by a subset of processes together with execution profiles for each of them. The execution profile of a process is mode dependent and includes:

- The activation period.
- The phase, i.e. the delay for the first execution.
- The priority, which indicates the relative execution order.

The scheduler is based on the above parameters and is organized in the following way:

- The major cycle is the execution scheme for an application execution mode and it is periodically repeated. Its length is equal to the lowest common multiple of the periods - for this mode - of the processes present in it. This major cycle is divided into one or more minor cycles.

- A minor cycle is a sequence of processes and it is timed by a minor cycle clock. The minor cycle clock period must be greater than or equal to the maximum duration of all the processes executed in the greatest minor cycle.

- A frame is a minor cycle division wherein a process is executed.

For every set of processes that belongs to a mode, a major cycle or major schedule is constructed according to their corresponding execution profiles.

The *cyclic executive* manages the process execution with the above scheme and its main characteristics are:

- Mode management: a mode change involves a change in the set of processes and its periods, phases and priorities.

- Time management: time of the day clock and elapsed time clock as well as timers for time interval measurement are provided.

- Control of data size and computation time of process: when an overrun or an error is detected, the process in execution is aborted and replaced by its recovery process in all the application execution modes where the process was present. This concept extends to recovery groups, which a are set of processes related in such a way that if a process fails, the whole group is replaced by one recovery process.

- Error management: in addition to error recovery by recovery processes, error logging is performed and, in some situations, the executive stops the system safely.

- Background process: a never ending process is executed during the time that is not used by real-time processes.

2.1 Design issues

The components of the *cyclic executive* include data structures for schedule information. These data structures or *schedules* store the sequence of frames within minor cycles and the sequence of minor cycles within major cycles. Primary and recovery processes have associated frames according to their execution profiles. There is one *schedule* per application execution mode. *Schedules* are defined at system initialization time and they are maintained by the executive.

Mode change is performed by changing the schedule data.

Another data structure, which associates a process identifier with its failure state, is maintained in order to perform error recovery by recovery processes. This data structure is constructed from recovery group information at system initialization time.

The scheduler extracts the process to be executed from the current mode *schedule* and checks if this process is executable according to its failure state. If so, the process associated code is executed with a limited data area and a limited computation time. Once the process has been executed the scheduler repeats this for the next frame.

Before executing a process, the Ada run-time system storage limit is changed according to the process maximum data size. So, the Ada run-time system raises `Storage_Error` if the process tries to use more storage space. In a similar way and in order to control computation time, the scheduler sets a timer according to the process maximum computation time. If the process overruns its frame duration, the timer interrupt handler raises a `Frame_Overrun` exception through an Ada run-time system access point.

Therefore, if a process fails, an unhandled exception is raised. Then the scheduler catches it and updates the failure state data structure for this process and all the processes in its recovery group, in such a way that primary processes are not runnable any more. Then, the recovery process is made runnable for the rest of the life of the system. If the faulty process is itself a recovery process, then this scheme cannot be applied, and the secondary level recovery procedure is executed.

2.2 Executive components

The *cyclic executive* consists of a number of reusable components. Most of them are generic packages. They can be grouped in the following five groups:

Interface components: these components define a set of basic types, which depend on the target hardware and the development system. Interfaces are reusable, for they can be used in other projects, but they are not portable without modifications to other architectures or development systems.

Basic structures: these components provide a set of abstract data types for describing the *cyclic executive* behaviour. These components allow to define processes, modes, recovery groups and schedules. They are independent from the development system and the execution architecture.

Scheduler: this is the main part of the *cyclic executive.* Its function is to schedule application processes, to perform mode changes and to detect and recover failures. It is implemented by a set of components that isolate hardware, compiler and run-time system dependencies from the application software.

Basic executive extensions: a basic executive can be built with the described components. Additional components were selected in order to increase functionality. These components deal with error logging, user defined timers and a time-of-the-day clock.

Application templates: schemes for writing application processes and defining the system structure are included in this group.

2.3 Application development process

Figure 1 shows a layout of the *cyclic executive.* The lower levels represent the basic execution elements, i. e. the computer and Ada run-time system. Above these levels the first level of the *cyclic executive*, consisting of the *interface components*, is built.

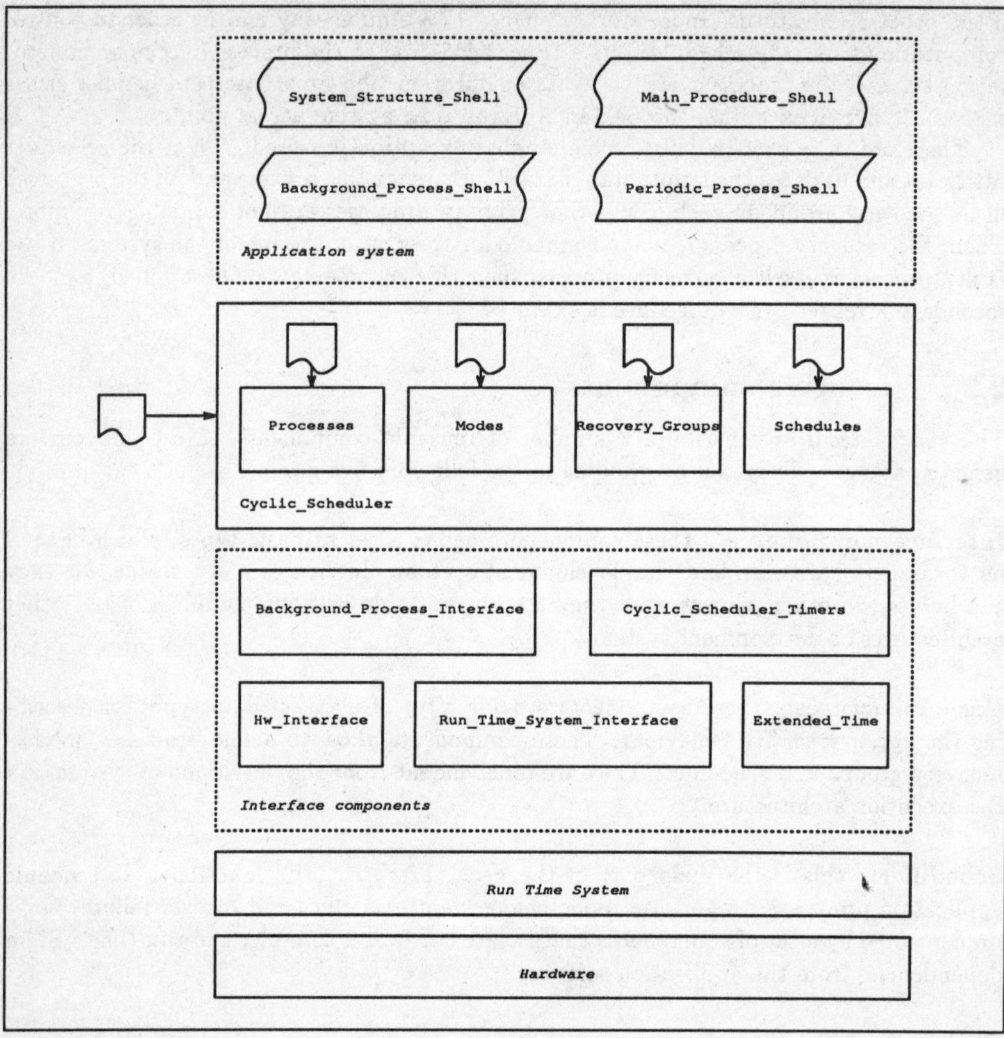

Figure 1: Layout of a system developed with the *cyclic executive*

The implementation of *interface components* is hardware and run-time dependent. If the programming environment or the target computer is changed, these components must be adapted to the new platform.

In order to build a real-time system the following steps are required:

1. To write `System_Structure`, which can be derived from the `System_Structure_Shell`. This package includes the definition of the structure of the whole system, and defines types for identifying and defining the *cyclic executive* objects. Procedures for performing special functions must be defined as well.

   This package instantiates the generic package `Cyclic_Scheduler` and, hence, instantiates the generic packages `Processes`, `Modes`, `Recovery_Groups` and `Schedules`, too.

2. To write the application process packages, which can be derived from `Periodic_Process_Shell` and `Background_Process_Shell`. One package per application process must be created.

   The process's identifier, code, computation time and data area must be defined, as well as the execution profiles, the recovery group and the process category (primary or recovery).

3. To write the main procedure derived from `Main_Procedure_Shell`. This procedure starts the system in some specific execution mode.

The *cyclic executive* user's manual [18] contains guidelines to build user's interrupt handlers, in order to avoid interference with the *cyclic executive*.

3 Tasking Executive

The *tasking executive* is based on Ada tasking. This executive reduces the complexity of developing concurrent systems, since it is based on tasks, which are of higher abstraction level than the basic objects in the *cyclic executive* model.

The executive theoretical foundations are the rate monotonic scheduling (RMS) and the deadline monotonic scheduling (DMS) methods. In the *tasking executive*, the deadline of every periodic process equals the period, and, in this situation, RMS and DMS are equivalent. The RMS method, first presented by Liu and Layland [10], assigns statically higher priorities to the shorter period processes. The deadlines of all the processes are guaranteed, provided that the total processor utilization lies below a maximum bound [8]. In this definition it is supposed that process deadlines are equal to the period and there is neither interprocess synchronization nor communication. Further research has been performed at SEI-CMU to adapt the method to systems with interprocess communication through monitors [16], sporadic processes [17], transient overloads [15] and mode changes [12]. Some guidelines for implementing the RMS algorithm and its extensions using Ada are suggested in [14].

The DMS method assigns statically higher priorities to the processes with shorter deadline [9]. This proposal has been further studied at University of York [5] in order to, among other issues, overcome the restrictions imposed in the original proposal, and to provide a schedulability test.

It is important to mention that in the executive documentation, the priority assignment and schedulability test are performed as in [5], because, although it is equivalent to the proposal related with RMS, sporadic processes are treated in a more natural way.

Some changes have been made in the above approaches in order to deal with the specific requirements and the development environment of the executive. It has also been necessary to make some minor changes in the Ada run-time system (RTS) to allow dynamic priorities and absolute time delays. The first is needed to perform mode changes and the second to precisely implement periodic processes. The reusable *tasking executive* has the following main characteristics:

- Periodic and sporadic processes are supported.
- The schedulability of the hard real-time processes can be analytically guaranteed.
- The system can have several execution modes. System mode can change during the system execution; then processes execute according to system mode.
- Processes communicate via monitors, which are designed following the priority ceiling protocol [16], in order to constrain priority inversion duration.
- Real-time processes detect possible failures: deadlines missing or storage violation of the size previously specified by the user.
- Failure recovery based in recovery groups.
- Background processes, i.e. processes without hard deadlines, can coexist with real-time processes.

3.1 Design issues

A real-time system based on the *tasking executive* consists of a set of concurrent processes. These processes are implemented as one or more Ada tasks.

Periodic processes execute an activity according to an execution profile, that includes: a period, a phase and a priority. The deadline is considered to be equal to the period. Every mode has an associated profile. When the system mode changes, the process executes the mode change protocol and sets the execution profile that corresponds to the new system mode. This approach is not the same as in the *cyclic executive*, because processes and profiles cannot be associated in a data structure since task identifiers do not exist in Ada. The process operational and mode control aspects are implemented using two tasks: activity task and control task. The activity task performs the main activity of the process, i.e. the periodic action, while the control task performs monitoring and mode change functions.

Sporadic processes execute an activity in response to an aperiodic event. Their profiles include an event interarrival time, a deadline and a priority. Their implementation follows the periodic process structure.

Fault recovery is based on the idea of the recovery group, that includes processes that have a common fault recovery behaviour. A recovery group is formed by a recovery process and a set of periodic and sporadic processes. When one process in the group fails, its control task communicates this fact to the recovery process and finishes. The other processes in the group stop as soon as they detect a failure. Then, the recovery process executes the recovery activity.

The recovery process exports operations to allow processes in its group to communicate failures and to check the error status of the group. These operations are used to instantiate the appropriate generic parameters of the processes in the group.

There must be a system supervisor process, which is the highest priority process and that executes system functions which include system mode and mode change management, system initialization and safe system stopping, in case of severe errors being detected. The system supervisor process exports the operations needed by other processes to execute according to the system mode. These operations, again, are used to instantiate generic parameters of user processes.

Background processes have a lower priority than any real-time process. Thus they only execute when there are no real-time processes ready.

Interprocess communication is carried out using monitors, which are server tasks with the necessary entry points to allow their clients to request the appropriate services. The design of those monitors is based on the priority ceiling protocol [16]. The priority of a monitor must be greater than its priority ceiling, which is the maximum priority of all its clients [13].

3.2 Executive components

This subsystem consists of 19 components. Most of them are generic packages. These components can be grouped as follows:

Interface components: these components define a set of basic types, which depend on the target hardware and the development system. Interfaces are reusable, for they can be used in other projects, but they are not portable without modifications to other architectures or development systems. The component `Run_Time_System_Interface` encapsulates run-time system modifications.

Basic process structures: a set of abstract data types is provided for defining sporadic and periodic process profiles and for associating them with execution modes.

Process constructors: components are provided to create periodic, sporadic and recovery processes and the system supervisor process.

Basic executive extensions: a basic executive can be built with the described components. Additional components were selected in order to increase functionality. These components deal with error logging, user defined timers and a time-of-the-day clock.

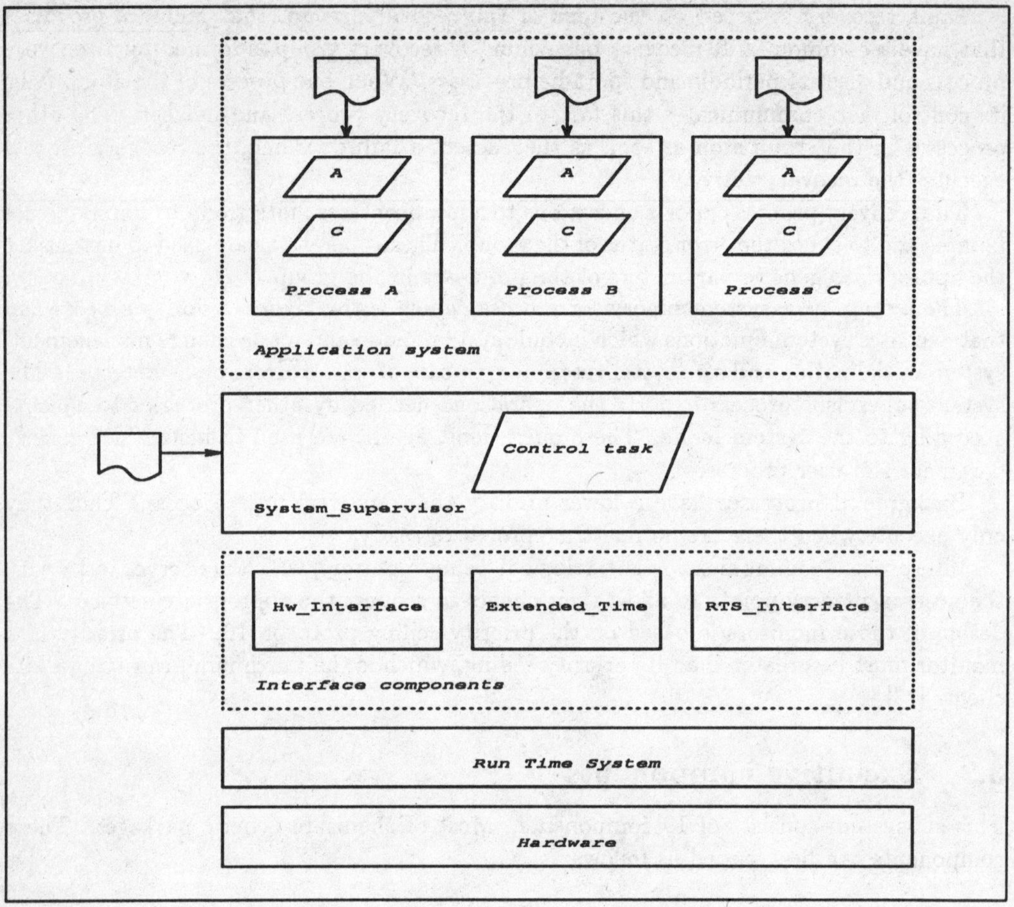

Figure 2: Layout of a system developed with the *tasking executive*

Application templates: the components used to create processes have several generic parameters. In order to give a model of how to instantiate them, a template for each type of process has been designed. In addition, templates are provided to create interrupt handlers, monitors and background processes.

3.3 Application development process

Figure 2 shows a simplified layout of a system developed with the *tasking executive*. Only the main elements are drawn in the picture. The *tasking executive* user's manual [1] fully describes the development steps required to build a real-time system. Those steps are now summarized. The following items specify the order in which the elements must be created, taking into account the 'use' relationship:

1. The **interface components** must be adapted to the underlying embedded computer and compiler specific Ada run-time system. This step is only needed the first time that a system is developed with this platform.

2. An enumeration type with one identifier per execution system mode, called hereafter `Mode_Type`

3. An instance of the **basic process structures**, to allow real-time processes to define their execution profiles. `Mode_Type` is the only generic actual parameter needed.

4. **System supervisor.** Its most important generic actual parameters are `Mode_Type`, the safe stop procedure and the initialization procedure.

5. **Monitors.** They must be created now because they could be used by a recovery process to communicate, when executing the recovery activity. The template `Monitor` is filled with the services provided.

6. **Recovery processes.** Their main generic actual parameters are the recovery activity, the execution profiles and procedures exported by the system supervisor.

7. **Interrupt handlers.** They are created using a component that is a template. The main items to fill in are the interrupt vector and the handling routine.

8. **Periodic Processes.** Their main generic actual parameters are the `Mode_Type`, execution profiles, periodic activity and subprograms to interact with the system supervisor and the recovery process in the group.

9. **Sporadic processes.** The main generic actual parameters are the same as in the periodic process and, in addition, a type with the information related with the event handled by each process.

10. **Background processes.** Those processes must have a priority lower than any real-time process and must not communicate with any of them.

4 Conclusions

The component library for both the cyclic and tasking executives has been released for distribution by the Spanish Ministry of Defense. The approximate size for each of the executive subsytems is about 8000 loc. The test code adds up to 50000 loc for each subsystem.

In our opinion, the development of reusable executive components has been made possible by such Ada features as tasking (for the tasking executive), packages, generics and low level constructions. These features are unique to Ada and provide a solid base for developing high quality reusable software components.

A large effort has been made in order to get a clear design and to provide the user with components that are close to his or her perception of the system to be developed. The abstraction level of the components is significantly higher than that provided by pure Ada.

Acknowledgements

We gratefully thank the members of the design team for their dedication and support:

Carlos Blanco	(U.P.M.)
Juan L. Freniche	(CASA)
Gonzalo Génova	(U.P.M.)
Enrique Martín	(CASA)
Juan L. Redondo	(U.P.M)
Luis Redondo	(CASA)
Jose I. Tortosa	(U.P.M.)

We appreciate and would like to thank the support of the contracting agency's representative Mr. Manuel Golmayo (Centro de Investigación y Desarrollo de la Armada).

We gratefully thank Till Kahle for his helpful suggestions during the preparation of this paper.

References

[1] A. Alonso, J. L. Redondo, C. Blanco, J. I. Tortosa, and J. A. de la Puente. *Ejecutivo multitarea. Manual de Usuario*, Jan. 1992.

[2] T. Baker and A. Shaw. The cyclic executive model and Ada. *Real-Time Systems*, 1(1), 1989.

[3] G. Booch. *Software components with Ada.* Benjamin Cummings, 1987.

[4] R. Bousley. Reusable avionics executive software. In *IEEE National Aerospace and Electronics Conference*, 1981.

[5] A. Burns and A. Wellings. Hard Real-Time Operating Systems Kernel. Task 1 Deliverable on Estec Contract 9198/90/NL/SF, Department of Computer Science, University of York, UK, Sept. 1991.

[6] J. L. Fernández and J. A. de la Puente. Constructing a pilot library of components for avionic systems. In D. Christodoulakis, editor, *Ada: The Choice for '92.* Ada Europe, Springer-Verlag, 1991.

[7] R. Holzapfel and G. Winterstein. Ada in safety critical applications. In S. Heilbrunner, editor, *Ada in Industry.* Cambridge University Press, 1988.

[8] J.P.Lehoczky, L. Sha, and Y. Ding. The rate monotonic scheduling algorithm — exact characterization and average case behavior. In *IEEE Real-Time Systems Symposium*, 1989.

[9] J. Leung and J. Whitehead. On the complexity of fixed-priority of periodic real-time tasks. *Performance Evaluation*, 2(4), 1982.

[10] C. Liu and J. Layland. Scheduling algorithms for multiprogramming in a hard-real-time environment. *J. ACM*, 20(1), 1973.

[11] C. Locke, D. Vogel, and T. Mesler. Building a Predictable Avionics Platform in Ada: A Case Study. In *IEEE Real-Time Systems Symposium*, 1991.

[12] R. Rajkumar and L. Sha. Accomplishing mode changes in Ada. In *3rd International Workshop on Real-Time Ada Issues*, 1989.

[13] L. Sha and J. B. Goodenough. Real-time scheduling theory and Ada. Technical Report CMU/SEI-89-TR-14;ESD-TR-89-22, Carnegie-Mellon University, Software Engineering Institute, 1989.

[14] L. Sha and J. B. Goodenough. Real-time scheduling theory and Ada. *IEEE Computer*, 23(4), 1990.

[15] L. Sha, J. Lehoczky, and R. Rajkumar. Solutions for some practical problems in prioritized preemptive scheduling. In *IEEE Real-Time Systems Symposium*, 1986.

[16] L. Sha, R. Rajkumar, and J. P. Lehoczky. Priority inheritance protocols, an approach to real-time synchronization. Technical Report CMU-CS-87-181, Department of CS, ECE and Statistics, Carnegie Mellon University, 1987.

[17] B. Sprunt, L. Sha, and J. Lehoczky. Aperiodic task scheduling for hard real-time systems. *Real-Time Systems*, 1(1), 1989.

[18] J. Zamorano, J. L. Redondo, C. Blanco, J. I. Tortosa, and J. A. de la Puente. *Ejecutivo cíclico. Manual de Usuario*, Jan. 1992.

Designing Hard Real-time Systems

A. Burns and A.J. Wellings

Real-time and Distributed Systems Research Group, Department of Computer Science
University of York, Heslington, York, Y01 5DD, UK

ABSTRACT

This paper presents a systems life cycle and a structured design method which are tailored towards the construction of real-time systems in general, and hard real-time systems in particular. The standard systems life cycle is modified to take into account the expression and satisfaction of non-functional requirements. The HOOD design method is extended to support abstractions which explicitly cater for the characteristics and properties of hard real-time systems. The new method is called HRT-HOOD (Hard Real-time HOOD).

1. Introduction

The most important stage in the development of any real-time system is the generation of a consistent design that satisfies an authoritative specification of requirements. Where real-time systems differ from the traditional data processing systems is that they are constrained by non-functional requirements (e.g. dependability and timing). Typically the standard design methodologies do not cater well for expressing these types of constraints.

The objective of this paper is to present a hard real-time systems life cycle, and a structured design method which is tailored towards the construction of real-time systems in general, and hard real-time systems in particular. Rather than developing a new method from scratch, the HOOD method is used as a baseline. HOOD (Hierarchical Object Oriented Design) has been chosen because it has a systematic mapping of the detailed design into Ada. The new method is called HRT-HOOD (Hard Real-time HOOD).

Section 2 of this paper presents the modified systems life cycle, and section 3 then discusses HRT-HOOD which has been designed to support the new life cycle. HRT-HOOD has also been developed to be compatible with the Ada 9X real-time tasking model[Intermetrics91]. Finally in section 4 we give our conclusions.

2. Overview of the Design Process

It is increasingly recognised that the role and importance of non-functional requirements in the development of complex critical applications has hitherto been inadequately appreciated[Burns91]. Specifically, it has been common practice for system developers, and the methods they use, to concentrate primarily on functionality and to consider non-functional requirements comparatively late in the development process. We believe that this approach fails to produce safety critical systems. For example, often timing requirements are viewed simply in terms of the performance of the completed system. Failure to meet the required performance often results in ad hoc changes to the system.

Non-functional requirements include dependability (e.g. reliability, availability, safety and security), timeliness (e.g. responsiveness, orderliness, freshness, temporal predictability and temporal controllability), and dynamic change management (i.e. incorporating evolutionary changes into a non-stop system). These requirements, and the constraints imposed by the execution environment, need to be taken into account throughout the system development life cycle. During development an early binding of software function to hardware component is required so that the analysis of timing and reliability properties of a still unrefined design can be carried out[Kopetz85].

Most traditional software development methods incorporate a life cycle model in which the following phases are recognised: Requirements Definition, Architectural Design, Detailed Design, Coding, and Testing. For hard real-time systems this has the significant disadvantage that timing problems will only be recognised during testing, or worse after deployment.

2.1. Addressing Hard Real-time Issues

We believe that if design methods are to address hard real-time issues adequately they must support:

- the explicit recognition of the types of activities/objects that are found in hard real-time systems (i.e. cyclic and sporadic activities);
- the explicit definition of the application timing requirements for each object;
- the definition of the relative importance of each object to the successful functioning of the application;
- the explicit definition and use of resource control objects;
- decomposition to a software architecture that is amenable to schedulability and timing analysis.

In addition, design methods must allow the schedulability analysis to influence the design as early as possible in the overall design process, and restrict the use of the implementation language so that worst case execution time analysis can be carried out.

2.2. The Hard Real-time Life Cycle

Our approach is to split the architectural design into two phases[Burns91]:

- logical architecture;
- physical architecture.

The logical architecture embodies commitments which can be made independently of the constraints imposed by the execution environment, and is primarily aimed at satisfying the functional requirements. The physical architecture takes these and other constraints into account, and embraces the non-functional requirements. The physical architecture forms the basis for asserting that the application's non-functional requirements will be met once the detailed design and implementation have taken place. It should be possible, for example, to prove that if all objects are built to their worst case timing and reliability constraints then the system itself will meet its safety requirements. In general, the physical architecture allows arguments to be developed that assess compliance with all the application's requirements.

In this paper we are primarily concerned with hard real-time systems, therefore the Physical Architecture Design is focused on timing requirements and the necessary schedulability analysis that will ensure (guarantee) that the system once built will function correctly in both the value and time domains. To undertake this analysis it will be necessary to estimate the execution time of the proposed code, and to have available the time dependent behaviour of the target processor and other aspects of the execution environment.

Once the Architectural Design Phases are complete, the detailed design can begin in earnest and the code for the application produced. When this has been achieved, the execution profile of the code must be measured to ensure that the estimated worst case execution times are indeed accurate. If they are not (which will usually be the case for a new application), the physical architecture design phase is revisited with the up-to-date information. If the system is not feasible then either the detailed design must be revised (if there are small deviations), or the designer must return to the logical architecture design phase (if serious problems exist). When the code measurement indicate that all is well, testing of the application proceeds. This should involve actual timing of code.

2.3. Logical Architecture Design

There are two aspects of any design method which facilitate the logical architecture design of hard real-time systems. Firstly, explicit supports must be given to the abstractions that are typically required by hard real-time system designers. Secondly, the logical architecture should be constrained so that it can be analysed during the Physical Architecture Design phase. These aspects are now discussed.

2.3.1. Supporting Common Hard Real-time Abstractions

The outcome of hierarchical decomposition, during the Logical Architecture Design phase, is a collection of terminal objects with all their interactions fully defined. It is assumed that some form of functional decomposition process has lead to the definition of these objects.

The terminal objects are characterised as:

- CYCLIC,
- SPORADIC,
- PROTECTED, or
- PASSIVE.

CYCLIC and SPORADIC activities are common in real-time systems; each should contain a single *thread* that is scheduled at run-time. The priority of the thread will be set during the schedulability analysis of the physical architecture phase. PROTECTED objects control access to data that is accessed by more than one thread (i.e. CYCLIC or SPORADIC object); in particular they provide mutual exclusion. On a single processor system this will be achieved by having a ceiling priority defined for each PROTECTED object that is at least the maximum of the threads that use it. When a thread accesses a PROTECTED object it will run with this ceiling priority and hence have mutually exclusive access over the data hidden within the PROTECTED object. PROTECTED objects are also similar to monitors in that they can block a caller if the conditions are not correct for it to continue. This will be used to hold a SPORADIC object until the release event has occurred. The final important object type is PASSIVE which is used for an object that is either used by only one other object or can be used concurrently without error.

All the above four objects types are admissible as terminal objects in a hard real-time system. It is however possible that a real-time system may have a subsystem that is not real-time. The objects in such a subsystem are either PASSIVE or ACTIVE. ACTIVE object types may also be used during decomposition of the main system but must be transformed into one of the above types before reaching the terminal level.

With these types of terminal objects the common paradigms used in hard real-time systems can be supported:

- Periodic activities — represented by CYCLIC objects
- Sporadic activities — represented by SPORADIC objects
- Precedence constrained activities — Precedence constrained activities involves a series of computations through terminal objects. They are likely to occur in a design which must reflect *transaction* deadlines.

The Logical Architecture Design Process may commence with the production of ACTIVE and PASSIVE objects, and by a process of decomposition will lead to the production of terminal objects of the appropriate character. For example, a required cyclic transaction from input to output may be first represented as a single ACTIVE object but may then be realised as a CYCLIC object followed by a series of SPORADIC objects linked by PROTECTED objects.

2.3.2. Constraining the Design for Analysis

In order to analyse the full design, certain constraints are required. These are mainly concerned with the allowed communication/synchronisation between objects. They are:

(a) CYCLIC and SPORADIC objects may not call arbitrary blocking operations in other CYCLIC or SPORADIC objects.

(b) CYCLIC and SPORADIC objects may call asynchronous transfer of control operations in other CYCLIC or SPORADIC objects.

(c) PROTECTED objects may not call blocking operations in any other object.

Points (a) and (b) require that CYCLIC and SPORADIC objects are only allowed to communicate via fully asynchronous message passing or PROTECTED objects. Fully asynchronous implies that neither the receiver or the sender is blocked. The preferred method is to use a PROTECTED object.

It is important to emphasise that any real-time design method must enforce these constraints during the logical design process.

2.4. Physical Architecture Design

For the purpose of this paper, the focus of the Physical Architecture Design is the timing requirements. The design process must support the definition of a physical architecture by:

1) allowing timing attributes to be associated with objects,
2) providing a framework from within which a schedulability analysis of the terminal objects can be undertaken, and
3) providing the abstractions with which the designer can express the handling of timing errors.

The physical design must of course be feasible within the context of the execution environment. This is guaranteed by the schedulability analysis. Issues of reliability must also be addressed during this phase. As we are not concerned with distribution here, many of the options for increased availability are not appropriate. There may be independent stand-by systems but they are outside the scope of the system actually being designed.

2.4.1. Object Attributes

All terminal objects have associated real-time attributes. Many attributes are associated with mapping the timing requirements on to the logical design (e.g., deadline, importance). These must be set before the schedulability analysis can be performed. Other attributes (such as priority etc.) can only be set during this analysis.

Each CYCLIC and SPORADIC object has a number of temporal attributes defined, for example:

- The period of execution for each CYCLIC object.

- The minimum arrival interval for each SPORADIC object.
- Deadlines for all sporadic and cyclic activities.

Two forms of deadline are identified. One is applied directly to a sporadic or cyclic activity. The other is applied to a precedence constrained activity (transaction); here there is a deadline on the whole activity and hence only the last activity has a true deadline. The deadlines for the other activities must be derived so that the complete transaction satisfies its timing requirements (in all cases).

To undertake the schedulability analysis the worst case execution time for each thread and all operations (in all objects) must be known. After the logical design phase these can be estimated (taking into account the execution environment constraints) and appropriate attributes assigned. Clearly, the better the estimates the more accurate the schedulability analysis. Good estimates come from component reuse or from arguments of comparison (with existing components on other projects). During detailed design and coding, and through the direct use of measurement during testing, better estimates will become available which will require the schedulability analysis to be redone.

2.4.2. Schedulability Analysis

Schedulability analysis is an integral part of the development of a physical architecture. The proposed design must be feasible; that is all deadlines must be guaranteed for all foreseeable circumstances. To do this requires knowledge of the processor speed, memory speed and memory capacity, plus kernel timings e.g. context switch. The timing behaviour of other hardware devices may also need to be known. If we assume the execution environment supports preemptive priority based dispatching of threads then the scheduling analysis is concerned with defining static priorities for the threads embodied within cyclic and sporadic activities. A number of formulae are available in the literature. If the system consists of mainly CYCLIC objects and they have period equal to deadline then the rate monotonic theories can be used[Lehoczky87]. A more flexible object structure is supported by deadline monotonic theory[Audsley91].

In summary, the schedulability analysis will add the following annotation to the terminal objects of the physical architecture:

- Priority of CYCLIC, SPORADIC threads (for each mode).
- Ceiling priority of PROTECTED objects.

In addition, budget times that have been derived from the worst case execution times will be available.

2.4.3. Handling Timing Error

The schedulability analysis described above can only be effective if the estimations/measurements of worst case execution time is accurate. Within the timing domain two strategies can be identified for limiting the effects of a fault in a software component:

- Do not allow an object to use more computation time than it requested.

- Do not allow an object to execute beyond its deadline.

One would expect a design method to allow a designer to specify the actions to be taken if objects overrun their allocated execution time or miss their deadlines. In both of these cases the object could be informed (via an exception) that a timing fault will occur so that it can respond to the error (within the original time frame, be it budget or deadline). There is an obligation on the execution environment to undertake the necessary time measurements and to support a means of informing an object that a fault has occurred. There is also an obligation on the coding language for language primitives that will allow recovery to be programmed.

3. Hard Real-time HOOD

In this section we present the Hard Real-time HOOD (HRT-HOOD) design method which has been developed to support the ideas introduced above. HRT-HOOD is an extension of HOOD[Agency89], and directly represents the abstractions considered in Section 2.

HRT-HOOD is based on the premise that:

1) it should be possible to express explicitly the characteristics and properties of hard real-time systems in the design method; and
2) it should be possible to distinguish at the design level the difference between an object which has an active thread of control and an object which is used to synchronise and pass data between active objects.

Consequently, HRT-HOOD has object types which represents the abstractions presented in Section 2.3.1. A hard real-time program will contain at the terminal level only CYCLIC, SPORADIC, PROTECTED and PASSIVE objects. ACTIVE objects, because they cannot be fully analysed, will only be allowed for background activity. There will, of course, be used during system decomposition to represent more abstract entities.

HRT-HOOD distinguishes between the synchronisation required to execute the operations of an object and any internal independent concurrent activity within the object. The synchronisation agent of an object is called the Object Control Structure (OBCS) (in Ada 9X this will normally be a protected record). The concurrent activity within the object is called the object's THREAD. The thread executes independently of the operations, but when it executes operations the order of the executions is controlled by the OBCS.

HRT-HOOD also has the concept of object attributes — which allow the expression of real-time attributes such as deadline, worst-case execution time etc.

In the following sections the details of the HRT object types and object attributes are discussed.

3.1. HRT-HOOD Objects

3.1.1. PASSIVE

PASSIVE objects which have no control over when invocations of their operations are executed, and do not spontaneously invoke operations in other objects Whenever an operation on a PASSIVE object is invoked, control is immediately transferred to that operation. Each operation contains only sequential code which does not synchronise with any other object (i.e. it does not block). A PASSIVE object has no OBCS and no THREAD.

3.1.2. ACTIVE

ACTIVE objects which may control when invocations of their operations are executed, and may spontaneously invoke operations in other objects. An ACTIVE object has may have an OBCS and one or more THREADs.

The operation available on ACTIVE objects are very similar to those provided by HOOD[Agency89].

3.1.3. PROTECTED

PROTECTED objects are used to control access to resources which are used by hard real-time objects. PROTECTED objects may control when invocations of their operations are executed, and do not spontaneously invoke operations in other objects; in general PROTECTED objects may *not* have arbitrary synchronisation constraints and must be analysable for their blocking times. The intention is that their use should constrain the design so that the run-time blocking for resources can be bounded (for example by using priority inheritance[Sha90], or some other limited blocking protocol such as the immediate priority ceiling inheritance associated with the Ada 9X[Intermetrics91] protected records).

PROTECTED objects are objects which do not necessarily require independent threads of control. A PROTECTED object does have an OBCS but this is a monitor-like construct: operations are executed under mutually exclusive, and functional activation constraints may be placed on when operations can be invoked. For example, a bounded buffer might be implemented as a PROTECTED object.

A single type of constrained operations is available on PROTECTED objects. It is:

- *Protected synchronous execution request* (PSER).

A constrained operation can only execute if no other constrained operation on the PROTECTED object is executing; it has mutually exclusive access to the object.

A PSER type of request can have a functional activation constraint which imposes any required synchronisation. However, for hard real-time systems these should not be used unless the time that a calling object may be blocked can be bounded.

PROTECTED objects may also have non-constrained operations, which are executed in the same manner as PASSIVE operations.

3.1.4. CYCLIC

CYCLIC objects represent periodic activities, they may spontaneously invoke operations in other objects, but the only operations they have are requests which demand immediate attentions (they represent asynchronous transfer of control requests). They are active objects in the sense that they have their own independent threads of control. However, these threads (once started) execute irrespective of whether there are any outstanding requests for their objects' operations. Furthermore, they do not wait for any of their objects' operations at any time during their execution. Indeed, in many cases CYCLIC objects will not have any operations.

In general CYCLIC objects will communicate and synchronise with other hard real-time threads by calling operations in PROTECTED objects. However, it is recognised that some constrained operation may be defined by a CYCLIC object because:

- other objects may need to signal a mode change to the cyclic object — this could be achieved by having CYCLIC objects poll a "mode change notifier" PROTECTED object, but this is inefficient if the response time required from the CYCLIC object is short (if mode changes can occur only at well defined instances then "mode change notifier" objects would be appropriate)
- other objects may need to signal error conditions to the cyclic object — this could again be achieved by having CYCLIC objects poll an error notifier PROTECTED object but this is again inefficient when the response time required from the CYCLIC object is short

Several types of constrained operations are therefore available on CYCLIC objects (each may have functional activation constraints). All of these, when open, require an immediate response from the CYCLIC's thread. The OBCS of a CYCLIC object interacts with the thread to force an asynchronous transfer of control. Available operations include an:

- *Asynchronous, asynchronous transfer of control request* (ASATC). This does not block the calling object but demands that the CYCLIC object responds "immediately". The request will result in an asynchronous transfer of control in the CYCLIC object's thread.

All CYCLIC objects have a thread, whereas only those with operations have an OBCS.

3.1.5. SPORADIC

SPORADIC objects represent sporadic activities; SPORADIC objects may spontaneously invoke operations in other objects; each sporadic has a single operation which is called to invoke the thread, and one or more operations which are requests which demand immediate attentions (they represent asynchronous transfer of control requests).

SPORADIC objects are active objects in the sense that they have their own independent threads of control. Each SPORADIC object has a single constrained operation which is called to invoke the execution of the thread. The operation is of the type which does not block the caller (ASER); it may be called by an interrupt. The operation which invokes the sporadic has a defined minimum arrival interval, or a maximum arrival rate.

A SPORADIC object may have other constrained operations but these are requests which wish to affect immediately the SPORADIC to indicate a result of a mode change or an error condition. As with CYCLIC objects, ASATC operations are possible. A SPORADIC object which receives a asynchronous transfer of control request will immediately abandon it current computation.

SPORADIC objects may also have non-constrained operations, which are executed in the same manner as PASSIVE operations.

3.2. Real-time Object Attributes

HOOD does not explicitly support the expression of many of the constraints necessary to engineer real-time systems. In the object description language there is a field in which the designer can express "implementation and synchronisation" constraints. Rather than use this to express an object's real-time attributes, a separate REAL-TIME ATTRIBUTES field has been added. These attributes are filled in by the designer normally at the TERMINAL object level. It is anticipated that many of the values of the attributes will be computed by support tools.

The following attributes are required:

- DEADLINE

  Each CYCLIC and SPORADIC object must have a defined deadline for the execution of its thread.

- OPERATION_BUDGET

  Each externally visible operation of an object must have a budget execution time defined.

  An operation which overruns its budgeted time is terminated. Each externally visibly operation of an object, therefore, must have an internal operation which is to be called if the operation's budget execution time is violated.

- OPERATION_WCET

  Each externally visibly operation of an object must have a worst case execution time defined. The worst case execution time for the external operation is the operation's budget time plus the budget time of the internal error handling operation.

- THREAD_BUDGET

  Each CYCLIC and SPORADIC object must have a budget execution time defined for each activation of its thread of execution. An overrun of the budgeted time results in the activity being undertaken by the thread being terminated.

  Each CYCLIC and SPORADIC object must have an internal operation which is to be called if its thread's budget execution time is violated.

- THREAD_WCET

  Each CYCLIC and SPORADIC object must have a worst case execution time defined for its thread of execution. The worst case execution time for the thread is the thread's budget time plus the budget time of the internal error handling operation.

- PERIOD

  Each CYCLIC object must have a defined period of execution.

- MINIMUM_ARRIVAL_TIME or MAXIMUM_ ARRIVAL_FREQUENCY

  Each SPORADIC object must have either a defined minimum arrival time for requests for its execution, or a maximum arrival frequency of request.

- PRECEDENCE CONSTRAINTS

  A THREAD may have precedence constraints associated with its execution.

- PRIORITY

  Each CYCLIC and SPORADIC object must have a defined priority for its thread. This priority is defined according to the scheduling theory being used (we are currently using deadline monotonic scheduling theory[Audsley91]).

- CEILING_PRIORITY

  Each PROTECTED, CYCLIC or SPORADIC object must have a defined ceiling priority. This priority is no lower than the maximum priority of all the threads that can call the object's constrained operations.

This list may be extended - for example some HRT approaches may require minimum/average execution times, utility functions etc.

4. Conclusions

In this paper we have presented a hard real-time life cycle and illustrated how the structured design method of HOOD can be modified to make it more appropriate for hard real-time system design. The HRT-HOOD method has been influenced by the tasking model of Ada 9X, and programs designed by the method have a systematic mapping to the language (see Burns and Wellings[Burns92] for details of the mapping).

Acknowledgement

The authors would like to thank Eric Fyfe and Chris Bailey of British Aerospace, Space Systems for their comments on the material presented in this paper. We would also like to thank Paco Gomez Molinero and Fernando Gonzalez-Barcia of the European Space Agency (ESTEC).

The work presented in this paper has been supported, in part, by the European Space Agency (ESTEC Contract 9198/90/NL/SF).

References

Agency89. European Space Agency, "HOOD Reference Manual Issue 3.0", WME/89-173/JB (September 1989).

Audsley91. N.C. Audsley, A. Burns, M.F. Richardson and A.J. Wellings, "Hard Real-Time Scheduling: The Deadline Monotonic Approach", *Proceedings 8th IEEE Workshop on Real-Time Operating Systems and Software*, Atlanta, GA, USA (15-17 May 1991).

Burns91. A. Burns and A. M. Lister, "A Framework for Building Dependable Systems", *Computer Journal* **34**(2), pp. 173-181 (1991).

Burns92. A. Burns and A.J. Wellings, *Hard Real-time HOOD: A Design Method for Hard Real-time Ada 9X Systems*, Towards Ada 9X, Proceedings of 1991 Ada UK International Conference, IOS Press (1992).

Intermetrics91. Intermetrics, "Draft Ada 9X Mapping Document, Volume II, Mapping Specification", Ada 9X Project Report (August 1991).

Kopetz85. H. Kopetz, "Design Principles for Fault Tolerant Real Time Systems", MARS Report, Institut für Technische Informatik, 8/85/2 (1985).

Lehoczky87. J.P. Lehoczky, L. Sha and V. Ding, "The Rate Monotonic Scheduling Algorithm: Exact Characterization and Average Case Behavior", Tech Report, Department of Statistics, Carnegie-Mellon (1987).

Sha90. L. Sha, R. Rajkumar and J. P. Lehoczky, "Priority Inheritance Protocols: An Approach to Real-Time Synchronisation", *IEEE Transactions on Computers* **39**(9), pp. 1175-1185 (September 1990).

Runtime System Support for Data-oriented Synchronization in Ada-9X

Prof.M.Gobin Dr.ir.M.Timmerman ir. F.J.A.Gielen

Dept. of Computer and Information Science
Royal Military Academy
Renaissance Av. 30,
B-1040 Brussels

Abstract

Ada is a high level language, designed for implementing large embedded systems. It became an ANSI standard in 1983 and in 1988 the Ada Joint Program Office established the ADA-9X project for the revision of the Ada standard. One of the specific areas addressed by the revision team deals with requirements posed by real-time applications and introduces a new building block for real-time Ada: the protected record. Protected records provide a low level data-oriented synchronization mechanism and are a primary support for real-time systems. They can be used to efficiently program solutions for real-time problems such as mutual exclusion, conditionally shared data, counting semaphores and signals. This paper compares two different approaches for the solution of a classical real-time problem: conditional critical regions. The first solution uses Ada83 tasking and the second one uses Ada9X protected records .Finally we will discuss the runtime support and some implementation issues for protected records on multiprocessor target systems.

1 Introduction

Ada is a modern, block structured algorithmic language designed for implementing large complex software systems. It supports real-time programming with facilities to define the synchronization and timing of parallel tasks, interrupt binding and low-level operations such as machine code insertion, unchecked conversion and representation clauses. In 1988, after some years of use, the Ada Joint Program Office established the Ada-9X project. The project goal is to revise the Ada standard in order to reflect current essential requirements with minimum problems and maximum advantage to the Ada community. The draft versions of the Ada 9X Mapping Documents, released in August 1991, give a snapshot of the work in progress and an in depth analysis of the enhancements of the language. The major change areas include real-time and parallel programming, object oriented programming and hierarchical libraries.
Although Ada83 was originally designed for real-time systems many people in the real-time community felt that special language constructs are necessary for more efficient programming. E.g. with the standard rendez-vous the calling task is always blocked until the server is finished. Moreover the rendez-vous server will take calls in FIFO order. This is often not desirable in real-time systems. On the other hand many modern real-time operating systems provide direct and fast support for mutual exclusion, non blocking communication and other system level functions. Some Ada compilation systems use a subset of such a real-time operating system for their basic runtime support (tasking, exception handling and resource management). In this case, the compilation system could also supply full access to the other features of the real-time operating system via Ada packages without violating the syntax and the semantics of Ada. Although this approach gives additional capabilities for one

particular compilation system it leads to the use of non standard, non portable and implementation dependent systems for the support of Ada83's real-time needs.
A first step towards the standardization of this support is presented in the Catalogue of Interface Features and Options (CIFO 3.0) by the Ada RunTime Environment Working Group (ARTEWG). The main objective of this document is to propose a common set of user-runtime interfaces in advance of some of the more general Ada-9X solutions. The effect of CIFO is to create an "extended runtime library" to supplement the original runtime library. The compilation system can draw the necessary routines from both libraries as directed by the user code.

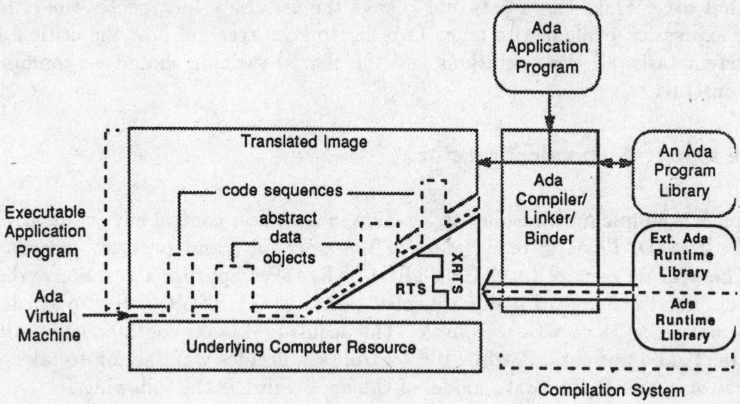

Figure 1: CIFO's extended runtime library.

In Ada-9X, the enhanced functionality is achieved by generalizing existing Ada83 features and adding new syntax elements to the language. This "core" language, which must be implemented in its entirety, will be upward compatible for most existing Ada applications. The extended features for specific application areas are defined in the Special Needs Annexes. These annexes do not define new syntax; they just provide tighter semantics for additional features by defining standards for specialized packages and implementation dependent pragmas and attributes.

2 Shared objects

2.1 Problem domain

Normally the communication between two Ada tasks is achieved through the use of parameters in the entry call. Other languages that support concurrent processing often use global shared data for this purpose. The use of shared data is normally not considered good programming practice and is not encouraged by the Ada language design. If despite this we need global shared data , their correct use requires extreme care (as in any other language) to provide the synchronization and mutual exclusion characteristics. While real-time operating systems provide semaphores to solve this problem, the Ada programmer has to realize both synchronization and mutual exclusion using the rendez-vous and some extra control task. This is a typical situation where the high level of abstraction of Ada tasking forces a programmer to use a combination of higher-level abstractions to express a lower level abstraction. This is known as "abstraction inversion" because the runtime system itself will require the use of mutual exclusion, scheduling and queueing for the implementation of the rendez-vous. Some real-time applications cannot tolerate the overhead of Ada tasking for simple resource control and need a lower-level mechanism that can be implemented in a very simple efficient way. The problem gets even more complicated if a task does not simply want exclusive access to the shared data but that it wants exclusivity only after a certain relation exists among the elements of the shared data.

This kind of synchronization primitives are conditional critical regions and have the following syntax:

region V when BARRIER do
statements
end;

where the barrier is a BOOLEAN expression and V is a shared variable. When a task enters the critical region the barrier expression is evaluated. Thus, the task might have to leave the critical region so that other tasks can access and change the variables, but reenter the critical region when the barrier expression evaluates to true. In order to keep track of how the critical regions are used by the different tasks all the operations and the shared variable should be combined in one single syntactic construct.

2.2 Case study: A chemical reactor

Our example is a simple multitasking application in a process control environment. Data acquisition tasks of the type DATAACQ read values of thermocouples and pressure sensors in the chemical reactor. The process control task, CONTROLLER, takes appropriate actions whenever the state of the system has to change. Finally a display task, VISUALIZER, will display all the control and status information on the operator console. The acquisition tasks continuously update the values of temperature, T, and pressure, P, while the control task decides what action to take next on the basis of the values of T and P. The data model of the application is the following:

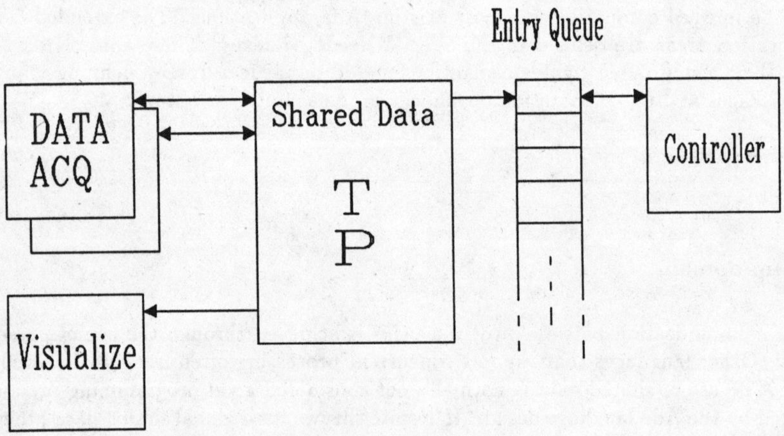

Figure 2: Data model of the chemical reactor.

During the initialization phase T and P are read by the sensors while the control task waits for some relation between T and P to hold before changing the system state to STEADYSTATE.

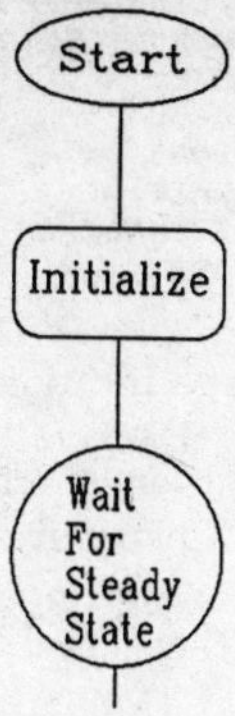

Figure 3: The first phase of the process control system.

2.3 The classical solution with Ada83

In Ada83 the protection against uncontrolled access would be achieved by encapsulating the data in a package as private types with a hidden data manager task. The package provides visible functions and procedures to manipulate the data (fig.4).

```
generic
        type ITEM is private;
        INITIAL_VALUE: ITEM;
        with  function EVALUATE(VALUE : ITEM) return BOOLEAN;

package PROTECTED_RECORD_TEMPLATE is
        type SHARED_DATA is limited private;
        function  VALUE_OF(OBJECT:in SHARED_DATA) return ITEM;
        procedure WRITE(OBJECT: in out SHARED_DATA;NEW_VALUE:in ITEM);
        procedure BARRIER_SYNCHRO(OBJECT : in SHARED_DATA);

private
        type SHARED_DATA is
                record
                    BARRIER_STATUS : BOOLEAN :=FALSE;
                    DATA         : ITEM;
                end record;
end PROTECTED_RECORD_TEMPLATE;
```

Figure 4: Package specification for controlled shared objects.

The implementation of a conditional critical region would require a second hidden barrier manager task (fig.5). This barrier manager would have the responsibility of managing the anonymous queue of suspended tasks that are waiting for the barrier expression to become true.

```
task BARRIER_AGENT is
        entry PULSE(OBJECT : in SHARED_DATA);
        entry QUEUE(OBJECT : in SHARED_DATA);
end BARRIER_AGENT;

task BIN_SEMAPHORE is
        entry WAIT;
        entry SIGNAL;
end BIN_SEMAPHORE;
```

Figure 5: Task specification of the hidden managers.

The correct programming of mutual exclusion, synchronization and barrier evaluation requires several entries to the hidden manager tasks in a particular pattern. The information hiding is obtained by putting the correct pattern of entries in a visible procedure. Our example uses the exported procedure WRITE (fig.6) for read-write access to the shared data.

```
procedure WRITE(OBJECT: in out SHARED_DATA;NEW_VALUE:in ITEM) is
begin
        BIN_SEMAPHORE.WAIT;
        OBJECT.DATA          := NEW_VALUE;
        OBJECT.BARRIER_STATUS := EVALUATE(OBJECT.DATA);
        BARRIER_AGENT.PULSE(OBJECT);
        BIN_SEMAPHORE.SIGNAL;
end WRITE;
```

Figure6: Procedure WRITE encapsulates entry calls.

The procedure requires encapsulation of two entry calls to the binary semaphore manager to obtain and release the lock on the data and it needs a third rendez-vous with the barrier to enforce consistent updating of the barrier expression before releasing the lock. The latest is implemented with a generic package subprogram parameter "function EVALUATE" (fig.4). When creating an instance of the generic package for the process control example, the application programmer must provide a function returning a BOOLEAN that depends only on the state of the elements of the shared data (fig.7).

```
        package REACTOR_PROTECTED_RECORD is
                new PROTECTED_RECORD_TEMPLATE
                        ( ITEM          => REACTOR_DATA_TYPE,
                          INITIAL_VALUE => (0,0),
                          EVALUATE      => REACTOR_EVALUATE);
end REACTOR_DATA;

package body REACTOR_DATA is

        function  REACTOR_EVALUATE(VALUE : REACTOR_DATA_TYPE) return BOOLEAN
        begin
                return VALUE.TEMPERATURE > TEMP_STEADY_STATE and
                    VALUE.PRESSURE > PRES_STEADY_STATE;
        end REACTOR_EVALUATE;
end REACTOR_DATA;
```

Figure 7: User defined evaluation function for the barrier expression.

Finally the management of the queue of tasks waiting at the barrier is programmed with a select statement that has two accept alternatives (fig.8). The first one, PULSE, is always open and is needed for the updating of the barrier after a modification of the shared data. The second accept, QUEUE, is open only when the barrier expression evaluates to TRUE. So any tasks calling the QUEUE entry via the visible procedure BARRIER SYNCHRO will be suspended if the barrier is FALSE because the rendez-vous server will simply not be waiting for this entry. When the barrier changes to TRUE the queue will be released in a FIFO order.

```
task body BARRIER_AGENT is

        BARRIER_OPEN : BOOLEAN := FALSE;
begin
loop
   select
        accept PULSE(OBJECT: in SHARED_DATA) do
                BARRIER_OPEN := OBJECT.BARRIER_STATUS;
        end PULSE;
   or
        when BARRIER_OPEN =>
        accept QUEUE(OBJECT: in SHARED_DATA) do
                null;
        end QUEUE;
   end select;
end loop;
end BARRIER_AGENT;
```

Figure 8: Suspension mechanism in the barrier task..

2.4 The Ada-9X solution : Protected records

In ADA-9X a new construct, called a "protected record", is introduced. A protected record consists of a protected record specification with a private part and a protected body (fig.9). The key features of a protected record are:
- They have components like any record but the components are locked against interfering actions.
- The operations are a syntactic part of the protected record declaration.
- Operations on the record are guaranteed to synchronize the state of the record.

```
protected_record_specification ::=
  protected [type] identifier [discriminant_part] is
    { protected_operation_declaration }
   private
   { protected_operation_declaration }
   record
    component_list
   end [record] [protected_record_simple_name]

protected_operation_declaration ::=
   subprogram_declaration
  | entry_declaration

protected_body ::=
  protected body protected_record_simple_name is
    { protected_operation_item }
  end [protected_record_simple_name];

protected_operation_item ::= subprogram_declaration
  | subprogram_body
  | entry_body
```

Figure 9: Protected record declaration.

The specification of a protected record contains a visible set of protected operations. There can be three kinds of operations:
- Protected functions provide read-only access to the record components.
- Protected procedures provide exclusive read-write access to the components.
- Protected entries also provide exclusive read-write access to the componets but in addition they specify a barrier, which is the BOOLEAN expression that depends on the components of the record.

Figure 10 shows how the protected records can be applied to code the controlled access to the shared data in the reactor example. The application programmer only has to specify what kind of operations are necessary while Ada9X is responsible for all the system level operations such as locking and maintaining queues.

```
protected type REAKTOR_DATA is
        function  VALUE_OF return REAKTOR_DATA_TYPE;
        procedure WRITE;
        entry     BARRIER_SYNCHRO;

private record
        DATA            : REAKTOR_DATA_TYPE;
end REAKTOR_DATA;


protected body REAKTOR_DATA is
        function VALUE_OF return REAKTOR_DATA_TYPE is
        begin
                return DATA;
        end VALUE_OF;

        procedure WRITE(NEW_VALUE: REAKTOR_DATA_TYPE) is
        begin
                DATA:= NEW_VALUE;
        end WRITE;

        entry BARRIER_SYNCHRO when ((DATA.TEMPERATURE > TEMP_STEADY_STATE)
                                    and DATA.PRESSURE > PRES_STEADY_STATE)) is
        begin
                null;
        end;
end REAKTOR_DATA;
```

Figure 10: Ada9X data structures for the reactor example.

Clearly this efficient construct eliminates abstraction inversion and tasking overhead and gives better protection against programming errors.
In addition protected records provide more user control over scheduler decisions. The specification makes explicit distinctions between read-only operations, read operations and possibly suspending operations. During the execution of a protected operation a task may not suspend for any reason.

3 Comparing the two alternatives

Apart from the number of lines of code which are needed to program the reactor example using Ada83 or Ada9X some more significant differences appear.

3.1 Tasking overhead and suspension

In Ada83 a write operation on the shared data requires 3 rendez-vous: two for mutual exclusion and synchronization and one for updating the barrier value. According to the LRM this implies that the requesting thread of control can be suspended -in the sense of enqueueing and scheduling another thread of control- at three different moments. On a 680x0 based microprocessor system this could mean up to nine full processor context switches!
With Ada9X, the thread of control is not allowed to be suspended when executing a protected procedure: the data synchronization must be implemented using low-level non-suspending primitives. This non-queueing property is a critical feature for the performance of the application and for asynchronous communication from hardware interrupt handlers.
For tasks that need suspension Ada9X allows queueing with a protected entry call. Only in this case the task is not suspended waiting for access to the data but will be waiting for the state of the protected record to change. The compiler or the runtime system will associate a waiting queue with every protected entry.

3.2 Efficiency and programming errors

Ada83 leaves the evaluation of the barrier expression and the queue management to the responsibility of the application programmer. Especially for complex data manipulations and multiple entries this can become an error-prone operation. Protected records allow the programmer to rely on a validated runtime system. Since this managment is done at a low-level it can be implemented in a very simple and efficient way which corresponds to the fast response requirements of modern real-time systems. Finally the entry mechanism improves performance because it reduces the number of context switches : the whole set of queued operations can be released by the one single task that detects a TRUE barrier condition for the entry queue.

3.3 Scheduling control

In the Ada83 example the user has little control over scheduler decisions. The implementation uses several entries to the (hidden) manager tasks in a particular pattern. Those operations involve many context switches and multiple calls to the scheduler. Hence the runtime behaviour of the Ada83 can be significantly influenced by the scheduling policy. For Ada9X protected records introduce a low overhead, data oriented synchronization mechanism. The protected operations allow two tasks to synchronize their operations using a set of nonqueuing locking mechanisms.

4 Multiprocessor implementation issues

4.1 Lock acquisition strategies

Since protected records are intended to be efficient, their implementation by the runtime system is of great importance. A call on a protected operation of a protected record proceeds by first evaluating the actual parameters. Then the caller tries to obtain the lock on the protected record. The lock acquisition algorithm has a major influence on the performance of a tightly coupled multiprocessor system (i.e. a shared memory multiprocessor system). A common implementation of the lock acquisition is the use of atomic instructions such as TAS (Test And Set). This instruction allows the processor to check and acquire the lock without being interrupted. If the lock is already held by another task or processor the situation is more complex. Typically in real-time operating systems the requesting task is put on the waiting queue until the lock becomes available. With this method, *Always Block*, the cost of queueing one task and activating another can be very high:
- The runtime system has to prepare an internal work request and send it to the scheduler. This allows the scheduler to verify the status of the lock and eventually reschedule the task.
- The scheduler must resynchronize. Scheduler resynchronization means that we have to inspect the local and global ready-task-chain in order to find the next schedulable task.
- Finally there is the overhead of the context switch.

Alternatively a task could busy wait until the lock is free. The *Always Spin* method is suggested by the Ada9X Mappping Document as a possible implementation for multiprocessor systems. This avoids the software overhead of the first method but many processor cycles can be wasted. Another possibility is to use *Competitive Spinning* strategies that combine both methods: the algorithm chooses to spin for a certain period and then blocks. Empirical studies of competitive strategies [7] show that their performance is not worse than some constant factor times the optimal off-line strategy that has complete knowledge about how long locks will be held.
Fixed Spin is the simplest competitive algorithm for spinning. The number of spins before blocking is a fixed fraction of the spins required for a context switch time. A fixed spin that equals the total context switch time has a competitive ratio of 2: the spin cost is always at most twice the optimal off-line algorithm. The deterministic nature of this algorithm makes the method particularly usefull for real-time Ada implementations.

4.2 Two stage locking with Write precedence

In a single processor system the lock acquisition could be implemented by inhibiting task preemption or by establishing a ceiling priority at the protected record. At the microscopic level only one protected operation can be executing at a time since there is only one processor.
In a tightly coupled multiprocessor more complex situations are possible: e.g. in a four processor system three tasks can execute protected read operations while on the fourth processor a task wants to execute a protected write. If we use only one binary lock to protect the data we will serialize the data access to the protected record and waste a lot of time probing the lock.
Our system uses two locks: a Read lock and a Write lock. The Read lock is implemented as a counting semaphore while the Write lock is a binary semaphore with the Write lock having precedence over the Read lock: every protected operation will always start with a fixed spin lock on the Write lock before proceeding.
If the Write lock is not held by another task a protected function will increment the R-lock, access the data and release the Write lock (i.e. decrement it by one).
A protected procedure or a protected entry will spin on the Read lock once it has acquired the Write lock (fig.11). This is necessary because we want all concurrent read operations to be finished before accessing the protected data in read-write mode. For the Read lock *Always Spin* may be the most efficient thing to do, since the lock will be released soon because the other processors are only reading the data. After the Read lock acquisition the protected operation modifies the protected data and evaluates the barrier expression. Finally it releases the Write lock.

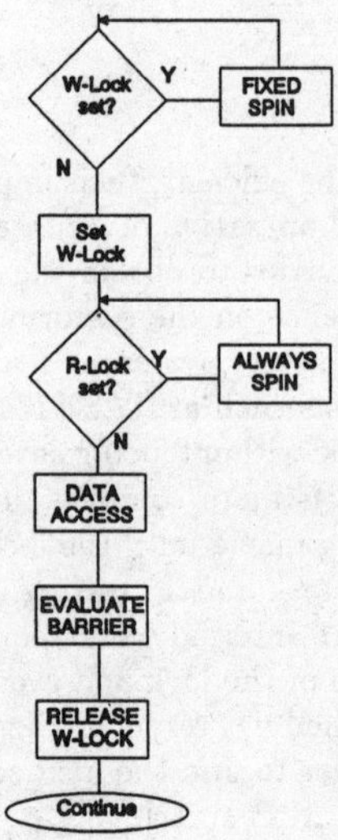

Figure 11: Read Write access to the protected data.

5 Conclussions and future work

We have shown that a lot of the Ada83 criticisms that are an obstacle towards the wide spread use of the language for real-time programming no longer holds for Ada9X. The combination of the revised language with the know-how of real-time operating system technology will allow Ada to become the standard real-time language. In a shared memory multiprocessor environment, a competitive spinning strategy in conjunction with two stage locking avoids serialization and optimizes processor utilization. The other improvements in the area of OOP and hierarchical libraries add extra arguments in favour of the use of Ada as a general purpose programming language that takes into acount the principles of modern software engineering.
Because the first validated Ada9X compiler will need some time to find its way to the marketplace the CIFO can provide an efficient and portable solution for specific needs. This investment will not be lost since ARTEWG and the Ada9X revision team have an efficient way for their synchronization and communication !

References

[1] RIPPS D. , *A Guide to Real-time Programming.*, Prentice Hall Inc., Englewood Cliffs,NJ,1989.

[2] ADA9X , *Mapping Document, Volume I, Mapping Rationale, vsn.3.1,*August 1991.

[3] ADA9X , *Mapping Document, Volume II, Mapping Specification, vsn.3.1,*August 1991.

[4] ELBERT T.F., *Embedded Programming in Ada,*

[5] LESTER K. , *The Ada9X project: progress report.*, Presented to the foundation meeting of Ada Belgium, October 3rd,1991.

[6] ARTEWG , *Catalog of Interface Features and Options for the Ada Runtime Environment.*, ACM Special Sigada edition Adaletters, Volume XI, Number 8, Fall 1991.

[7] KARLIN A., LI K., MANASSE M., OWICKI S., *Empirical Studies of Competitive Spinning for A Shared Memory Multiprocessor,* ACM 0-89791-447-3/91/0009/0041, 1991.

Decimal Arithmetic in Ada*

Benjamin M. Brosgol
brosgol@ajpo.sei.cmu.edu

Brosgol Consulting & Training
79 Tobey Road
Belmont, MA 02178
USA
+1-617-489-4027

Robert I. Eachus
eachus@d74sun.mitre.org

The MITRE Corporation
Burlington Road
Bedford, MA 01730
USA
+1-617-271-2614

David E. Emery
emery@d74sun.mitre.org

The MITRE Corporation
Burlington Road
Bedford, MA 01730
USA
+1-617-271-2815

1 Introduction

Although Ada was originally designed to meet the requirements of embedded real-time systems, it is in many respects a general-purpose language and is being adopted or considered for use in the traditional COBOL domain of business data processing. However, the apparent mismatch between Ada's arithmetic type facility and the exact decimal model for financial computation leaves a major impediment to a successful transition to Ada for Information Systems applications. This area is being given high priority in the Ada 9X revision ([1, Section 10.1], [2, Section G.4]), but users under the Ada mandate or evaluating Ada for financial systems need an approach that works with existing compilers and that achieves reasonable run-time efficiency. Ease of transition to the eventual Ada 9X solution is also important.

Support for financial processing requires suitable arithmetic facilities, representation control, and formatted output. This paper describes the possible approaches to the problem, the solution that the authors have developed, and the rationale for the choice. The main focus in this paper is on the computational issues. Further details on representation control and formatted output appear in [3].

---

* This work is sponsored by the Ada Joint Program Office's Ada Technology Insertion Program under the supervision of the U.S. Air Force.

2 Summary of Principal Issues

2.1 Computation

A major objective is to provide computational support for exact, decimal arithmetic based on capabilities found in COBOL. The principal needs are:

- A convenient way to express numeric literals
- Declaration of data items with at least 18 digits of precision (or compiler support for 64-bit integer arithmetic)
- Operations for addition, subtraction, multiplication, and division, with extra precision on intermediate results providing additional range rather than finer accuracy
- Programmer control over truncation versus rounding on a per-computation basis

Beyond the computational requirements there are also issues of programming style:

- Exploitation of Ada's strong typing (for example, having different types for, say, MONEY and PRICE_EARNINGS_RATIO)
- Ability to place logical range constraints on decimal data

2.2 Representation Control

The programmer needs to be able to precisely control data representation, both to exploit particular hardware instructions and to match the format of data stored on external files or databases.

A specific goal is to be able to deal with data formats found in files or databases created by COBOL programs. COBOL supplies an extensive and sometimes confusing set of options. Its PICTURE clause facility allows the programmer to specify the total number of digits of a numeric data item (we refer to this as the item's *precision*) and the number of digits to the right of the decimal point (the item's *scale*). COBOL's USAGE clauses then allow the programmer to specify whether the item's representation will be DISPLAY (character string) versus COMPUTATIONAL. An example in COBOL:

```
05   SOME-ITEM  PICTURE 9(8)V9(2)  USAGE COMP.
```

SOME-ITEM has 10 digits of precision, a scale of 2, and is represented in binary (COMP) format. The "V" indicates the position of the virtual decimal point, which is not stored explicitly in the data.

Some COBOL compiler vendors supply representations beyond those in the language standard; COMP-3, otherwise known as packed decimal, is perhaps the best-known example. Defining a common way to deal with packed decimal representations in an Ada program is one of our project's objectives.

2.3 Formatted Output

Producing human-readable forms for numeric data is of obvious importance, and the "edited output" feature of COBOL gives a large set of options for achieving this. For example, a COBOL program can specify which currency symbol is to be used (such as a dollar versus pound sign) and allow its placement in the output to "float" based on the value of the quantity to be printed so that it immediately precedes the leftmost digit. An Ada solution needs to provide similar functionality.

3 Decimal Computation through Ada Numeric Types

The two main approaches to realizing decimal arithmetic in Ada are (1) through the existing numeric facilities or (2) through a package with a private type and appropriate operations.

With Ada's numerics, we have a choice among integer, floating-point, and fixed-point. In some sense integer arithmetic provides the most appropriate computational model, since it matches the requirements for exact results. For example, one might consider using an integer type PENNIES to represent monetary values. However, this would be impractical for several reasons, both stylistically (keeping track of implicit scaling is awkward) and pragmatically (most compilers do not support 64-bit integer arithmetic).

Floating-point is unacceptable because of the inherent inexactness of representing decimal quantities. Consider the following program fragment, where X is a floating-point variable:

```
X := 0.0;
for I in 1 .. 10 loop
   X := X + 0.10;
end loop;
```

After execution of the loop using typical floating point hardware, X will not equal 1.00. Moreover, 64-bit floating point does not have enough mantissa bits to represent 18 decimal digits.

At first glance, fixed point seems no better. The apparent motivations behind the fixed point facility in Ada were to deal with scaled data coming in from sensors in real-time applications, and to provide a substitute for floating point in target environments lacking floating-point hardware. Indeed, the inherent bias toward powers of 2 for 'SMALL in Ada's fixed-point model seems at odds with the needs of decimal computation. However, fixed point provides a closer fit than might be expected [4, 5]. The Ada 83 unification of floating-point and fixed-point under the category of "approximate" computation is more artificial than real, since the model-number inaccuracy that is appropriate in the floating-point case because of differences in target hardware is not applicable at all to fixed point. The fixed-point arithmetic operations "+", "-", "*", "/" are exact, and through a 'SMALL representation clause the programmer can specify decimal scaling. Thus consider a COBOL declaration

```
05    SALARY PICTURE S9(6)V9(2) USAGE COMPUTATIONAL.
```

which defines SALARY as a signed binary data item comprising 8 decimal digits, of which 2 are after the assumed decimal point. This can be simulated in Ada:

```
type MONEY is range -999_999.99 .. 999_999.99 delta 0.01;
for MONEY'SMALL use 0.01;

SALARY : MONEY;
```

The programmer-specified 'SMALL not only provides the required decimal scaling, it also prevents the implementation from supplying extra fractional digits. This is important in financial applications: if the programmer requests 2 fractional digits, it would be incorrect for a compiler to provide 3.

There are several benefits to using fixed point to obtain decimal arithmetic:

- Real literals are automatically available.
- The Ada fixed-point rules requiring explicit rescaling of the result of a multiplication or division correspond to what programmers would expect in practice and avoid the need to define rules for intermediate scales and precisions of arithmetic expressions.

- Good run-time performance is to be expected (that is, there is no need for a compiler to perform fancy optimizations of run-time values for scale and precision).
- Providing different fixed-point types for different kinds of decimal data (such as money versus interest rates) preserves Ada's strong typing model while still allowing mixed-type multiplication and division.
- The programmer can specify logical range constraints for decimal data. For example, a variable representing a percentage could be declared with an explicit upper bound of 100.00 rather than implicitly having the bound 999.99 as in COBOL.

On the other hand, fixed point also has several anomalies and drawbacks:

- The Ada fixed point model leads to occasional surprises, even in the presence of a 'SMALL representation clause. For example, one or both endpoints supplied in the definition of a fixed point type may be absent from the implemented range for the type.
- The fixed-point rules require conversions of real literals (and named numbers of type *universal_real*) that appear as factors in multiplication or division. Without the programmer providing an explicit declaration of an applicable "*" operator, it would be illegal to write:

  ```
  SALARY := 1.05 * SALARY;
  ```

  Instead, something like the following circumlocution is required:

  ```
  SALARY := MONEY ( SOME_TYPE(1.05) * SALARY );
  ```

  Although the conversion to MONEY might be palatable, the need for an explicit conversion of the literal 1.05, or for an explicit overloading of "*", is somewhat embarrassing.
- The previous example illustrates another serious problem: Ada fixed point does not give a well-defined result for the conversion of values. That is, the language does not guarantee whether the result of a fixed-point conversion is to be rounded versus truncated. In fact, different evaluations of the same expression in the same program could yield different results, an unwelcome nondeterminism. Probably the cleanest solution, but one that requires a new facility in Ada 83, is to have attribute functions 'TRUNCATE and 'ROUND available for any fixed-

point type; each of these functions takes as its parameter a value from any fixed point type. Thus in the above example, we would write MONEY'TRUNC(...) or MONEY'ROUND(...) rather than just MONEY(...).

- Since fixed point types do not automatically come with I/O operations or conversions to and from STRING, the programmer will need to obtain them through generic instantiations. If the program needs to declare many fixed point types, the resulting generic instantiations will add compilation time, code space, and program clutter.

- The decimal 'SMALL representation clause is not widely supported in current Ada '83 compilers, in part because of the difficulty in efficiently implementing the accuracy requirements for conversions of fixed-point products and quotients with arbitrary (and possibly incompatible) 'SMALLs [6, 7].

These problems are not insurmountable; indeed, the approach being adopted for decimal arithmetic in Ada 9X introduces decimal types (with attributes 'TRUNCATE and 'ROUND, as well as other operations) as a special category of fixed-point types. However, since usage of fixed point for decimal in Ada 83 would require compiler support, we were led to reject this approach in favor of one based on supplemental packages.

4 Decimal Computation through Packages

The alternative to using Ada's numeric type features for decimal is to supply a package with a private type and a set of operations. Actually there are several ways in which this may be obtained, depending on whether the precision (or range) and scale are established as subtype characteristics of a single type, or are intrinsic to the type and are supplied as generic actual parameters.

4.1 Precision and Scale as Discriminants

Ada's data abstraction facility offers one approach to realizing decimal semantics. We can define a private type, with discriminants for precision and scale, and a set of subprograms to yield the needed operations. The following is a skeletal version of such a package (for a complete version, see [3, Section A.3.1]). Note that the package name BINARY reflects the fact that this package corresponds to the binary computational format.

```
package BINARY is
   MAX_PRECISION : constant := 18;
   subtype PRECISION_RANGE is POSITIVE range 1 .. MAX_PRECISION;
   type SIGNED ( PRECISION : PRECISION_RANGE;
                 SCALE     : INTEGER ) is private;
   ...
   -- Operations:
   --  Rescaling
   --  Construction of SIGNED from string, integer, or float
   --  Generics for conversion to/from numeric
   --  Procedures for arithmetic operations
   --  Relationals
   --  "Edited output" of formatted strings
private
   ...
   -- Implementation as variant record with 32- or 64-bit integer
end BINARY;
```

A package PACKED_DECIMAL has an analogous structure and likewise declares a private discriminated type SIGNED. The Ada programmer's choice of BINARY versus PACKED_DECIMAL corresponds to the COBOL programmer's choice between COMP and COMP-3 (in an environment supporting packed decimal).

Note that the arithmetic operations are obtained via procedures versus infix operators. Although this yields a style that perhaps resembles COBOL more than Ada, the alternative of defining operators and specifying result precision and scale was considered and rejected. The issue of result precision and scale has proved to be an extremely difficult problem for other programming languages, especially for division. Languages that attempt to give well-defined semantics, such as PL/I, invariably yield anomalies; in PL/I, the well-known example is that the simple-looking expression 10 + 1/3 will yield an overflow. Moreover, the Ada rules for assignment of discriminated objects (requiring equality of corresponding discriminants in source and target) have an unpleasant interaction with the rules for result scale and precision. Intuitively, one would expect that the scale of a product is the sum of the scales of the two factors. However, this implies that a simple assignment like

```
SALARY := SALARY * OVERTIME_RATE; -- Assume OVERTIME_RATE.SCALE > 0
```

will raise CONSTRAINT_ERROR because of the SCALE discriminant mismatch between source (the result of the multiplication) and target. Languages that leave the rules unspecified (for example, SQL) avoid these sorts of anomalies but at a sacrifice in portability. The use of procedures rather than operators or functions avoids these problems.

An example usage of the package:

```
SALARY     : BINARY.SIGNED ( PRECISION => 8, SCALE => 2);
ADJUSTMENT : BINARY.SIGNED ( PRECISION => 5, SCALE => 4);
...
MULTIPLY ( SALARY, ADJUSTMENT, ROUNDED, GIVING => SALARY );
```

4.2 Range and Scale through Generics

An alternative to defining precision and scale as run-time specifiable discriminants is to supply them through a generic instantiation. In skeletal form (for a complete version see [3, Section A.5.1]):

```
generic
   type INTEGER_TYPE is range <>;
   type FLOAT_TYPE is digits <>;
package GENERIC_DECIMAL is
   generic
      DECIMAL_PLACES : in INTEGER_TYPE;   -- Scale
      FIRST, LAST    : in FLOAT_TYPE;     -- Range
   package SHORT_DECIMAL is
      type DECIMAL is private;
      ...
      -- Operations including conversions to/from STRING,
      -- binary operators "+", "-"
   private
      ...
      -- Implementation as 32-bit integer type
   end SHORT_DECIMAL;
   -- Analogous declaration of generic LONG_DECIMAL
   -- Declarations of generics for multiplication and division,
   -- rescaling conversions, and I/O
end GENERIC_DECIMAL;
```

The programmer instantiates the outer generic once, using the longest integer type and the floating point type with the largest mantissa, to obtain a non-generic package. A set of instantiations of the inner generics is now needed, based on the number of differently scaled decimal types required by the application. As an example:

```
package DECIMAL is new GENERIC_DECIMAL( LONG_INTEGER, LONG_FLOAT );

package MONEY is new DECIMAL.LONG_DECIMAL ( DECIMAL_PLACES => 2,
                                            FIRST => -100_000.00,
                                            LAST  =>  100_000.00 );

package PERCENTAGE is new DECIMAL.SHORT_DECIMAL
   ( DECIMAL_PLACES => 4,
     FIRST => -1.0000,
     LAST  =>  1.0000);

package MONEY_PERCENTAGE_OPERATIONS is
   new DECIMAL.MULTIPLY_OPERATIONS ( MONEY, PERCENTAGE, MONEY );

SALARY      : MONEY.DECIMAL;
ADJUSTMENT : PERCENTAGE.DECIMAL;
...
SALARY := SALARY * ADJUSTMENT;
```

5 Evaluation of Alternatives for Decimal Computation

Although a solution through Ada's fixed point mechanism provides the best long-term solution for Ada 9X, the need for a readily implementable approach in Ada 83 dictates a choice of one or both of the package techniques. The two approaches differ significantly in style.

The discriminated type approach is the simpler of the two in practice. Since there is a single type BINARY.SIGNED, the package BINARY can explicitly provide subprograms that convert to/from external representations and that generate formatted (report) output. There is no need to instantiate generics for this purpose. A programmer wishing to exploit Ada's strong typing can derive new types from BINARY.SIGNED; it is not necessary to declare all decimal data to be from one type.

Drawbacks to the discriminated type approach are the inability to associate logical range constraints with a data object as part of the declaration, a sacrifice of performance due to the passing and interrogation of precision and scale as run-time discriminants, and the need to perform arithmetic with a procedural versus expression syntax. Also, if derived types are used, then a generic instantiation or explicit overloading is required in order to obtain mixed-type multiplication and division.

The generic range and scale approach offers the opposite tradeoffs. Run-time performance is likely to be much better than with a discriminated type, the programmer can specify a logical range at the instantiation that will apply to the type, and infix expression syntax is available at least for addition and subtraction, and for multiplication and division where one of the factors is an integer or floating point value. On the other hand, the generic approach is somewhat more complicated to use, and requires explicit instantiations to obtain the needed operations. The use of nested generics may tax the capabilities of some existing Ada implementations, and compilation performance could be an issue in some environments.

Rather than selecting between these alternatives, the authors are recommending that both be supplied. Although the provision of two techniques appears redundant, the differences in how they achieve the functionality of decimal computation correspond to differences in requirements for users. It is thus appropriate for the users themselves to choose the technique that is more appropriate for their backgrounds and their needs. In general we expect that programmers coming from COBOL who are new to Ada will find the discriminated type approach easier to learn and use, while those with more experience in Ada will tend towards the generics-based approach.

6 External Representations and Report Output

In a typical financial application, data exists in an external file or database, the program reads it and processes it, and then writes the updated data back to the external file and/or outputs it in human-readable format to a report. The issue is how to model these external representations in Ada.

To model COBOL-based external representations, the approach developed by the authors is a package EXTERNAL (see [3, Section A.1]) that declares a set of array types. This achieves some amount of type protection, since a data field declared as, say, TRAILING_SEPARATE, will be correctly interpreted when passed to a conversion procedure that moves the data into a computational format.

As an example of the so-called "edited output" problem, suppose that we have a decimal data item whose value is 12345.67 and we want to output this to a report in a field that is 12 characters wide; moreover, we want to suppress leading 0's, have a dollar sign immediately precede the leftmost digit, and have a comma separating the thousands. That is, the desired output is `ѢѢ$12,345.67` where the `ѢѢ` indicates blank characters.

In Ada we can do this through a subprogram that takes the decimal value as one parameter and a "picture string" as a second parameter. The picture string reflects the desired 0 suppression, currency symbol placement, etc. The result of the subprogram (an **out** parameter if a procedure, or the returned value if a function) is a STRING.

The approaches to external representations and edited output are common to both the discriminated private type and generic package technique for decimal computation.

7 Conclusions and Status

The requirement to have a solution to decimal arithmetic for Ada 83 that could be used without compiler modifications dictated an approach based on external packages rather than on fixed point and has served as a "stress test" of Ada's definitional facilities. Ada's private types and generics proved to be sufficient to obtain the needed abstract behavior, and derived types are of course valuable in helping to exploit the language's strong typing for data that are logically different but that happen to share a common precision and scale.

Three principal sacrifices are made when a package (versus a numeric type) is used for decimal computation. One is the absence of literals, necessitating explicit conversions. The second is that run-time performance will not be as efficient as when the compiler directly implements the code sequences for the decimal constructs. Third, there is no way to specify range as subtype constraints for a private type. However, these drawbacks are manageable. Overloading unary "+" for conversion of literals can help make the notation fairly unobtrusive; there is nothing to prevent a compiler from optimizing the handling of decimal; and at least with the generic approach to computation the programmer can supply logical range bounds on a per-type basis.

Thus a package approach to decimal arithmetic enables Ada 83 to meet the immediate requirements of Information Systems applications. The choice between a discriminated type and a generic package solution will depend upon project-specific characteristics, with each approach serving a different constituency.

Prototype implementations exist for the components described in this paper, together with examples of the approaches for some sample financial programs. The Information Systems ad hoc Rapporteur Group (IRG) has been established under ISO/IEC JTC1/SC22 WG9 Ada to investigate possible standardization for the proposed packages.

Acknowledgements

The background for this work has been an ongoing exchange of electronic mail and a number of meetings involving the authors and Robert Dewar (NYU), Ken Fussichen (Computer Sciences Corporation), Marc Graham (Software Engineering Institute), Jim Moore (IBM), Tucker Taft (Intermetrics), and Brian Wichmann (NPL). Meetings of SIGAda's Commercial Ada Users Working Group have also elicited some useful ideas.

The authors gratefully acknowledge the support and encouragement of MAJ Tom Croak (USAF) and Dr. John Solomond (AJPO).

References

[1] Office of the Under Secretary of Defense for Acquisition, Ada 9X Project Report, *Ada 9X Requirements*, December 1990.

[2] Intermetrics, Inc.; *Ada 9X Mapping Document, Volume II (Mapping Specification)*, Version 4.0, December 1991.

[3] Emery, David E., Robert I. Eachus, and Benjamin M. Brosgol; *Ada Decimal Arithmetic: Interim Report*, The MITRE Corporation, January 1992.

[4] Dewar, Robert; *The Fixed-Point Facility in Ada*; Software Engineering Institute Special Report SEI-90-SR-2, February 1990.

[5] Wichmann, Brian A., and Terry Froggatt; *Fixed Point and Decimal in Ada 9X*; October 1991

[6] Terry Froggatt, "Fixed-point Conversion, Multiplication, & Division, in Ada(R)"; *Ada Letters* Vol. 7, No. 1 (January-February 1987); pp 71-81.

[7] Paul N. Hilfinger, *Implementing Ada Fixed-point Types Having Arbitrary Scales*; Report No. UCB/CSD 90/#582; University of California , Berkeley; June 1990.

Task Dependence Net as a Representation for Concurrent Ada Programs

Jingde Cheng

Department of Computer Science and Communication Engineering
Kyushu University
6-10-1 Hakozaki, Fukuoka 812, Japan

Abstract

This paper proposes two new types of basic program dependences in concurrent programs, named the synchronization dependence and the communication dependence, and a new program representation for concurrent Ada programs, named the Task Dependence Net (TDN). The task dependence net can be used as a unified representation in a concurrent Ada programming environment.

1. Introduction

Program dependences are dependence relationships holding between statements in a program that are determined by control flow and data flow in the program, and therefore, they can be used to represent the program's behavior. There are two types of basic program dependences in the literature, i.e., the control dependence that is determined by control flow of a program, and the data dependence that is determined by data flow of a program. Informally, a statement S is control dependent on the control predicate C of a conditional branch statement (e.g., an if statement or while statement) if the value of C determines whether S is executed or not. A statement S_2 is data dependent on a statement S_1 if the value of a variable computed at S_1 directly or indirectly has influence on the value of a variable computed at S_2.

In general, a concurrent program consists of a number of processes, and therefore, it has multiple control flows and data flows. Moreover, these control flows and data flows are not independent because of the existence of interprocess synchronization and communication in the program. It is obvious that only using the control and data dependences is inadequate to represent the full behavior of a concurrent program.

Dependence-based program representation has many applications in software development activities including program optimization, parallelization, understanding, testing, debugging, and maintenance [1,7,8,10,11,14-17]. For example, program dependence graph [7,10,14], which explicitly represents both control and data dependences in a sequential program, has been developed as an important program representation tool used in compiler construction and software testing, debugging, and maintenance. However, the program dependence graph itself and its various variations have been proposed for representation of only sequential programs. Until recently, there is no dependence-based representation proposed for concurrent programs.

This paper proposes two new types of basic program dependences in concurrent programs, named the *synchronization dependence* and the *communication dependence*, and a new program representation for concurrent Ada programs, named the *Task Dependence Net* (TDN), which extends the usual program dependence graph for sequential programs to the case of concurrent Ada programs. Our primary motivation in developing the task dependence net is to develop a unified representation tool useful in knowledge-based debugging of concurrent Ada programs. The representation can also be used in understanding, testing, maintenance, and complexity measure/metrics of concurrent Ada programs.

It is assumed that any Ada program considered in this paper consists of some single tasks (i.e., such task types as have the only instance). In order to simplify discussion, here we do not consider abort, block, subprogram, and package facilities in Ada. We also assume that every object in a program has a unique name statically and no object is created dynamically.

The rest of this paper is organized as follows: Section 2 defines the terminology used in this paper, Section 3 defines the control and data dependences in a task, Section 4 defines the synchronization and communication dependences between tasks, Section 5 presents the Task Dependence Net and its applications, and Section 6 points out some future research problems.

2. Terminology

Definition 2.1 A *digraph* is an ordered pair (V, A), where V is a finite set of elements, called *vertices*, and A is a finite set of elements of the Cartesian product $V \times V$, called *arcs*, i.e., $A \subseteq V \times V$ is a binary relation on V. For any arc $(v_1,v_2) \in A$, v_1 is called the *initial vertex* of the arc and said to be *adjacent to* v_2, and v_2 is called the *terminal vertex* of the arc and said to be *adjacent from* v_1. A *predecessor* of a vertex v is a vertex adjacent to v, and a *successor* of v is a vertex adjacent from v. The *in-degree* of a vertex v, denoted in-degree(v), is the number of predecessors of v, and the *out-degree* of a vertex v, denoted out-degree(v), is the number of successors of v. A *simple digraph* is a digraph (V, A) such that $(v,v) \notin A$ for any $v \in V$. □

Definition 2.2 An *arc-labeled digraph* is an n-tuple $(V, A_1, A_2, ..., A_{n-1})$ such that every (V, A_i) $(i=1, ..., n-1)$ is a digraph. A *simple arc-labeled digraph* is an arc-labeled digraph $(V, A_1, A_2, ..., A_{n-1})$ such that $(v,v) \notin A_i$ $(i=1, ..., n-1)$ for any $v \in V$. □

Definition 2.3 A *path* in a digraph (V, A) or an arc-labeled digraph $(V, A_1, A_2, ..., A_{n-1})$ is a sequence of arcs $(a_1, a_2, ..., a_\ell)$ such that the terminal vertex of a_i is the initial vertex of a_{i+1} for $1 \leqq i \leqq \ell-1$, where $a_i \in A$ $(1 \leqq i \leqq \ell)$ or $a_i \in A_1 \cup A_2 \cup ... \cup A_{n-1}$ $(1 \leqq i \leqq \ell)$, and ℓ $(\ell \geqq 1)$ is called the *length* of the path. If the initial vertex of a_1 is v_I and the terminal vertex of a_ℓ is v_T, then the path is called a path from v_I to v_T, or v_I-v_T path for short. A path in a digraph or an arc-labeled digraph is said to be *simple* if it does not include the same arc twice. A path in a digraph or an arc-labeled digraph is said to be *elementary* if it does not include the same vertex twice. □

Definition 2.4 A *deterministic control flow graph* is a quadruple (V, A, s, t), where (V, A) is a simple digraph such that out-degree(v) $\leqq 2$ for any $v \in V$, $s \in V$ is a unique vertex, called *start vertex*, such that in-degree(s) $=0$, $t \in V$ is a unique vertex, called *termination vertex*, such that out-degree(t) = 0, and for any $v \in V$ ($v \neq s$, $v \neq t$), there exists a path from s to v and a path from v to t. Any arc $(v_1, v_2) \in A$ is called a *control flow arc*. □

Definition 2.5 A *nondeterministic control flow graph* is a quadruple (N, V, A, s, t), where $N \subset V$ is a finite set of elements, called *nondeterministic vertices*, (V, A) is a simple digraph such that out-degree(v) $\leqq 2$ for any $v \in (V - N)$ and $2 \leqq$ out-degree(v) $\leqq k$ for any $v \in N$, $s \in V$ is a unique vertex, called *start vertex*, such that in-degree(s) = 0, $t \in V$ is a unique vertex, called *termination vertex*, such that out-degree(t) = 0, and for any $v \in V$ ($v \neq s$, $v \neq t$), there exists a path from s to v and a path from v to t. Any arc $(v_1, v_2) \in A$ is called a *control flow arc*. □

A deterministic control flow graph can be regarded as a special case of nondeterministic control flow graphs where nondeterministic vertex set N is the empty set.

Definition 2.6 Let (V, A, s, t) be a deterministic or nondeterministic control flow graph, and u and v be any two vertices in V. u *forward dominates* v iff every path from v to t contains u; u *properly forward dominates* v iff u forward dominates v and $u \neq v$; u *strongly forward dominates* v iff u forward dominates v and there exists an integer k ($k \geqq 1$) such that every path from v whose length is greater than or equal to k contains u; u is the *immediate forward dominator* of v iff u is the first vertex that properly forward dominates v in every path from v to t. □

Definition 2.7 A *deterministic or nondeterministic definition-use graph* is a quadruple (G_C, Σ_V, D, U), where G_C is a deterministic control flow graph (V, A, s, t) or a nondeterministic control flow graph (N, V, A, s, t), Σ_V is a finite set of symbols, called *variables*, and D: $V \rightarrow 2^{\Sigma_V}$ and U: $V \rightarrow 2^{\Sigma_V}$ are two functions from V to the power set of Σ_V. □

Definition 2.8 A *control flow net* is a 8-tuple (G_{CS}, b, e, L_s, L_t, Σ_C, S, R), where G_{CS} = (N_S, V_S, A_S, S_S, T_S) is a finite set of deterministic and nondeterministic control flow graphs, where $N_S = N_1 \cup N_2 \cup \ldots \cup N_n$, $V_S = V_1 \cup V_2 \cup \ldots \cup V_n$, $A_S = A_1 \cup A_2 \cup \ldots \cup A_n$, $S_S = \{s_1, s_2, \ldots, s_n\}$, and $T_S = \{t_1, t_2, \ldots, t_n\}$, $b \in S_S$ is a unique vertex, called *entry vertex* of the net, $e \in T_S$ is a unique vertex, called *exit vertex* of the net, $L_s \subseteq V_S \times S_S$ and $L_t \subseteq T_S \times V_S$ are two binary relations, any $(v_1, v_2) \in L_s$ is called a *start link arc*, and any $(v_1, v_2) \in L_t$ is called a *termination link arc*, Σ_C is a finite set of symbols, called *channels*, S: $V_S \rightarrow \Sigma_C$ and R: $V_S \rightarrow \Sigma_C$ are two partial functions, and for any $v \in V_S$ ($v \neq b$, $v \neq e$), there exists a path from b to v and a path from v to e, where the paths may consist of control flow arcs, start link arcs, and termination link arcs. □

Definition 2.9 A *definition-use net* is a quadruple (N_C, Σ_V, D, U), where N_C = ((N_S, V_S, A_S, S_S, T_S), b, e, L_s, L_t, Σ_C, S, R) is a control flow net, Σ_V is a finite set of symbols, called *variables*, and D: $V_S \rightarrow 2^{\Sigma_V}$ and U: $V_S \rightarrow 2^{\Sigma_V}$ are two functions. □

Note that all above definitions are graph-theoretical, and therefore, they are independent of programming languages.

3. Control and Data Dependences in a Task

For any task in a concurrent Ada program, we can construct its deterministic or nondeterministic control flow graph by using vertices to represent simple statements including assignment, exit, goto, delay, raise, and return statements, and control predicates in conditional branch statements including if and loop statements, using nondeterministic vertices to represent points where nondeterministic selection are performed, and using arcs to represent possible control transfers between the statements.

Moreover, the following techniques are necessary in the construction of deterministic or nondeterministic control flow graph for Ada tasks.

First, unlike the usual method in construction of control flow graph for sequential programs, we can not necessarily use s and t to represent the first and the last statements in the body of a task, respectively. Instead, we must use s to represent the start point of the elaboration of the declarative part of the task, and use t to represent the termination point of execution of the task, respectively. Also, if the task has some exception handlers, then there should be an arc from the vertex representing the last statement of each exception handler to the vertex representing "end" (i.e., the termination point) of the task. These are because of the following two reasons: (1) before the execution of the first statement in the body of a task, the elaboration of the declarative part of the task may include creations of some tasks, initializations of some variables, and synchronization and/or communication with other tasks, and (2) if the body of a task has an exception handling part, then the execution of the task may complete after the execution of a statement in an exception handler but not after the execution of the last statement in the body of the task.

Second, an exit statement with a condition (e.g., "**exit** L **when** C") can be treated as an if statement with a goto statement (e.g., "**if** C **then goto** L **end if**"), which is semantically equivalent to the original exit statement. A case statement can also be equivalently treated as an if statement whose each conditional branch corresponds to a choice alternative of the original case statement.

Third, a loop statement without an iteration scheme can be treated as the sequence of statements in the loop statement following a goto statement "**goto** L" such that the first statement in the sequence is labeled with label name "L".

Fourth, for an accept statement with a sequence of statements, it is necessary to use two vertices to represent "begin" and "end" of the accept statement respectively. If the sequence of statements includes a return statement, then there should be an arc from the vertex representing the return statement to the vertex representing "end" of the accept statement.

Finally, for a selective wait statement, a nondeterministic vertex having more than one successor should be used to represent "begin" (i.e., the nondeterministic selection point) of the selective wait statement such that each successor of the nondeterministic vertex corresponds to a select alternative or the else part of the selective wait statement. There should be an arc from the vertex representing the last statement of each select alternative (excluding terminate alternative) or the else part to the vertex representing the statement following the selective wait statement. If the selective wait statement has a terminate alternative, then there should be an arc from the vertex representing the terminate alternative to the vertex representing "end" of the task having the selective wait statement. A similar technique can be used to treat a conditional or timed entry call statement.

We say that a variable V is *defined* at an assignment, entry call, or accept statement S if V is assigned a value at S. We say that variable V is *used* at statement S if V occurs in an expression computed at S.

For any task in a concurrent Ada program, we can construct its definition-use graph (G_C, Σ_V, D, U) based on its deterministic or nondeterministic control flow graph by defining the two functions D and U explicitly, i.e., by assigning two sets D(v) and U(v) of variables to every vertex v of the control flow graph such that D(v) is the set of all variables defined at v, and U(v) is the set of all variables used at v. In particular, for a vertex v representing an entry call statement, we define D(v) as the set of all "out mode" and "in out mode" parameters of the called entry; for a vertex v representing "begin" of an accept statement, we define D(v) as the set of all "in mode" and "in out mode" parameters of it; for a vertex v representing "end" of an accept statement, we define U(v) as the set of all "out mode" and "in out mode" parameters of the accept statement.

Fig. 1 shows a task, named "T", which has two child tasks, named "PERCENT" and "FACT", and the definition-use graph of task PERCENT. Fig. 2 shows the definition-use graph of task FACT.

The control dependence in a task then can be defined based on the task's control flow graph as follows.

Definition 3.1 Let u and v be any two vertices in the deterministic or nondeterministic control flow graph of a task. u is *directly strongly control dependent* on v iff there exists a path from v to u such that the path does not contain the immediate forward dominator of v. u is *directly weakly control dependent* on v iff v has two successors v' and v" such that u strongly forward dominates v' but does not strongly forward dominates v". □

```
t1   task body T is
t2       R : INTEGER := 1;
         task FACT is
             entry E1(I : in INTEGER);
             entry E2(O : out INTEGER);
         end FACT;
         task PERCENT;
     begin
t3       FACT.E2(R);
t4       PUT(R);
t5   end T;

p1   task body PERCENT is
         X, Y, P : INTEGER;
         MINUS_OPERATOR,
         ZERO_DIVIDE : exception;
     begin
p2       GET (X);
p3       GET (Y);
p4       if X<=0 or Y<=0 then
p5           raise MINUS_OPERATOR;
p6       elsif Y=0 then
p7           raise ZERO_DIVIDE;
         else
p8           P:=(X/Y) * 100;
         end if;
p9       FACT.E1 (P);
     exception
         when MINUS_OPERATOR =>
p10          PUT ("MINUS_OPERATOR");
p11          PUT (X);
p12          PUT (Y);
         when ZERO_DIVIDE =>
p13          PUT ("ZERO_DIVIDE");
p14          PUT (Y);
p15  end PERCENT;
```

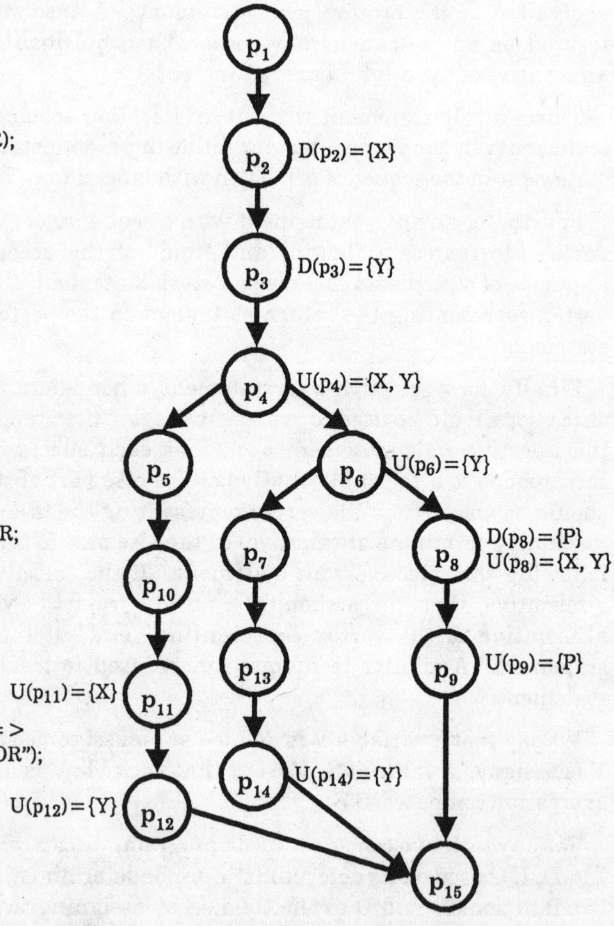

Fig. 1 Task T, task PERCENT, and the definition-use graph of task PERCENT

Note that according to the above definition, if u is directly strongly control dependent on v, then u is also directly weakly control dependent on v, but the converse is not necessarily true.

Informally, if u is directly strongly control dependent on v, then v must have at least two successors v' and v" such that if the branch from v to v' is executed then u must be executed, while if the branch from v to v" is executed then u may not be executed. If u is directly weakly control dependent on v, then v must have two successors v' and v" such that if the branch from v to v' is executed then u is necessarily executed within a fixed number of steps, while if the branch from v to v" is executed then u may not be executed or the execution of u may be delayed indefinitely. The difference between strong and weak control dependences is that the latter reflects a dependence between an exit condition of a loop and a statement outside the loop that may be executed after the loop is exited, but the former does not.

```
f1   task body FACT is
         N, F : INTEGER;
     begin
f2       GET (N);
f3       F := 1;
f4       while N /= 0
         loop
f5           F := F * N;
f6           N := N - 1;
         end loop;
f7       select
f8           accept E1 (I : in INTEGER) do
f9               F := F * I;
f10          end E1;
         or
f11          accept E2 (O : out INTEGER) do
f12              O := F;
f13          end E2;
         end select;
f14  end FACT;
```

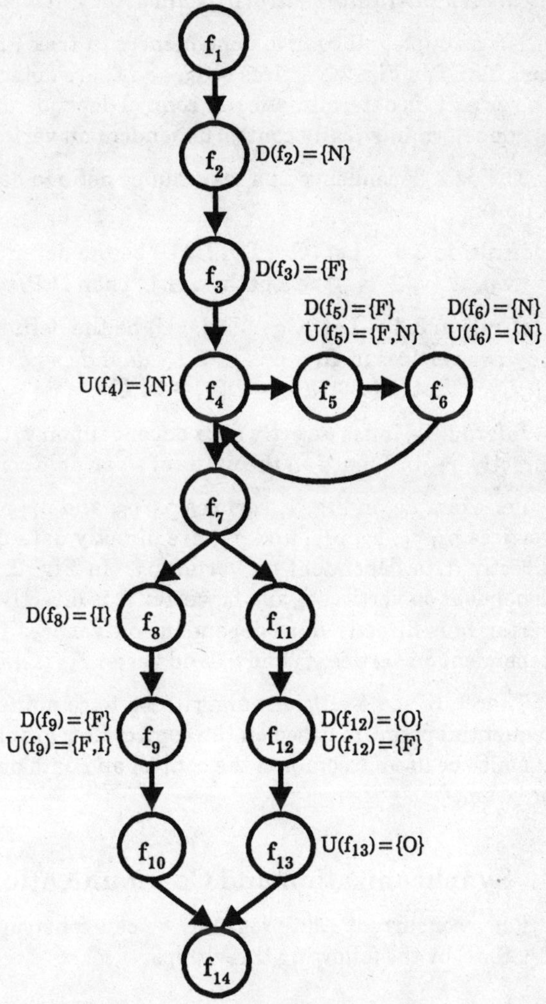

Fig. 2 Task FACT and its definition-use graph

For example, in Fig. 1, vertices p_5 and p_6 are directly strongly (weakly) control dependent on vertex p_4, vertices p_{10}, p_{11}, and p_{12} are also directly strongly (weakly) control dependent on vertex p_4, vertices p_7 and p_8 are directly strongly (weakly) control dependent on vertex p_6, and vertices p_9, p_{13}, and p_{14} are also directly strongly (weakly) control dependent on vertex p_6. In Fig. 2, vertices f_5, f_6, and f_4 are directly strongly (weakly) control dependent on vertex f_4, vertex f_7 is directly weakly control dependent on vertex f_4 but not directly strongly control dependent on f_4, and any of vertices $f_8 \sim f_{13}$ is directly strongly (weakly) control dependent on vertex f_7.

Obviously, there are some semantic difference between a control dependence caused by a deterministic control transfer and a control dependence caused by a nondeterministic selection. Therefore, we give the following definition.

Definition 3.2 Let u and v be any two vertices in the deterministic or nondeterministic control flow graph of a task, and u be directly weakly control dependent on v. u is *deterministically control dependent* on v iff v is not a nondeterministic vertex; u is *nondeterministically control dependent* on v iff v is a nondeterministic vertex. □

For example, all control dependences in task PERCENT in Fig. 1 are deterministic. In task FACT in Fig. 2, vertices f_5, f_6, and f_4 are deterministically control dependent on vertex f_4, vertex f_7 is deterministically control dependent on vertex f_4, and any of vertices $f_8 \sim f_{13}$ is nondeterministically control dependent on vertex f_7.

The data dependence in a task can be defined based on the task's definition-use graph as follows.

Definition 3.3 Let (G_C, Σ_V, D, U) be the definition-use graph of a task, and $P=((v_1,v_2), (v_2,v_3), ..., (v_{n-1},v_n))$ be a path in G_C. Then $D(P)=D(v_1) \cup D(v_2) \cup ... \cup D(v_n)$. □

Definition 3.4 Let (G_C, Σ_V, D, U) be the definition-use graph of a task, and u and v be any two vertices in G_C. u is *directly data dependent* on v iff there is a path P from v to u in G_C such that $(D(v) \cap U(u)) - D(P) \neq \Phi$. □

Informally, if u is directly data dependent on v, then the value of a variable computed at v directly has influence on the value of a variable computed at u.

For example, in Fig. 1, vertices p_4, p_8, and p_{11} are directly data dependent on vertex p_2, vertices p_4, p_6, p_8, p_{12}, and p_{14} are directly data dependent on vertex p_3, and vertex p_9 is directly data dependent on vertex p_8. In Fig. 2, vertices f_4, f_5, and f_6 are directly data dependent on vertices f_2 and f_6, vertex f_5 is directly data dependent on vertices f_3, f_6, and f_5, vertex f_9 is directly data dependent on vertices f_3, f_5, and f_8, vertex f_{12} is directly data dependent on vertices f_3 and f_5, and vertex f_{13} is directly data dependent on vertices f_{12}.

There are some efficient algorithms to compute the control and data dependences in a sequential program based on the control flow graph of the program [2,7]. Those algorithms can also be used to compute the control and data dependences in a task of a concurrent Ada program.

4. Synchronization and Communication Dependences between Tasks

For a concurrent Ada program, we can construct its control flow net $(G_{CS}, b, e, L_s, L_t, \Sigma_C, S, R)$ by the following three steps:

(1) Construct a deterministic or nondeterministic control flow graph for every task in the program. The result is the set G_{CS} of deterministic and nondeterministic control flow graphs of tasks in the program, where $G_{CS}=(N_S, V_S, A_S, S_S, T_S)$, $N_S=N_1 \cup N_2 \cup ... \cup N_n$, $V_S=V_1 \cup V_2 \cup ... \cup V_n$, $A_S=A_1 \cup A_2 \cup ... \cup A_n$, $S_S=\{s_1, s_2, ..., s_n\}$, and $T_S=\{t_1, t_2, ..., t_n\}$.

(2) For any i and j, where i and j ($1 \leqq i \leqq n$, $1 \leqq j \leqq n$) are the identification number of any two tasks, define L_s and L_t as follows:

1) $(b,s_i) \in L_s$ if i is a task that is declared in the declarative part of the main program,

2) $(s_i,s_j) \in L_s$ if i is a task and j is a task that is declared in the declarative part of i,

3) $(t_i,e) \in L_t$ if i is a task that is declared in the declarative part of the main program, and

4) $(t_j,t_i) \in L_t$ if i is a task and j is a task that is declared in the declarative part of i.

(3) For any $v \in V_S$ and $E \in \Sigma_C$, define $S(v)=E$ if v represents an entry call statement for entry E or v represents the end of the body of an accept statement for entry E, and define $R(v)=E$ if v represents an accept statement for entry E or v is a successor of v' that represents an entry call statement for entry E.

For a concurrent Ada program, we can construct its definition-use net (N_C, Σ_V, D, U) based on its control flow net by using the techniques described in Section 3 to define the two functions D and U explicitly.

In order to define synchronization dependence in a concurrent Ada program, it is necessary to identify those vertices representing the first statements in the body of every task.

Definition 4.1 Let $(G_{CS}, b, e, L_s, L_t, \Sigma_C, S, R)$ be the control flow net of a concurrent Ada program, where $G_{CS}=(N_S, V_S, A_S, S_S, T_S)$. $F: \{1, 2, ..., n\} \rightarrow V_S$ is a function, called *first-statement function*, such that for any task i, $F(i)$ is the vertex representing the first statement in the body of the task. □

Fig. 3 shows the definition-use net of the three tasks T, PERCENT, and FACT, where those vertices representing the first statements in the body of every task are marked by a star "*".

Now, we define synchronization and communication dependences in a concurrent Ada program based on the control flow net and definition-use net of the program.

Definition 4.2 Let $(G_{CS}, b, e, L_s, L_t, \Sigma_C, S, R)$ be the control flow net of a concurrent Ada program, F be the first-statement function of the control flow net, and u and v be any two vertices in G_{CS}. u is *directly synchronization dependent* on v iff any of the following three conditions holds:

1) there exists a start link arc $(s_i,s_j) \in L_s$ such that $F(i)=u$ and $F(j)=v$,

2) there exists a termination link arc $(v,u) \in L_t$, and

3) there exists a vertex v' such that v' is directly synchronization dependent on v, u properly forward dominates v', and $S(v'')=\Phi$ and $R(v'')=\Phi$ for any vertex v'' in any v'-u path. □

Informally, if u is directly synchronization dependent on v, then the start or termination of execution of v directly determines whether or not the execution of u starts or terminates.

For example, in Fig. 3, vertex t_3 is directly synchronization dependent on vertices p_2 and f_2, vertices t_4 and t_5 are also directly synchronization dependent on vertices p_2 and f_2, and vertex t_5 is directly synchronization dependent on vertices p_{15} and f_{14}.

Definition 4.3 Let (G_{CS}, b, e, L_s, L_t, Σ_C, S, R) be the control flow net of a concurrent Ada program, and u and v be any two vertices in G_{CS}. u is *directly possibly synchronization dependent* on v iff S(v) = R(u). □

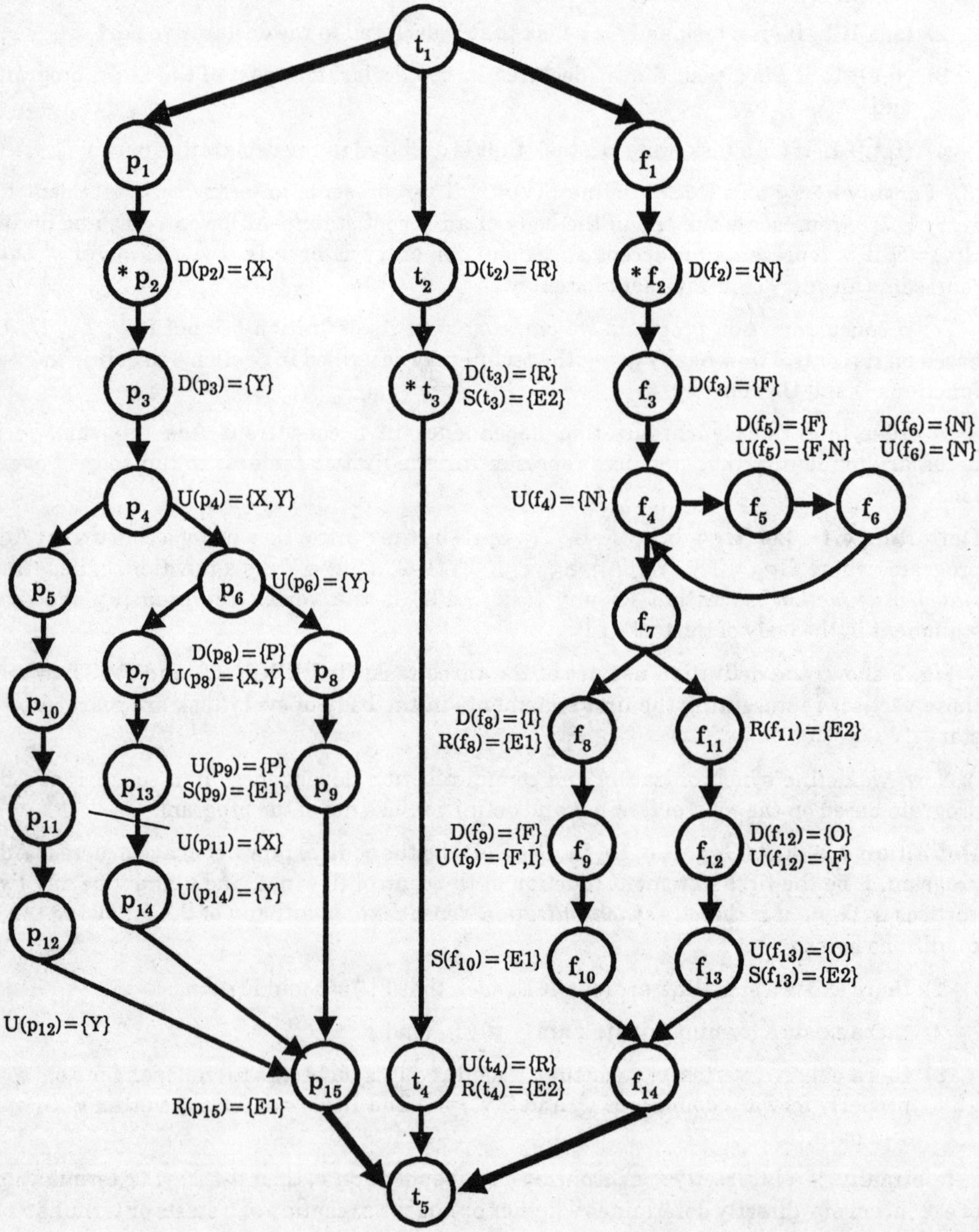

Fig. 3 The definition-use net of the three tasks T, PERCENT, and FACT

Informally, if u is directly possibly synchronization dependent on v, then the start or termination of execution of v possibly directly determines whether or not the execution of u starts or terminates. Note that the difference between the direct synchronization dependence and direct possible-synchronization dependence is that the former reflects a dependence which exists certainly, but the latter only reflects a dependence which exists possibly.

For example, in Fig. 3, vertex f_8 is directly possibly synchronization dependent on vertex p_9, vertex p_{15} is directly possibly synchronization dependent on vertex f_{10}, vertex f_{11} is directly possibly synchronization dependent on vertex t_3, and vertex t_4 is directly possibly synchronization dependent on vertex f_{13}.

Definition 4.4 Let (N_C, Σ_V, D, U) be the definition-use net of a concurrent Ada program, and u and v be any two vertices in N_C. u is *directly possibly communication dependent* on v iff any of the following conditions holds:

1) there exist two vertices v' and v" such that u is directly data dependent on v', R(v') = S(v"), and v" is directly data dependent on v,
2) there exist three vertices v', v", and v"' such that u is directly data dependent on v', v" is a successor of v', R(v") = S(v"'), and v"' is directly data dependent on v, and
3) $D(v) \cap U(u) \neq \Phi$ for $v \in V_i$ and $u \in V_j$ $(i \neq j)$. □

Informally, if u is directly possibly communication dependent on v, then the value of a variable computed at v possibly directly has influence on the value of a variable computed at u.

For example, in Fig. 3, vertex f_9 is directly possibly communication dependent on vertex p_8, and vertex t_4 is directly possibly communication dependent on vertex f_{12}.

5. Task Dependence Net and Its Applications

Definition 5.1 The *Task dependence Net* (TDN) of a concurrent Ada program is an arc-labeled digraph (V, Con, Dat, Syn, Com), where V is the vertex set of the control flow net of the program, Con is the set of control dependence arcs such that any (u,v) ∈ Con iff u is directly weakly control dependent on v, Dat is the set of data dependence arcs such that any (u,v) ∈ Dat iff u is directly data dependent on v, Syn is the set of synchronization dependent arcs such that any (u,v) ∈ Syn iff either u is directly synchronization dependent on v or u is directly possibly synchronization dependent on v, Com is the set of communication dependence arcs such that any (u,v) ∈ Com iff u is directly possibly communication dependent on v. □

Note that the above definition of TDN is not constructive. A transformation algorithm is indispensable in order to transform a concurrent Ada program into its TDN.

For example, Fig. 4 shows the TDN of the three tasks T, PERCENT, and FACT.

As a representation for concurrent Ada programs, the TDN has many potential applications in concurrent Ada programming.

The most direct application of TDN is slicing concurrent Ada programs because the explicit representation of various program dependences in a concurrent Ada program makes the TDN very ideal for constructing slices of the program.

Definition 5.2 A *static slicing criterion* of a concurrent program is a 2-tuple (s, V), where s is a statement in the program and V is a set of variables used at s. The *static slice* **SS**(s, V) of a concurrent program on a given static slicing criterion (s, V) consists of all statements in the program that possibly affect the beginning or end of execution of s and/or affect the values of variables in V. *Statically slicing* a concurrent program on a given static slicing criterion is to find the static slice of the program with respect to the criterion. □

Note that there is a difference between the concept of program slice given above for concurrent programs and that given in the literature [1,8,10,11,16,17] for sequential programs, i.e., the above definition includes a condition on the beginning or end of

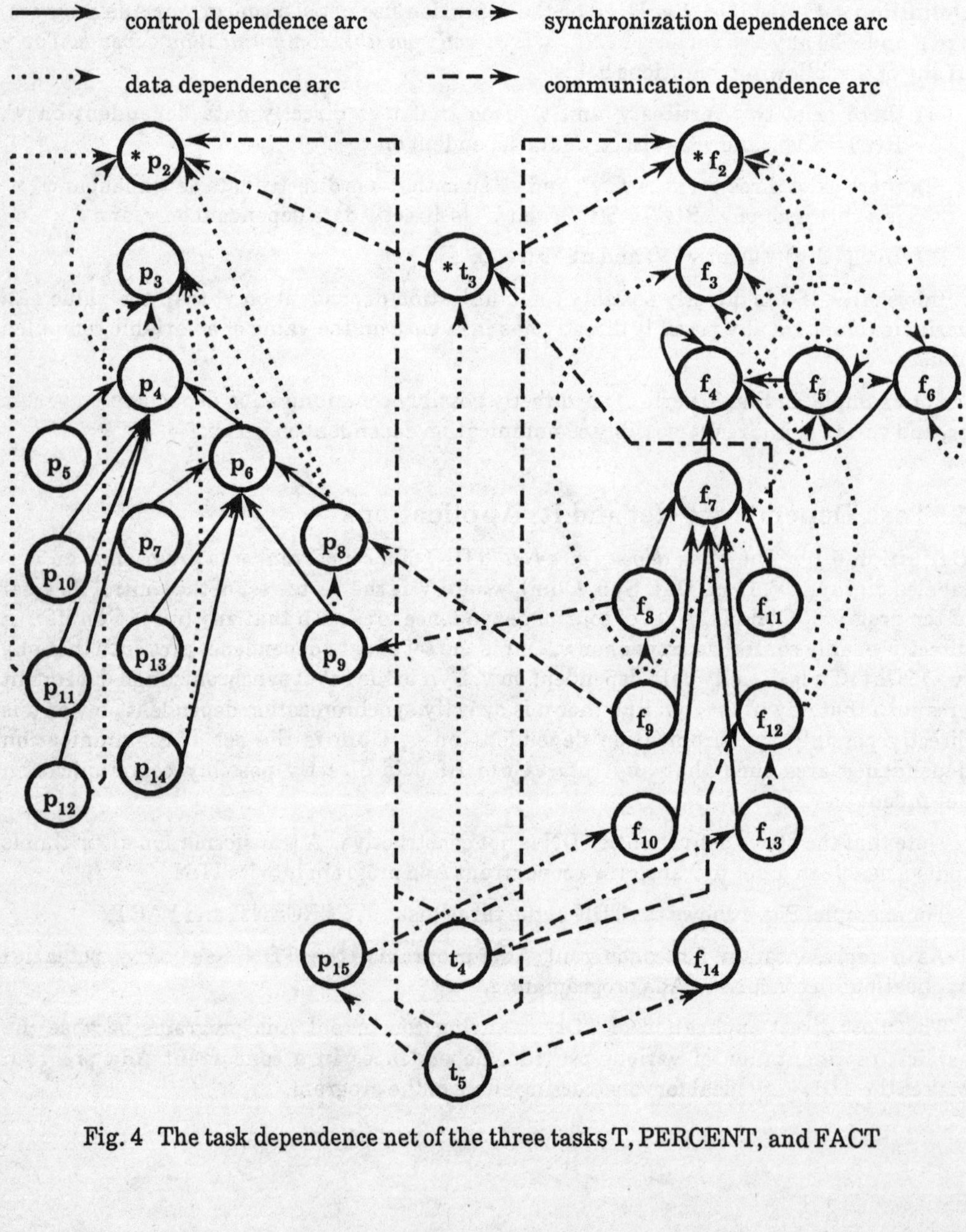

Fig. 4 The task dependence net of the three tasks T, PERCENT, and FACT

execution of s, and therefore, it is meaningful even if V is the empty set. This makes the concept useful in analysis of deadlocks and livelocks in concurrent programs.

It is obvious that once a concurrent Ada program is represented by its TDN, the static slicing problem of the program is simply a vertex reachability problem in the net.

Definition 5.3 A *dynamic slicing criterion* of a concurrent program is a quadruplet (s, V, H, I), where s is a statement in the program, V is a set of variables used at s, and H is a history of an execution of the program with input I. The *dynamic slice* DS(s, V, H, I) of a concurrent program on a given dynamic slicing criterion (s, V, H, I) consists of all statements in the program that actually affected the beginning or end of execution of s and/or affected the values of variables in V in the execution with I that produced H. *Dynamically slicing* a concurrent program on a given dynamic slicing criterion is to find the dynamic slice of the program with respect to the criterion. □

Note that for a concurrent program, two different executions with the same input may produce different behavior and histories because of unpredictable rates of processes and existence of nondeterministic selection statements in the program. This is the reason why we use a program's execution history H produced with an input I to define the concept of dynamic slicing criterion.

The dynamic slicing problem of a concurrent Ada program can be reduce to the vertex reachability problem in its TDN with the program's execution history information that can be collected by an execution monitor [5,6].

Static and dynamic slicing are useful in concurrent program debugging because they can be used to find all statements that possibly or actually caused the erroneous behavior of the execution occurring an error.

A program error is a difference between a program's actual behavior and the behavior required by the specification of the program. A "bug" relative to an error is a cause of the error. Debugging is the process of locating, analyzing, and correcting bugs in a program by reasoning. It begins with some indication of the existence of an error, repeats the process of developing, verifying, and modifying hypotheses about the bug causing the error until the location of the bug is determined and the nature of the bug is understood, corrects the bug, and ends in a verification of the removal of the error [3,13]. In general, about 95% of effort in debugging has to be spent on locating and understanding bug because once a bug is located and its nature is understood, its correction is often easy to do [13]. Therefore, the most important problem in debugging is how to know which statements possibly and/or actually cause the erroneous behavior of the execution occurring an error.

Most current debugging methods and tools for concurrent programs provide programmers with only facilities to extract information from programs and display it in textual or visual forms, but no facilities to support the localization, analysis, and correction of bug in an automatic or semi-automatic manner [9,12]. Until recently, there is no systematic method used for bug location in debugging concurrent programs [3,12].

Having the TDN as a representation for concurrent Ada programs, static and dynamic program slicing based on the representation can provide us with a systematic method to support the bug location in debugging concurrent Ada programs. A static slice SS(s, V) of a program covers all statements possibly cause the error occurred at statement s, i.e., all "possible candidates" of bugs. A dynamic slice DS(s, V, H, I) of a program covers all statements actually caused the error occurred at statement s, i.e., all "actual candidates" of bugs. However, the static and dynamic slices of a program only cover those "candidates" of bugs but neither locate the bugs nor give some hints on the nature of the bugs. In order to develop more powerful debugging methods and tools to support bug localization, analysis, and correction in concurrent program debugging, we are constructing a entailmental logic calculus [4] for causal reasoning about bugs in concurrent programs and developing a knowledge-based approach to debugging concurrent programs.

Static and dynamic slicing are also useful in maintenance of concurrent programs in the sense that they are helpful for us to know what statements affect a modified statement.

In program understanding and maintenance, we often want to know what statements would be affected by the execution of a statement of interest. The needs can be satisfied by forward-slicing of program.

Definition 5.4 A *static forward-slicing criterion* of a concurrent program is a 2-tuple (s, v), where s is a statement in the program and v is a variable defined at s. The *static forward-slice* SFS(s, v) of a concurrent program on a given static forward-slicing criterion (s, v) consists of all statements in the program that would be affected by the beginning or end of execution of s and/or affected by the value of v at s. *Statically forward-slicing* a concurrent program on a given static forward-slicing criterion is to find the static forward-slice of the program with respect to the criterion. □

Definition 5.5 A *dynamic forward-slicing criterion* of a concurrent program is a quadruplet (s, v, H, I), where s is a statement in the program, v is a variable defined at s, and H is a history of an execution of the program with input I. The *dynamic forward-slice* DFS(s, v, H, I) of a concurrent program on a given dynamic forward-slicing criterion (s, v, H, I) consists of all statements in the program that are actually affected by the beginning or end of execution of s and/or affected by the value of v at s in the execution with I that produced H. *Dynamically forward-slicing* a concurrent program on a given dynamic forward-slicing criterion is to find the dynamic forward-slice of the program with respect to the criterion. □

In order to obtain forward-slices of a concurrent Ada program, it is necessary to have a representation for the program that explicitly represents influence relationships holding between statements in the program. In fact, we can obtain this representation as a "reverse" of task dependence net.

Definition 5.6 The *Task Influence Net* (TIN) of a concurrent Ada program is an arc-labeled digraph (**V**, **Con**, **Dat**, **Syn**, **Com**), where **V** is the vertex set of the control flow net of the program, **Con** is the set of control influence arcs such that any (u,v)∈**Con** iff v is directly weakly control dependent on u, **Dat** is the set of data influence arcs such that any (u,v)∈**Dat** iff v is directly data dependent on u, **Syn** is the set of synchronization influence arcs such that any (u,v)∈**Syn** iff either v is directly synchronization dependent on u or v is directly possibly synchronization dependent on u, **Com** is the set of communication influence arcs such that any (u,v)∈**Com** iff v is directly possibly communication dependent on u. □

It is obvious that once a concurrent Ada program is represented by its TIN, the static forward-slicing problem of the program is simply a vertex reachability problem in the net, and the dynamic forward-slicing problem of the program can be reduce to the vertex reachability problem in the net with the program's execution history information.

Static and dynamic forward-slicing based on the TIN are useful in understanding of concurrent Ada programs in the sense that they are helpful for us to know what is the total affect of a statement of interest. They are also useful in maintenance of concurrent Ada programs in the sense that they are helpful for us to know what statements will be affected by a modified statement.

Since the TDN and TIN of a concurrent Ada program represents control and data dependences in every task and synchronization and communication dependences among tasks, they can also be used to define dependence-coverage criterion for testing concurrent Ada programs, and to define metrics for measuring complexity of concurrent Ada programs.

6. Concluding Remarks

We have proposed two new types of basic program dependences and a new program representation for concurrent programs. Although here we presented the program dependences and the representation in terms of concurrent Ada programs, the concepts are general and easy to be applied to those concurrent programs written in other high-level concurrent programming languages. As we showed in Section 5, the representation would play an important role in concurrent programming. It is not quite clear now what role the representation will ultimately play in concurrent programming. The significance of the representation in concurrent programming depends on how we develop the representation itself and apply it to practices of concurrent programming.

We are developing a group of tools including a tool to transform concurrent Ada programs into their task dependence nets, a tool to slice concurrent Ada programs based on their task dependence/influence nets, a knowledge-base to story knowledge about program dependences and influences in concurrent Ada programs, and a causal reasoning engine based on entailmental logic to reason about properties of bugs in concurrent Ada programs. All of the tools will use the task dependence net as a unified representation for target concurrent Ada programs.

The following are some future research problems.

First, the four types of basic dependences presented in this paper do not cover all possible program dependences in a concurrent Ada program. For example, a statement S_1 in a task may synchronization dependent on a statement S_2 in another task and S_2 may control dependent on a statement S_3. Obviously, there is some dependence between S_1 and S_3 that cannot be regarded as any of the four basic types of dependences. An important research problem is how to deal with all possible program dependences in a concurrent Ada program.

Second, in this paper the task dependence/influence net is presented in terms of simple Ada programs. Some technical issues must be treated in order to define the task dependence/influence net of a regular Ada program that includes task types, abort and block statements, subprograms, packages, and dynamic creation of objects.

Finally, the size of the task dependence/influence net of a practical Ada program is crucial to the application of the net in practices. How to measure the size of a task dependence/influence net and how to reduce the size of the net on the condition that the dependence/influence information is not lost are also important research problems.

Acknowledgements

The author would like to thank the anonymous referees for their helpful comments on an extended abstract of this paper.

References

[1] H. Agrawal and J. R. Horgan, "Dynamic Program Slicing", Proc. ACM SIGPLAN'90, pp.246-256, 1990.

[2] A. V. Aho, R. Sethi, and J. D. Ullman, "Compilers: Principles, Techniques, and Tools", Addison-Wesley, 1986.

[3] K. Araki, Z. Furukawa, and J. Cheng, "A General Framework for Debugging", IEEE-CS Software, Vol.8, No.3, pp.14-20, 1991.

[4] J. Cheng, "Logical Tool of Knowledge Engineering: Using Entailment Logic rather than Mathematical Logic", Proc. ACM 19th Annual Computer Science Conference, pp.228-238, 1991.

[5] J. Cheng, K. Araki, and K. Ushijima, "Development and Practical Applications of EDEN – An Event-Driven Execution Monitor for Concurrent Ada Programs", Transactions of IPSJ, Vol.30, No.1, pp.12-24, 1989 (in Japanese).

[6] J. Cheng, Y. Kasahara, and K. Ushijima, "A Tasking Deadlock Detector for Ada Programs", Proc. IEEE-CS 15th Annual COMPSAC, pp.56-63, 1991.

[7] J. Ferrante, K. J. Ottenstein, and J. D. Warren, "The Program Dependence Graph and Its Use in Optimization", ACM TOPLAS, Vol.9, No.3, pp.319-349, 1987.

[8] K. B. Gallagher and J. R. Lyle, "Using Program Slicing in Software Maintenance", IEEE-CS TOSE, Vol.17, No.8, pp.751-761, 1991.

[9] G. S. Goldszmidt, S. Temini, and S. Katz, "High-Level Language Debugging for Concurrent Programs", ACM TOCS, Vol.8, No.4, pp.311-336, 1990.

[10] S. Horwitz, T. Reps, and D. Binkley, "Interprocedural Slicing Using Dependence Graphs", ACM TOPLAS, Vol.12, No.1, pp.26-60, 1990.

[11] B. Korel and J. Laski, "Dynamic Program Slicing", Information Processing Letters, Vol.29, No.10, pp.155-163, 1988.

[12] C. E. McDowell and D. P. Helmbold, "Debugging Concurrent programs", ACM Computing Surveys, Vol.21, No.4, pp.593-622, 1989.

[13] G. J. Myers, "The Art of Software Testing", John Wiley & Sons, 1979.

[14] K. J. Ottenstein and L. M. Ottenstein, "The Program Dependence Graph in a Software Development Environment", ACM Software Engineering Notes, Vol.9, No.3, pp.177-184, 1984.

[15] A. Podgurski and L. A. Clarke, "A Formal Model of Program Dependences and Its Implications for Software Testing, Debugging, and Maintenance", IEEE-CS TOSE, Vol.16, No.9, pp.965-979, 1990.

[16] M. Weiser, "Programmers Use Slices When Debugging", CACM, Vol.25, No.7, pp.446-452, 1982.

[17] M. Weiser, "Program Slicing", IEEE-CS TOSE, Vol.SE-10, No.4, pp.352-357, 1984.

Detection and Avoidance of Elaboration-time Problems for Multi-unit Real-time Ada Applications

Leslie C. Lander, Sandeep Mitra

Department of Computer Science, Thomas J. Watson School of Engineering and Applied Science, State University of New York, Binghamton NY 13902-6000

Abstract. This paper describes three significant problems that may occur due to the elaboration order of the compilation units of a large Ada program. One concern is the possibility of *access-before-elaboration* errors. A second issue is *priority inversion* amongst library tasks—a possibly serious problem for real-time systems, for example, in the implementation of the Priority Ceiling Protocol. A third problem is *elaboration-time deadlock*—the situation where elaboration cannot be completed because a non-task entity calls a task entry before the activation of the task. In this paper we outline a set of coding practices which, if rigorously followed, eliminate most elaboration-time problems. Also, we briefly describe a scheme to determine a proper elaboration order on the basis of source code analysis and show how such a scheme can be used, if our coding practices are followed, to detect potential elaboration-time deadlock situations.

1 Introduction

According to the Ada Language Reference Manual (LRM) [1], the process by which a declaration achieves its effect is called the *elaboration* of the declaration; this process occurs during program execution. Ada rules also require that a program entity (e.g., type, variable, procedure, etc.) be elaborated before it is used, otherwise an *access-before-elaboration* (ABE) error, indicated by the exception PROGRAM_ERROR, should arise. The rules also require elaboration of entities during the elaboration/execution of their enclosing unit, and permit reference to other entities during the elaboration process itself. Consequently, to run an Ada program, an *elaboration order* of compilation units must be found so that every entity used at elaboration-time is certain to be elaborated before its use. We call such an elaboration order *proper*. However, due to the complexity of the interactions between entities that are possible at elaboration-time, it is hard to formulate rules that ensure a proper elaboration order. Therefore, validated Ada compilers are not required to produce a proper elaboration order. The 1983 Ada standard provides a means for manual control of elaboration order, through the pragma ELABORATE. However, such manual control, even if fully implemented, is not adequate for large programming projects

```
package P1 is
-- authored by programmer A
        function Fun1 return integer;
end P1;

package P2 is
-- authored by programmer A
        type T2 is new integer range ... ;
        procedure Proc2;
end P2;

package P3 is
-- authored by programmer B
        type T3 is new integer range ... ;
        procedure Proc3;
end P3;

with P3, P2;
package body P1 is
-- authored by programmer A
        Obj1 : P2.T2;
        Obj2 : P3.T3;
        function Fun1 return integer is ... ;
end P1;

with P1, P3;
-- the pragma ELABORATE (P1) placed
-- here would prevent ABE
package body P2 is
-- authored by programmer A
        Obj2 : P3.T3;
        procedure Proc2 is
        J : integer;
        begin
                J := P1.Fun1;
                ...
        end Proc2;
end P2;

with P2, P1;
-- the pragma ELABORATE (P1) placed
-- here would also prevent ABE
pragma ELABORATE (P2);
package body P3 is
-- authored by programmer B
        procedure Proc3 is
        begin
                P2.Proc2;
                ...
        end Proc3;
        ...
begin
        Proc3;
end P3;

with P3, P2, P1;
-- authored by programmer B
procedure Main_Pgm is begin
        ...
end Main_Pgm;
```

Fig. 1. The problem of using pragma ELABORATE in a multi-programmer environment.

as it is difficult to discover if a unit needs the pragma by a mere inspection of the source code. Elaboration-time problems are significant ones for the Ada community, particularly for large projects, as indicated in [18]. The ABE problem has received attention in various Ada fora, including Ada 9X [2]. An example of the ABE problem, and the difficulty of using pragma ELABORATE to rectify it, is given in Fig. 1.

The code skeleton in Fig. 1 shows only those subprogram calls that cause elaboration-time dependencies. Programmer B recognizes the need to insert pragma ELABORATE (P2) as shown because P3.Proc3 is called during the elaboration of package body P3, and P3.Proc3 calls P2.Proc2. However, the need to use pragma ELABORATE (P1) on the body of package P3 is not evident, as the internal implementation details of package body P2 are not known to programmer B. The pragma ELABORATE (P1) placed before package body P2 would also prevent ABE in this example, assuming the compiler respects the pragma for user packages, but programmer A sees no need to do so as P2.Proc2 is not called

```
package P1 is
        task T1_pr4 is
                pragma priority (4);
        end;
        task T2_pr10 is
                pragma priority (10);
        end;
end P1;

package P2 is
        task T1_pr1 is
                pragma priority (1);
        end;
        task T2_pr2 is
                pragma priority (2);
        end;
end P2;
```

Fig. 2. Tasks which are susceptible to priority inversion due to elaboration order.

during the elaboration of package body P2. Thus, the proper placement of all pragmas would require knowledge of internal implementation details by diverse programming teams, which is contradictory to the good software engineering practices that Ada seeks to promote. Therefore, ensuring that no ABE errors will arise calls for either a strict coding discipline, adherence to which avoids complex declaration or initialization code, or an automatic determination of elaboration order that takes into account all inter- and intra-unit elaboration-time dependencies.

In [10] and [17], the definition of *priority inversion* is given as any situation where low priority tasks are served before higher priority tasks. These papers, as well as [14], report various forms of priority inversion that may occur during the execution of an Ada program due to the FIFO nature of entry queues and the scheduling of selective wait statements. We have recognized a form of priority inversion that occurs at "start-up time" and arises due to the elaboration order chosen by the compiler. We call such priority inversion *priority inversion during elaboration* (PIDE) ([13], [15]). This form of priority inversion arises on account of the rules for activation and commencement of execution of tasks. A task enclosed by a library package, for example, begins activation after the completion of elaboration of the package body's declarative part. As reported in [4], [9] and [21], such tasks then begin to execute concurrently with the initialization statements of the package, at elaboration time, and priority inversion is observed. Consider the example in Fig. 2.

If the body of package P2 is elaborated before the body of package P1, then the initial order in which the tasks begin to run will be P2.T2_pr2, P2.T1_pr1, P1.T2_pr10, P1.T1_pr4. Priority inversion is evident. This paper reports on the impact of such priority inversion on real-time systems implemented, using Ada tasks, in accordance with recommendations outlined by Sha and Goodenough in [19]. Note that we assume that the main program has been given the lowest available priority for that particular implementation. For the Ada systems we have tested, the behaviors reported and coding practices suggested are valid only if such is the case.

During the elaboration phase of a unit a situation may arise, e.g. during the execution of the initialization part of a package body, where despite the absence of an ABE error, the elaboration cannot be effectively completed before the main program begins to execute because of a task entry call to a task that has not yet been activated. The elaboration of the current unit cannot complete until the task entry call is satisfied, which in turn cannot happen until the called task is activated as part of the elaboration of its containing unit.

```
package P1 is                          package body P2 is
...                                    ...
end P1;                                task body T is
                                           ...
package P2 is                          begin
    task T is                              ...
        entry E;                           accept E do
    end T;                                     ...
end P2;                                    end E;
                                           ...
with P2;                               end T;
package body P1 is                     ...
    ...                                end P2;
begin
    P2.T.E;
end P1;
```

Fig. 3. Packages that may deadlock during elaboration.

This latter elaboration cannot commence, however, until the current elaboration is completed. Thus there is an *elaboration-time deadlock* situation, as illustrated by Fig. 3.

If package body P2 is not elaborated before package body P1, then a deadlock occurs. Such deadlocks are not easy to detect, in general, at compile- or link-time. We present a suggestion in this paper which would make it possible to warn the programmer about the *possibility* of such deadlocks arising on account of elaboration-time communication with library tasks.

2 Scheme for Automatic Determination of a Proper Elaboration Order

Extensive detailed analysis is necessary to determine all possible elaboration-time dependencies amongst the library and secondary units of an Ada program. The analysis involves program *units* and *entities*, which include, for example, type marks, objects, subprogram declarations, subprogram bodies, block statements, etc.. To determine a proper elaboration order, the compiler and linker must identify all situations where ABE errors are possible; namely, those situations where the elaboration of a program unit U1 causes the elaboration of one of its sub-entities U1.E1, which in turn uses some entity U2.E2 from another program unit U2. In such a case, it must be ensured that U2 be elaborated before U1. Reference [15] is a complete report on this analysis and the associated algorithm for proper elaboration order that could be incorporated into a compiler and linker. Some of the salient features are reported in this section.

The following notation identifies certain program units and entities explicitly. The symbol **X** indicates a unit or entity of the kind stated in parentheses:

Table I. Example of the eps and psd of Ada program entities.

Declaration in unit U	eps	psd
type T is record A : P1.T1 := P1.X; B : P1.T1; C : P2.T2; end record;	eps(U.T) = {$P1_s$.T1, $P2_s$.T2}	psd(U.T) = {$P1_s$.X}
Obj : T;	eps(U.Obj) = {U.T, $P1_s$.X} -- using psd(U.T)	not applicable

function Fun
(Parm : P1.T1 := P1.Fun1)
return P2.T2 is
begin
...
P2.Proc1;
...
end;
	eps(U.Fun_d) =
	{U.Fun_d.Parm, $P2_s$.T2}
	eps(U.Fun_d.Parm) = {$P1_s$.T1}
	eps(U.Fun_b) =
	{U.Fun_d, U.Fun_b.*exec*}
	eps(U.Fun_b.*exec*) = {$P2_b$.$Proc1_b$}
		psd(U.Fun_d) =
		{$P1_s$.$Fun1_b$}

X_b : *body* of X (subprogram, task or package)
X_d : *declaration* of X (subprogram)
X.*exec*: *sequence of executable statements* in X (subprogram, task, package, block)
X_s : *specification* of X (task or package)

Example: The entity named $P1_b$.$Proc_b$.N could be an object N declared inside the body of the procedure Proc which appears in the body of the package P1.

During the processing of an Ada program by the compiler and linker, the following sets are created:

1. The *entity prerequisite set* of unit or entity E, denoted eps(E) and created by the compiler and extended by the linker, is the set of units and entities that must be elaborated or executed before or during the elaboration or execution of E.
2. The *prerequisite set for defaults* for a unit or entity E, denoted psd(E) and created by the compiler, is the set of units and entities which provide default values in E. Note that this set is distinguished from the *explicit initialization* value in an object declaration which causes an entry in the entity prerequisite set. The set psd(E) may contribute to eps(E'), for some other entity E', when default values have to be computed, as shown in Table I.
3. The *initial unit prerequisite set* for a library or secondary unit U, denoted iups(U) and created by the compiler, is the initial set of all entities occurring immediately within U that create transitive elaboration-time dependencies and must be elaborated or executed during the elaboration of U. Therefore, an entity such as a subprogram body is not included in this set, as its elaboration only establishes that this body can

be used for later execution of the subprogram; the subprogram itself is not executed during elaboration of its body unless it is called.

4. The *unit prerequisite set* for a library or secondary unit U, denoted ups(U) and created by the linker, is the set of all units and entities (including those generated by transitive elaboration-time dependencies) that must be elaborated or executed before or during the elaboration of U.

The rules for determining the entity prerequisite sets, the prerequisite set for defaults and the initial unit prerequisite sets are determined in accordance with the rules stated in the LRM. Full details about these rules are provided in [15] where an algorithm *ada_elab* for the determination of a proper elaboration order is described. Some examples of these sets for typical Ada program constructs are shown in Table I. Entity prerequisite sets and initial unit prerequisite sets provide a taxonomy of elaboration dependencies in Ada which is the input to the algorithm. An experimental implementation of *ada_elab* has been written in Ada and tested. The implementation does not handle Ada source code as yet. The philosophy of *ada_elab* is that a graph of elaboration-time dependencies needs to be built up on the basis of the prerequisite sets, and not the dependencies indicated by the context clauses. This graph, in turn, determines a set of possible elaboration orders. The general structure of *ada_elab*, which is designed to be part of a linker is as follows:

1. For each non-generic, non-package entity or non-generic subprogram declaration or body unit, extend the entity prerequisite to its transitive closure to create the set of all units and entities on which this unit or entity depends, even indirectly, at elaboration time.
2. For each non-generic library or secondary unit, form its unit prerequisite set as the union of the initial unit prerequisite set and the entity prerequisite sets of all the units or entities in that initial unit prerequisite set.
3. For each unit U of the program, ups(U) is used to determined the set of *required compilation units*, rcu(U). Each element of rcu(U) will be a unit containing one or more of the entities in ups(U), excluding consideration of entities that are formal parameters of a subprogram declaration unit. For example, if $ups(P2_b) = \{P2_b.exec, P1_s.T1\}$ then $rcu(P2_b) = \{P2_b, P1_s\}$.
4. A graph G is created whose nodes are the units of the program; a directed arc is inserted from each node U to all other nodes that are in rcu(U). Other such arcs are inserted in G in order to obey Ada rules such as the specification of a unit having to be elaborated before its body. Some nodes may have self-loops and these are removed if a check shows that they are not caused by direct or indirect forward references. A topological order of G would provide a proper elaboration order (in reverse). If a circularity of dependencies is detected, then no such order can be found.

An example of the application of *ada_elab* to a program similar to Fig. 1 can be found in [15]. Compile- and link-time determination of a proper elaboration order will preclude the need for elaboration checks at run-time, thus improving real-time performance.

3 Priority Inversion amongst Library Tasks and its impact on a Real-Time Implementation

In [13] there is a report on the priority inversion that is observed when a program has multiple packages each containing multiple tasks: we observe that a low priority library task activates and begins execution before a high priority task if the package containing the former is earlier in the elaboration sequence. Such priority inversion will be true to Ada semantics if the affected high priority tasks can be considered *ineligible for execution* (LRM, paragraph 9.8(4)) as the enclosing package body has not yet been elaborated. It should be noted, however, that an entry of a task may be called after the elaboration of the task specification, but before the activation, without raising an exception, unlike an entry call to a terminated task.

To illustrate how the presence of PIDE upsets otherwise sound approaches by preventing them from even beginning to execute properly, consider the implementation, using Ada tasks in a uniprocessor environment, of the Rate Monotonic Scheduling theory, including the Priority Ceiling Protocol, as described by Sha and Goodenough [19], [20]. In a tasking model where tasks communicate through binary semaphores, the Priority Ceiling Protocol assigns a *ceiling* to each semaphore, which is the highest task priority amongst all tasks that use the semaphore. Despite the fact that high priority tasks can preempt lower priority tasks, the Protocol does not allow a task to enter its *critical region* unless its own priority is higher than the ceilings of all semaphores currently locked by other tasks. Thus, a low priority task LT can only block a high priority task HT, with priority p, when the situation is such that HT is trying to enter its critical region and LT currently holds the lock on a semaphore S that HT, or some other task with priority greater than or equal to p, uses. The Protocol ensures that any task T is not allowed to enter its critical region unless it will not request any semaphore that is currently locked by any other preempted task T ' and hence a deadlock between T and T ' cannot occur. Sha and Goodenough suggest appropriate design approaches and coding practices in Ada to implement this methodology. The basic idea in this technique is to implement the semaphores, which are the sole means for communication between other "client" tasks, by using "monitor" Ada tasks. Each monitor task has a selective wait. When a call from a client task is accepted in the selective wait, the code executed during the rendezvous by the monitor task actually executes the critical region on behalf of the client task. When a client task wishes to enter its critical region, it makes a task entry call to the appropriate accept of one of the monitor tasks.

In any Ada system that does not have a special "Rate Monotonic Scheduler," Sha and Goodenough have reported that, in order for the correct implementation of the Priority Ceiling Protocol, it is necessary to eliminate the priority inversion amongst Ada tasks that arises on account of FIFO entry queues and selective waits. They have suggested that monitor tasks be given a priority *one level higher* than the maximum priority of all their clients. Also, they have stated that monitor tasks should also not be suspended during rendezvous. Thus, a monitor task will always be ready to rendezvous with any of its clients and the problems of priority inversion due to FIFO queuing and selective waits are both avoided.

```
package P1 is
      task T is
            pragma priority(2);
      end T;
end P1;

package P2 is
      task T is
            pragma priority(1);
      end T;
end P2;

package P3 is
      task Sem is
            entry E1;
            entry E2;
            pragma PRIORITY (3);
      end;
end P3;

package P4 is
      task Sem is
            entry E1;
            entry E2;
            pragma PRIORITY (3);
      end;
end P4;

-- context clauses ...
package body P1 is
task body T is
begin
      delay (Task_start_time - Calendar.Clock);
      loop
            ...block of code (A)
            P3.Sem.E1;
            ...block of code (B)
      end loop;
end T;
end P1;

-- context clauses ...
package body P2 is
task body T is
begin
      delay (Task_start_time - Calendar.Clock);
      loop
            ...block of code (A)
            P4.Sem.E1;
            ...block of code (B)
      end loop;
end T;
end P2;

-- context clauses ...
package body P3 is
task body Sem is
begin
      loop select
            accept E1 do
                  ...block of code (C)
                  P4.Sem.E2;
                  ...block of code (D)
            end E1;
      or
            accept E2 do
                  ...block of code (E)
            end E2;
      end select;
      end loop;
end Sem;
end P3;

-- context clauses ...
package body P4 is
task body Sem is
begin
      loop select
            accept E1 do
                  ...block of code (C)
                  P3.Sem.E2;
                  ...block of code (D)
            end E1;
      or
            accept E2 do
                  ...block of code (E)
            end E2;
      end select;
      end loop;
end Sem;
end P4;

-- context clauses ...
procedure Main_Pgm is
...
begin
      ...;
end Main_Pgm;
```

Fig. 4. An implementation template of the Priority Ceiling Protocol.

These recommendations, however, do not take into account the priority inversion that arises amongst Ada tasks in a multi-package environment on account of the elaboration order of the enclosing packages. We have observed that due to priority inversion during elaboration, there is a possibility that, during the first execution cycle, both FIFO queues will build up and multiple accepts in a selective wait will have tasks waiting to rendezvous. Thus critical regions may be entered in a manner inconsistent with the requirements of the Priority Ceiling Protocol and deadlocks may occur. We have used the suggestions by Sha and Goodenough [12], [19] and Borger [6] to create the Ada code template given in Fig. 4 (the Figure also includes the delay mechanism [6], outlined at the end of this section). In our experiments we used a simple environment consisting of a single processor/single user system where the Ada run-time support was suspended during I/O. To simulate the base scheduling algorithm, for example the Rate Monotonic Scheduling, the different approaches outlined in [6] were used.

Suppose we have two periodic tasks T1 and T2. In addition, there are two binary semaphores S1 and S2, used by both tasks. Suppose T1 locks the semaphores in the order S1, S2, while T2 locks them in reverse order. Further, assume T1 has a higher priority than T2. Thus,

T1: {...P(S1)...P(S2)...V(S2)...V(S1)...}
T2: {...P(S2)...P(S1)...V(S1)...V(S2)...}

According to the priority ceiling protocol, since both semaphores are used by T1 and T2, neither task will be allowed to enter any critical region if the other holds the lock on a semaphore. Thus deadlocks will be prevented. The Ada code skeleton template in Fig. 4 is expected to model this behavior, P1.T corresponds to T1, P2.T to T2, P3.Sem to S1, and P4.Sem to S2. Note that monitor tasks have been given priorities higher than all their clients and our Ada run-time support is such that these tasks are not suspended during rendezvous.

A particular Ada implementation may use the context clauses to determine the following elaboration order of package bodies: P1, P2, P3, P4. Note that this order may not be unique and different implementations may compute different orders. We shall make an assumption about the choice made by the Ada implementation when a selective wait is executed for the *first* time in a task during program execution. We shall assume that the entry which is being called and which appears *earliest*, lexically, in the task specification, is always accepted. The Ada implementations we have used do make some arbitrary choice of this kind. Then the blocks of code that have been labeled for this example are first executed as follows:

P1.T(A), P2.T(A), P3.Sem(C), P4.Sem(C), DEADLOCK

When P3.Sem and P4.Sem accept their entries labeled E1, they execute within the accept blocks the critical regions on behalf of P1.T and P2.T respectively. Each accept block contains a nested entry call. If the higher priority tasks P3.Sem and P4.Sem ran earlier, then the program would prevent deadlock correctly. However, P1.T and P2.T are elaborated, activated and execute earlier. Subsequently, they block on their entry calls to monitor tasks. Note that such blocking is not sanctioned by the Priority Ceiling Protocol. When P3.Sem becomes ready to run upon activation and executes, there is an entry call waiting and when P4.Sem executes similarly it has two entry calls pending. However, the priority profile of all participating tasks as suggested by Sha and Goodenough is supposed to preclude tasks waiting at one or more entries of the monitor tasks. The deadlock now occurs because, making an arbitrary choice in the selective wait in a manner consistent with current Ada semantics, P4.Sem accepts the call to entry E1 resulting in a nested entry call to P3.Sem which is blocked on an entry call to P4.Sem.

The sole reason for this abnormal behavior arising despite giving monitor tasks higher priority is that the effect of higher priority is nullified by priority inversion during elaboration. The activation rules for Ada tasks are such that, in a uniprocessor environment, the assigned priorities may be respected in the order of activation only if the concerned tasks are in the same enclosing compilation unit. An obvious, albeit unsatisfactory, remedy for the problem stated above would be to require all participating client and monitor tasks to be in the same package or subprogram. For example, it is quite likely that the behaviors of each of the client tasks in their respective critical regions corresponding to a semaphore are such that this set of client tasks writes to the guarded shared variables in the same manner. The monitor task corresponding to this semaphore may thus be developed by a separate programmer, and would ideally be placed in a separate package.

It is possible to counter the effect of priority inversion during elaboration through the use of some reasonable coding practices. Borger *et al.*, [6] discuss several design approaches for implementing periodic tasks, that however, are not adequately equipped to handle this problem cleanly. The concept of a user-written "Dispatcher" task they discuss is a possible approach. A central Dispatcher task makes all client tasks ready to run. Also, a TIMER_INTERRUPT from a timer that is initialized by the main program is used--the main program begins to execute after all package bodies are elaborated. This approach serves the purpose that all monitor tasks will be ready to rendezvous whenever they are called, thus effectively countering the malevolent effects of priority inversion during elaboration for the above implementation template, but it is over-centralized and restrictive. For example, the Dispatcher must know the identities of all the client tasks, each of which must be given an entry which the Dispatcher can call. This structure precludes client tasks from being wholly declared within library package bodies. Besides, this model requires the user to explicitly manage the scheduling of tasks; ideally, this function should be abstracted out of the application program [6]. The model that uses the Ada delay statement to delay the tasks' commencement of useful execution until a pre-defined, user-specific start time and the DELAY_UNTIL model suggested in [6] as the best approach (for other reasons such as lack of jitter) is also not "ideal" insofar as this priority inversion problem is concerned. Both these models require the tasks to be delayed until an absolute Task_Start_Time (possibly different for each task). This value must be computed, in order to avoid the effects of priority inversion during elaboration, by taking into consideration the elaboration (and activation) time of certain other program components. In other words, Task_Start_Time should have a value such that elaborations, and activations of concerned tasks, are completed before it is reached, for otherwise, a "client" periodic task may begin useful execution before the higher priority monitor task, as described above. In the absence of a unique elaboration order, this absolute value will differ over various Ada implementations. It may also have to be changed when modifications, that otherwise do not affect the computation time of client tasks but which change the elaboration order/time, are made to the application program. We suggest a coding practice in a subsequent section that totally eliminates the problem of priority inversion during elaboration for any Ada program with prioritized tasks. Our approach ensures that the order in which all library tasks begin to run respects the assigned priorities.

4 Classification Strategy and Activation Rules for Tasks

The termination rules for library tasks are such that they are not explicitly required to terminate. It is stated in [2] RI-2016: the automatic termination of library tasks when the main program completes is fundamentally at odds with the paradigm of having a "vacated" main program and doing all the work in library tasks. It is also stated in [2] that this paradigm is frequently used in real-time systems. It seems evident that the possibility of having the library tasks constitute the single set of all actors in a real-time system was intentionally included by the language designers. Now note that the manner in which this set of actors activates is extremely ill-structured. The LRM states that a task object declaration results in the activation of the task immediately after passing the reserved word following the enclosing declarative part or the begin following the declarative part of the corresponding package body; if, however, the task object is created by the evaluation of an allocator, then the task is activated by this evaluation itself. Therefore, library tasks are activated and may commence execution when the initialization parts of their enclosing package bodies begin to execute during elaboration, and the assigned priorities for these tasks play no role whatsoever in determining the activation/execution order. We suggest a model to rectify these problems.

We propose a classification strategy for tasks based on the method of creation of tasks and the nature of the direct masters of tasks.

1. A task that is not created by an allocator and whose direct master is a library package is classified as a *pervasive* task.
2. A task that is not created by an allocator and whose direct master is a task, block statement or subprogram is classified as a *non-pervasive* task.
3. A task created by an allocator is classified as an *anomalous* task, as such a task depends directly on the unit that elaborates the corresponding access definition and not on the entity whose execution creates the task.

Since non-pervasive tasks exist only in the execution lifetime of the ephemeral entity (subprograms, block statements and tasks, all of which can complete execution and/or terminate) the current activation and termination rules are appropriate for them. For anomalous tasks the current rules may also be considered appropriate for it is assumed that such tasks will be created only in the event that we do not know how many tasks we shall eventually need, or if we need to exchange task identities at some point during elaboration.

We now discuss an activation mechanism whereby priority inversion during elaboration for *pervasive* tasks can be eliminated. All pervasive tasks should be activated *after* the elaboration of the declarative part of the main program and just after the reserved word begin. Thus, the Ada Run-time scheduler will ensure that no priority inversion takes place when pervasive tasks begin to execute. The consequences of this restriction are discussed next. In [4], Barnes, while discussing the structure summary and main program of a typical Ada system, states that a model of the "complete" program can be understood in terms of one where the package STANDARD is declared inside a "declare" block statement that appears in the body of the environment task, and all library packages and package bodies are considered to be declared as subpackages immediately within the package body STANDARD. These library packages and package bodies appear in an order consistent with the context clauses and the pragmas ELABORATE. The main program is called as one of the "initialization" statements of package body STANDARD. Barnes states that this model captures the fact that tasks that depend on a library package (and are not designated by an access value) are started at the end of the declarative part of STANDARD and before the main program is called. If this were to be true, then priority inversion during elaboration would certainly be precluded. However, we have observed that this is not the behavior provided by several Ada compilers. The relevant reason can be found in the LRM, which states the following: "If an object declaration that declares a task object occurs *immediately* within a declarative part, then the activation of the task object starts after the elaboration of the declarative part (that is, after passing the reserved word begin following the declarative part)." Thus, it appears that the activation of a task is determined by the *enclosing lexical entity* and not the master of the task, which is not always the same. As we have reported earlier, many authors of Ada textbooks state that the immediate subsequent execution of the task begins concurrently with the parent (i.e., the enclosing entity), though this is not explicitly stated in the LRM. If the task under consideration is a non-pervasive or anomalous task, this rule makes sense, but not for pervasive tasks that are not required to terminate (as packages do not really "complete their execution and get exited from"). Therefore, Barnes' perception is appropriate, though apparently not universally implemented. The lack of explicit instructions in the LRM on the commencement of execution and the non-orthogonality in Ada whereby the termination, but not the activation, of a task is related to its master, is the root cause of the problem.

Through our classification strategy and modified activation rules, we are making a case for the activation of a task to also be related to its master, and suggesting a new master for pervasive tasks. In [4], Barnes states that a package is merely a passive scope wall and has no dynamic life. Thus, the execution of the initialization statements in a package body is somewhat qualitatively different from the execution of a task, subprogram or "declare" block. Pervasive tasks should therefore depend on the environment task and not the enclosing library package, and this should be made clear in the LRM.

```
package P1 is
    ...
end P1;

package P2 is
        task T is
                entry E1;
                entry E2;
        end T;
end P2;

with P2;
pragma ELABORATE(P2);
package body P1 is
...
begin
        ...
        P2.T.E2;
        ...
end P1;
```

```
package body P2 is
        task body T is
        ...
        begin
                ...
                accept E1 do
                        ...
                end E1;
                accept E2 do
                        ...
                end E2;
                ...
        end T;
        ...
end P2;
```

Fig. 5. A situation of elaboration-time deadlock.

5 Elaboration-time Deadlock

Under our suggested new activation rules, a pervasive task will not be activated until the main program starts to execute, any task entry call to a pervasive task from non-task code (e.g., a procedure) executing during the elaboration of a library unit or unit body will surely result in an elaboration-time deadlock, unlike the current situation where such a call may or may not result in deadlock depending on whether the appropriate package body has been elaborated or not before the call is made. It should, however, be noted that using current elaboration control mechanisms it is not possible to preclude such deadlocks by merely ensuring earlier elaboration, for other factors such as the order of accept statements in the called task may still cause such a deadlock. For example, in Fig. 5 the pragma ELABORATE(P1) on package body P2 may not eliminate the deadlock for there may be no earlier caller to entry E1 of T. Very sophisticated control flow analyses are necessary to predict such deadlocks correctly and some may not be detectable.

Our suggested activation rules simplify the elaboration-time deadlock problem, as now, whatever the elaboration order, any elaboration-time call to entries of pervasive tasks will result in deadlock. Data computed for the algorithm *ada_elab* can be utilized to detect possible elaboration-time deadlocks that may be caused on account of entry calls to pervasive tasks. Full details are provided in [16]; briefly, these detection techniques involve checking for the presence of pervasive tasks in entity prerequisite sets of other calling entities (such as a subprogram that executes during elaboration).

We are thus making a case for disallowing task entry calls from the initialization statements of a package body. The justification for this is that the execution of the package body is qualitatively different from that of a task or subprogram and hence, needs different rules.

6 Coding Practices

We now discuss some coding disciplines can achieve the effect of avoiding many of the elaboration-time problems mentioned above in current Ada programs.

1. For ABE errors:
   a. Do not create elaboration dependencies between packages by using an object from another package to constrain or otherwise declare a type or subtype, as an actual parameter to a subprogram called during elaboration, in an expression evaluated during elaboration, or to assign an explicit initialization value to an object.
   b. Do not create elaboration dependencies between packages by calling a subprogram from another user-defined package, directly or indirectly, from the executable statements of a package initialization part or the body of a task object activated in the package.
   c. If cross-package initializations are unavoidable, restrict them to operations that can be carried out at the beginning of the main program.

2. For elimination of priority inversion during elaboration:
   It is necessary that, irrespective of the order of activation, pervasive tasks must begin to perform useful work in the order of their assigned priorities. To achieve this effect, require all pervasive tasks to make an entry call to a common task as their first executable instruction in the sequence of statements that appears after the reserved word begin in their bodies. The common task is in a package which has the specification shown in Figure 6a.

   All compilation units that contain tasks request visibility to this package via a context clause. The main procedure calls the entry "start" which is accepted as the first executable instruction in the sequence of statements that appears after the reserved word begin in the body of task T. This call to "start" in the main procedure must not occur before all pervasive tasks have begun execution; in the Ada systems we have tested, this can be ensured by giving the main procedure the lowest priority. The sequence of executable statements of T then consists of a succession of loops. Each inner loop has a selective wait with an else option. The entry index for the accept statement in a selective wait evaluates to a priority value and the inner loops are executed in decreasing order of priority, see Figure 6b.

   Every other pervasive task calls entry "gate(*p*)" of T, where *p* is the priority of the calling task. Each loop accepts an entry call from a pervasive task in the program, and the sequence of loops and point of initiation of task T ensure synchronization

```
package Starting_gate is
        task T is
                entry Gate (Lowest_priority..Highest_priority - 1);
                entry Start;
                pragma priority (Highest_priority);
        end T;
end Starting_gate;
```

(a)

```
task body T is
begin
        accept Start;
        for Priority_value in reverse Lowest_priority..Highest_priority - 1
        loop
                Inner: loop
                        select accept Gate (Priority_value);
                        else exit Inner;
                        end select;
                end loop Inner;
        end loop;
end T;
```

(b)

Fig. 6. Scheme to eliminate PIDE among library tasks

in order of priority. An obvious limitation of this scheme is that the highest priority provided by the implementation cannot be used by a "client" task.

3. For elimination of elaboration-time deadlock:
Do not (directly from the initialization part of a package body or indirectly via a procedure call that executes during elaboration) call an entry of a pervasive task or use such a task as an actual parameter to a procedure that executes during elaboration. This will preclude deadlocks arising on account of calls to pervasive tasks.

7 Conclusions

We believe that our studies demonstrate the feasibility of automatic determination of elaboration order and detection of possible elaboration failure due to circularities of dependencies and many elaboration-time deadlock situations. Despite the success of Rate Monotonic Scheduling and the Priority Ceiling Protocol for real-time Ada systems and general correctness of the existing model of implementing semaphores with high priority monitor tasks, there remains the problem that the task activation and initial execution order may be able to destroy the proper functioning of the model during the first execution cycle. Safe implementations using the Ada-83 language may benefit from applying the coding practices outlined above. More consideration of task activation rules is appropriate by the Ada 9X teams.

Acknowledgement

We thank IBM Owego for support of the State-Oriented System and Software Engineering Project, under which this paper was developed.

References

1. Ada Programming Language Reference Manual (LRM), *ANSI/MIL-STD 1815 A*, U.S. Government, Ada Joint Program Office, 1983.
2. Ada 9X Project Report, Requirements Issue 4017, Ada 9X Revision Issues Release 1, April 1990, Ada 9X Project Office.
3. Approved Ada Language Commentaries, *ACM Ada Letters*, Volume IX, no. 3, Spring 1989.
4. J.G.P. Barnes, *Programming in Ada*, 3rd Ed., Addison-Wesley, 1989.
5. P. Belmont, "On the access-before-elaboration problem in Ada," *Proceedings of the 1982 AdaTEC Conference on Ada*, ACM, New York, 112-119.
6. M. W. Borger, M. H. Klein, R. A. Veltre, "Real-time software engineering in Ada: Observations and guidelines," Software Engineering Institute, Carnegie-Mellon University, Tech. Rep. No. CMU/SEI-89-TR-22, 1989.
7. D.L. Bryan and G.O. Mendal, *Exploring Ada*, Volume 1, Prentice-Hall, 1990.
8. A. Burns and A.J. Wellings, "Real-time Ada issues," *Proc. 1st Int. Workshop on Real-Time Ada Issues, Ada Letters VII*, no. 6, pp. 43-46, 1987.
9. N.H. Cohen, *Ada as a second language*, McGraw-Hill, 1986.
10. D. Cornhill, "Session summary: tasking," *Proc. 1st Int. Workshop on Real-Time Ada Issues, Ada Letters VII*, no. 6, pp. 29-32, 1987.
11. T. Elrad, "Comprehensive scheduling controls for Ada tasking," *Proc. 2nd Int. Workshop on Real-Time Ada Issues, Ada Letters VIII*, no. 7, pp. 12-19, 1988.
12. J.B. Goodenough and L.Sha, "The priority ceiling protocol: A method for minimizing the blocking of high priority Ada tasks," *Proc. 2nd Int. Workshop on Real-Time Ada Issues, Ada Letters VIII*, no. 7, pp. 20-31, 1988.
13. L.C. Lander, S. Mitra, and T.F. Piatkowski, "Priority inversion in Ada programs during elaboration," *Proc. 7th Washington Ada Symp.*, June 1990, pp. 133-41.
14. L.C. Lander, S. Mitra, and T.F. Piatkowski, "Deterministic priority inversion in Ada selective waits," *ACM Ada Letters*, vol. 10, no. 7, pp. 55-62, 1990.
15. L.C. Lander, S. Mitra, N. Singhvi, and T.F. Piatkowski, "The elaboration order problem of Ada," Dept. of Computer Science, SUNY Binghamton, Tech. Rep. No. CS-TR-90-57, 1990 (to appear in *Software–Practice and Experience*).
16. L.C. Lander, S. Mitra, "Detection and avoidance of elaboration-time problems for multi-unit real-time Ada application," Dept. of Computer Science, SUNY Binghamton, Tech. Rep. No. CS-TR-90-58, 1990.

17. D. Locke, L. Sha, R. Rajkumar, J. Lehoczky and G. Burns, "Priority inversion and its control: an experimental investigation," *Proc. 2nd Int. Workshop on Real-Time Ada Issues, Ada Letters VIII*, no. 7, pp. 39-42, 1988.
18. P.E. McMahon, "Lessons learned on the fringe of Ada," *Interservices Training Systems Conference*, Fort Worth, Texas, November 1989.
19. L. Sha and J.B. Goodenough, "Real-time scheduling theory and Ada," *IEEE Computer*, vol. 23, no. 4, pp. 53-62, 1990.
20. L. Sha, R. Rajkumar, J.P. Lehoczky, "Priority inheritance protocols: An approach to real-time synchronization," Computer Science Dept., Carnegie-Mellon University, Tech. Rep. CMU-CS-87-181, 1987.
21. D.A. Watt, B.A. Wichmann and W.Findlay, *Ada language and methodology*, Prentice-Hall, 1987.

Simulation of Mosca specifications in Ada

Arlet Ottens Hans Toetenel

Delft University of Technology
Faculty of Technical Mathematics and Informatics
P.O. Box 356, 2600 AJ Delft The Netherlands
email: toet@dutiba.tudelft.nl

February 6, 1992

Abstract

MOSCA is an experimental language to extend the Vienna Development Method specification language VDM-SL to be applicable in the area of developing distributed, parallel and real-time systems. As is generally known, plain VDM is not adequate for these application areas since it lacks facilities to specify multiple threads of control and it does not allow the use of time within specifications. MOSCA is designed to overcome these restrictions.

The paper reports on the development of a mechanical transformation of MOSCA specifications into executable Ada programs. The paper highlights the transformation of MOSCA types, the implementation of pattern matching, the realisation of MOSCA agents through Ada tasks and the realisation of time.

1 Introduction

This paper presents an overview of the process specification capabilities of MOSCA[1] [14, 15] and their transformation into Ada.

It is assumed that the reader has some working knowledge of the VDM specification language [2, 3, 8]. Further it is an advantage to have at least some knowledge of process algebraic specification notations, like CCS [10, 11] and CSP [6]. Baeten [1] presents an overview of the basic mathematical properties developed around the process algebras (in dutch).

The MOSCA specification language builds on VDM-SL[2] [7] and process algebra, in particular CCS. The model-oriented specification language of VDM is embedded within MOSCA by acting as the process algebra's value manipulation language. The combination is further extended with capabilities to describe *structure* and *time*.

A MOSCA specification describes four aspects of complete systems of communicating processes: their data-containment, their functional behaviour, process-structure and time characteristics. In this paper we will concentrate on the process defining and time handling constructs in MOSCA and their transformation into Ada.

MOSCA is an experimental language. The concrete syntax applied in this paper is based on the VDM-SL concrete mathematical syntax notation and the CCS notation. This syntax

[1] Mosca stands for Model-Oriented Specification of Communicating Agents.

[2] The specification language for VDM for which an ISO standard is currently being developed (ISO SC22/WG19) in cooperation with the British Standardisation Institute.

acts more or less as a vehicle to demonstrate the capabilities of the language. The complete concrete and abstract syntax of MOSCA is given in [15], together with a formal semantics, based on the dynamic semantic model for VDM-SL [9] and Plotkin's labelled transitions systems [13] extended to handle time in a manner inspired by Wang Yi's work [17].

The basic element in the MOSCA model is a process, which is called *agent*. In the following two sections an overview is presented of the various kind of attributes a standard process can obtain through various definitions. Section 2 shows some of the constructs available for agent behaviour specification. The overview of MOSCA is closed in section 3 with a short presentation of the constructs in MOSCA to specify real-time behaviour.

The remaining sections describe the work done on the design and implementation of a MOSCA simulator tool. This tool accepts a MOSCA specification, and transforms it into an executable Ada program that simulates the behaviour of this specification. Section 4 presents the mapping of MOSCA types into Ada, section 5 highlights the transformation of patterns and discusses pattern matching. Section 6 is devoted to the translation of agent expressions. Section 7 addresses the realisation of time. The paper is concluded with some remarks on our results so far.

2 A short overview of MOSCA

2.1 Agent Behaviour

The behaviour of agents is defined using a *BehaviourExpression*^{CS}. [3] A behaviour expression is built from classic CCS construct like prefix and choice constructs and compound constructs like agent-if and agent-let. In the following these constructs are introduced by example to describe the various aspects of agent definition. We will only enumerate the constituents of behaviour expressions relevant to the present presentation.

2.2 Agent Definition

Agents are defined by the *AgentDefinition*^{CS} construct. Agent definitions can be given in various styles, ranging from simple agents without any means to handle values, through agents with value parts, to agents with local state and associated operations that act on the state of the agent. Table 1 summarises the capabilities.

CAPABILITY	TYPE 0	TYPE 1	TYPE 2
Value Passing Actions	No	Yes	Yes
Value Part Specification	No	Yes	No
State Part Specification	No	No	Yes
Value Manipulation	—	functions	operations

Table 1: Agent / Value combinations

[3]Syntactical classes are highlighted by postfixing the name of the class with the ^{CS} symbol.

The general form of the most simple style agent definition is depicted in specification 2.1. This style involves no value passing, neither through actions, value parts nor the state of the agent, and is referred to as Type 0.

MOSCA 2.1 Type 0 Agent

Agent_name
ports syn portname_1
...
syn portname_n

Agent_name ≜ *Agent-Behaviour-Expression*

An agent definition consists of three parts: an agent heading, a port specification and the behaviour of the agent. An *AgentHeading*^{CS} starts with an identifier. It is the name of the agent. In the Type 0 style the heading is limited to the name of the agent. The *PortSpecification*^{CS} of an agent definition specifies the interface of the agent with the surrounding system. It enumerates the ports of the agent. In Type 0 agents the ports are used for synchronisation only. The *AgentBehaviour*^{CS} consist of the agent name and the ≜ symbol followed by the definition of the behaviour in the form of a *BehaviourExpression*^{CS}.

Example 2.1 Suppose we want to model a simple semaphore device (specification 2.2), only capable of undertaking a series of *p* and *v* actions.

MOSCA 2.2 Semaphore

Semaphore
ports syn p
syn v

Semaphore ≜ p ⊙ v ⊙ *Semaphore*

First we state the name of the agent, which is *Semaphore*, followed by the port specifications. The specification syn p specifies a port dedicated to synchronisation purposes only. The behaviour of the semaphore is given by p ⊙ v ⊙ *Semaphore*. It defines the agent *Semaphore* to be able to perform an action p followed by an action v after which the agent becomes itself again. Here we have an example of a *recursive agent definition*. □

Syntactically the behaviour consists of two prefix expressions p ⊙ (v ⊙ *Semaphore*) and v ⊙ *Semaphore*. The prefix operator '⊙' is equivalent with the CCS prefix operator '.'. The action, represented syntactically by an *Action*^{CS} construct, specifies a communication through the designated port. The behaviour expression following the '⊙' symbol specifies a replacement behaviour for the agent. For Type 0 agents the action is restricted to a single label. The next class of agents, Type 1 agents, can handle parameterised actions.

The ability to store values within an agent can be modelled in two different ways: through a value part and through a full state definition. Both entities allow the storing of values within an agent. The main difference between the two approaches is the way the stored values are manipulated. Agents equipped with value parts are referred to as Type 1 agents. Agents with state definitions are called Type 2 agents. The most flexible agent is the combination of Type 1 and Type 2.

The definition of a Type 1 agent starts with an identifier to name the agent, followed by a type specification that states the type of the value part of the agent. A value part specification has the form of a MOSCA type expression. The value can be set through agent instantiation by means of an agent-service construct, which binds a value to the value part. The general form of a Type 1 agent is given in specification 2.3.

MOSCA 2.3 Type 1 Agent

Agent_name ⟨ *Valueparttype*⟩
ports in `inportname` : *Type*
out $\overline{\texttt{outportname}}$: *Type*

Agent_name ⟨*valuepartpattern_1*⟩ $\triangleq$ *Agent-Behaviour-Expression_1*

...

Agent_name ⟨*valuepartpattern_n*⟩ $\triangleq$ *Agent-Behaviour-Expression_n*

The port specification for value passing ports consists of a direction specifier, a port name and a port value type. For example:

in `set`: $\mathbb{N}$

specifies a port `set` that can be used to read natural numbers.

The third part of a Type 1 agent definition again specifies the behaviour of the agent. In general the behaviour is specified through a series of $AgentBehaviour^{CS}$ constructs. Each construct defines the behaviour of the agent for a specific set of values of the value part of the agent. This set of values is fixed by a $Pattern^{CS}$ construct. The set of patterns must match all possible values for the value part type. Patterns with overlapping associated value sets are allowed, and specify loose behaviour.

Example 2.2 MOSCA can be used to model a wide variety of concurrent systems. In small grain concurrent systems even memory cells could be modelled as independent entities. This example assumes that a memory cell can store integer values, and can be accessed through the normal read and write operations. We model the storage capability of a memory cell with a value part. The read operation is modelled by the output action $\overline{\texttt{get}}$, the write operation by the input action `set`. Specification 2.4 shows the details.

MOSCA 2.4 Memory Cell

MCell ⟨$\mathbb{Z}$⟩
ports in `set` : $\mathbb{Z}$
out $\overline{\texttt{get}}$: $\mathbb{Z}$

$$MCell\,\langle val\rangle \triangleq \texttt{set}(x) \odot MCell\,\langle x\rangle \oplus \overline{\texttt{get}}(val) \odot MCell\,\langle val\rangle$$

The agent *MCell* has an integer value part, so the value patterns in the agent behaviour construct must match integer values. The actual pattern *val* matches all possible integer values, thereby bundling the behaviour into one agent behaviour construct. The behaviour construct of the *MCell* agent applies a $Choice^{CS}$ expression. This expression is formed with the choice operator '⊕'. It is equivalent to the CCS summation construct. □

Generally the value pattern in the agent behaviour construct may introduce a collection of variable names. The scope of these names reaches to the end of the associated behaviour expression. The actions of a Type 1 agent are used to pass values from one agent to another. The value parameters of actions are patterns for input actions and expressions for output actions. Note that:

- The pattern in an input action has a *defining nature*. The names in these patterns define a new scope region, that starts with the occurrence of the name and reaches to the end of the prefix expression. In the prefix construct

  $$\mathtt{in}(x) \odot A$$

  x acts as a value binder in a similar way as in a lambda term. The agent A will behave as $A[v/x]$ after the input v is received through port $\mathtt{in}$.

- Names in an output action have an *applied nature*, and do not introduce scope regions. They are just identifiers in a value expression, conforming to a call by value semantics.

The initial value of the value part of the memory cell cannot be specified within the agent itself. It is set through the behaviour expression that introduces the agent, which is syntactically an $AgentService^{CS}$. It resembles the function call in the value part of MOSCA. An agent service construct has two parts, namely the agent name it invokes, and an actual value for the value part, if present of course. The expression

$$MCell\ \langle 0 \rangle$$

is an agent service expression that behaves like the agent *MCell*, with its value part set to 0.

Example 2.3 The next specification uses sequence patterns and gives a model for a simple unbounded buffer that buffers natural numbers (adapted from Milner [11]).

MOSCA 2.5 Buffer

$Buffer\ \langle \mathbf{N}^* \rangle$
ports in $\mathtt{in}$: $\mathbf{N}$
out $\overline{\mathtt{out}}$: $\mathbf{N}$

$$Buffer\ \langle [\,] \rangle \triangleq \mathtt{in}(x) \odot Buffer\ \langle [x] \rangle$$

$$Buffer\ \langle [x] \frown s \rangle \triangleq \overline{\mathtt{out}}(x) \odot Buffer\ \langle s \rangle \oplus \mathtt{in}(y) \odot Buffer\ \langle [x] \frown s \frown [y] \rangle$$

The agent *Buffer* has a single value part that holds sequences of natural numbers, $\mathbf{N}^*$. It offers two ports: one input port $\mathtt{in}$ that accepts a number, and an output port $\overline{\mathtt{out}}$ that delivers a value from the buffer. The sequence patterns $[\,]$, and $[x] \frown s$ are used to mark the two cases of behaviour for the buffer. An empty buffer can only accept values at the input port, whereas a non-empty buffer can both accept a value for buffering and deliver a value from the buffer to the environment. □

3 Time handling in MOSCA

The time model starts from the ideas in Timed CCS [4], and TCCS [16]. It is built around the following issues:

- There is no external clock, no ticking device to register time.
- The passing of time is measured related to *actions*: from the start of an action to the end of an action. Let

  $$a, \star t \odot P$$

  denote an agent waiting for the environment to synchronise on a and then become $P[d/t]$ in doing so, where d represents the time delay before synchronisation on a takes place.
- Time delay results from *idle* actions. The transition

  $$idle(x) \odot P \xrightarrow{\epsilon(y)} idle(x-y) \odot P$$

  is valid for each $y \leq x$ where x and y are time expressions, and $\epsilon(y)$ is the action label expressing the amount of time spent idling.
- Time is only spent by idling and by waiting for synchronisation on the ports.

Example 3.1 Stopwatch A particular model of a stopwatch has two buttons for control: a start button and a stop button. Reading must be done after stopping the stopwatch. Specification 3.1 presents a MOSCA model.

MOSCA 3.1 Stopwatch

SW

ports syn `start`
  syn `stop`
  out $\overline{\texttt{display}}$: T

$$SW \triangleq \texttt{start} \odot \texttt{stop}, \star t \odot \overline{\texttt{display}}(t) \odot SW$$

After the stopwatch is started, the agent SW is ready to accept `stop`. The time elapsed between start and stop is registered in time variable t. □

Time delay is measured in time units from a time-domain T. The time-domain, with least element 0 can be dense or discrete. In the sequel it is assumed to be the domain $\mathbf{R}^+$.

Example 3.2 Another Stopwatch A more realistic stopwatch can be started and stopped with one button, reset with another and constantly read. The accuracy of the stopwatch is 1 centisecond. Specification 3.2 shows the details.

The stopwatch can be in one of three states, ready for a fresh start — RSW, ticking — $RSWR$ and ready to be restarted after a previous ticking status, retaining the current reading — $RSWS$. In the expression

$$(idle(tick) \odot RSWR\ \langle tick + t\rangle\ ) \oplus \texttt{ss}, \star d \odot idle(tick - d) \odot RSWS\ \langle t + d\rangle$$

MOSCA 3.2 Realistic Stopwatch

values
  $tick\ :\ \mathsf{T} = 0.01$
end

$RSW\ \langle \mathsf{T} \rangle$
ports syn `ss`
  syn `reset`
  out $\overline{\texttt{display}}$: T

$$RSW\ \langle t \rangle \ \triangleq\ \texttt{ss} \odot RSWR\ \langle t \rangle$$

$$RSWR\ \langle t \rangle \ \triangleq\ (idle(tick) \odot RSWR\ \langle tick + t \rangle\ ) \oplus$$
$$\texttt{ss}, \star d \odot idle(tick - d) \odot RSWS\ \langle tick + t \rangle \oplus$$
$$\overline{\texttt{display}}(t), \star d \odot idle(tick - d) \odot RSWR\ \langle tick + t \rangle$$

$$RSWS\ \langle t \rangle \ \triangleq\ \texttt{ss} \odot RSWR\ \langle t \rangle\ \oplus \texttt{reset} \odot RSW\ \langle 0 \rangle$$

either the idle action runs to completion, after which the first prefix will be active, or within the time span of a tick the start/stop button is pressed, after which the second prefix will be activated. □

The remaining sections present some of the more interesting aspects of the MOSCA compiler. The full report is given in [12].

4 The translation of the MOSCA type system

The MOSCA data types are adopted from the VDM-SL data types, and include: basic types, sets, sequences, maps, unions, product types, records and optional types.

At first sight it may seem best to implement MOSCA types by Ada generic packages, using a dedicated package for each of the type constructors shown above. However, it turns out that this approach leads to serious difficulties.

Suppose for example that we design a package to implement set types, and another package to implement sequence types. Both packages contain functions to manipulate sets and sequences. Now consider the function elems (a built-in MOSCA function that returns the set of sequence elements). This function cannot be part of either of the two packages and must be provided separately. This either results in exporting implementation details about the sets and sequences or in extremely inefficient code. Apart from generating function calls to implement the MOSCA operations, the compiler also has to generate code to declare the types and the functions that operate on these types. If the implementation of a type changes, the compiler itself has to be modified.

Another problem is associated with the implementation of union types. Suppose we have the following declarations:

$$A\ =\ \mathsf{N} \mid \mathsf{B}$$
$$B\ =\ \mathsf{N} \mid \mathsf{Char}$$

Suppose further that variables x of type A and y of type B are declared. The expression $x + y$ is now legal in MOSCA, provided that both x and y are of type N at time of evaluation. To implement these types in Ada a variant record could be used:

```
type nat_bool is ( nat, bool, undefined );
type A( base: nat_bool := undefined ) is record
   case base is
      when nat       => nat_val  : nat_type;
      when bool      => bool_val : bool_type;
      when undefined => null;
   end case;
end record;
```

Type B would be implemented likewise. The problems are caused by the + function. A potentially very large combination of types can be used for arguments and return types. This may result in a large number of different + functions.

To overcome these problems we have introduced an alternative in the form of a universal type, called 'T'. This type can hold all MOSCA values. Using only one type has a great advantage: the run-time system (which contains routines for built-in functions, pattern matching and agent communication) can be written separately and then simply linked to the Ada code that is generated by the compiler. The type 'T' is organised as a special record and looks like this:

```
type base_type is ( undefined, char, int, bool, set, seq, tuple );
type T( base: base_type := undefined ) is record
   case base is
      when char      => char_val : char_type;
      when int       => int_val  : int_type;
      when bool      => bool_val : bool_type;
      when set       => set_val  : set_of_T;
      when seq       => seq_val  : seq_of_T;
      when tuple     => tuple_val: seq_of_T;
      when undefined => null;
   end case;
end record;
```

For clarity not all fields are shown here. The types mentioned in the fields must be defined in a suitable way. Notice that the product type (tuple) is implemented using the sequence type. This is possible because the elements of the tuple are all represented using the single type 'T'. Representing union types using this record is straightforward, type 'T' is already a union of all types. As an example of a type 'T' application, consider the implementation of the card function, that returns the cardinality of an arbitrary set:

```
function card( arg: T ) return T is
   card: int_type := 0;
   list: set_of_T;              -- set_of_T is a linked list.
begin
   list := arg.set_val;         -- the linked list itself
   while list /= null loop      -- while there are elements ...
      card := card + 1;         -- count element
      list := list.next;        -- next element
   end loop;
   return( int(card) );         -- return card as T.
end card;
```

A disadvantage of this method is the absence of any form of type checking by the Ada compiler. The MOSCA compiler has to perform all checks itself, or generate explicit code for the checks.

5 Patterns and pattern matching

Patterns are widely used in MOSCA. They can be found in the multiple behaviour expression and in the *AgentLet* construct. Our implementation does not attempt to produce in-line code to perform pattern matching. Instead a general back-tracking procedure `match` is provided:

```
procedure match( expr    : in T;
                 pattern : in pattern_type;
                 bind    : out bind_list;
                 matched : out boolean );
```

The parameters have the following meaning:

- `expr`: this is the expression that must match the pattern. A full implementation of MOSCA patterns would be able to cope with recursive definitions like

  let $x = f(x)$ in ...

  In the semantic approach taken here x is a fixpoint of the function f. In such an implementation a simple expression would not suffice. In the current implementation we demand that the expression can be evaluated before the actual pattern matching takes place.

- `pattern`: this is the pattern. It is represented by a special tree. This tree also contains information about the current state of the matching process.

- `bind`: this structure is the result of a successful match. It consists of a list of pattern identifier, together with their values. If the pattern does not match, the bind list is undefined.

- `matched`: this parameter tells whether or not the match succeeded.

The above match procedure finds only one successful match (if there are any). When more matches are possible it is not defined which one will be chosen. Internally the pattern matching procedures must be able to find all matches. Consider for example the following pattern:

let $[a \curvearrowright b, a] = [\,[10,20],[10]\,]$ in ...

The pattern matching routine divides this pattern into 2 sub-patterns, $a \curvearrowright b$ and a, that are matched separately. They are however not independent, because they share the same symbols. Suppose that the left sub-pattern is tried first. This results in 3 possible matches:

a	b
[]	[10, 20]
[10]	[20]
[10, 20]	[]

The procedure works by trying them one by one and, using the partly filled-in bind list, trying to match the right sub-pattern. To do the job an internal procedure is provided:

```
procedure match( expr      : in T;
                 pattern   : in out pattern_type;
                 in_bind   : in bind_list;
                 out_bind  : out bind_list;
                 matched   : out boolean;
                 first     : in boolean );
```

Some new parameters are introduced:

- `in_bind`: the current bindings. These are the results from previous calls to the `match` routine.
- `out_bind`: the new bindings. This list is identical to the `in_bind` list, except that some of the previously unbound symbols may now have a value.
- `first`: this parameter must be set to `true` on the first call to this procedure. In subsequent calls to this procedure (to obtain a different bind) this parameter must be `false`.

To show what the actual generated code looks like, we will now present a realistic example from the *Buffer*-agent (specification 2.5):

$$Buffer\ \langle[\,]\rangle \triangleq \mathrm{in}(x) \odot Buffer\ \langle[x]\rangle$$

$$Buffer\ \langle[x] \curvearrowright s\rangle \triangleq \overline{\mathrm{out}}(x) \odot Buffer\ \langle s\rangle \oplus \mathrm{in}(y) \odot Buffer\ \langle[x] \curvearrowright s \curvearrowright [y]\rangle$$

The resulting Ada code has the following structure:

```
pat0 := mk_pat( matchvalue, empty_seq ); -- create [] pattern
match( val, pat0, bind, matched );       -- val contains value part
IF matched THEN                          -- if val = []
   -- first behaviour expression
ELSE
   pat0 := mk_pat( id, 1 );              -- x pattern
   pat1 := mk_pat( enum, (1=> pat0) );   -- [x] pattern
   pat2 := mk_pat( id, 2 );              -- s pattern
   pat3 := mk_pat( conc, pat1, pat2 );   -- [x] ^ s pattern
   match( val, pat3, bind, matched );    -- match value part
   IF matched THEN
      x := bind( 1 );                    -- get value of x
      s := bind( 2 );                    -- get value of s
      -- second behaviour expression
   ELSE
      RAISE match_failed;                -- no match at all
   END IF:
END IF;
```

Using the run-time support function `mk_pat`, a pattern tree is built bottom-up. The numbers in the id-nodes correspond to the numbers in the array `bind` that contains their values after pattern matching.

6 From MOSCA agents to Ada tasks

The most interesting part of the translator concerns the translation of agents to Ada-tasks. Every MOSCA agent is implemented using an Ada task type. Each agent service results in the allocation of a new task of the proper type. It is not possible to simply translate MOSCA communication to Ada rendez-vous for the following reasons:

- In every Ada rendez-vous the caller must explicitly specify the task it calls (the callee). This is not the case in MOSCA, here the agents communicate through *ports*. The agent does not have an idea how this port is connected to other agents. In fact, this can change at any moment.
- Using an Ada `select` construct, a task can wait for a number of `accepts`. However, it is not possible to try and call more than one entry at a time, nor is it possible to mix entry calls and accept statements. This asymmetry in Ada has caused many problems in the implementation.

It is clear that we need a special way to implement the MOSCA communication in Ada. Therefore we have introduced a special task, the *communication server*, or simply *server*. This task supervises all communication between the agents. It also keeps track of the current set of active agents and maintains a clock to implement the timing facilities. Except for the central server, no other task knows anything about its environment.

It is acknowledged that using a central server constitutes a potential bottleneck, especially when used on a distributed system. It has been studied whether or not such a centralised server could be replaced by a number of smaller, distributed tasks. Apart from the problems involved with communication between agents that arise from such a system, it is not clear how the central clock mechanism could be distributed.

If an Ada task wishes to communicate through a port it sends a request to the server. After one or more requests have been sent, it notifies the server that it is waiting for reply. Immediately after that the task waits for the action using an `accept`-statement.

All requests are stored by the server. When all tasks are waiting for reply, the server examines the stored requests. If two matching requests are found (two syn-actions or read/write-actions), the involved tasks are notified.

1. When a syn-action is possible, both tasks are notified by an entry call, and they can now continue evaluating their behaviour expressions.
2. When a read/write-action is possible, the server calls the writer agent and provides it with the identification of the reader agent. The writer agent can then send its data to the reader. Note that the central server does not handle the messages itself, it only provides a one-time channel between the two tasks.

In either case, the server removes all pending requests of the two tasks. For reasons of fairness [5, 12], it is not possible to handle the requests as soon as communication is possible. Slow tasks must be allowed to communicate with any other task. Therefore the server has to wait for all tasks to send requests before they can be served. Due to this approach, we usually find very few tasks running, typically only two or three. This greatly reduces the possibilities of distributed processing.

Translating the semaphore device. Let us examine how the *Semaphore* device is translated to an Ada task. The semaphore agent has two syn-ports, namely p and v. Every port has an internal representation, which is used internally by the agent and an external representation, which is used by the server. The need for the two representations is a direct consequence of the *Relabelling*^{CS} operation, which is not discussed in this introduction.

The representation of a port (internal or external) is an integer value, the numbering of the ports is done by the compiler. Every internal number can be transformed into an external number using the call `map( my_map, internal )`.

The first action of the semaphore device is a synchronisation using the p-port. This is done in three steps:

1. The agent sends a request to the server, saying that it is willing to communicate via port p. This is done in the following way:

   ```
   server.request( myself, (syn, 1, map(my_map, p_port)) );
   ```

   This call uses 2 arguments: the first one (`myself`) is an identification of the calling task. Using this identification the task can be called back later. The second argument is an aggregate consisting of three elements. The first element is the type of request that is desired. The second element is an index, when a request is granted this index is returned so that the the calling task can identify the original request. The third element is the external port identification.

2. The agent tells the server that it has no more requests:

   ```
   server.wait;
   ```

3. The agents awaits reply from the server:

   ```
   ACCEPT receive( val: in T; index: IN positive ) DO
      NULL;
   END data;
   ```

   The parameter `val` is used to send data through the port. It is not used in synchronisation actions. The `index` is the same value that was used in the request above.

The second part of the behaviour expression (synchronisation through the v-port) is translated in the same way.

6.1 Choice expressions

A choice expression is a non-deterministic choice between two behaviour expressions. The compiler generates port requests that arise from both options, it waits for reply and uses the returned index parameter to decide what to do next.

As an example, let us examine the generated code for a simple *Choice* expression that can be found in the description of the memory cell agent:

$$\mathtt{set}(x) \odot MCell\langle x\rangle \oplus \overline{\mathtt{get}}(val) \odot MCell\langle val\rangle$$

There are two possible ways of communication: the first one is reading a value through the set-port. The second one is writing a value through the get-port. Therefore the following requests are generated:

```
server.request( myself, (read, 1, map(my_map, set_port)) );
server.request( myself, (write, 2, map(my_map, get_port)) );
server.wait;
```

The server will queue both requests, and can reply in two different ways:

1. The agent can receive some value through the **set**-port. It gets this value directly.
2. The agent may have to send a value through the **get**-port. In this case it receives the identification of its partner. The partner is called 'peer' in the compiler.

For each of those two answers, the agent provides an **accept**-statement.

```
SELECT
   ACCEPT send( peer : IN peer_type; index, peer_index : IN positive ) DO
      my_peer := peer;
      my_peer_index := peer_index;
      my_index := index;
   END agent;
OR
   ACCEPT receive( val : IN t; index : IN positive ) DO
      read_val := val;
      my_index := index;
   END data;
END SELECT;
```

The actual rendez-vous is kept as short as possible, in order to avoid excessive delays on the server. The actions are restricted to copying the parameters.

Using the **index** parameter, the agent is able to determine the chosen alternative in the choice expression. If the index equals 1, then **read_val** contains the value that was read through the **set**-port. If the index is 2, the agent has to send a value to its peer. This is done with the following call:

```
my_peer.receive( val, my_peer_index );
```

As can be seen, the task also sends the peer's index. Using this index the peer task can also determine the chosen alternative.

7 On the realisation of time

The server is also responsible for maintaining a clock. It is implemented using an Ada **float** type. Time handling in the server is implemented in the following way:

1. The server keeps track of the total number of tasks that are still running. These are the tasks that are not idling or waiting for communication.
2. As soon as a task performs an idle action it is placed in the idle queue. This queue is sorted according to wake-up time, and can be compared to a calendar. The task becomes suspended, and the number of running tasks is decreased by one.

3. If a task notifies the server that it is waiting for reply using the `server.wait` call, this task becomes suspended too.

4. When the total number of running tasks equals zero, the system first examines the communication queue to see if there is any communication action possible. If this is not the case the system cannot continue without spending some time and the idle queue is examined. The first entry in the idle queue is removed as well as all the subsequent entries with equal wakeup times. The clock is advanced to this wakeup time. The associating tasks are all notified by a synchronisation action and become 'running'.

Translation of idle actions. The *idle* actions are sent to the server as requests, very much like ordinary requests for communication. Consider for example the following behaviour expression:

$$\mathit{Timer}\ \langle t\rangle \quad \triangleq \quad \mathit{idle}(1) \odot \mathit{Timer}\ \langle t+1\rangle \oplus \overline{\mathtt{put}}(t) \odot \mathit{Timer}\ \langle t+1\rangle$$

The generated Ada code for the request looks like this:

```
server.request( myself, (idle, 1, int(1)) );
server.request( myself, (write, 2, map(my_map, put_port)) );
server.wait;
```

The `idle`-request looks very much like any ordinary request, the first element of the aggregate is the word `idle`, the second is again the index, and the third is the amount of time.

Measuring passed time. In MOSCA it is possible to measure the amount of time that has passed when waiting for communication. It is straightforward to implement this in Ada. This can be demonstrated using a small fragment of code from the *Stopwatch* example. The behaviour expression:

$$\mathtt{ss}, \star d \odot \mathit{idle}(\mathit{tick} - d) \odot \mathit{RSWS}\langle \mathit{tick} + t\rangle$$

results in the following structure for the Ada code:

```
server.start( d );
server.request( myself, (syn, 1, map(my_map, ss_port)) );
-- accept syn action
server.stop( d );
server.request( myself, (idle, 1, tick - d) );
-- accept syn action
```

The `server.start` entry call initialises the argument with the current clock value. The call `server.stop` calculates the difference between the contents of the clock and the argument. The result is returned in the argument.

8 Conclusion

The MOSCA compiler is far from complete. It does not support all VDM-SL constructs, most notably it does not implement looseness, inductive definitions, and explicit operation definitions. Although the current supported subset of MOSCA is small, it contains enough process defining facilities to experiment with. One of the purposes of the simulator is to assess the functionality of the MOSCA process defining primitives.

References

[1] J.C.M. Baeten. *Procesalgebra.* Kluwer Programmatuurkunde, 1986.

[2] D. Bjørner. Towards a meaning of 'M' in VDM. In J. Diaz and F. Oregas, editors, *Tapsoft-89*, volume 352 of *LNCS*, pages 1–35. Springer Verlag, 1989.

[3] D. Bjørner and C.B. Jones. *Formal Specification & Software Development.* PHI. Prentice Hall, 1982.

[4] L. Chen, S. Anderson, and F. Moller. A timed calculus of communicating systems. Technical Report LFCS-90-127, University of Edinburgh, 1990.

[5] N. Francez. *Fairness.* Texts and Monographs in Computer Science. Springer Verlag, 1986.

[6] C.A.R. Hoare. *Communicating Sequential Processes.* PHI. Prentice Hall, 1985.

[7] ISO SC22/WG19. *VDM Specification Language — Proto-Standard*, 1991. Draft dated 9th March.

[8] C.B. Jones. *Systematic Software Development Using VDM, 2-nd edition.* PHI. Prentice Hall, 1990.

[9] P.G. Larsen, A. Tarlecki, W. Pawlowski, and M. Borzyszkowski, Wieth. The dynamic semantics of the BSI/VDM specification language. Technical report, IFAD, The institute of Applied Computer Science, Munkebjergsvaenget 17, DK-5230 Odense M, Denmark, August 1990.

[10] R. Milner. Calculi for synchrony and asynchrony. *TCS*, 25:267–310, 1983.

[11] R. Milner. *Communication and Concurrency.* PHI. Prentice Hall, 1989.

[12] A. Ottens. The design and implementation of a MOSCA compiler. Master's thesis, Delft University of Technology, department of Technical Mathematics and Informatics, 1991.

[13] G. Plotkin. A structural approach to operational semantics. Technical Report DAIMI FN-19, Aarhus University, 1981.

[14] W.J. Toetenel. Model-oriented specification of communicating agents. In J. van Leeuwen, editor, *Computing Science in the Netherlands, proceedings, part II.* SION, 1991.

[15] W.J. Toetenel. *Model Oriented Specification of Communicating Agents.* PhD thesis, Delft University of Technology, Faculty of Mathematics & Informatics, 1992. (in preparation).

[16] Y. Wang. An interleaving model for real time systems. In K.G. Larsen and A. Skou, editors, *2nd Nordic Workshop on Program Correctness.* The University of Aalborg, October 1990.

[17] Y. Wang. Real-time behaviour of asynchronous agents. In J.C.M. Baeten and J.W. Klop, editors, *CONCUR'90 Theories of Concurrency: Unification and Extension*, volume 458 of *LNCS*, pages 502–520. Springer Verlag, 1990.

CONSIDERATIONS WITH REGARD TO VALIDATION OF ADA DEBUGGERS

Steen Silberg
DDC International A/S
Gl. Lundtoftevej 1B, DK-2800 Lyngby, Denmark

Abstract: Today, it is possible to ensure that an Ada compiler conforms to the Ada programming language, but it is not possible to verify the Ada aspects of a symbolic Ada debugger. This paper presents a number of Ada related debugging features, and shows thereby that a symbolic Ada debugger may contain quite a lot of Ada functionality. In fact, one can conclude that the debugger functionality must grow with the number of language constructions available. As Ada is a complex programming language, it is necessary with a verification of the Ada related debugging facilities. A check list and a test suite are suggested as possible tools for Ada debugger evaluations. Finally, it is concluded that an Ada compiler system without a symbolic Ada debugger is not a full featured development environment.

1. Introduction

Although Ada is developed in order to help programmers write correct programs, a need for debugging facilities still exists. For example the elimination of erroneous conditions can be a difficult and time consuming process, but equipped with a full featured symbolic Ada debugger, the problems can be found and corrected as they occur. Therefore, a good symbolic Ada debugger is an important component of an Ada compiler system, and it should be evaluated along with other components before purchasing an Ada compiler system. A symbolic Ada debugger contains a number of Ada related features like debugging generic instantiations, packages, exceptions, and tasking. It is not a simple case for an Ada debugger to handle programs containing all these Ada constructions. The number of features which must be supported increases even more when debugging at machine level in cross environments. Nevertheless, no symbolic Ada debugger evaluation schemes exist today ensuring that the novel aspects of Ada can be debugged.

When a project or a company is going to select its future Ada development environment, a number of well-known Ada test suites usually form the basis for selecting an Ada compiler system. The support of chapter 13 features and performance measurements are the most frequently chosen subjects in these test suites. It is the user's decision to select the basis for the evaluation of other Ada development tools like symbolic debuggers. Some debuggers are ineffective when debugging large and complex applications due to lack of important debugging functionality, and the situation gets worse if the debugger commands are difficult to remember.

The Ada Compiler Validation Capability ensures that the Ada compiler generates code which conforms to the Ada programming language. As regards the Ada debugger the support of the Ada programming language could be validated, if the Ada functionality of the debugger is large enough for reasoning a validation. But the Ada Reference Manual does not mention how an Ada debugger should support the Ada Programming Language. In the present situation the user of a symbolic Ada debugger can be helped in two ways. The first one is to make and publish a debugger check list making it possible to identify whether important debugger features are included in the product. The check list can also be used by the debugger supplier to ensure that the product meets the market requests. The second way of helping the user is to define an Ada debugger test suite based on a set of pseudo Ada debugger commands. The two tools can be combined so that the test suite can ensure the achievement of the checklist. The user will then be able to check if the vital requirements to his project are actually met.

This paper presents a number of features for debugging Ada applications showing that quite a lot of features are needed in order to debug complex Ada programs. These Ada debug features can form the basis of a test suite or simply be used as a check list by the purchaser and developer of an Ada compiler system. It is discussed whether a standard for a development tool like a symbolic Ada debugger should be defined, and whether it is at all possible to define a basis for validation of symbolic Ada debuggers.

This paper strictly concerns symbolic debugging of programs at run time after they have been compiled and linked. Interpreters of the source code and tools like in-circuit emulators or logic analyzers are not the subject of this paper. A good symbolic (cross) debugger can, in most cases, replace these tools and provide a much richer environment.

2. The Functionality of a Symbolic Ada Debugger

A debugger is a development tool which controls and monitors the progress of an executing program. The debugger accomplishes its task through the definition and subsequent encounter of eventpoints in the program code. At such control points the debugger must provide display, modification and evaluation functionality with regard to program data.

By symbolic debugging is meant that it is possible to refer to program locations and data by use of the symbols defined in the program.

During compilation, the compiler saves the symbolic information needed for debugging, instantiations, inline expanded code, etc. The symbols include names of constants, variables, subprograms, packages, tasks, exceptions as well as operators and line numbers. When the program is compiled with the debug option address information about code (breakpoints) is generated. The information needed by the debugger consists of these symbols, address information, and the object files generated by the compiler.

3. The Validation Problem

When an Ada compiler is validated it means that a number of Ada aspects have been checked for conformity with the Ada Reference Manual by passing the ACVC test suite. However, this does not mean that all possible requirements have been checked. But, the validation test suite ensures a certain quality of the product. Therefore, the supplier must issue a quality control which should be based on a check list and additional tests.

The overall problem of validating Ada debuggers is that no standard for a symbolic Ada debugger has been defined. Not even the functionality of the symbolic Ada debuggers has been specified in a standard. The debuggers available on the market have a functionality ranging from being very simple in the sense of Ada debugging support to being quite advanced symbolic cross debuggers. The most advanced ones supports debugging of tasks by being able to break just one task at a time which enables the program to continue serving interrupts and to meet its deadlines.

An Ada debugger which is unable to break on Ada names, recognize Ada constructions, support Ada expressions, debug instantiations, exceptions, inline expanded programs, overloaded names and tasking can certainly not be said to be a full featured symbolic Ada debugger, and such debuggers are useful only when debugging very simple Ada applications. Better quality debuggers are needed as Ada debuggers with limited Ada support result in increased project risk.

This can be achieved by defining a set of Ada related debugger requirements. These requirements should be strictly Ada related. They should not be concerned with e.g. the user interface of the debugger. I think that an easy usable set of tools for evaluation of symbolic Ada debuggers should be made before setting up a set of Ada debugger requirements. Talking about Ada compilers, these tools would for example be the PIWG, ACEC and MICHIGAN evaluation test suites. In the area of symbolic Ada debuggers these tools could be a check list and a test suite which can easily be adapted to a particular debugger. If such requirements are to be made it would be a good idea to introduce them before the Ada9X compiler systems appear on the market, because the Ada related debugger requirements will increase with the additional language constructs.

4. An Ada Debugger Test Suite

The basic requirement to a debugger test suite is that it is possible to specify and supply the debugger with a debugging command sequence and collect the result of this sequence in a file which can be compared with a reference file containing the expected result of the command sequence.

This means that the debugger test suite could consist of:

- a number of Ada source files which can be compiled and linked
- a number of corresponding debugging command files written in a pseudo command language ready to be substituted by the debugger command language
- a number of reference files in text format describing the expected result

Due to the different command language syntaxes of the available Ada debuggers it is not possible to define a portable debugger test suite. But the test suite could be based on the philosophy of the Ada Compiler Validation Capability, ACVC.

It can be assumed that a serious Ada compiler system supplier has developed a regression test suite for their Ada debuggers. This implies that it is possible to define a debugger test suite and perform a partly computerized debugger evaluation which can be used for evaluation of the symbolic Ada debuggers on the market.

The main problem left is that there should not be a way in which tailoring can change the pass/fail of an applicable test. This problem can be solved if it is easy to locate the modifications of the test suites, and the validation suite is characterized by debugging a fixed set of Ada source texts.

The test suite should cover most, if not all, Ada related cases of the debugger knowing that the test suite cannot be a complete test of all possible inputs. The test suite should be easy to use, and the individual test must indicate pass or fail. Each test, or related sets of test, shall include comments stating the test objective, the test method and the expected results. The requirements for the test or the arguments from which the requirements are derived should also be stated in the comments to the test.

The test suite could be provided together with the debugger in order to prove the quality of the debugger, and as a predefined set up for white box testing at Ada level.

To my knowledge the only public debugger test suites are the ACEC 2.1 and the AES test suites. The ACEC 2.1 test suite is first of all a compiler test suite. The debugger part of the ACEC test suite is closely linked to the native Ada debugger from DIGITAL. As the functionality of this debugger is limited, the existence of a number of important features found in the other Ada debuggers is not verified.

5. The Basis for an Evaluation of a Symbolic Ada Debugger

The suggested features of Ada debugging described in the following are meant to be used as input to an Ada debugger check list or to create the basis for a Ada debugger test suite. For example documentation related things cannot be tested. Therefore, intestable things should be included in the check list. Performance and capacity tests have been defined. Those features which are common to debuggers in general are not described in this paper in order to limit the size of the paper. Such features could for example be the ability to step over, into and out of subprograms.

A multi-language debugger should be able to detect the language being debugged and allow the use of the corresponding set of debugger commands. The allowed debugger expressions should also be language sensitive. This ensures that special language constructs can be supported and that it feels natural to use the debugger depending on the language being debugged.

In the following sections the debugging evaluation subjects are divided into a number of groups:

- User Interface Subjects
    - Debugger Symbols and Subprograms
- Ada Level Debugging
    - Handling Eventpoints
    - Debugging Exceptions
    - Debugging Tasks
    - Debugging Instantiations
    - Debugging Inline Expanded Code
- Machine Level Debugging
- Error Handling
- Performance
- Capacity
- Debugger Implementation Subjects
- Debugging Multi-processes and Multi-processors
- Cross Environment Support

The user interface subjects, machine level debugging and other not language related groups should not be included in a validation suite ensuring the conformance of the debugger with an Ada debugging standard. But these groups are natural and important elements in a debugger evaluation suite, and therefore included in this section.

5.1 User Interface Subjects

It should be checked whether the window system supports:

- Both keyboard and pointing device input
- Interaction with the user in a separate window
- Recall of a number of debugger commands
- Machine instructions and source code displayed in separate windows
- Tasks to be debugged from different windows
- Scrolling up and down in the source code
- A program pointer visible in the source code for each task
- Breakpoints emphasized in the source code
- To switch from full symbolic debugging to machine instruction debugging at any time

5.1.1 Debugger Symbols and Subprograms

Debugger symbols and subprograms serve the purpose of improving the usability of the debugger. The debugger symbols are meant to represent expressions or to be used as abbreviations in debugger commands. It should be checked whether it is allowed to define, display and delete debugger symbols.

Example: Symbol definition

```
DEBUG> DEFINE SYMBOL SYM := A + 8
```

A symbol is here defined by assigning a value to it, and the type of the symbol depends on the type of the expression defining the symbol (integer, real, enumeration, boolean, task, access or address). A symbol can also be use for an abbreviation:

```
DEBUG> DEFINE SYMBOL SEC := "DISPLAY PACKAGE_TIME.SECONDS"
```

If debugger subprograms containing a number of debugger commands can be defined, it should also be checked whether support for execution of a debugger subprogram with a number of named parameters is provided. It should also be allowed to define, execute, display, and delete debugger subprograms.

Example: How to generate debugger test files by using debugger subprograms

```
DEBUG> DEFINE SUBPROGRAM LOG_ON(LOG_FILE) BEGIN
DEBUG>        DEFINE TARGET OUTPUT "LOG_FILE.TRG"
DEBUG>        SET LOG ON "LOG_FILE.DBG"
DEBUG>        DISPLAY DATE
DEBUG> END

DEBUG> DEFINE SUBPROGRAM LOG_OFF BEGIN
DEBUG>        SET LOG OFF
DEBUG>        DEFINE TARGET OUTPUT ""
DEBUG>        RESTART
DEBUG> END

DEBUG> EXECUTE LOG_ON(TEST1)
...           Issue the debugger commands of the test
DEBUG> EXECUTE LOG_OFF
```

Debugger commands which are read from a file or defined in a debugger subprogram need some features to control the flow of debugger commands. At least the following four constructions could be supported:

- Conditional execution	IF <condition> THEN <statements> {ELSIF <condition> THEN <statements>} ELSE <statements> END IF
- Repetition of commands	LOOP <statements> END LOOP
- Execute a conditional exit of a loop	EXIT [WHEN <condition>]
- Termination of a command file or subprogram	RETURN

5.2 Ada Level Debugging

A symbolic Ada debuggger is expected to be able to refer to all visible items according to the visibility rules of Ada. The debugger can be expected to handle debugging of the elaboration code of a program. The debugger should be able to display the value of an object independent of the type of the object. If it is a structured object every component is expected to be displayed, and they should then be displayed in terms of Ada names. A symbolic Ada debugger can also be expected to support the displaying of the value of an Ada expression. A symbolic Ada debugger may be able to handle the attributes defined by the Ada language. The capability of a symbolic Ada debugger with regard to these Ada debugging features should all be verified.

Due to optimizations of the generated code it may not always be possible to display the value of an object. In such cases the debugger should report a message to the user saying that optimizations have taken place making it impossible for the debugger to obtain the value, thus indicating that the user should debug at machine level in order to fully understand the generated code. But generally it should not be necessary to debug Ada code on machine level.

The Ada debuggers should be able to display the constraints for a given type or object. This could for example be a dynamic array passed to a procedure or subtypes defined with non-static constraints. This facility must be verified, too.

It should be checked whether the debugger supports display of the call chain of the current task. The call chain could include subprogram calls, accepts and packages.

A possible feature is that the debugger supports dumping the contents of the stack and the heap and is able to express the dump in terms of Ada names.

5.2.1 Handling Breakpoints and Tracepoints

The term eventpoints is used in the following when both breakpoints and tracepoints are referred.

Eventpoints in a symbolic Ada Debugger can in general be related to:

- Source code positions
- Ada names
- Exceptions
- Task events
- Physical memory addresses
- Object modifications

This means that the program/task will be suspended whenever one of these conditions occurs, and the debugger is then ready for input in case of a breakpoint. Therefore the debugger support of these items should be investigated.

Because a symbolic Ada Debugger is expected to support the Ada programming language, it should be checked whether eventpoints can be defined at the following source code positions:

- Main program entrance
- Declaration
- Statement

- Package
- Task
- Block statement
- Begin or end of a subprogram
- Elsif
- Select guard in a select statement
- Entry name
- Delay expression
- Instantiation
- Inline expanded subprogram
- Overloaded subprograms

The ability of setting eventpoints on declarations and statements irrespective of the result of an optimization should be investigated, because some users would like to have a feeling of where the breakpoints will be and can be set when stepping through the source code.

For subprograms, packages and tasks it should be checked whether the debugger supports dedicated eventpoints before and after the elaboration part and before the end of the program unit.

The capability of setting eventpoints, before the first accept statement, and before the End statement, should also be investigated. This feature could be achieved by using the name of the task entry. If there is more than one accept statement for the task entry in a task body it can be handled as an overloaded Ada name.

Example: Break on an accept statement

```
accept WAKEUP(MESSAGE : in DATA; LENGTH : in INTEGER) do
        COMMAND := CHECK_COMMAND(MESSAGE,LENGTH,STATUS);
end WAKEUP;

DEBUG> SET BREAKPOINT AT NOTE.WAKEUP
```

It should also be checked whether a breakpoint can be specified so that the accept statement is activated only when the event occurs in a certain task.

It should be checked whether the Ada debugger support:

- Conditional eventpoints on object values and task status
- Counted eventpoints
- Deletion of both all and single eventpoints
- Definition, activation, deactivation and deletion of a set of eventpoints

It should also be checked whether the debugger supports setting eventpoints at a specified source code position; e.g. at a line number and construct number.

Example: Setting a breakpoint at statement 2 in line 27 of unit CHECK.

```
DEBUG> SET BREAKPOINT AT CHECK #27 # 2

        23          A : INTEGER;
        24          B : CHARACTER;
        25
        26      BEGIN
B       27          A := CHARACTER'POS(B); B := CHARACTER'VAL(61)
        28      END CHECK;
```

5.2.2 Debugging Exceptions

In many cases real time systems are designed to run forever. The design of such systems requires the ability to handle those exceptions which will inevitable occur during the life time of the system. Exception handling is a part of Ada and therefore a symbolic Ada debugger must be expected to handle exceptions in a useful way.

Therefore, it should be checked whether the Ada debugger supports the definition of eventpoints in case any exception or a set of named exceptions is raised.

It should also be checked whether the debugger supports raising of both pre-defined and user-defined exceptions with the effect that the current task is resumed with the specified exception raised.

When an exception is not handled within a task or main program an event can be generated. It should be checked whether the debugger supports capturing such events. This feature can for example be used to detect deadlocks caused by exceptions.

If an exception is propagated out of a block containing dependent tasks, it would be useful with an eventpoint to examine the dependent tasks, especially with regard to a deadlock.

5.2.3 Debugging Tasks

Ada provides a high level facility for concurrent programming. This is called tasking. Several task debugging features can be identified, but the two basic task breaking modes are:

1) Break All Tasks: The entire program becomes suspended when a breakpoint is reached. This means that interrupts (including the timer interrupt) are not served until the broken task is resumed.

2) Break One Task: Only the task reaching the breakpoint is suspended while the remaining tasks continue their execution and interrupts are being served.

The Break One Task mode must naturally support that more than one task can be suspended at a breakpoint at the same time. It should be checked whether the Ada debugger supports these task debugging modes.

As implied above most debugger commands will refer to a single task. In this paper this task is called the current task, and it is this task that will execute when for example a STEP or a GO command is given.

It is interesting whether it is possible to specify the current task by using a debugger command in such a way that it is easy to swap between the breaked tasks. It should also be checked whether the user can select a non-breaked task for examination.

Support for changing the task characteristics of a set of tasks in a program could be provided by the debugger, although the use of these features might cause the program to behave in a non-intended manner. It should be checked whether the following task characteristics are available for modification:

- Suspend the executing tasks
- Resume a suspended task
- Abort a suspended or executing task
- Changing the priority of a task
- Modify the time slice value

The Ada language defines the following attributes specific to tasks which a symbolic Ada debugger may be able to display:

- T'Callable	It is FALSE when the task is completed or terminated.
- E'Count	Number of entry calls presently queued on the task entry.
- T'Terminated	TRUE if the task is terminated.
- T'Storage_size	Number of storage units reserved for each activation of a task.
- T'Size	Number of bits used to hold the task object.
- T'Address	Address of the local copy of the task.

A number of task events can be used to set breakpoints and tracepoints in tasks. A general feature would be the possibility to specify a set of tasks or task types to indicate that the eventpoints should be activated only when the event occurs in the specified tasks.

It should, of course, be checked whether it is possible to monitor the execution of communicating tasks by setting eventpoints on entry calls and accept statements. The functionality in connection with communicating tasks could be the possibility to set breakpoints or tracepoints:

- Immediately before the rendezvous is initiated.
- Before the first statement in the accept statement.
- After the statement list in the accept statement.

The debugger could also be expected to handle a number of task initialization requirements. The following task initializations events should occur before and when a task is about to run:

- A **start of activation event** occurring before the elaboration of the first declaration in the task body.
- An **end of activation event** occurring before the BEGIN statement in the task body.
- A **creation event** occurring when a task is created by a declaration of a task object or by an allocator.
- An **activation event** occurring in a task immediately before it starts the activation of a number of created tasks.

A number of task termination events could also be present as debugger eventpoints:

- A **normal completion event** occurring before the completion of a task (before the END statement in the task body).
- An **exception event** occurring when a task is terminated due to an exception.
- An **abort event** occurring when a task is terminated due to an abort.
- A **termination event** occurring when a task is terminated either normally, by abort, or by exception.

A preempted event occurring when a task is being preempted could also be an available debugger eventpoint.

Whether the debugger provides these task initialization and termination features should be checked along with the ability to have an event occurring when a task is leaving a block or body containing tasks. The last feature is important in order to detect deadlocks.

As regards combined task and exception events, a block-exit by exception event could occur when an exception is propagated out of a block containing dependent tasks. A completion by exception event occurring when an exception is not handled within a task or main program is also useful. The rendezvous exception event should occur just before an exception is propagated out of a rendezvous. It should be checked whether the debugger provides support for these combined task and exception events.

The capability with regard to displaying task information should also be investigated. It should in this connection be checked whether it is possible to select a list of tasks, all the tasks, the suspended tasks or the breaked tasks to be displayed. It should be checked whether the following task information can be displayed:

- Object name
- The current state of a task
- Whether it is suspended, breaked or aborted
- The corresponding task type
- The current priority of the task
- The master or creator of the specified task
- Task dependencies
- Entry queues
- The stack size and location
- Rendezvous and called entries

5.2.4 Debugging Instantiations

Subprograms and packages in Ada can be generic. An instantiation with a set of actual parameters of a generic subprogram or package can be used like any other subprogram or package. The great advantage of this generic facility is that a subprogram or package must not be written for each element type it can be used with, simplifying a tedious aspect of other programming languages. It is important to be able to ensure that all aspects of a generic body work as expected, and therefore the symbolic Ada debugger should support debugging of instantiations.

It should be checked that a breakpoint in a generic body causes a break in all its instantiations. A breakpoint in the instantiation should on the other hand only cause the program to break in the particular instantiation. How easy it is for the Ada debugger to support the features depends on whether the compiler support generics by expansion or by code sharing.

5.2.5 Debugging Inline Expanded Code

PRAGMA inline is defined in the Ada Reference Manual and a symbolic Ada debugger should therefore be able to support debugging of inline expanded subprograms.

When setting breakpoints in inline expanded subprograms it should be checked whether the debugger provides additional information to specify which calls of the subprogram should be affected, for example by including the source code position of the call.

Example: Setting breakpoints in not fully inline expanded programs.

```
13          FUNCTION FAC(I : INTEGER) RETURN INTEGER IS
14          BEGIN
15                IF I = 0 THEN
16                      RETURN 1;
17                ELSE
18                      RETURN I * FAC(I-1);
19                END IF;
20          END FAC;
21
22          PRAGMA INLINE(FAC);
23      BEGIN
24          RES := FAC(10);
```

It is legal to set a breakpoint in line 15, because FAC is recursive and can therefore not be fully inline expanded:

DEBUG> SET BREAKPOINT AT FAC #15

However, part of the function is expanded at each call, therefore a breakpoint in inline expanded code could look like:

DEBUG> SET BREAKPOINT AT MAIN #24 INLINE FAC #15

5.3 Machine Level Debugging

Machine code debugging may be needed to examine machine code insertions and routines written in assembler. It is also important to be able to display and modify the memory and the registers when a program is being investigated.

It should be checked whether the debugger supports alignment of the source code and the machine code windows to each other in order to swap between Ada and machine level debugging.

It should be checked whether the debugger supports display of the:

- Disassembly of the memory
- Physical address of a source text position
- Physical address of an object by using the ADDRESS attribute
- Memory layout, start address and size of an object
- Memory dump
- CPU registers

It should be checked whether the debugger supports modifications of the:

- Memory
- Stacks and the heap
- CPU registers

5.4 Error Handling

The debugger should be checked with regard to the generation of error messages when:

- Using an incorrect debugger command syntax
- Referring to non-existent source lines
- Referring to non-existent symbols

The evaluation criteria for accuracy and helpfulness of these error messages could be the same as for the Ada Compiler Systems (The B-tests of ACVC).

It should be checked whether the debugger is capable of handling the following error situations:

- Errors generated while evaluating Ada expressions
- Failure of the host-target communication line during a debugging session

5.5 Performance

The timing figures for debugging operations can be determined by letting a specially designed test program write the current time while debugger commands are supplied from a file.

It should be verified that the following operations take place right after the commands are issued:

- Displaying source text
- Single stepping
- Displaying the contents of Ada objects
- Displaying the memory content
- Open and close debug windows

The timing differences between a program compiled with and without the compiler debug option enabled could also be measured. The load time can be measured in order to select proper communication support.

5.6 Capacity

It should be checked that no unreasonably low limits exist owing to the size of the program being debugged. Therefore, a number of tests should be made verifying that quite a number of eventpoints can be defined. Capacity test programs showing that a large number of tasks can be monitored should be made.

Test programs which investigate that the debugger can handle large programs in terms of source lines should also be made as part of a debugger evaluation.

5.7 Debugger Implementation Subjects

Certain debuggers may use supplementary instructions inserted in the object code (instrumented code) to achieve its required functionality. This may change the real-time behaviour of the program, and it should therefore be verified whether the code is instrumented.

When large applications are to be debugged it should be verified that it does not take minutes to start a debugging session. This indicates how the symbol information is collected during startup of a debug session and the time for loading.

It should be checked whether the development system includes debugger support for:

- Two debugging sessions using the same Program Library.
- Debugging a program while its units are compiled.
- Interaction with the services of the underlaying operating system.
- Interface with an editor so that the user may enter the editor from the debugger, modify source, recompile, relink, and restart with the new version, with the same set of debugger commands.
- Interface with an editor so that the user may enter the editor from the debugger and have the editor cursor positioned in the same place.

Some Ada debuggers are able to run in sequential mode without windows and in batch mode, taking its input from a file. Batch mode capability is important when setting up a regression test suite for the debugger. Therefore, suppliers with a regression test suite will be able to collect the debugger commands in a file forming a debug script ready to be executed.

5.8 Debugging Multi-processes and Multi-processors

It should be checked whether the debugger supports the two dimensional concepts of debugging task and processes when the operation system supports multi-processes.

As regards cross debuggers, it should be checked whether the debugger is capable of supporting debugging of several target boards simultaneously.

It should be investigated whether the debugger (and the Run Time System) supports a program which has its tasks executing on more that one processor. This is interesting because, in this situation, the tasks may communicate using a common bus.

5.9 Cross Environment Support

This section concerns cross debugger features. Cross debugger commands given by the user are processed by the debugger running on the host and usually broken down into sequences of basic commands which are sent to the Debug Monitor situated on the target board.

Example: The Cross Debugging Environment

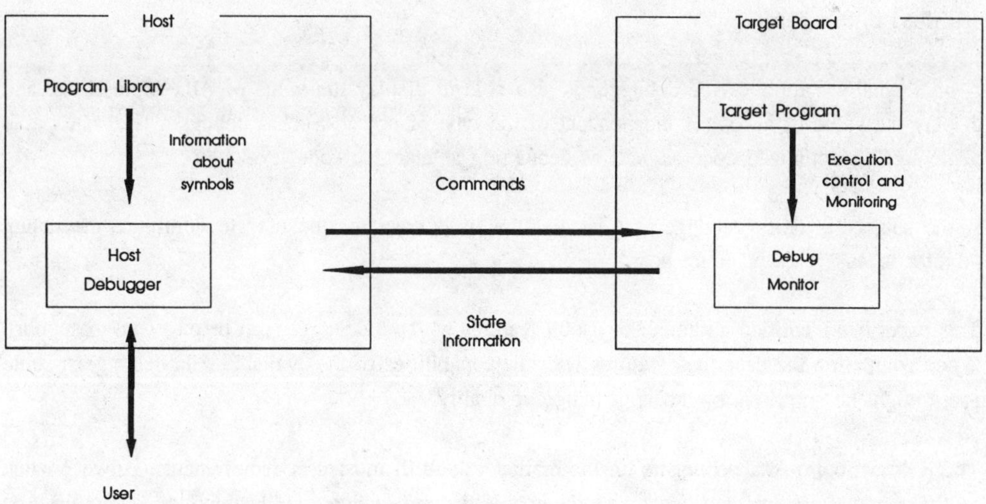

The Debug Monitor can be said to interact with the debugger running on the host while it monitors and controls the user program running on the target board.

The Debug Monitor, which also loads the program from the host to the target board, is normally PROMed on the target board. It must be well-documented how much RAM the debug monitor is using in order to be able to download applications correctly. The size of the Debug Monitor should also be documented in order for the user to select a target board and decide the memory layout of the firmware.

Furthermore, the communication line requirements must be well-documented so that the communication devices can be configured correctly.

It is important that the Debug Monitor is designed in such a way that it can be configured for those target boards containing the microprocessor for which the code is generated. This means that the modules which have to be modified must:

- be user accessible
- be small
- have a simple functionality
- be well-documented

6. Conclusion

I conclude that a full featured symbolic Ada debugger must at least provide debugging capabilities with regard to debugging tasks, packages, exceptions, instantiations, inline expanded code, etc. as described in this paper.

A high quality symbolic Ada debugger is also able to display the value of Ada expressions, and display the value of an object independent of the type of object. Such a debugger is also capable of debugging optimized code as well as debugging at machine code level.

If the subject is cross debuggers, it is vital that it is easy for the user to configure the debug monitor to any relevant target board.

This paper has identified a number of useful features which a debugger can be expected to support. When comparing the described features with the capabilities of the available Ada debuggers, some users might be surprised by the large range of quality.

The best symbolic Ada debuggers on the market can fulfil most user requirements. However, due to the productivity improvements and the many features which a full supported symbolic Ada debugger is expected to provide, it can be concluded that it is important to evaluate the Ada debuggers.

It is concluded that it is more important with debugger evaluation tools than defining a set of Ada debugger requirements, because the best symbolic Ada debuggers fulfil the user requirements. The number of Ada features which a debugger can be expected to support indicate that it is relevant with an Ada debugger validation suite.

It is suggested that the tools used in order to evaluate a symbolic Ada debugger are a checklist and a debugger test suite. The debugger features identified are meant to be included in an evaluation checklist, but they can also form the basis for a debugger test suite.

It is suggested that the debugger test suite should be based on a test script available to anyone. It is also suggested that a generic debugger test suite should be based on a pseudo debugger command language easy for anyone familiar with debuggers to adapt to their symbolic Ada debugger.

The work in setting up the debugger test suite is a time consuming task due to the number of features which should be checked. Therefore, the next task in creating this debugger test suite will be to form a special debugger interest group.

Anyway, I hope that this paper has convinced you that a symbolic Ada debugger is an important component of an Ada compiler system and that it, therefore, should be evaluated as carefully as the Ada compiler.

References

Symbolic Debugging of Ada in Embedded Environments,
B. Berland and H.J.H. Larsen, DDC International A/S, 1991

DACS VAX/VMS to 680x0 Bare Symbolic Ada Cross Debugger, User's Guide,
DDC International A/S, September 1991

DACS VAX/VMS to 80x86 Bare Symbolic Ada Cross Debugger, User's Guide,
DDC International A/S, June 1991

DACS VAX/VMS to 80860 Bare Symbolic Ada Cross Debugger, User's Guide,
DDC International A/s, September 1991

Symbolic Debugging System for MIPS R3000, User's Guide, DDC-Inter, Inc.,
October 1991

Developing Ada Programs on VAX/VMS, Digital Equipment Corporation, 1985
Ada Evaluation, Reader's Guide, BSI Quality Assurance, 1989

Technical Operating Report, User's & Reader's Guides, Ada Compiler Evaluation Capability (ACEC), Release 2.0, 1990

Reference Manual for the Ada Programming Language,
ANSI/MIL-STD 1815A, January 1983

SWG APSE Test Support Toolset

(Assessment of the CAIS-A Interface Set)

W. Treurniet

TNO Physics and Electronics Laboratory

P.O. Box 96864, 2509 JG The Hague, The Netherlands

Email: Willem.Treurniet@fel.tno.nl

1. INTRODUCTION

1.1 Project Context

One of the participants in the NATO Ada Programming Support Environment (APSE) project is the Netherlands Ministry of Defense. The Royal Netherlands Army assigned the development of one of the APSE tools (the Test Support Toolset (TST)) to the Physics and Electronics Laboratory of the Netherlands organization for applied scientific research (TNO FEL).

The main goal of the APSE project is to investigate the feasibility of building a portable APSE using Interface Set technology.

1.2 Goal and structure of the Paper

The objective of this paper is to assess the facilities of the APSE and the underlying Interface Set with respect to portability and integration of the environment. For this assessment our experience in developing the TST will be used.

The paper is structured as follows. First we will discuss two well-known models in this area: the APSE model described in [1] and the ECMA reference model desicribed in [2]. After that we will discuss the APSE implementation the TST is part of. Special attention will be given to the Interface Set constituting the framework of this APSE. In the next part we will describe the requirements of the TST and how the TST has been implemented and integrated in the APSE. After the actual assessment we will end with some concluding remarks.

2. CASE TECHNOLOGY - AN OVERVIEW

Software systems have become more and more complex. The number of requirements and constraints systems are to meet tend to increase, as well as the size of the system development teams. Usage of automated tools supporting system development is one of the ways to cope with the increasing complexity. By helping to manage this complexity, development tools support development teams in achieving quality and productivity.

Examples of tools are: tools supporting analysis of requirements, tools supporting system design, (language sensitive) editors, code management systems, compilers, linkers, debuggers, quality assurance support tools, project management tools, and cost estimation tools.

The next logical step is to integrate a useful set of tools. Tool integration has several benefits. If the user interfaces of the tools are integrated, the presentation and usage of all tools is the same. A user being familiar with one of the tools can soon become familiar with another. If the tools work on the same dataspace, conversion or transition of data can be avoided, and work can be done more efficiently. When a set of tools is fully integrated, the borders between the tools disappear. The toolset presents itself to the user as one tool. A job to be done with such a toolset is no longer a series of tool invocations. Such a tool is rather task-oriented than tool-oriented.

2.1 APSE model

The Stoneman report ([1]) describes an architectural model of an Ada Programming Support Environment (APSE). According to this report, an environment consists of three layers: a Kernel APSE (KAPSE), a Minimal APSE (MAPSE) and a number of other tools that can eventually be added (figure 1).

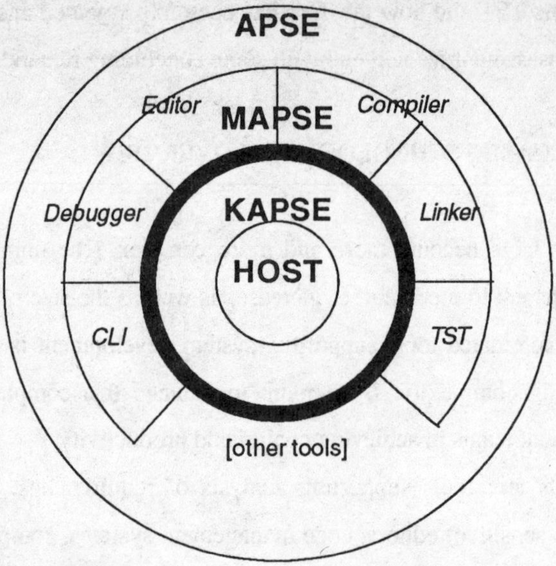

Figure 1: The APSE model

The KAPSE layer provides host and operating system independent data management, process control, and interprocess communication services. The KAPSE is the only host and operating system dependent part of the environment. Current examples of KAPSEs are CAIS-A and ECMA PCTE.

The MAPSE consists of a minimal set of tools necessary for software development. A MAPSE should contain for example a compilation system, an editor and a command interpreter. This layer must be portable as much as possible.

A MAPSE can eventually be extended by other tools like project management tools and quality assurance tools. In this way it is possible to extent the APSE to an environment supporting all activities of the life-cycle of a product.

2.2 ECMA reference model

Functionality supporting integration and portability of an environment is concentrated in the framework[1] of that environment. A framework reference model can be helpful to assess such a

1 In this paper 'framework', 'interface set', and 'KAPSE' are used as synonyms.

framework with respect to support of integration and portability. The APSE model however emphasizes the tools in the environment rather that the framework of the environment. The tools within the environment are described more differentiated. Distinction is made between tools constituting the MAPSE and the other tools for example.

A model that is complementary to the APSE model is the Reference model for Frameworks of Computer-assisted Software Engineering Environments of the European Computer Manufacturers Association (ECMA) ([2])[2]. Figure 2 (the "Toaster Diagram") shows the overall structure of the reference model.

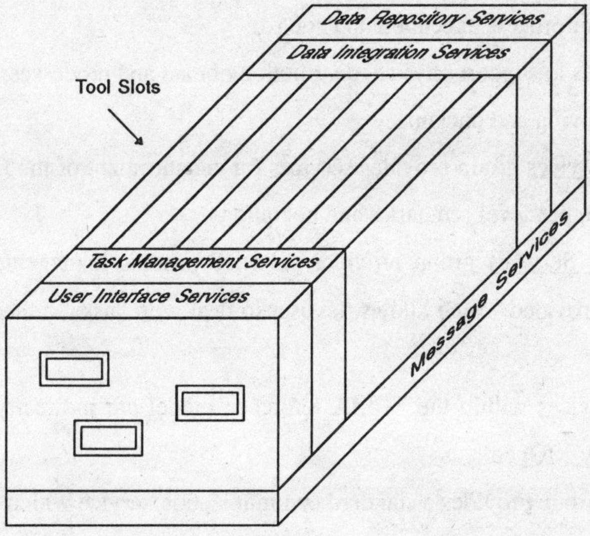

Figure 2: The ECMA reference model ("Toaster Diagram")

This reference model models the framework in which tools can be embedded. In general terms such a framework corresponds with the KAPSE in the APSE model. According to [2] the ECMA reference model should be suitable for describing, comparing, and contrasting existing

2 A new version of this model is currently under development with the (US) National Institute of Standards and Technology.

and proposed environment frameworks. In this paper we will use the reference model to assess a framework.

In the ECMA reference model, the framework consists of five groups of services: Data Repository Services, Data Integration Services, Task Management Services, User Interface Services, and Message Services. Some of these groups also enable various kinds of integration to be discussed: presentation integration (User Interface Services); control integration (Task Management Services plus the Message Services); and data integration (Data Repository plus Data Integration Services).

The Data Repository Services group provides services for:

- management of data entities and relationships among them;
- basic support for process execution and control;
- location services to support physical distribution of data and processes;
- support of archiving and backup.

The Data Integration Services group provides services for enhancement of the Data Repository Services by providing higher-level semantics and operations.

The Task Management Services group provides software process management services. A layer of abstraction is provided which allows the user to deal with 'tasks' rather than 'series of tool invocations'.

The User Interface Services within the ECMA reference model are indirectly based upon a framework developed by X/Open.

The Message Services group provides a standard communication service which can be used for inter-tool and inter-service communication.

3. THE SWG APSE

An example of an integrated set of tools supporting software development is the SWG APSE (Ada Programming Support Environment)[3]. The SWG APSE project has two important goals.

---

3 Work on the SWG APSE was initiated by a Statement of Intent signed by the National Armaments Directors of several NATO nations for a cooperative program to develop an initial capability for an APSE. The work was formalized by a Memorandum of Understanding (MOU) and a Special Working Group (SWG) was established to manage the work.

Firstly, the project is to show that it is possible to develop a portable APSE. In this context there are two aspects of portability. The PSE has to support both interoperability[4] and transportability[5]. Secondly, the project has to result in a usable APSE.

The SWG APSE contains nine tools ([7]): Command Language Interpreter, Requirements Analyzer, Syntax Directed Editor, Compiler, Symbolic Debugger, Linker, Loader, Test Support Toolset, and Version Controller. The Command Language Interpreter (CLI) consists of two parts. The actual CLI processes statements expressed in the SWG APSE Command Language. The second part is a common user interface for all of the SWG APSE tools.

3.1 General Requirements

The most important requirement of the SWG APSE in the context of this paper is: All tools in the SWG APSE must use the services provided by the SWG Common APSE Interface Set (CAIS) Implementation. Any deviation must be reviewed by the Tools and Integration Review Board. In [3] this general statement is further elaborated. The APSE shall be Open Ended (it shall permit improvements, updates and replacement of tools), User Helpful, Rehostable, Portable (Operating System and hardware dependencies shall be isolated in CAIS as much as possible), Robust, Usable, Maintainable, Secure, and Integrated.

The purpose of the last elaboration is to show that the tools will work in a well coordinated way. That means that all tools must communicate with the underlying operating system and with each other through the SWG CAIS as much as possible.

3.2 CAIS-A

In the SWG APSE the SWG CAIS ([5], [6]) forms the KAPSE. The SWG CAIS is an implementation of CAIS-A. According to [4] the goal of the CAIS-A is to promote

---

4 In [4] *interoperability* is defined as the ability of APSEs to exchange database objects and their relationships in forms usable by tools and user programs without conversion.

5 In [4] *transportability* of an APSE tool is defined as the ability of the tool to be installed on a different Kernel Ada Programming Support Environment (KAPSE); the tool must perform with the same functionality in both APSEs. Transportability is measured in the degree to which this installation can be accomplished without reprogramming. Portability and transferability are commonly used synonyms for transportability.

interoperability and transportability. CAIS-A is intended to provide the transportability interfaces most often required by common software development tools. It standardizes those tool-to-tool interfaces that are most crucial for tool portability. Other less frequently used or inherently host-dependent interfaces must complement CAIS-A. For example: the SWG CAIS implementation of CAIS-A provides a package SWG_CAIS_HOST_TARGET_IO for communication with a target system, not included in CAIS-A.

CAIS-A includes the following interface areas:

- Node Model - entity relationship model in which CAIS entities are defined and manipulated;
- Process - process and transaction services;
- Input and Output - input, output, device control, interprocess communication services within and between CAIS-A instances;
- Status Management - allows programs to obtain detailed status and exception information.

Let us try to relate CAIS-A to the reference model.

Recall that the ECMA reference model identifies five groups of services provided by an environment framework: Data Repository Services, Data Integration Services, Task Management Services, User Interface Services, and Message Services. The Data Repository Services group is fully covered by CAIS-A.

The Data Integration Services group is partly covered by CAIS-A. The services in this group are sub-divided as follows:

- versioning;
- configuration management;
- query;
- metadata (data about data);
- state-monitoring (database state and state transformations);
- sub-environment (limiting the view of an application);
- data interchange (between environment frameworks).

Of these sub-groups only the metadata, sub-environment and data interchange services are (to a certain extent) supported by CAIS-A.

The Task Management Services group isn't supported at all by CAIS-A.

CAIS-A provides very low-level User Interface Services. These services cannot provide a reasonable extent of presentation integration. A common user interface (APSE_MMI) provided by the Command Language Interpreter tool of the SWG APSE resolves the lack of User Interface Services with the KAPSE.

The Message Services group is partly supported. Inter-tool communication is possible. There is no central part, however, where tools can be registrated or where tools can register their interest in certain messages. The coupling between tools is very tight and inflexible.

4. TEST SUPPORT TOOLSET - REQUIREMENTS

One of the tools integrated in the SWG APSE is the Test Support Toolset (TST, [8]). The TST assists in testing Ada applications throughout all levels, i.e. from unit testing up to integration and acceptance testing. The TST supports several dynamic testing techniques such as performance, coverage, assertion, and prediction analysis. In addition the TST provides functions to generate stubs, create test drivers and simulators. They create an environment for the software item under test. Moreover, functions to maintain a test database and to generate test reports are offered.

An important requirement of the TST is already mentioned in section 3.1: the TST shall be portable as much as possible, using services provided by the SWG CAIS.

Testing can be defined as the process of determining whether a program behaves in accordance with a predefined reference model. Four different categories of testing tools can be identified ([11]):

1. Static analysis tools (testing code without actually executing it);
2. Dynamic analysis tools (testing code by executing it);
3. Test data generation tools;
4. Test data management tools.

The Test Support Toolset that is part of the SWG APSE was required to be a combination of two forms of test tools: a dynamic analysis tool with data management facilities.

Two categories of dynamic analysis techniques can be distinguished. Firstly, we can distinguish black box testing, i.e. testing of the functional specification of a piece of software to ensure that, given certain inputs, the expected outputs are generated. Secondly, we can distinguish white box testing i.e. testing based on a detailed knowledge of the structure of a program.

The SWG APSE Test Support Toolset is required to provide the following facilities:

a. coverage and timing analysis facilities (white box testing);

b. assertion analysis facilities (white box testing);

c. prediction analysis (black box testing)

d. stub generation facilities (permitting analysis of syntactically correct but incomplete code).

e. test bed generation facilities (e.g. simulation of a target-specific environment);

f. test driver generation facilities

The testing methodology supported by the TST consists of four steps:

1. Design test - a test design specifies the details of the test approach for a set of software features. The purpose of the test design stage is to select the testing techniques associated with the test approach and to generate an executable test item out of the software item indicated on the test plan.
2. Create test - a test consists of a set of test cases and a set of test procedures. The purpose of the test creation stage is to compose tests out of newly entered data and previously defined test cases and test procedures.
3. Execute test - the purpose of the test execution stage is to execute a test and to collect the generated output.
4. Evaluate test - the purpose of the test evaluation stage is to analyze and present the collected test results.

5. TEST SUPPORT TOOLSET - IMPLEMENTATION AND INTEGRATION

5.1 Architecture

The input of the TST is an Ada program library containing the software items under test. The program library contains both the library units and source code of the software items. Some parts of the TST use the source code of the software. Other parts extract structural information of the software items using an intermediate representation of it. This so called DIANA ([9]) representation is also stored in the program library.

5.1.1 System architecture

The Test Support Toolset consists of four major parts, controlled by a main unit ([10], figure 3). The first part is the user interface part (Manage_Dialogue). The user interface is a window oriented interface using the APSE_MMI window manager. This window manager is a character oriented window manager, developed within the SWG APSE project as part of the Command Language Interpreter (refer to section 5.2). The second part is a database manager (Manage_Database). This part provides interfaces to the test database. This unit intends to hide the implementation details of the database. The third part consists of the implementation of the test facilities of the TST (Apply_Test_Techniques). The test techniques contained in this part can be started by the main unit of the TST. After that they will run under user control. Commands issued by the user result in events generated by the user interface intended for the application program. The event dispatcher part (Dispatch_Events), the fourth and last major part, routes the generated events to the application parts they were meant for.

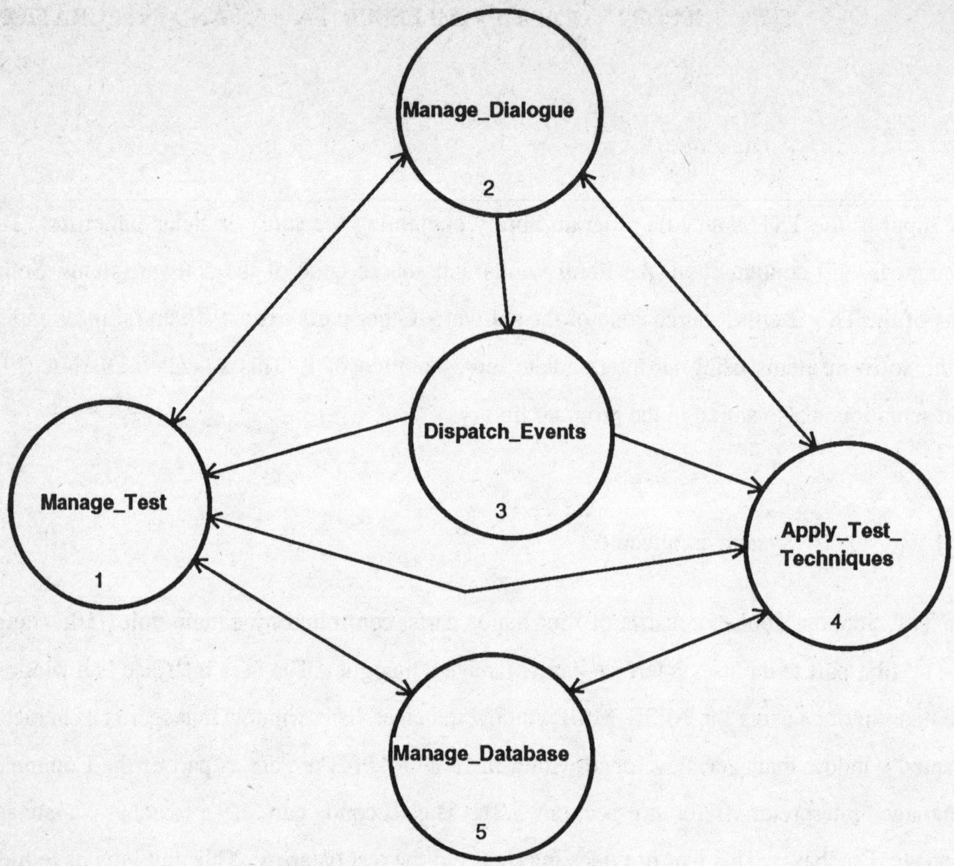

Figure 3: High level architecture of the TST

5.1.2 Conceptual model of the test database

The persistent data generated by and with use of the Test Support Toolset is stored in a test database (figure 4). The structure of the database reflects the testing methodology the TST supports.

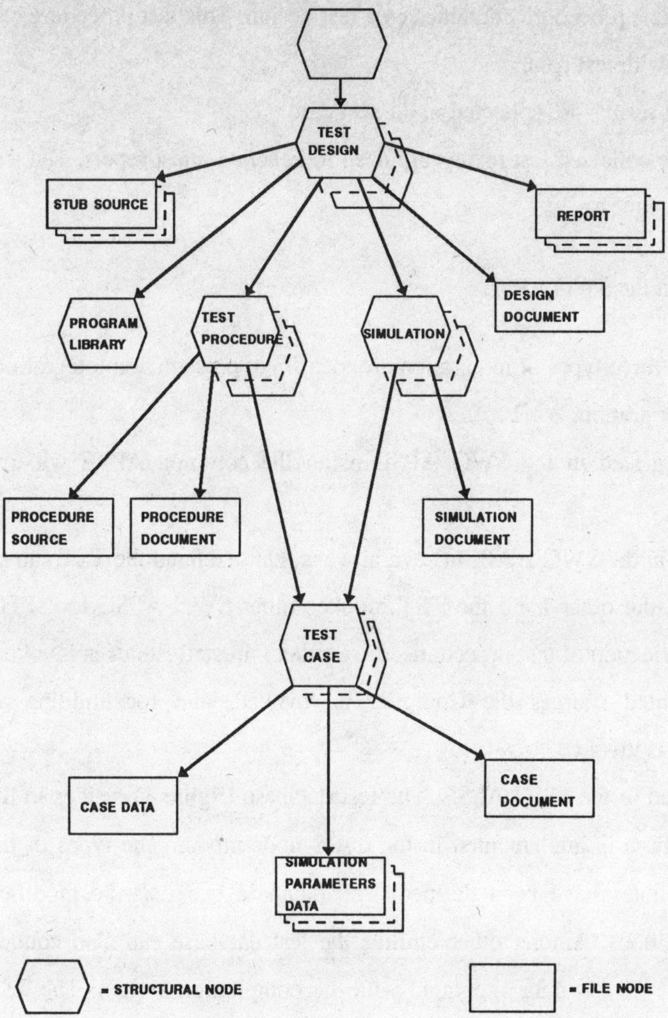

Figure 4: Conceptual model of the test database

Each test design results in a test design in the test database. Within each test design one or more generated simulators can be contained. Beside these simulators the generated test driver, the instrumented Ada source code (coverage- and performance analysis), the asserted source code (assertion analysis), and the generated stubs are contained in the test design. After generation the source code will be compiled in an Ada program library contained in the test design.

Each test creation results in a test procedure contained in a test design. This test procedure can contain one or more test cases with test data.
During a test execution the test results are collected in the test case.
In the test evaluation phase the collected test results are used to generate a test report. The test reports are stored in the test design.

5.2 Integration in the SWG APSE

In the ECMA reference model three types of integration are identified: presentation integration, control integration and data integration.
The TST is presentation integrated in the SWG APSE using the common APSE window manager (refer to chapter 3).
The TST is control integrated in the SWG APSE in several ways. On one hand the TST can be invoked by the CLI tool. On the other hand the TST invokes other SWG APSE tools. For example: for creation or modification of test procedures the Syntax Directed Editor is invoked, for compilation of instrumented sources the Compiler is invoked, and for building an executable test item the linker is invoked.
The TST is also data integrated in the SWG APSE. The test database (figure 4) resides in the CAIS database. The test database is implemented in the CAIS node model. The types of the nodes, relationships and attributes have been defined. The database can only be modified according to these type definitions. Among other entities the test database can also contain program libraries. As such the TST is data integrated with the compilation system. The TST can access the internal structure of the library (to extract sources or dependency information) by using a DIANA interface to the library structure.

6. ASSESSMENT

In the previous part of the paper, we discussed the APSE, an APSE implementation (SWG APSE), a KAPSE (CAIS-A), a KAPSE implementation (SWG CAIS), and one of the tools contained in the SWG APSE (the Test Support Toolset). In this part we will assess the SWG APSE and its kernel with respect to integration, portability, and support for it.

6.1 Integration

Presentation Integration, nor Control Integration, nor Data Integration of a tool within the APSE is a trivial job. In case of the TST the least complex type of integration was Presentation Integration, although CAIS-A only provides a window oriented TEXT_IO-like package for this type of integration. This is related to the development path we choose. We started developing the TST as a VMS tool. A VMS based implementation of the common APSE window manager was used for the user interface. As far as that goes, porting the TST to the APSE was practically a matter of recompilation.

For Control Integration CAIS-A only provides process invocation primitives. This type of integration within the APSE is indeed rather primitive. Tools are only Control Integrated by invoking each other. For this purpose an Ada package is available. Including this package in the context clause, the various parts of the APSE can be invoked just like you can do it from the desktop. Dynamic integration of tools is only possible at the desktop.

Data Integration is achieved mostly using 'rough' SWG CAIS facilities. For this purpose the TST maintains private definitions of nodes (entities), relationships and attributes. Also some common APSE definitions (to be shared among tools) can be used. Conceptually the facilities provided by CAIS-A for this purpose appeared to be sufficient (recall that the Data Repository Services group of the ECMA reference model is fully covered by CAIS-A). However, the Database Definition Language the SWG CAIS implementation provides is a very primitive and error-prone language. Beside usage of CAIS-A facilities, Data Integration with the compilation system is achieved using a DIANA interface to the internals of the Ada libraries.

It appeared to be rather hard to integrate a set of tools that are under development. One of the means we used for this purpose is an Interface Control Document. It is very important for such a document to be kept up to date.

6.2 Portability

The SWG APSE TST doesn't contain any host or operating system dependencies. From that point of view the tool is fully portable. However, the tool does contain some SWG CAIS implementation dependencies instead.

In section 3.2 we mentioned that less frequently used or inherently host-dependent interfaces must complement CAIS-A. The SWG CAIS implementation contains such inherently host-dependent parts. Recall that for communication with a target system a package SWG_CAIS_HOST_TARGET_IO has been included.

A second SWG CAIS implementation dependency is caused by the Database Definition Language. This language doesn't belong to CAIS-A. So when you try to port the TST to another CAIS-A implementation you have to translate the scripts written in the SWG CAIS Database Definition Language.

Finally, the level of portability of the TST highly depends on the level of portability of the tools invoked by the TST. For example: it is obvious that a compilation system is highly host dependent. The TST invokes (parts of) a compilation system. The level of portability of the TST depends on the level of portability of the compilation system.

The SWG CAIS has been hosted to VAX/VMS and to SUN-3/UNIX. Our first experience is that the TST runs on both implementations without changing the code. The SUN version of the TST is still under test, however.

7. CONCLUSIONS

The following conclusions can be drawn from the previous discussion:

- CAIS-A covers only a small part of the framework functionality modelled in the ECMA reference model. Practically, only Data Integration is supported by CAIS-A;
- Despite of this, it appears to be possible to build a Test Support Toolset (as part of an APSE) on top of it with no host, or operating system dependencies. The integration of this tool within the APSE is primitive and is practically restricted to Data Integration. This type of integration already appears to provide much benefit;
- Dependency on the CAIS-A implementation used is introduced instead of host and operating system dependency. This stems from the fact that CAIS-A does not intent to shield the host and the underlying operating system fully. Within an APSE implementation, specific, non CAIS-A functionality may be added to the KAPSE;
- Another fact that moderates tool portability is the fact that, when a tool invokes another tool, portability of the tool depends on the portability of the invoked tool;

8. REFERENCES

[1] Requirements for Ada Programming Support Environments, STONEMAN, United States Department of Defense, February 1980

[2] European Computer Manufacturers Association, A Reference Model for Frameworks of Computer-assisted Software Engineering Environments, ECMA, December 1990

[3] NATO Special Working Group on APSEs, NATO SWG APSE REQUIREMENTS version 1, December 1987

[4] Military Standard, Common Ada Programming Support Environment (APSE) Interface Set (CAIS), Revision A, MIL-STD-1883A, United States Department of Defense (Ada Joint Program Office), 1989

[5] VAX/VMS SWG APSE CAIS User and Installation Manual (version 5.5E), August 1991

[6] Common APSE Interface Set (CAIS) Proposed DOD-STD-1838A VAX/VMS CAIS Implementation Design Document, February 1990

[7] NATO Special Working Group on APSEs, NATO SWG APSE SYSTEM SPECIFICATION (NATO-SWG-APSE:TISO:SPC:001), October 1990

[8] Canjels, Ir. I. et al., Test Support Toolset Requirements Specification (NATO-SWG-APSE:TST:SRS:0001), September 1989

[9] Goos, Wulf, Evans and Butler, DIANA An Intermediate Language for Ada (revised version), Springer-Verlag 1983

[10] Canjels, Ir. I. et al., Test Support Toolset Design Description Information (NATO-SWG-APSE:TST:DDI:0001), April 1989

[11] SWG APSE Evaluation Document

COMPILATION INTEGRATION: A SOLUTION FOR THE CHALLENGE OF DEVELOPING AND REUSING ADA SOFTWARE ON DIFFERENT PLATFORMS

Thanh-Nu Do
Rational
16, rue Henri Régnault
La Défense 6
F-92411 Courbevoie Cedex
Tel: 33(1)47.17.41.77
Email: tdo@rational.com
Fax: 33(1)47.17.41.55

1. INTRODUCTION

With Ada already around so long that its first major standardization revision is imminent, and with major application projects under way which will well reach into the next century, practical software engineering challenges replace the often too theoretical discussions around Ada in the past. Today Ada users have made their first experience and successfully terminated their first major projects. Some have even built a business on using Ada in specific application domains. In such cases where a capital of existing software has been developed and is to be put to fruitful use, the evolution of computer systems and hardware often leads to one or both of the following situations:

- the software is reused for different targets than its original one,
- the software is reused or adapted to deliver more complex software systems on heterogeneous platforms.

Thanks to Ada's excellent support for reusability and portability which has been presented many times at Ada conferences, an organization can cope with these situations much better in the case of Ada software than in the case of software developed in any other language. However, the task is far from being without challenges. There is no single Ada compilation system today which offers code generation for all possible targets. In fact, most of the Ada compiler vendors concentrate on a well-chosen number of target architectures. This means that users are generally confronted with differences in compilation and library systems as well as subtle discrepancies between the results of host and target code generation when their Ada business grows and their applications spread on many platforms.

In this article we present a proven solution to the problem of managing the development of Ada software for any variety of targets. This solution is a universal host approach based on the integration of any Ada compiler. The integration described is not only a tool integration in a framework IPSE, merely providing a common user interface and management services, but it is a true integration in which the host has knowledge of the behavior of the foreign compiler integrated, and exploits this knowledge to provide an effective answer to the challenges mentioned.

Section 2 sets the stage with the description of a concrete user situation. In section 3, the challenges are summarized. In section 4, the solution of compilation integration is described by discussing host/target development, compiler compatibility, and library management issues. In section 5, a simple development synopsis will summarize the functional characteristics of the Rational Compilation Integration. Section 6 describes briefly the compiler integration method. The conclusion will report on experiences.

2. A TYPICAL USER SITUATION

An air traffic control organization is faced with the replacement of software for an operational display system. This system involves a peripheral computer complex of five identical minicomputers and operator workstations built around a VME-bus architecture with Motorola boards. The development work can be performed from development workstations which act as hosts and interfaces to the target systems. For the minicomputers, host and target compilers are different, and there is no cross-compiler available. In the words of the user: "For (final) compilation, linking and testing, sources have to be transferred to the target where they are subjects of a specialized operating system, a local Ada compiler system with own utilities." For the Motorola targets, there is a host compiler and a cross compiler available on the development workstations.

The user is painfully aware of the challenges involved in his development situation. In his own words: "Despite the general portability of Ada programs the development of the software for the minicomputer targets is negatively affected mainly by the necessity to maintain two consistent project libraries. The host library structure has to reflect the dependencies of the programs on the different compilers and the different operating systems. The complexity of the handling misleads programmers to short term solutions by taking copies of the units to be 'withed'. Already in the current local situation, software management and control is only supported by means of the involved Ada library systems and the discipline of the developers, a 'Sisyphus job': with the increasing number of library units during application development; library management becomes complex and error prone. The situation would be worse and probably unmanageable in a team of more than five developers, or if the coexistence of different releases composed of different versions would have to be controlled."

Currently, reuse of programs, developed for either target, in the development for the other target is achieved by file transfer copies and management with the means of Unix utilities. This is today possible since the development team is still small. However, the user is aware of the challenge which he will be confronted with when configuration and version control will have to be applied to ensure a consistent overall system between the peripheral computer complex and the operator workstations.

3. THE CHALLENGES

In the case of development for different platforms, a productive and reliable approach guaranteeing a well-controlled development of quality software must provide a solution to the following challenges:

- Establishing a uniform development environment and process regardless of the different hosts, targets, and compilers used.
- Eliminating the burden of code transfers by automatically moving sources to the appropriate compilation platforms, and automatically invoking the target compiler in the right order.
- Redirecting target compiler output to the host environment.
- Managing the library consistency between host and target.
- Applying uniform configuration management, and allowing the propagation of changes from one platform to another in either direction.
- Providing a host-based semantic analysis following the target compiler semantics for semantic checking.

4. RATIONAL COMPILATION INTEGRATION

The Rational Environment, an integrated Ada development system used on major Ada projects all over the world, offers a solution to the situation outlined. It is a universal host development environment which has the capability to integrate any commercial Ada compiler. This paper is not meant to provide commercial exposure but to present a concrete solution to an important real-life problem. Both the paper and the solution are geared towards improving the usability and acceptance of Ada. The fact that this solution is proven and available commercially should make the discussion only more interesting and relevant.

4.1. HOST/TARGET DEVELOPMENT

Most organizations follow today a host/target approach. Target-independent development takes place on a comfortable development host which offers all the development tools necessary besides the target code generator. The host is also the repository for any software delivered or to be reused. Code generation for the target is then accomplished either by cross-compilation from the host, or by cross-compilation from a separate compilation platform, or by native compilation on the target itself. Given that software development is very labour-intensive, the host/target approach makes enormously sense in several cases:

- the target has no suitable development environment,
- multiple different targets have to be serviced,

- a host environment exists which offers advantages in terms of productivity, quality, and risk reduction such that they outweigh any inconveniences due to the separation of host and target.

The following discussion is based on a host/target approach where the target compiler is different from the native host compiler and runs on a platform different from the host. This compilation platform can be any workstation or server, including the target itself. We call the compiler running on the target platform the *foreign* or *remote* compiler with respect to the native development compiler running on the host.

4.2. COMPILER COMPATIBILITY

Differences in compilation between host and target compilers can be very costly. Recompilation is already relatively expensive in Ada, but it is greatly annoying if a program does not compile at all or executes differently on the target after it has been developed, unit-tested, and perhaps even system-tested successfully on the development host. Incompatibility between Ada compilers can have many sources:

- Compiler-specific representation clauses and attributes
- Implementation-defined pragmas (naming, arguments, and legality of pragmas differ from one compiler to another).
- References to compiler-specific predefined types, objects, and subprograms, most notably packages Standard and System.
- Support of generics and inlined subprograms.

Because of these features, semantic checking differs slightly between compilers. The Rational Environment embodies technology which enables the semantic analysis of programs according to the compilation features of a foreign compiler.

4.3. VARIANTS OF THE NATIVE COMPILER FOR TARGET-DEPENDENT SEMANTIC CHECKING

Semantic analysis consists of target-dependent and target-independent checking. The Compilation Integration tool provides mechanisms to create variants of the native compiler so that semantic analysis can be performed according to the features of the foreign compilers. Each of these variants acquire the semantics specific to a remote compilation system and therefore, can mimic the semantic checking of the corresponding compilers.

Part of the integration process is the creation of this so-called variant native compiler. This process is called *customization* of the Compiler Integration tool. The semantic information which can be customized include:

- The predefined libraries of the foreign compiler such as:
  - Package Standard
  - Package System

— Package Machine_Code

— Any other implementation-defined units

- Implementation-dependent features such as pragmas and attributes.

- Support of representations Clauses

- Dependency among Ada units due to the handling of generics and inlining.

The benefit of having this semantic analysis performed on the host is that the development process is not defocused by network problems or target resource availability. Once a unit successfully passes semantic analysis, there is a high level of confidence that it will also compile under the foreign compiler, unless there are flaws on the remote platform such as bugs in the foreign compiler, or resource problems.

4.4. TARGET CODE GENERATIONS

Our goal being to provide the users with a single interface to control any compilation systems, it is necessary that the compiler commands remain the same whether the compilation process is achieved by the native compilation system or the remote one. From the user's perspective, invoking the compile command should cause the unit or the entire library to be compiled by the desired compilation system. It becomes interesting to look behind the screen to see what happens when a compilation command is invoked. When the user issues the command "compile", which compiler must be invoked among numerous integrated compilers, including the native one? What happens behind the command that invokes the remote compiler?

Whilst semantic analysis is performed on the host machine by variants of the native compiler as mentioned above, the code generation is actually done by the remote compiler in a totally transparent manner. Each host library contains an attribute which indicates which compilation system should be used (see Chapter 4.5.1). If the selected compiler is foreign, the compilation process of an Ada unit will consist of the following steps:

- The Compilation Integration tool checks whether the requested units in the closure have been successfully compiled; if not, the tool will attempt to compile them, providing that those units have passed the semantic check.

- The first unit in the compilation order is downloaded to the remote machine using the remote connection information initially setup by the user. If the connection or downloading fails, an error message is displayed.

- The Compilation Integration tool issues a command to the remote compiler for that unit. The command is constructed according to the information provided by the customization process. The Compilation Integration tool waits for the compilation to complete before progressing to the next step. Standard output from the remote compiler, including errors, is displayed in a log window of the host development environment. If errors occur, the remote compilation process terminates without requesting compilation for any other units. Among the errors that can prevent a unit from being compiled are:

— Network errors

- — Incorrect setup of remote communications (invalid remote user name and password, unknown remote machine or directory names)
- — Resource limitation or remote compilation failures

- When a unit is successfully compiled, the assembly code and various files can be uploaded automatically.

- The previous four steps are repeated for each unit in the closure.

After all these steps, the program is now ready to be linked.

Similarly, the remote linker can be invoked from the host development environment. Standard output from the remote linker is redirected to a log window at the host platform. After a successful link, the linked executable module is created on the remote machine with the name specified by the user as he/she issued the link command. This linked executable module is uploaded to the host and saved as an associated file of the Ada unit. This module is not executable on the host, but it can be controlled and managed by taking advantage of the powerful configuration management and version control offered by the Rational Environment. The remote library management is also controlled from the host platform as described in the following chapter.

4.5. LIBRARY MANAGEMENT

The Rational Environment offers a very elaborate Ada program library system which is integrated with the configuration management and version control facilities [Morgan 1988]. Subsystems, providing recompilation barriers, and incremental compilation reduce the compilation efforts on the development host which automates recompilation completely. Parallel development paths which allow for managing the evolution of common units are an effective approach to multiple host and target variants of the software and its related products. These beneficial capabilities are propagated as far as possible to the final compilation process with the foreign compiler.

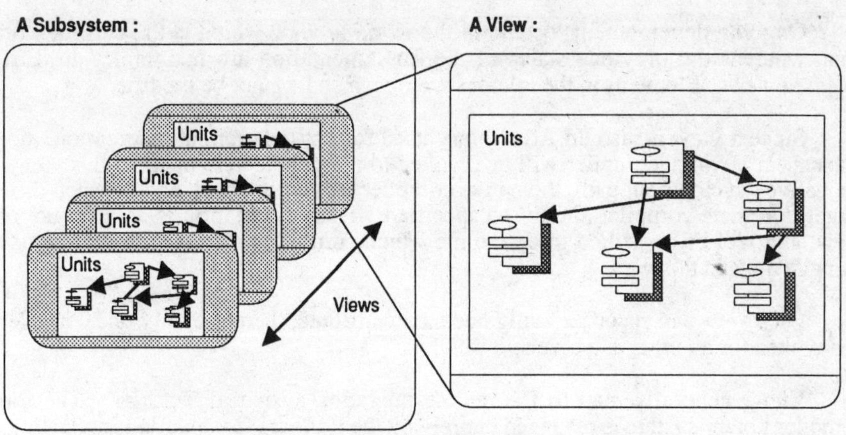

Figure 1. Ada libraries/Views

4.5.1. The host library structure

Host development libraries in the Rational Environment are generally called *views* in order to stress their being subject to a controlled evolution (Figure 1). In the Rational Environment, *views* are both the repository for configuration-management purposes and program libraries that can be used for compilation. They are used to group and compile sets of logically related generations of objects.

For instance, different views in a project can represent alternate implementations for different target machines or different major versions. The user can thus separate the host and targets development path as shown in figure 2.

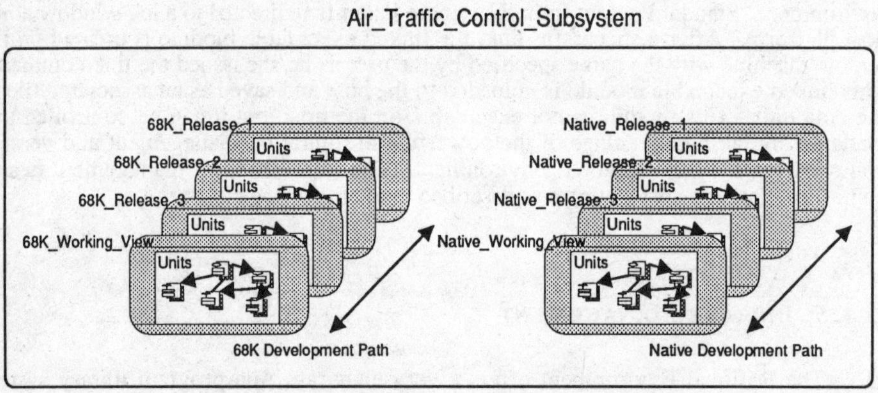

Figure 2. Parallel Development Paths

The source-control functions have been designed to track the development history of the elements in a view, and provide facilities to coordinate the activities of multiple developers by prohibiting any conflict reservation of a given element. Changes made from one view can be automatically propagated into other views in different paths, thus avoiding the 'Sisyphus job' situation.

Ongoing development occurs in the *working view* which is the current working area, whereas the previous states of the implementation are maintained in different *released views*. Elements in the releases are frozen and cannot be modified.

Since a view is also an Ada library used for compilation, at its creation, the user must specify which compiler will be invoked to compile the elements in this view. For the native development path, the native compiler will be selected, and for each different target, a remote compiler should be specified. This information is an attribute of the view, and will be consulted to determine which compilation system should be used to compile units in this view.

Each view can specify exactly one target attribute, therefore only one compiler can be invoked for all units in a given view.

Views generally map to the remote operating system directories. The foreign compiler library system is managed entirely by the Rational Compilation Integration, and is totally transparent to the user as described in the following chapter.

4.5.2. Managing the remote library structure

As mentioned above, development for a target platform is made in a view dedicated to this target. The creation of such a view in the host will automatically trigger the creation of the corresponding remote library on the remote platform.

Figure 3 illustrates this automatic creation of the remote library. Note that the remote directory organization was initially setup by the customizer of the Compiler Integration tool. The example given in Figure 3 is just an arbitrary organization. The customizer can decide to organize the source code directory and Ada libraries at his convenience.

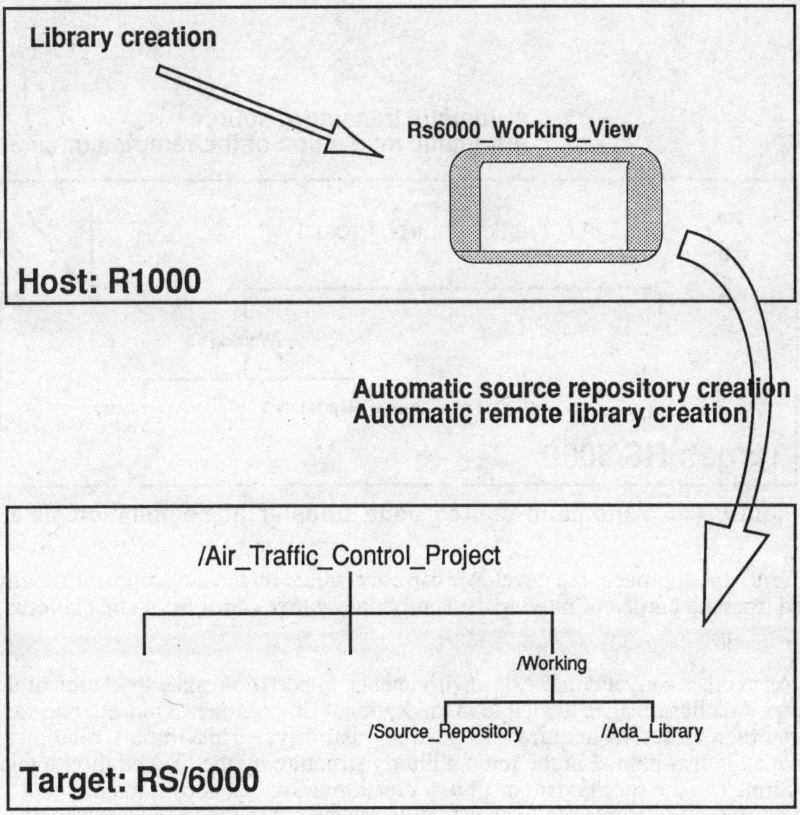

Figure 3. Automatic creation of the remote library and source code repository

The development process will then take place in the host view; the developer writes Ada programs using the syntax and semantics-driven editor of the Rational Environment. Semantic analysis is performed by the native compiler variant which mimics the semantic checking of the target compiler as described above. Once all units are semantically correct, the developer issues the compilation command which will automatically transfer the contents of the library to the remote library, where the remote compiler will be invoked as described in the section "target code generations" above. Note that there is no manual file transfer; downloading and uploading between host and target platforms are totally encapsulated in the compilation commands (Figure 4).

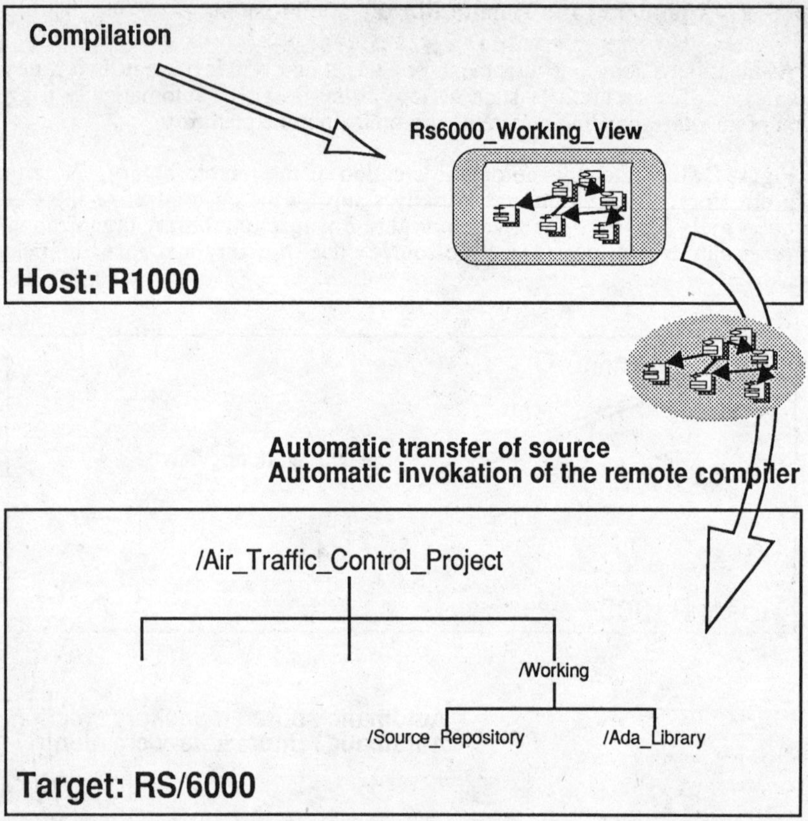

Figure 4. Automatic source code transfer at compilation time.

With this approach, the developer can concentrate on the development activity, and is freed from the burden of moving the appropriate source codes from one platform to the others.

As in other conventional Ada environments, importation and exportation of units to and from Ada libraries are available in the Rational Environment. Indeed, one view can import other views to acquire the desired visibility. This import relationship is automatically maintained in the remote library structure by the Compilation Integration tool. Similar to the mechanism of library creation described above, maintaining import relationship on the remote platform is totally transparent to the user. The remote import operations are performed in parallel with the host operations, and are encapsulated in the host import commands. Thus, adding imports to a host view can cause imports to be automatically added to the remote library's import list, and removal of imports from the host view causes automatic removal of imports from the remote library's import list.

As the source codes reside on both host and remote platforms, maintaining the consistency between the host and target program libraries is challenging. According to the host/target development synopsis proposed in this paper, the user is advised to only modify the source program from the host; once the program is compiled, it is automatically downloaded to the target platform. In this manner, the remote program libraries are always up-to-date, and consistent with the host. However, if an undisciplined user has modified the source codes from the target platform, the Compilation Integration tool is smart enough to report this remote modification to the user, and provides him/her facilities to update the host libraries by accepting the remote changes. At any time, the user can run commands to check for consistency between the host and target libraries, and perform updates if necessary.

4.6. CUSTOMIZATION METHODS

The customization of the Compilation Integration tool essentially consists of modifying existing templates. Templates are simply Ada record type declarations, and users will merely create instances of these records to describe the target dependent semantics such as: pragmas, attributes, representation clauses. This information will ultimately be consulted by the Compilation Integration tool to simulate the foreign compiler's semantics.

For instance, the following Ada record type is used to describe the implementation-dependent pragmas of any integrated compiler:

```
type Pragma_Specification is
      record
         Name: Text;
         Valid_Locations: Location_Array;
         Arguments: Argument_Array (1..32);
         Arg_Count: Natural:= 0;
      end record;

type Pragma_List is array (Natural range <>)
                             of Pragma_Specification);
```

Thus, to specify the pragmas supported by a foreign Ada compiler, the customizer will create instances of the above record as shown below:

```
Foreign_Implementation_Dependent_Pragmas: Pragma_List (1..2):=
      (1 => (Name => "Comment",
             Valid_Locations => (Compilation_Unit => false,
                                  others => true),
             Arg_Count => 1,
             Arguments => (1 => (Name => " ",
                                 The_Type => String_Type))),
       2 => (Name => "Images",
             Valid_Locations => (Decl_Level => true,
                                  others => false),
             Arg_Count => 2,
             Arguments => (1 => (Name => " ",
                                 The_Type => Id_Type))),
                           2 => (Name => " "),
                                 The_Type => Constant_Type))));
```

Target compiler commands and the remote Operating System characteristics are specified in the same manner. In addition, the predefined libraries (Standard, System, Calendar) of the target compiler should also be entered by the customizer. This information will ultimately be consulted by the Compilation Integration tool to issue commands to the foreign compiler.

The "customization" process is performed by Rational field personnel or any knowledgeable user.

5. A SIMPLE DEVELOPMENT SYNOPSIS

Now that the functional characteristics of the Compilation Integration tool are described, the host/target development cycle is best illustrated by a simple development synopsis:

- The developer writes Ada unit using the syntax and semantics-driven editor of the Rational Environment, in a view dedicated to target development with the right target library attribute setup.

- He/she checks the units for semantic correctness. The semantic analysis is performed according to the features of the foreign compiler. Thus programs which are not portable due to specific predefined types, pragmas, etc. can nevertheless be checked for correctness in the Environment even in the absence of the foreign compiler, reducing the risk of a late detection of problems and the rejection of the units in the generally costly phase of compilation with the foreign compiler for the target.

- When all units are semantically valid, code is generated for the target. The Compilation Integration automatically determined the compilation order for the foreign compiler. It then transfers any modified source to the platform where the foreign compiler resides, and invokes the compiler in the proper compilation order. The output of the compilation (progress, warnings etc) is redirected to a window of the Rational Environment.

- After the successful compilation the foreign linker is invoked. The executable produced is uploaded to the Environment for configuration management purposes.

- The developer logs on the target for execution and debugging of the program.

- At any time he can check for consistency of sources and program libraries that reside on the platform running the foreign compiler, with respect to the host ones, and performs updates if necessary.

In addition, the Compilation Integration includes subunits not written in Ada (assembly language, C, etc.) in the configuration management and compilation process.

The host/target interaction of the Compilation Integration is accomplished in either of two ways. For the common workstation platforms (Sun, IBM RS/6000, HP, DEC), the interaction is based on an extension of the object management system of the Rational Environment to include remote objects and operations residing on these remote platforms. This extension offers high level integration services and is based on relevant TCP/IP layers. For any other platform which offers a full Telnet capability above TCP/IP, the interaction is accomplished with the help of Telnet. The latter solution is more widely available, and more easily portable.

6. CONCLUSION

A large number of Rational customers have made good experiences with a less comfortable compilation integration than the one described. In many cases, this kind of approach has been instrumental to the success or even the feasibility of a development.

Examples of projects where this approach has been especially helpful are the Advanced Automation System, the North American air traffic control system, under development by IBM for the FAA, and the Stanfins-R project, a rewrite of the US Army financial accounting system, completed by Computer Sciences Corporation. In both cases, the targets are IBM mainframes or workstations. In Europe, the software development for the French-German helicopter "Tiger" by Eurocopter follows this approach.

The good qualities of Ada combined with the appropriate support to solve the kind of real-life problem described could be extremely useful in other situations where huge amounts of money are wasted due to out-of-date software engineering. For instance, a major car manufacturer develops a lot of software in FORTRAN. Once the FORTRAN programs are made to run on the development host - if they ever run reliably - they have to be ported to a large number of different platforms ranging from small workstations to supercomputers. The poor portability combined with poor compilation and configuration management turns this operation into a major risk and resource sink. It is time that Ada reach out beyond its traditional user community, and bring its benefits to new industries and services!

7. ACKNOWLEDGEMENTS

I would like to thank Knut Ripken for providing me a good abstract to write this paper, and Pascal Leroy for reviewing it.

8. REFERENCE

[Morgan 1988] *Thomas M. Morgan, Configuration Management and Version Control in the Rational Programming Environment,* Proceedings of the Ada-Europe Conference Munich, 7-9 June 1988, Ada Companion Series, Cambridge University Press, 1988.

EXTENDING WORKING ENVIRONMENTS FOR THE DEVELOPMENT OF REACTIVE/ADAPTIVE SYSTEMS WITH INTELLIGENT CONTROLS

Tzilla Elrad, Sungyoung Lee and Ufuk Verun
Department of Computer Science
Illinois Institute of Technology
Chicago, IL 60616, U.S.A.

e-mail:
cselrad@harpo.iit.edu
leesung@harpo.iit.edu
veruufu@harpo.iit.edu

Abstract

It is very common for reactive/adaptive systems to face a situation where the system has to make a choice among a set of possible contending reactions. Several events may occur simultaneously and an intelligent choice is crucial. Moreover, this intelligent choice might depend on system mode or some data values. Race controls are those controls that enable an intelligent choice.

Several working environments exist for the specification, analysis, design, and development of reactive systems. Statecharts [H] is a visual formalism that enables a user to specify, analyze, and debug diagrammatic, yet precise, descriptions of real-time embedded systems, and control and communication systems. We choose Statecharts as our extension for two reasons. First it is designed to be capable of a complete description of the system under development so that the developed system can be checked for crucial dynamic properties. Second, an Ada running code can be generated automatically.

The objective of this paper is to extend the expressive power of such working environments to encompass specifications for intelligent behavior and to extend their semantics to enable an automated Ada code generation that implements it. Impact on Ada-9X to facilitate translation of an entire conceptual model, including intelligent controls, into Ada is provided.

This work supported in part by a grant from the U.S. Army Research Office under scientific contract number 1800.

1. Introduction

Statecharts is a visual formalism designed to specify the behavior of reactive systems [H]. It is intended for use in defining real-time reactive systems and it is appropriate for the embedded applications. The term *reactive systems* describes a wide class of software systems which are, to a large extent, event-driven, constantly having to react to external and internal stimuli. These systems are considered complex and problematic in many aspects concerning specifications. The term *adaptive systems* describes also an event-driven system, but it adapts itself to the changes both in the environment and in the system itself. The term *intelligent systems* is given to those systems that not only are capable of distinction among available reactions, but also when faced with more than one possible reaction are competent of making an intelligent choice. Specifying this aspect of an intelligent behavior and programming it is a challenge. The language mechanisms to implement intelligent behavior are the race controls.

Racing commonly appears in nondeterministic (conflicting) situations in reactive systems. In most reactive real-time systems some control over indeterminate behavior constructs is needed to recognize the overall system behavior. Note that while controlled nondeterminism might be important for efficient concurrent system constructs, uncontrolled nondeterminism usually results in erroneous program behavior that is hard to debug. Thus, the lack of such a control mechanism in the specification language provides the users (programmers) no means of control which may cause the system to be unfair or unpredictable as well as erroneous. These types of controls are classified as availability controls and they answer the question ***what could or could not be done next?*** Availability controls resolve race conditions which might cause an erroneous reaction. In this paper we are not concerned with availability controls but assume that the language is capable of expressing such controls so that we are not faced with erroneous reactions. Both Statecharts and Ada are competent of expressing availability controls. Yet in some situations the system might face a choice among a few reactions where each reaction is consistent with the system specification (i.e., none of these reactions is erroneous). An intelligent choice might be crucial in some situations, and at this point of decision making, race controls play a role by incorporating intelligence into the resolution of conflicting cases.

The rest of the paper is organized as follows: Section 2 provides the basic rationale for using intelligent controls in the specification and implementation languages. Section 3 gives an overview of Statecharts. Section 4 extends Statecharts to incorporate specification of intelligent choices and to produce Ada code that utilizes the explicit race controls. Section 5 shows how to consistently express these intelligent choices specifications as Ada's race controls and projects the implications of race controls on the semantics of Ada-9X's Protected Record.

2. Statecharts, Ada, Intelligent Specification and Race Controls

The controls on indeterminate behavior must map to the target applications of the language and must be applied consistently. Otherwise, the result is a concurrent language with inconsistencies that do not solve problems in the intended domain. In many applications the indeterminate behavior is characteristic to the problem domain and; therefore, must be expressed within the solution domain. Indeterminate behavior controls are best expressed naturally by language constructs; whereas, others currently incorporate these controls within the runtime system. High-level notations are closer to the specification of problem solutions than the low-level notations [CK]. High-level notations can provide encapsulation of different aspects of a system into syntactically recognizable units, which makes the development, correctness analysis, portability and maintenance of concurrent programs much more tractable [E89].

Statecharts does not have a complete set of race control specifications and hence it is not always possible to express directives to an intelligent choice. The paper will show how to extend Statecharts to specify race controls and how to map these controls into an Ada code.

The definition of the race controls first appears in [E89, E90]. Race controls answer the question ***among all eligible alternatives which one to choose?*** or ***what should be done next?*** However, in the notion of Statecharts, the racing can be detected among the events that are triggered (enabled) at the same time from a source state, or among the events that are sensed by the active states in orthogonal components (priority control), among the compound events that occur simultaneously (preference controls), and among the conditions which are true when an event just occurs (forerunner control). Our goal is not to provide another specification language but to enhance the expressive power of existing languages, such as Statecharts.

3. Features in Statecharts

The semantics of Statecharts are described in [H]. In this section, we briefly explain the semantics of states and transitions which are the most challenging parts of semantics and which form the basis for the possible extensions using intelligent control mechanisms.

3.1. General Information about Statecharts

Statecharts is a part of a working environment to analyze, specify and test the functional, behavioral and structural aspects of a reactive system under development. As a final output the working environment provides a running code in Ada or C language from the visual specifications that are proven to be correctly reflecting the system requirements which can be concurrent in nature.

Statecharts is used to model the state-wise transitions in the system. To overcome the difficulty of expressing exponentially increasing state transitions, an abstraction called depth is added to the visual representation formalism. Depth gives the ability to keep the size of the state transition diagram manageable by providing right amount of abstraction on the process. Statecharts can be viewed as state transition diagrams with depth that allows abstract yet precise specification of concurrent activities with possibly broadcasting capabilities. In that sense, Statecharts seems like a good visual counterpart to the tasking model which is used by most concurrent programming languages like Ada.

The basic components of Statecharts are the states and transitions among these states. A state stores the relevant system information that is specific to the part of the system that it resides in. Associated with each transition there is a triple α[C]/ACT, an event α whose occurrence triggers the transition only when the condition C evaluates to true. As an output, action ACT is generated, which inturn may trigger some other events. All of the items in the transition triple are optional.

In expressing the real-time system requirements, Statecharts provides special delay and timeout events and transitions which operate on states that are bounded with timing restrictions [H].

3.2. Abstractions

Abstractions are used to reduce the complexity and exponential growth of ordinary state diagrams.

XOR Decomposition

XOR decomposition is a graphical abstraction which enables the specification of mutual exclusive states. The system can be in only either one of the states that are in the same XOR decomposition.

XOR decomposition is used to dicipt depth and structure by grouping states that lead to the same next state under the occurrence of the same event.

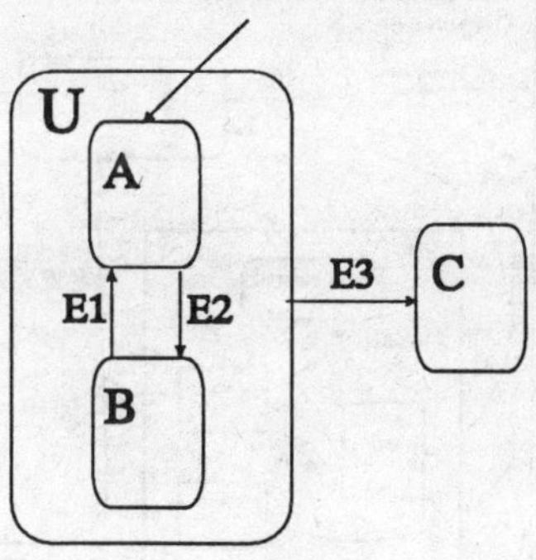

Figure 1. XOR Decomposition

In Figure 1, when the system is in state U, it can be either in state A or B, but not both.

AND Decomposition

AND decomposition is the other abstraction provided by Statecharts which enables the specification of concurrently existing system states.

AND decomposition is used to capture the orthogonality among states and it represents concurrency.

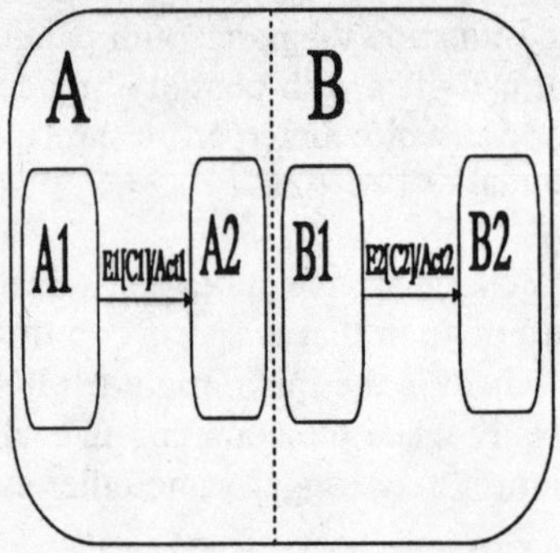

Figure 2. AND decomposition

In Figure 2, the system must be both in states A and B. Being in state A implies being in either state A1 or A2, and being in state B implies being in either state B1 or B2. Hence, the possible states for the system is the cartesian product of substates in A and B.

AND and XOR decompositions provide an abstraction that closely resembles the tasking model. Mutually exclusive activities can be represented by XOR graphs, and concurrently running activities which are also said to be orthogonal can be represented by AND decompositions.

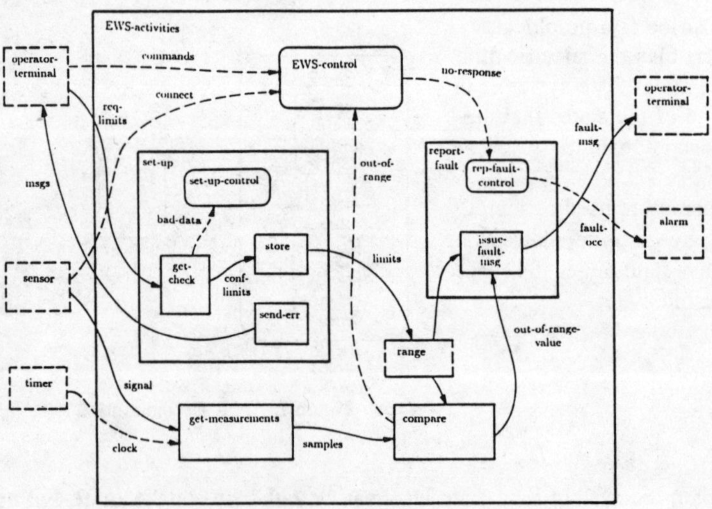

Figure 3. Activity-Chart of the Early Warning System

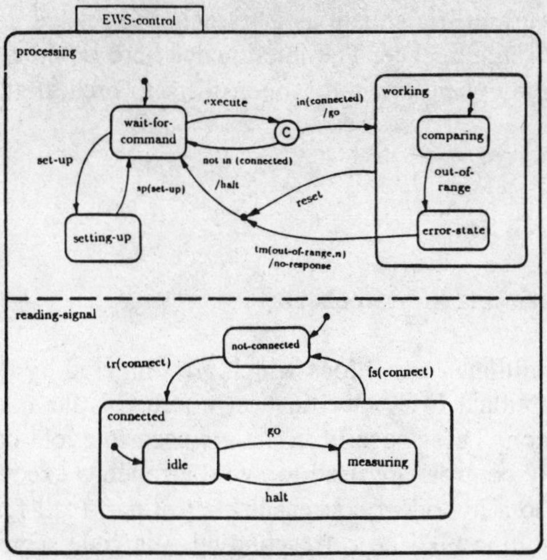

Figure 4. Statechart for the High Level Activity of the Warning System

3.3. Nondeterminism

A nondeterministic situation in Statecharts is characterized by the following cases:

■ Nondeterminism due to transitions from orthogonal states (Race among alternative orthogonal transitions). The occurrences of triggering events on transitions exiting from different states that are orthogonal to each other (i.e., in different components in an AND decomposition). Please see Figure 2.

Currently there is no way to express an explicit intelligent choice among these racing transitions.

■ Nondeterminism due to multiple transitions from a state (Race among alternative transitions from a state). The occurrences of triggering events on more than one transition exiting from a state whose associated conditions are all found to be evaluated to true.

Currently there is no way to express an explicit intelligent choice among these racing transitions.

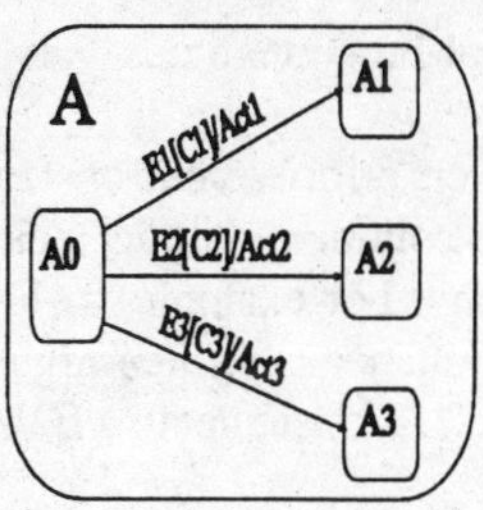

Figure 5. Race Situation among Alternative Transitions from a State.

A control over these nondeterministic situations is essential to realize the requirements of a Reactive/Adaptive system with intelligence. The intelligence here is to be able to pick up a reasonable and smart alternative by using a control mechanism to orchestrate nondeterministic situations.

4. Intelligent Controls in Statecharts

4.1. Avoiding Erroneous Transitions in Statecharts

In Statecharts, we have conditioned transitions which are triggered by the occurrences of events. Each transition has an optional E[C] specification where C is the condition and E is the event that enable the transition. These specifications are used to avoid erroneous transitions just as the availability controls are used to avoid erroneous executions [E89, E90]. E[C] specification corresponds to a hybrid of consensus control part (call for entry E) and private control part (barrier condition C). The corresponding Ada code segment to E[C] specification will look like

```
when C => accept E(...) do ... end;
```

where entry E is accepted only when the condition C evaluates to true, and then the alternative becomes eligible as being in a path of a possible future.

4.2. Race Controls in Statecharts

Multiple transitions from a specific state and transitions from orthogonal components form the major sources of indeterminate behavior in Statecharts. In this section, we present priority and preference controls, and modify Statecharts to address these control mechanisms to control the nondeterministic behavior.

We have already shown that erroneous transitions are eliminated by transition specifications that closely resemble to a subset of availability controls. Once all the possible transition patterns are determined by the use of availability controls then comes the race control mechanisms to pick up a reasonable and intelligent alternative among the possible set of futures.

4.2.1. Implicit Race Control in Statecharts

Statecharts has an implicit priority control. If more than one transition occur simultaneously which are in common state in their source set, the priority of transition depends on the state hierarchy. For example, in Figure 6, assume that system is in state S1. If events E1 and E2 occur simultaneously, then higher level transition E2/Act2 has priority over the internal transition E1/Act1. Consequently, E2/Act2 occurs first.

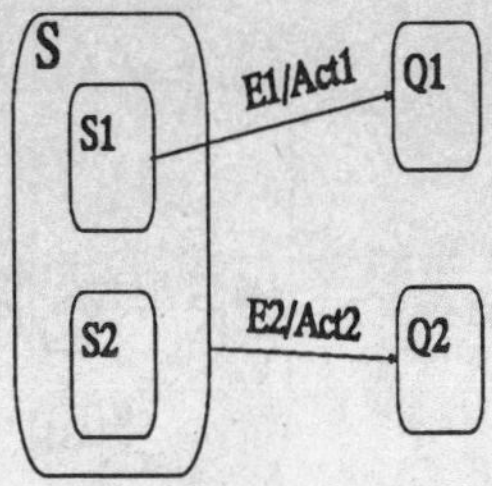

Figure 6. Implicit Priority Control in Statecharts

In the following sections we present our extensions to Statecharts for incorporating explicit race controls.

4.2.2. Explicit Priority Control in Statecharts and Ada

Priority control is introduced as a mechanism to resolve races among orthogonal transitions whose conditions all evaluate to true and whose enabling events are activated at the same time. It controls the nondeterminism due to transitions from states that are orthogonal to each other.

Priority control provides a mechanism to prioritize the orthogonal components in Statecharts just as it is used to prioritize tasks in Ada. Priorities can be assigned to orthogonal components in Statecharts by using special definition fields so that when a decision is to be made among conflicting alternative transitions, priority information plays a role to control the nondeterminism.

Priority control in Statecharts is a control mechanism to control the races among components that are orthogonal to each other.

As a counterpart, the definition of priority control in Ada tasking model is a mechanism to resolve races in task level, among the alternative tasks that are eligible for execution. An example of mapping the extended Statecharts specification with priority information into Ada code is as follows:

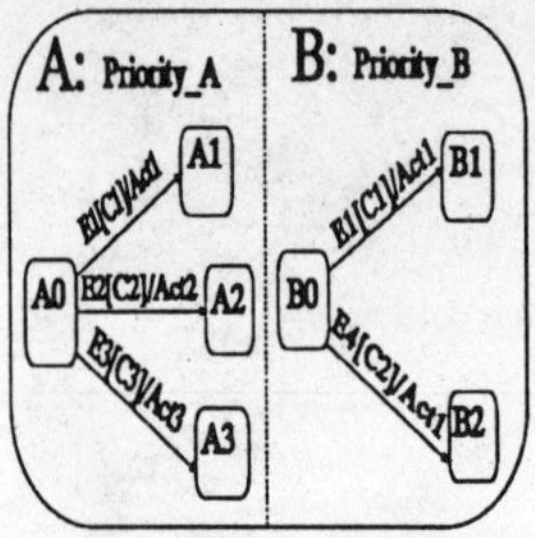

Figure 7. Explicit Priority Control among Orthogonal Components

Corresponding Ada code for prioritized orthogonal components (only the task specification parts are relevant for the specification of priorities among tasks):

```
task A is
    pragma priority Priority_A:=2; -- Can be modified dynamically
    entry E1( );
    entry E2( );
    entry E3( );
end A;

task B is
    pragma priority Priority_B:=1; -- Can be modified dynamically
    entry E1( );
    entry E4( );
end B;
```

4.2.3. Explicit Preference Control in Statecharts and Ada

Preference race is characterized by nondeterminism due to multiple transitions from a state. Here, preference control is proposed as an extension mechanism to Statecharts in order to resolve races that result from the simultaneous enabling of more than one transitions from a specific state.

To explicitly control the nondeterminism due to multiple transitions from a state, one can associate relative preference values to each transition so that in a conflicting case this preference information plays a role in determining which future to take among the possibilities. In a sense, preference control is a part of the intelligent control provided by the race control mechanism.

As a counterpart, the definition of preference control in Ada tasking model is a mechanism to resolve races within task level, inside a select construct, among the eligible alternatives.

Figure 8. Preference Control in Statecharts

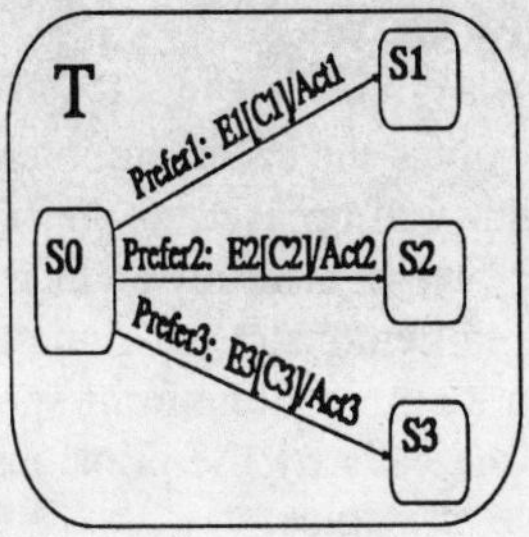

Mapping the extended Statecharts specification into Ada code is as follows:

```
task T is
    entry E1( );
    entry E2( );
    entry E3( );
end T;

task body T is
    ...
    loop
        select
            prefer1: when C1 ==> accept E1( ) do transition_to_S1 end;
        or
            prefer2: when C2 ==> accept E2( ) do transition_to_S2 end;
        or
            prefer3: when C3 ==> accept E3( ) do transition_to_S3 end;
        end select;
    end loop;       -- S1, S2, and S3 may modify preference values
    ...
end T;
```

This code can be simulated by using the count attribute in Ada-83. Explicit preference control can be used among different protected record entries and procedures. Currently there is an implicit preference control for entries over procedures. These implicit race controls are intelligent in most cases but, when the user needs a different strategy of controls he/she would need to fight the language semantics (as happened to us before with Ada-83 implicit control over pending calls to an entry; FIFO strategy which is suitable for most applications, but inconvenient for some real-time applications).

Explicit preference control over protected record operations is consistent with user control over scheduling and flexibility of these controls.

4.2.4. Explicit Forerunner Control in Ada

Explicit forerunner control resolves the races among pending calls that are queued on an entry by specifying the strategy that will be used in the ordering of the calls by outer tasks. Ada-83 has an implicit forerunner race control mechanism. The implicit strategy, which is FIFO ordering of the calls, has been demonstrated in many circumstances to be fraught with problems [E90]. Ada-9X seems to be more flexible in specifying different strategies for the forerunner control (like, ordering the calls by the priorities of the callers), but still lacks the power of supporting user-definable strategies.

An example Ada code utilizing explicit forerunner control mechanism could be:

```
task T is
    entry E1(Urgency: urgency_type);
    entry E2(Distance: distance_type)
end T;

task body T is
    ...
    loop
        select
            when C1 ==> accept E1(Urgency: urgency_type) by (Urgency) do ... end;
        or
            when C2 ==> accept E2(Distance: distance_type ) by (-Distance) do ... end;
        end select;
    end loop;
    ...
end T;
```

5. Impact on Ada-9X: Protected Record and Intelligent Race Controls

A major requirement of Ada-9X is flexibility and user control over scheduling [DoD]. Race controls are programmers agents to express these controls where ever intelligent decisions are needed. As such race controls are major semantics issues for the tasking model and protected records. Protected Records are the proposed Ada-9x lightweight synchronization mechanism. We assume that the reader is familiar with the Ada-9X proposal for PR. References may be obtain from [DoD, DPW, BW]. Current Ada-9X scheduling controls over protected records operations are not flexible enough. Implicit language defined semantics prevents (or at least results with an unacceptable simulations) some intelligent controls. An example is the real-time resource allocation [BW]. The following is a solution to the problem assuming the comprehensive race controls [E89, E90]. Here we use **onlywhen** as a barrier which permits references to parameters of mode **in** passed by the caller (the reason for a new key word is to indicate that different pending calls may have different barrier value). This control is classified as **mutual control** [E89, E90]. (Current protected record simulates mutual control by introducing a new key word and operation called **requeue**). We use the **by** construct for forerunner control as provided in Concurrent-C [GR].

<u>The problem:</u> Consider a resource manager which allocates resources from a pool of identical resources. Two controls are needed here; mutual control (only if the manager has enough resources he can grant a specific request but, until he identifies how many resources are requested he does not know whether or not the request could be serviced), forerunner control (order the calls to an entry according to any strategy, priority in this case).

Our solution:

```
package resource_control is
    subtype resources is integer range 1..MAX;
    protected manager is
        procedure free(I: resources); -- free resources held by the caller
        entry allocate(I: resources); -- request to allocate I resources
    record
        resources_available : resources := MAX;
    end manager;
end resource_control;

package body resource_control is
    protected body manager is
        procedure free(I: resources) is
        begin
            resources_available := resources_available + I; ...
        end;
        entry allocate(I: resources) onlywhen (I <= resources_available) by (Priority) is
        begin
            resources_available := resources_available - I; ...
        end allocate;
    end manager;
end resource_control;
```

The reader is challenged to compare this solution to the one given in [BW].

Simple modification would allow blocking of low priority tasks calling allocate until the manager collects enough resources to serve the highest priority task waiting for allocation.

```
package resource_control is
  subtype resources is integer range 1..MAX;

  protected manager is
```

```
      procedure free(I: resources); -- free resources held by the caller
      entry allocate_high(I: resources); -- to be called by high priority tasks
      entry allocate_medium(I: resources); -- to be called by medium priority tasks
      entry allocate_low(I: resources); -- to be called by low priority tasks
   record
      resources_available : resources := MAX;
   end manager;
end resource_control;

package body resource_control is
   protected body manager is

      procedure free(I: resources) is
      begin
         resources_available := resources_available + I; ...
      end;

      entry allocate_high(I: resources) onlywhen (I <= resources_available) is
      begin
         resources_available := resources_available - I; ...
      end allocate_high;

      entry allocate_medium(I: resources)    when allocate_high'count = 0
                                             onlywhen (I <= resources_available) is
      begin
         resources_available := resources_available - I; ...
      end allocate_medium;

      entry allocate_low(I: resources)    when (allocate_high'count = 0 and
                                                allocate_medium'count = 0)
                                          onlywhen (I <= resources_available) is
      begin
         resources_available := resources_available - I; ...
      end allocate_low;
   end manager;
end resource_control;
```

The reader is challenged to compare this solution to the one given in [BW], particularly considering tasks within the equivalent priority classes. In this particular example there is no need for explicit preference specifications for the entries since the preferences are specified automatically by the condition checks (e.g., allocate_high'count = 0).

The **onlywhen** construct is similar to **suchthat** construct in Concurrent-C [GR]. The semantic difference between these two becomes apparent in checking the barrier conditions.

when is used to check a condition which applies to all the requests in the entry queue (i.e., **when** is associated with the entry queue. If the **when** condition evaluates to true, it makes the entry accessible to outer tasks), whereas **onlywhen** is used to check a condition which applies to individual pending calls in a queue (i.e., **onlywhen** is associated with the individual calls arriving to an entry).

5.1. Flexibility for Real-Time Applications

Assume all tasks have the same priority.

Modification A: Serve tasks requesting many resources first; (to avoid starvation of such tasks)

```
entry allocate(I: resources)
        onlywhen (I <= resources_available)
        by (I) is ....
```

Modification B: Serve tasks requesting minimum number of resources first; (to improve average performance).

```
entry allocate(I: resources)
        onlywhen (I <= resources_available)
        by (MAX - I) is .......
```

Modification C: Serve tasks requesting urgent service first; (to improve response time for such requests)

```
entry allocate(I: resources, URGENT: urgency_level)
        onlywhen (I <= resources_available)
        by (URGENT) is ........
```

Modification D: Serve tasks requesting resources for the shortest estimate period first; (to improve performance).

```
entry allocate(I: resources, PERIOD: period_type)
        onlywhen (I <= resources_available)
        by -(PERIOD) is .......
```

The degree of scheduling flexibility and programmer control over different race decision policies is an important goal for a language used for reactive/adaptive systems exploiting intelligence. Moreover, the intelligent control is syntactically encapsulated with the rest of the controls, the module functionality and structure within a cohesive block that supports a simple interface.

6. Conclusion

The development of reactive/adaptive systems can be accomplished by incorporating functional, structural and behavioral aspects into a syntactically recognizable component. Intelligent controls come in to play when the behavioral system requirements are to be specified in these syntactic units, especially to specify the resolution of conflicting cases that can be encountered during the actual runtime. We have already proposed the intelligent control mechanisms as an extension to Ada task scheduling. In this paper, we extended Statecharts, which is a part of a working environment for reactive/adaptive systems, to facilitate our proposed extensions in the final Ada output code that it automatically generates from the visual specifications. Intelligence in the race controls is encapsulated in the visual specifications, hence the final output code reflects the system behavior.

As an impact on Ada-9X Protected Record, we gave an example which uses the intelligent race control mechanisms. The implications of the intelligent race controls on the semantics of the Ada-9X Protected Record entries and procedures are stated.

References

[BW] A. Burns, A.J. Wellings, "In Support of the Ada 9X Real-Time Facilities", Ada Letters, Jan/Feb 1992, Vol.12, No.1, pp.53-64.

[CBS] B. Chandrasekaran, R. Bhatnagar, D.D. Sharma, "Real-Time Disturbance Control", Communications of the ACM, August 1991, Vol.34, No.8, pp.32-47.

[CK] K.M. Chandy and C. Kesselman, "Parallel Programming in 2001", IEEE Software, November 1991, pp. 11-20.

[DoD] Ada 9X Mapping v3.1, Technical Report, Office of the Under Secretary of Defense for Acquisition, Department of Defense, Washington, D.C., August, 1991.

[DPW] R.A. Duff, O. Pazy, W.A. White, "Lightweight Task Synchronization: The Protected Record Mechanism in Ada 9X", Proceedings of TRI-Ada 91, San Jose, CA, USA, October 21-25, 1991.

[E89] T. Elrad, "Comprehensive Race Controls: A Versatile Scheduling Mechanism for Real-Time Applications", Proceedings of the Ada Europe Conference, ADA The Design Choice, Ed. Angel Alvarez, Cambridge University Press, June 1989.

[E90] T. Elrad, Final Report on Comprehensive Race Controls, Prepared for U.S. Army HQCECOM, Center for Software Engineering Advanced Software Technology, CIN:C08092KU 000100, February 1990.

[H] D. Harel, "Statecharts: A Visual Formalism for Complex Systems", Science of Computer Programming 8 (1987), North-Holland, pp.231-274.

[GR] N. Gehani, W.D. Roome, The Concurrent-C Programming Language, Silicon Press, Summit, NJ, 1989.

Predicting the Speedup of Parallel Ada Programs

Lars Lundberg
Department of Computer Engineering,
Lund University, P.O. Box 118, S-22100 Lund, Sweden
e-mail: larsl@dit.lth.se

Abstract: A method for predicting the speedup of parallel Ada programs has been developed. For this purpose the states Active and Blocked are used to characterize a task during program execution. Of the active tasks, some may be waiting for a processor to be available. Transitions between the two states may be caused only by certain tasking constructs that can be statically identified in the source code. The execution of a task forms a list of Active and Blocked time segments. Segments in different tasks may depend on each other through task synchronizations, thus forming a dependency graph.

Using this graph and certain assumptions about the way tasks are scheduled, one can determine how the number of active tasks varies during the execution. Disregarding hardware and system overheads, speedup is limited either by the number of processors or by the number of active tasks. That is, dependency graphs make it possible to compare the speedup of different programs solving the same problem. This method can also be used for selecting a multiprocessor system with a suitable number of processors for a certain program.

By inserting probes at certain tasking constructs and executing the program on a single-processor, we are able to record the dependency graph. This method has been used for predicting the speedup of a parallel Ada program containing 80 tasks.

1. Introduction

A process in a parallel program, e.g. a task in a parallel Ada program [1], can be in any of the three states Running, Ready or Blocked [2]. An active process is a process which is in the Ready or the Running state.

The transitions between the Ready and the Running states are controlled by the scheduling policy. In global multiprocessor scheduling all processes which are in the Ready state are kept in one global ready queue. In global time-sliced round-robin scheduling each processor inserts the process it was executing last into the ready queue and picks a new process from this queue, at the expiration of each time slice. Theoretically, using an infinitely small time slice on a system with a set of identical processors and no cost for context switching, there are two cases: first case, there are at least as many processors as active processes, and in this case all active processes execute in parallel at full speed, i.e. the same execution speed as if each active process had its own processor. Second case, there are more active processes than processors, in this case all active processes still execute in parallel. The execution speed for each process is, however, reduced due to the sharing of processors, e.g. for 10 active processes and 6 processors the execution speed would be 60% of full speed.

In a multiprocessor system with a set of identical processors the *speedup* of a parallel program is the ratio of the execution time using one processor to that of using a number of processors. If there are N processors in the system then the maximum speedup is simply N. In real systems, this ratio is reduced by different types of overhead costs, e.g. communication, synchronization and context switching overhead. However, even in an ideal multiprocessor system, i.e. a system with no such overhead costs, the maximum speedup will not be reached if there are less active processes than processors.

Ideal speedup is the speedup on an ideal multiprocessor using global time sliced round-robin scheduling with an infinitely small time slice. Speedup measurements can only be done on multiprocessor systems. Ideal speedup can, however, be measured on a single-processor system. Consequently, approximating speedup with ideal speedup makes it possible to do speedup predictions without using any multiprocessor.

For parallel programs with a constant number of active processes, the ideal speedup is simply the minimum of the number of active processes and the number of processors in the ideal system. However, determining the ideal speedup of parallel Ada programs is more complicated, because the number of active tasks may vary during the execution. These variations are not only due to the fact that tasks in Ada may be dynamically created and terminated during the execution; the number of active tasks may vary even in programs with a constant number of tasks depending on the way tasks synchronize. For instance, the number of active tasks decreases when a task becomes blocked at an accept statement.

Here, a method for measuring the ideal speedup of parallel Ada programs is presented. This method uses recordings from previous executions of the program, i.e. the program has to be executed at least once before we can do any speedup predictions. Consequently, this approach is only relevant for programs which will be executed more than once, e.g. programs in embedded computer systems where one single program often is executed endlessly over and over again.

2. Method Overview

Figure 1 shows how three tools (instrumentation tool, postprocessing tool and ideal speedup analyzer tool) enable the calculation of the ideal speedup of a parallel Ada program.

First, the instrumentation tool takes the parallel program to be analyzed and inserts software probes at all tasking constructs, e.g. accept statements and entry calls, thus generating an instrumented version of the Ada program. This program is then compiled, linked and executed in a standard single-processor environment. When the instrumented program is executed, a trace containing recordings of the synchronizations is created, e.g. rendezvous synchronizations, aborts, task creations and terminations are recorded. At each synchronization, the type of synchronization, the identity of the synchronizing tasks and the current time are recorded. This trace is then restructured by the postprocessing tool, producing a format more suitable for ideal speedup analysis.

The ideal speedup analyzer tool, i.e. the last tool in the flow described in figure 1, takes three inputs: the dynamic tasking behavior of the monitored program, the number of processors in the ideal multiprocessor system and the processing speed (instructions per second) for each of these processors (the processing speed of each processor is only needed for programs containing delay statements, this will be explained in section 4). From these three inputs the ideal speedup is calculated

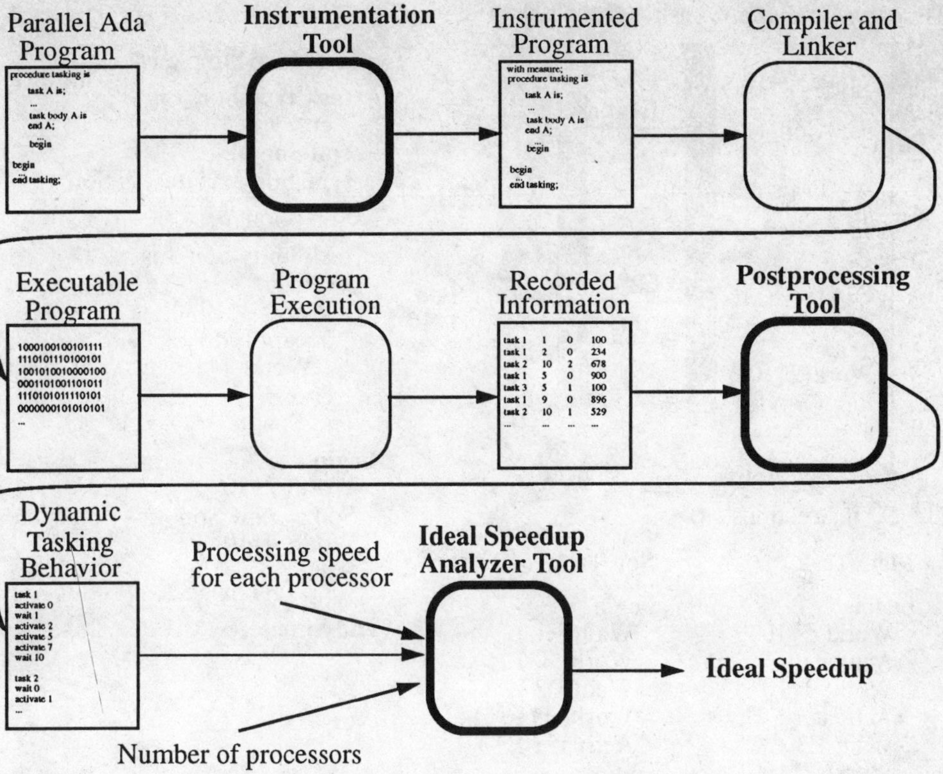

Figure 1: A flowchart describing a set of tools which enable the calculation of the ideal speedup of parallel Ada programs.

3. Dynamic Tasking Behavior

When defining dynamic tasking behavior the simple Ada program depicted in the right part of figure 2 will be used as an example. The program consists of two tasks: the Main task and the Son task. Son is an instance of the task type Son_t. Sequential processing is represented by *Work(k)*, where *k* denotes the number of instruction cycles executed in the procedure Work. The upper left part of figure 2 shows a graphical representation of the Ada program, using a two processor system. Synchronization overhead, e.g. rendezvous overhead and overhead for task creation, has been omitted in this example; a processing speed of $1*10^6$ instructions per second is assumed.

The lower left part of figure 2 shows a textual representation of the Ada program using two simple synchronization primitives: *Activate(Event)* and *Wait(Event)*. The parameter Event couples a certain Activate to a certain Wait. When a task executes an Activate on an event, then we say that the event has occurred. Each event acts as a binary semaphore. Thus, if a task executes a Wait on an event which has not yet occurred then that task becomes blocked until another task executes an Activate on the same event. However, a task executing a Wait on an event which already has occurred does not become blocked.

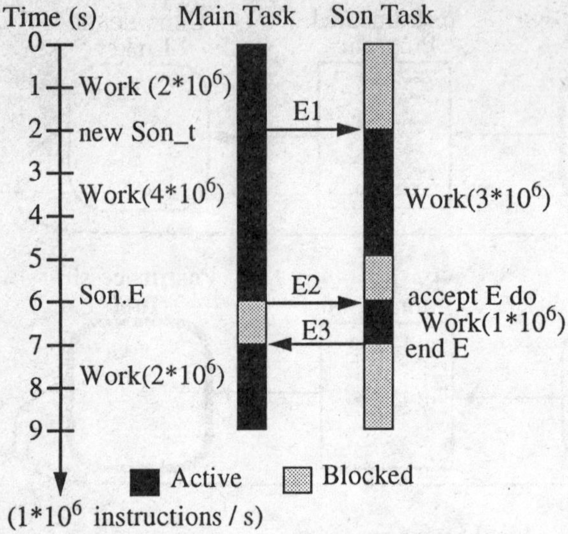


```
procedure Simple is
  task type Son_t is
    entry E;
  end Son_t;
  type Son_p is access Son_t;
  Son : Son_p;
  task body Son_t is
  begin
    Work( 3*10^6 );
    accept E do
      Work( 1*10^6 );
    end E;
  end Son_t;
begin
  Work( 2*10^6 );
  Son := new Son_t; -- Son is created
  Work( 4*10^6 );
  Son.E;
  Work( 2*10^6 );
end Simple;
```

```
Main Task                 Son Task

begin                     begin
  Work( 2*10^6 )            Wait( E1 )
  Activate( E1 )            Work( 3*10^6 )
  Work( 4*10^6 )            Wait( E2 )
  Activate( E2)             Work( 1*10^6 )
  Wait( E3 )                Activate( E3 )
  Work( 2*10^6 )          end
end
```

Figure 2: Three representations of the same parallel program.

In the textual representation there is a list of *sequential segments* for each task. Segments are separated by an *Activate(Event)*, a *Wait(Event)* or a *Delay(Time)* statement; Delay simply blocks the task for a fixed period of time. The length of each segment, i.e. k in Work(k), is the number of instruction cycles the task has spent executing between two synchronization events. Some segments may have zero length, e.g. the Main task has 4 segments: one before the first activation, one between the first and the second activation, one segment with zero length between the second activation and the Wait statement and one segment after the Wait statement. The length of a segment is assumed to be independent of the number of processors and the scheduling policy, i.e. segment lengths can be measured on a single-processor system using a simple scheduling policy. *Dynamic tasking behavior is the set of these lists of segments*; one list for each task. That is, the textual representation in the lower left part of figure 2 is the dynamic tasking behavior of the Ada program.

In this representation, all tasks are created at time 0. The Son task in the simple Ada program is, however, not created until the Main task has executed $2*10^6$ instructions. In order to model this in the dynamic tasking behavior the Son task is initially blocked on an event E1 (Wait(E1)). The new-statement in the Main task corresponds to an Activate on the event E1. This is a simplification of the semantics of task creations in Ada thus making the example more comprehensive. The rendezvous is modeled by two events (E2 and E3). Reaching the accept statement in the Son corresponds to executing a Wait on event E2. The entry call in the Main task (Son.E) corresponds to an Activate on event E2 followed by a Wait on event E3. The end of the accept statement in the Son task corresponds to an Activate on event E3.

According to the full semantics for task termination the Son must notify the Main task that it has terminated before the Main task can terminate. Again, the full semantics are handled by the method, but these semantics have been simplified thus making the example more comprehensive. The full synchronization patterns for task creation and termination are discussed in sections 5 and 6.

Dynamic tasking behavior is obtained from a trace of one monitored execution of the parallel program, i.e. it represents that particular execution. Therefore, dynamic tasking behavior is deterministic, and there is no way to represent variations. If the amount of sequential processing between two synchronization events varies from one execution to another then this cannot be seen in the dynamic tasking behavior. For instance, an if-statement which has considerably more processing in the then-part than in the else-part may be executed between two synchronization events. The value of the condition in this if-statement could be determined by the input to the program, i.e. this value could change from one execution to another. In this situation, the length of the corresponding sequential segment in the dynamic tasking behavior (Work(k)) is the amount of processing measured during the monitored execution of the program, i.e. for different inputs to the program the length of this segment may vary, thus yielding different dynamic tasking behaviors.

Except for the select statement, all tasking constructs can be modeled by the three synchronization primitives (Activate, Wait and Delay). However, the Wait primitive cannot wait for more than one event at a time whereas a task which is blocked in a select statement is waiting for any of a number of events. Therefore, select statements are represented by the alternative chosen during the monitored execution of the parallel program, i.e. a select statement inside a loop may be represented differently in different iterations. Figure 3 shows an Ada program, with a select statement inside a loop, and the corresponding dynamic tasking behavior.

This program consists of two tasks (Main and Son). Disregarding the full semantics for task creation, both tasks are active at program start-up. The Main task makes an entry call to the Son. This is represented by an Activate followed by a Wait. The Son executes two iterations in a loop. In the first iteration the accept alternative in the select statement is chosen, i.e. the recordings of the monitored execution will show that the accept alternative was chosen in the first iteration.There are no statements inside the entry. Therefore, the accept statement is represented by a Wait directly followed by an Activate. When the select statement is reached in the second iteration there is no active task which could call entry E. Consequently, the delay alternative is chosen.

As discussed previously, some programs may yield different dynamic tasking behaviors depending on the input to the program or on the way tasks are scheduled. One of the basic requirements for the success of the described method is that these variations are limited or predictable. Consequently, this method is not applicable to programs for which the dynamic tasking behavior varies vastly between different executions. Ways to handle limited variations in dynamic tasking behavior will, however, be discussed later.

```
procedure Iteration is

task Son is
  entry E;
end Son;

task body Son is
begin
   for I in 1..2 loop   -- 2 iterations
      Work(I*10^6);
      select
         accept E;
      or
         delay 10.0;
      end select;
   end loop;
end Son;

begin
   Son.E;
end Iteration;
```

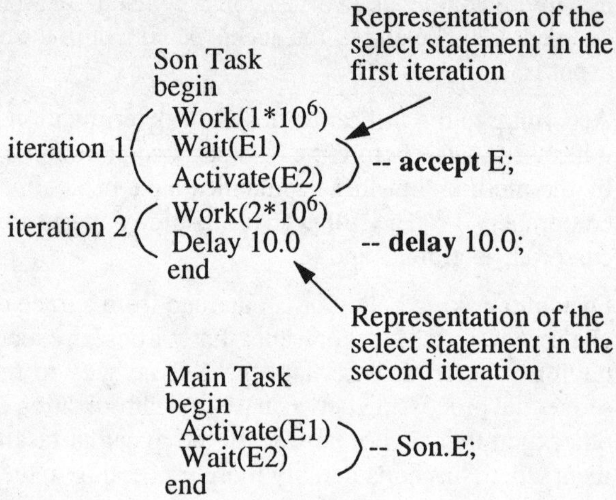

Figure 3: A parallel Ada program and the corresponding tasking behavior. The select-statement in the Son task is represented differently in the two iterations.

4. Ideal Speedup Analysis

The execution time for a parallel program executing on an ideal multiprocessor using time sliced scheduling with an infinitely small time slice is denoted T_i where i is the number of processors. The ideal speedup using i processors (SP(i)), is calculated as SP(i) = T_1 / T_i, where T_1 is the execution time using one processor.

Delay lengths are expressed in seconds, whereas segments lengths are expressed in instruction cycles. However, if the processing speed for each processor is known then the length of the sequential segments can be expressed in seconds instead of instruction cycles, thus facilitating a common unit (seconds) for both segment lengths and delay lengths.

In order to calculate T_i some variables are needed: For each task, there is a variable indicating the local time, i.e. the time a task has spent executing. Each event is represented by a boolean flag, which is initially false. The flag becomes true when a task has reached an Activate on that event.

The following algorithm calculates T_i:

1. Set T_i to 0.

2. Find the next event that will occur.

   For each active task, the time to the next event is investigated; this time can easily be determined from the lists representing the task and the variable indicating the local time for that task. Due to the time sliced scheduling policy, all tasks execute with equal speed, and the next event in the system can therefore be easily determined.

3. Adjust the state of the system.

   Potentially, this includes updating the value of an event flag or changing the state of a task from active to blocked or the opposite. T_i and the local execution times for the active tasks are also advanced with the time it took to reach the occurred event. It will generally take less time to reach the next event if we have a lot of processors. The reason for this is that if the number of active tasks exceeds the number of processors then the tasks will have to share the processors instead of having one processor each.

4. If there are any tasks which have not reached the end of their list of sequential segments then go back to 2.

The calculations of T_i are now finished, and the ideal speedup using *i* processors (SP(i)) is obtained by dividing T_1 with T_i.

Using two CPUs with a processing speed of $1*10^6$ instructions per second, the Ada program shown in figure 2 has a T_2 of 9 seconds; T_1 is 12 seconds, i.e. SP(2) = 12 / 9 = 1.33.

5. Instrumentation

The instrumentation tool takes a correct (parallel) Ada program and automatically inserts software probes monitoring the dynamic tasking behavior in the source code, thus generating an instrumented version of the Ada program. The software probes are written in assembly language, thus reducing the overhead to 20-30 instruction cycles for each recording. For most programs the number of instruction cycles between two synchronizations is much larger than this. Therefore, the overhead for doing the recordings is generally small compared to the length of the segments, i.e. the dynamic tasking behavior is not significantly affected by the instrumentation.

All the measurement facilities are encapsulated in a package called *Measure*; the body of this package is written in assembly language. Figure 4 shows the specification of the package Measure, which exports one procedural and one functional version of a recording routine *Rec*. The functional version of Rec is used when a value should be returned by the measurement routine, e.g. at task creation a unique task identification number is returned. Moreover, the Ada syntax does not permit procedural calls in the elaboration parts of procedures, functions, tasks etc. When recording events in such elaboration regions the functional version has to be used even if only a dummy value is returned. However, in normal code bodies the procedural version is used.

```
package Measure is
  procedure Rec( Probe : in Natural;
                 Para1 : in Natural;
                 Para2 : in Natural := 0);

  function Rec( Probe : Natural;
               Para1 : Natural) return Natural;
end Measure;
```

Figure 4: The specification of the package measure.

Probe Name	Parameters	Semantics
BeforeSelect	TaskId	The task has reached a select statement
BeforeAccept	TaskId	The task has reached an accept statement
Accepted	TaskId, AcceptedTask	The task has entered an accept statement
EndAccept	TaskId, AcceptedTask	The task has reached the end of an accept
BeforeEntryCall	TaskId	The task has reached an entry call
AfterEntryCall	TaskId	The task has completed an entry call
FirstInTask	TaskId	The task has started to execute its body
LastInTask	TaskId	The task as reached the end of its execution
BeforeDelay	TaskId	The task has reached a delay statement
AfterDelay	TaskId, Time	The task has started to execute after a delay
ElaborateTask	FatherId **return** TaskId	A task has started its elaboration
ElaborateTaskType	FatherId **return** TaskId	A task type object has started its elaboration
AfterNew	TaskId	The task has executed a new-statement
ElaborateBlock	TaskId	The task is elaborating a block
EnterBlock	TaskId	The task has entered a block
ExitBlock	TaskId	The task is leaving a block
AfterBlock	TaskId	The task has left a block
AfterAbort	TaskId	The task has executed an abort-statement

Table 1:Synchronization events monitored by the instrumentation tool.

Table 1 shows the 18 different types of probes that are used for monitoring the execution of a parallel Ada program. These probes capture the full dynamic tasking behavior of an Ada program including rendezvous, task creation, task termination, delay and abort.

Figure 5 shows the instrumented version of the example program discussed previously (see figure 2). The new code inserted in the instrumentation process is indicted in italics.

The figure shows that all tasks in the instrumented program share the local state of the package Measure. However, there is no risk for harmful interference, because the Ada compiler guarantees that the scheduling policy used during the monitored execution is non-preemptive, i.e. context switches occur only at the synchronization points. In this case the Alsys Ada compiler version 4.4.1 and an ordinary IBM PC were used.

In the following we will comment on the main aspects of the instrumentation shown in figure 5. The instrumentation probes used in this example can be divided into four groups: First, instrumentation for establishing a unique identification for each task. Second, instrumentation monitoring the rendezvous. Third, instrumentation monitoring task creation. Fourth, instrumentation monitoring task termination.

```
with Measure;
procedure Simple is
  MyId : Positive := Measure.Rec(ElaborateTask, 0);   -- Main task has no father
  task type Son_t is
    entry E( Id : Positive );
  end Son_t;
  type Son_p is access Son_t;

  Son : Son_p;

  task body Son_t is
    Dummy : Positive := Measure.Rec(ElaborateTaskType, MyId);   -- Father's identity
    MyId : Positive := Dummy;
  begin
    Measure.Rec(FirstInTask, MyId);
    Work( 3*106 );
    Measure.Rec( BeforeAccept, MyId);
    accept E( Id : Positive ) do
      Measure.Rec(Accepted, MyId, Id);
      Work( 1*106 );
      Measure.Rec(EndAccept, MyId, Id);
    end E;
    Measure.Rec(LastInTask, MyId);
  end Son_t;

begin
  Measure.Rec(FirstInTask, MyId);
  Work( 2*106 );
  Son := new Son_t;
  Measure.Rec(AfterNew, MyId);
  Work( 4*106 );
  Measure.Rec(BeforeEntryCall, MyId);
  Son.E( MyId );
  Measure.Rec(AfterEntryCall, MyId);
  Work( 2*106 );
  Measure.Rec(LastInTask, MyId);
end Simple;
```

Figure 5: The instrumented version of the parallel Ada program shown in figure 2

Task identification: All tasks in the parallel program, including instances of task types, have a unique identification number. This number is used for coupling the recording of a probe to a certain task. During the instrumentation process, each task gets a new variable *MyId* which is initialized with the task's identification number. This initialization is done through a call to Rec with the probe *ElaborateTask* or *ElaborateTaskType* depending on if it is a task type or not. Now, Rec does two things: first, it makes a recording indicating the current time (a high resolution real-time clock is required) and the type of probe, in this case either *ElaborateTask* or *ElaborateTaskType.* Second, it returns the identification number for the new task. Moreover, the counter indicating the next identification number is incremented thus guaranteeing a unique number for all tasks in the system. In the program in figure 5, the Main task gets the identity 1 and the Son gets the identity 2.

A new rendezvous parameter (*Id : Positive*) is added in all entries. This parameter makes it possible for the accepting task to determine the identity of the calling task, thus making it possible to couple a certain entry call to a certain accept. In the example program, the Main task passes its own identity (denoted by *MyId*) to the Son through this parameter.

The *Dummy* variable in the body of the task type Son_t is used to overcome the visibility rules of Ada. Ideally one would have liked to write:

MyId : Positive := Measure.Rec(ElaborateTaskType, MyId);

That is, the parameter MyId in the call to Rec should denote the identity of the surrounding task, which is the father of the task, and the new variable MyId should denote the identification number of the new task. The visibility rules of Ada do, however, not permit this. Therefore, a dummy variable is used for storing the returned task identification. On the next line this identification is passed to the local variable MyId.

Both tasks in the example program start their execution with recording the probe *FirstInTask.* These two recordings can be separated through the values of the variable MyId, which will be 1 for the Main task and 2 for the Son task.

Rendezvous: The probe *BeforeAccept* records the time when the Son reaches the accept statement (see figure 5). In the postprocessing phase, this information makes it possible to determine the length of the segment before the accept, i.e. Work($3*10^6$).

When the Main task reaches the entry call (Son.E*(MyId), MyId* is used for communicating the callers identity to the called task) then this is recorded by the *BeforeEntryCall* probe. The time for the start of the rendezvous is recorded by the probe *Accepted.* The last parameter in this probe (*Id*) makes it possible to decide the identity of the accepted task. Similarly, the time when the rendezvous is completed is recorded by the probe *EndAccept.* The probe *AfterEntryCall* indicates the start of the execution of the Main task after the entry call. Extracting the dynamic tasking behavior from the recordings of these probes will be described in section 6.

Task creation: The *AfterNew* probe makes it possible to determine when a new instance of a task type is created; in this case the Son task. Task creation has been simplified in the previous discussion, where it was treated as one *Activate* (see figure 2). Actually, the semantics of task creation are more complicated than this, i.e. the creator may not continue until the created task (or tasks) have elaborated all local variables (see figure 7).

For statically declared tasks the identity of the creator is determined in the recording of the *ElaborateTask* probe, i.e. the last parameter in the *ElaborateTask* probe denotes the creator. For instances of a task type the situation is more complicated. The creator of an instance of a task type does not have to be the same task as the one indicated in the recording of *ElaborateTaskType* (see figure 5).

There are two ways to determine, from the trace, the identity of the creator of a task instance: first, a number of possible candidate creators can be calculated. A task can only create a new task with a new statement, in its elaboration part or during the elaboration of a block, e.g. a procedure. These events are recorded by the probes *AfterNew, ElaborateTask, ElaborateTaskType* and *ElaborateBlock.* Consequently, when encountering an *ElaborateTaskType* in the recorded trace, one can determine which tasks could have elaborated the new task by looking at the other probe recordings in the trace. The problem with this method is that, theoretically, one could find more than one possible creator.

The second method for finding the creator of a task type is more pragmatic; one simply looks at the identity of the task making the first entry call to the newly created task, i.e. one has to make a sequential search forward in the trace until the first rendezvous with the created task is found. The problem with this method is that the first task making an entry call does not have to be the creator, however, no such Ada program is known to us. In all programs investigated thus far the father has been established using the first method, i.e. there has only been one possible candidate. Should there be more than one possible father, then the second method will be used for selecting the creator from the list of candidates.

It is not necessary to have a probe indicating that a task has reached a "**new** *TaskType*" statement, i.e. no *BeforeNew* probe is needed. The reason for this is that it is always possible to indirectly, in the postprocessing phase, determine when a task reaches a **new** statement. The reason for this is that when the creator is suspended after the new-statement (see figure 6) then there is at least one active task in the system, i.e. the created task. The instrumentation guarantees that all the starting points of sequential segments are recorded. Therefore, one can determine when a creator reaches a new-statement indirectly by looking at the starting time for the task executing immediately after the creator has been blocked waiting for the created task to elaborate.

However, in the case of a rendezvous one must record the time when the tasks reaches the entry and accept points, i.e. the *BeforeAccept, BeforeSelect* and *BeforeEntryCall* probes. The reason for this is that in these cases one cannot guarantee that there are any active tasks in the system, e.g. in the case of *BeforeEntryCall* the accepting task may be blocked in a delay-statement. In that case it would not be possible to determine exactly when the calling task actually reached the entry call, i.e. it would not be possible to determine the length of the sequential segment proceeding the Activate in the entry call (see figure 2).

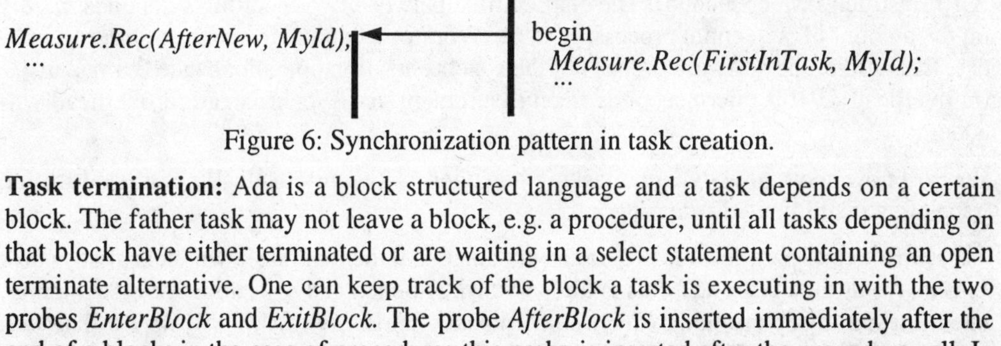

Figure 6: Synchronization pattern in task creation.

Task termination: Ada is a block structured language and a task depends on a certain block. The father task may not leave a block, e.g. a procedure, until all tasks depending on that block have either terminated or are waiting in a select statement containing an open terminate alternative. One can keep track of the block a task is executing in with the two probes *EnterBlock* and *ExitBlock.* The probe *AfterBlock* is inserted immediately after the end of a block; in the case of procedures this probe is inserted after the procedure call. In order to reduce the amount of instrumentation, only blocks containing tasks or task types are instrumented, e.g. the procedure Work in the example program is not instrumented.

Usually, an instance of a dynamic task type depends on the block where it was created, e.g. when the instance is denoted by a local variable. However, if an instance of a task type is created dynamically through a new-statement then it depends on the block where the pointer type denoting the task type is declared, i.e. the task may not depend on the block where it was created but on a surrounding block. Separating these cases requires major program analysis. There is, however, a pragmatic approach which yields correct results in most cases.

We assume that all tasks depend on the block where they have been created. However, if there is evidence in the trace that the task actually has been executing after the creator has left the block then the created task is assumed to depend on the block surrounding the block where it was created, and so on. Depending on the way tasks are scheduled during the monitored execution, a task which actually depends on a surrounding block may have terminated before the creator has left the block where it was created. In that case this method would yield a slightly pessimistic result concerning the amount of parallelism in the program, i.e. we would wrongly assume that the creator has to wait for the created task before it can leave the inner block.

In practice we expect that this potential source of error will have very little effect. If the created task is short lived then making this type of incorrect assumption will only have a marginal impact on the overall dynamic tasking behavior of the program. On the other hand, if the created task executes for a substantial amount of time then the risk for making these kinds of false decisions is small, because the created task will probably continue to execute after the creator has left the inner block. Thus far we have not encountered this error in any of the programs being analyzed.

6. Postprocessing

The output from the instrumentation phase is an instrumented Ada program, which is then executed on a single-processor system. During the execution of the instrumented program a trace is produced. Figure 7 shows the trace produced by the instrumented program shown in figure 5. The time column in figure 7 is expressed in microseconds (the processing speed is 10^6 instructions per second). The elapsed time between two recordings depends mainly on the amount of sequential processing in the Work procedure. However, in order to indicate that neither the software probes nor the synchronization operations take 0 time, an extra overhead of 100 micro seconds for measurement and synchronization overhead was added.

We will now show how dynamic tasking behavior can be automatically extracted from a trace of an instrumented Ada program.

The semantics of parallel Ada programs guarantee that the main task, which is always task 1, is active at time 0. In fact, this is the only task which is active at time 0. Consequently, one must start by determining which synchronization primitive task 1 will start with (Wait, Activate or Delay) and how long it will execute before it reaches this primitive.

Probe Id	TaskId	Param	Time (μs)
ElaborateTask	1	0	0
FirstInTask	1	0	100
ElaborateTaskType	2	1	2000200
FirstInTask	2	0	2000300
BeforeAccept	2	0	5000400
AfterNew	1	0	5000500
BeforeEntryCall	1	0	9000600
Accepted	2	1	9000700
EndAccept	2	1	10000800
LastInTask	2	0	10000900
AfterEntryCall	1	0	10001000
LastInTask	1	0	12001100

Figure 7: The execution trace of the instrumented Ada program in figure 5.

Looking at the trace we see that no synchronization primitive is encountered until time 2000200, when task 2 starts elaborating. The creator of task 2 must be task 1, because at this point in the execution there is no other task in the program. The number of instruction cycles executed between time 0 and time 2000200 can easily be determined, because the processing speed is known (10^6 instructions per second). From this information we are able to construct the first parts of the lists describing dynamic tasking behavior, i.e. we know that the lists will start like this.

```
task 1                          task 2
begin                           begin
  Work( 2000200 )                 Wait( Event_1 )
  Activate( Event_1 )
  Wait( Event_2 )  <--
                          task 1 is blocked waiting
                          for task 2 to elaborate
```

After this we see that the Son (task 2) is executing for 100 microseconds before it reaches the *FirstInTask* probe. From the example in figure 6 we know that the creator may continue when the created task has elaborated, which is approximately the same as when the created task has reached the probe *FirstInTask*.

The Son continues to execute until it reaches the accept statement. From the trace we see that the time from the *FirstInTask* probe to the *BeforeAccept* probe is 3000100 microseconds. Now we know a little more about the dynamic tasking behavior.

```
task 1                          task 2
begin                           begin
  Work( 2000200 )                 Wait( Event_1 )
  Activate( Event_1 )             Work( 100 )
  Wait( Event_2 )                 Activate( Event_2 )
                                  Work( 3000100 )
                          -->     Wait( Event_3 )
task 2 is blocked waiting for
an entry call
```

When the Son becomes blocked at the accept statement the Main task starts to execute, thus first making a recording of the probe *AfterNew.* The time required for reaching the entry call can be calculated to 4.0001 seconds from the recordings of *AfterNew* and *BeforeEntryCall* (9000600 - 5000500 = 4000100). By looking at the parameters in the recording of the *Accepted* probe we know that the Main task made the entry call to the Son task. At this time the dynamic tasking behavior looks like this.

```
task 1                      task 2
begin                       begin
  Work( 2000200 )             Wait( Event_1 )
  Activate( Event_1 )         Work( 100 )
  Wait( Event_2 )             Activate( Event_2 )
  Work( 4000100 )             Work( 3000100 )
  Activate( Event_3 )         Wait( Event_3 )
  Wait( Event_4 )  <-- task 1 is blocked waiting
                       for the rendezvous to finish
```

Now, the Son starts executing the code inside the accept statement. The length of this segment is 1.001 seconds; this is calculated from the recordings of *Accepted* and *EndAccept.* After the end of the rendezvous the Son spends an additional 100 microseconds executing before it reaches the *LastInTask* probe, thus completing its execution. The last part of the trace shows how the Main task executes the last sequential segment before it terminates. Finally, we have the complete dynamic tasking behavior of the example program.

```
task 1                      task 2
begin                       begin
  Work( 2000200 )             Wait( Event_1 )
  Activate( Event_1 )         Work( 100 )
  Wait( Event_2 )             Activate( Event_2 )
  Work( 4000100 )             Work( 3000100 )
  Activate( Event_3 )         Wait( Event_3 )
  Wait( Event_4 )             Work( 1000100 )
  Work( 2000100 )             Activate( Event_4 )
  Wait( Event_5 );            Work( 100 )
end                           Activate( Event_5 )
                            end
```

Comparing this dynamic tasking behavior with.the one in figure 2, one sees that there are some minor simplifications in figure 2. The semantics of task creation and task termination were somewhat simplified in figure 2. Moreover, the processing time for executing the synchronization statements was also omitted in figure 2.

7. Method Example

In this section we will demonstrate the described technique by predicting the speedup of a parallel Ada program. The speedup was predicted using the described tools (see figure 1), the Alsys compiler and an IBM PC. The example shows how this technique makes it possible to select a multiprocessor with a suitable number of processors for a certain parallel program.

The parallel program being analyzed is an Ada implementation of an algorithm for generating all prime numbers smaller than or equal to a number N. The algorithm generates the prime numbers in increasing order starting with prime number 2 and ending with the largest prime number smaller than or equal to N. A number M is a prime number if it is not divisible by any prime number smaller than M. For instance, 7 is a prime number, because it is not divisible by any of the prime numbers 2, 3 or 5, i.e. testing 7 for primality is really three divisibility tests. Such divisibility tests are carried out by autonomous filter stations; each station has a prime number assigned to it.

Figure 8 shows how the algorithm works: the filter stations form a line with a number generator at the front feeding numbers into the line. Each station filters out numbers which are divisible by its prime number, e.g. the first station filters out all even numbers. If a filter station cannot divide a number then that number is forwarded to the next station. Prime numbers are not divisible by any number and will therefore reach the end of the line. When a prime number reaches the end of the line then a new filter station is created, i.e. the line of filter stations grows for each new prime number.

The Ada implementation of this algorithm has been described separately [3]. This prime sieve consists of a number generator task and a number of filter tasks (see figure 8). There is one filter task for each generated prime number, i.e. the number of filter tasks grows dynamically during the execution. The first number generated is 2, thus immediately creating the first filter task. The number generator task stops by generating number 397, which is the 79th prime number. Therefore, the maximum number of tasks, which is reached at the end of the execution, is 80, i.e. 79 filter tasks and the number generator task.

Numbers are passed from one filter task to another as rendezvous parameters, i.e. the arrows between the filter tasks in figure 8 correspond to entry calls. Consequently, filter tasks are blocked in select-statements when they are waiting for new numbers.

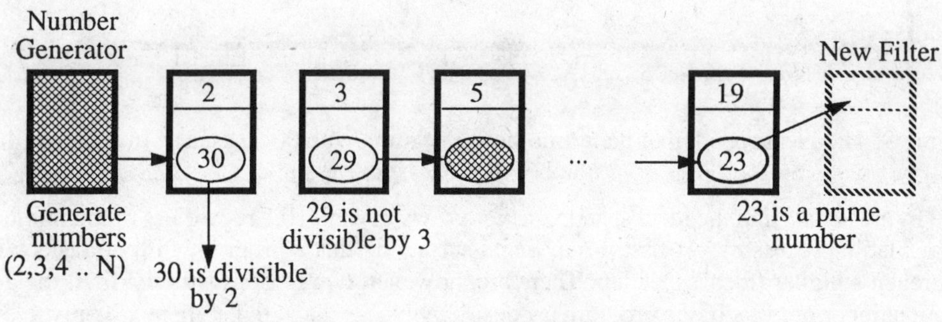

Figure 8: The algorithm for generating prime numbers.

The filter tasks are programmed using the open terminate construction [1]. Using this programming technique, all 80 tasks terminate in parallel at the end of the program. The program ends when all filter tasks are waiting in an open terminate; this happens when the 79th filter task has been created.

All filter tasks are instances of the same task type, i.e they all execute the same code. New filter tasks are created by a new-statement in the filter task which is currently last in the line. Therefore, it is not easy to see, in the source code, how the number of tasks grows during the execution or how much work each filter task performs. Consequently, it would be very difficult to do any accurate speedup predictions by looking at the source code of the program.

Figure 9 shows the ideal speedup of the prime sieve program. This is a typical example of a speedup curve. The speedup grows almost linearly when the number of processors is small. However, after a certain number of processors the speedup stops growing. For this type of speedup curves there are (at least) two values of interest: the maximum speedup value and the number of processors when the speedup stops growing. These two values are indicated in figure 9.

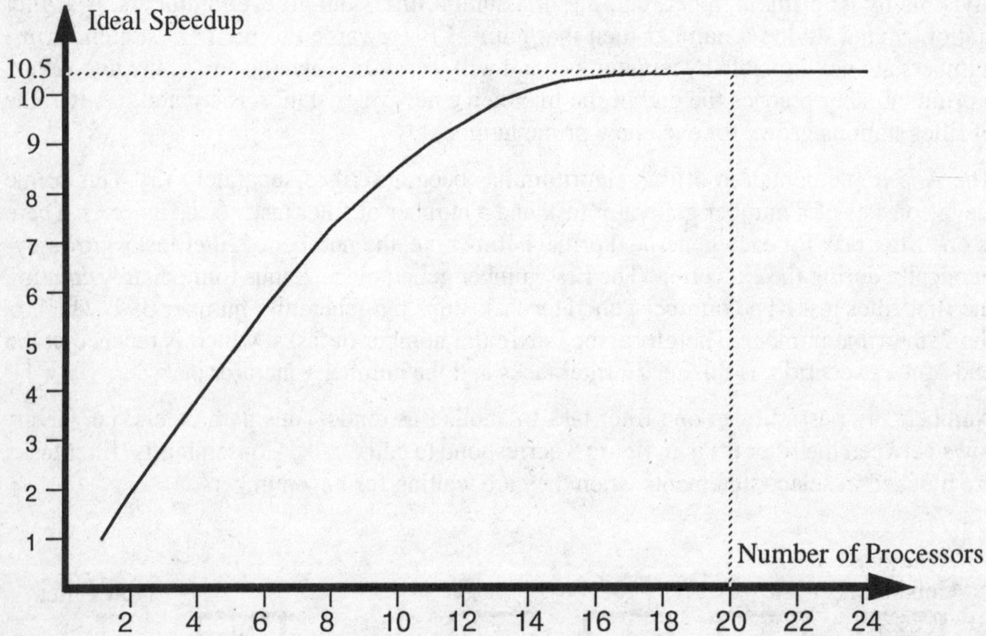

Figure 9: The ideal speedup of the prime sieve program, with 80 tasks, as a function of the number of processors.

The figure shows that the ideal speedup never grows beyond 10.5 regardless of the number of available processors. At first it may seem surprising that a program with 80 tasks will not reach a higher (ideal) speedup. There are, however, two reasons for this: first, the average number of tasks in the program is considerably less than 80, i.e. there are only a few tasks in the beginning of the program's execution and the number of tasks does not reach 80 until the last fraction of the execution. Second, the work is not evenly distributed between all tasks. The reason for this is that most of the generated numbers are filtered out by the tasks in the first part of the chain, i.e. filter tasks in the first part of the chain execute considerably more than filter tasks further down the chain.

The speedup stops growing when the number of processors reaches 20 (see figure 9), i.e. although there are considerably more than 20 tasks during the last part of the program's execution there are never more than 20 active tasks at the same time. This can be understood from the second observation above, i.e. since most numbers are filtered out by the first tasks, filter tasks at the end of the chain are blocked waiting for new numbers most of the time.

When calculating the ideal speedup, global time sliced scheduling using an infinitely small time-slice is assumed. The execution time of a parallel program executing in a multiprocessor system is affected by the scheduling policy. However, for global scheduling, which is often used in multiprocessor systems [4][5], these variations in execution time are bounded by a factor 2, i.e. the execution time using the worst global scheduling policy cannot be more than twice as long as the execution time using the best global scheduling policy [6]. For most programs, this difference is much smaller.

Ideal speedup is, therefore, a reasonable approximation of the speedup using any global scheduling policy, i.e. figure 9 is useful when one wants to decide how many processors this prime sieve program would need in a real multiprocessor system. The figure shows that there is no reason for using more than 20 processors. This number (20) could, however, be somewhat smaller or larger, depending on the scheduling policy in the real system.

8. Conclusions

The method described here is very useful if we have a parallel program and want to select a multiprocessor system for this program. Generally, the speedup of a parallel program increases with the number of processors in the multiprocessor. However, the price for the multiprocessor will also grow with the number of processors. In order to do price-performance trade-offs we have to predict how much speedup we will gain by buying a larger multiprocessor system. The presented method makes it possible to do this kind of prediction.

Most multiprocessor systems lack good programming and debugging facilities. Consequently, parallel programs are often developed on ordinary single-processor work-stations, and not in their target multiprocessor environment. Two different programs solving the same problem may have vastly different speedup properties. In most cases, we want to select the program with the best speedup properties. Unless there is some way of predicting the speedup, the parallel program has to be ported to the target environment in order to get any performance measures; this type of porting is generally very time-consuming. The described method makes it possible to compare the speedup of different programs without porting the programs to the multiprocessor. Therefore, the speedup of prototype implementations can be easily evaluated, thus making it possible to select an efficient structure early.

Dynamic tasking behavior corresponds to one execution of the parallel program. When doing the speedup predictions we assume that the dynamic tasking behavior obtained from this single monitored execution is representative for all executions of the program. Therefore, this method is only applicable to programs for which the dynamic tasking behavior does not change very much from one execution to another. Variations in dynamic tasking behavior can, however, be represented through multiple dynamic tasking behaviors for the same program, i.e. a parallel program could be monitored during a number of different executions, thus producing a set of dynamic tasking behaviors. From these dynamic tasking behaviors a set of ideal speedup curves can be calculated, one curve for each dynamic tasking behavior. If the variation between these speedup curves is limited then useful statistical measures, e.g. mean and standard deviation, describing the speedup can be obtained.

One way of extending the technique described here would be to abandon the ideal multiprocessor model and add system and hardware overhead when calculating the speedup, thus making it possible to do more realistic speedup predictions.

A similar approach to the one described in this paper has been used for predicting the speedup of parallel FORTRAN programs [7]. However, the instrumentation and postprocessing phases were quite trivial in that case, because the parallelization mechanisms in the FORTRAN environment were very simple. Also, a tool using similar techniques for predicting the execution times of parallel algorithms has been described in the literature [8]. This tool is based on a high level description of the parallel algorithm.

Acknowledgments

I am deeply indebted to Lars Philipsson for his advice and support. This project was sponsored by the Swedish National Board for Technical Development (STU) under contract number 87-2427.

References

[1] Department of Defense, USA. *Ada reference manual,* February 1983. ANSI/MIL-STD-1815A.

[2] James L. Peterson and Abraham Silberschatz, *Operating System Concepts (second edition),* Addison-Wesley Publishing Company, 1985.

[3] Gordon E. Anderson, *An Ada Multitask Solution for the Sieve of Erathosthenes,* ACM, Ada Letters Vol 7 September/October 1988.

[4] V. F. Rich, *Parallel Ada for Symmetrical Multiprocessors,* In proceedings of the distributed Ada symposium held at university of Southampton, pp 61-70, December 1989.

[5] Susan Flynn Hummel, *SMARTS - Shared-memory Multiprocessor Ada Run Time Supervisor*, Ph.D. thesis, Published as technical report 495 at the Department of Computer Science, New York University, February 1990.

[6] R.L. Graham, *Bounds for Certain Multiprocessor Timing Anomalies,* SIAM Journal of Applied Mathematics, 17, 2 (1969), pp 416-429.

[7] K. So, A.S. Bolmarcich, F. Darema and V.A. Norton, *A Speedup Analyzer for Parallel Programs,* In proceedings of the 1987 International Conference on Parallel Processing, pp 653 - 662, August 1987.

[8] Anselmo A. Lastra and C. Frank Starmer, *POET: A Tool for the Analysis of the Performance of Parallel Algorithms,* In proceedings of the 1988 International Conference on Parallel Processing, pp 126 - 129, August 1988.

A Highly Parallel Ada Task Scheduler

Susan Flynn Hummel*
CRI, Ecole Nationale Supérieure des Mines de Paris
35, rue Saint-Honoré, 77305 Fontainebleau, France

1 Introduction

Although the tasking model of Ada was mainly aimed at embedded systems, its rich set of tasking features together with Ada's support for programming in the large make Ada attractive for writing large-scale parallel programs for computationally intensive applications. These applications benefit from (and may even require) the power provided by machines with hundreds of processors. To harness such highly parallel machines, a common programming idiom is to create a large number of nearly identical tasks (declared with an array in Ada) that operate on a shared data structure (such as a matrix).

VLSI advances have made the construction of highly parallel machines feasible, however, similar techanological advances have not yet occurred in the software arena and their software environments remain a challenge. For Ada, the concern is that the cost of managing large numbers of tasks will negate the speedup obtainable from their parallel execution. Indeed, a run-time supervisor for Ada must contend with many potentially expensive serialization points, that is, constructs that may take time proportional to the number of tasks involved.

SMARTS (Shared-memory Multiprocessor Ada Run Time Supervisor) [1] is the run-time supervisor for a descendent of the NYU Ada/Ed compiler ([2], [3], [4]) that has been ported to the Ultracomputer [5], which is a scalable shared-memory machine also being designed and built at NYU. SMARTS has been implemented and tested on an eight processor Ultracomputer prototype.

The implementation exploits the atomic increment and swap instructions, `fetch&add` and `fetch&store`, supported by the Ultracomputer and other multiprocessors (e.g., BBN GP-1000 [6]). (These instructions can also be simulated with other read-modify-write instructions.) Indeed, because it is specifically targeted to scalable machines, SMARTS implements all the tasking features of Ada in a highly parallel manner. The overhead of Ada tasking is reduced further by user-mode scheduling, i.e., the explicit scheduling of a family of Ada tasks on a specified number of processors. Thus, Ada tasks are implemented as lightweight processes managed by SMARTS, rather than as full-blown operating system processes.

*On leave from Polytechnic University, Brooklyn, New York, hummel@mono.poly.edu.

In previous papers, we have described the highly parallel task termination algorithm [7] and the shared data management of SMARTS [8]. Here, we concentrate on its highly parallel scheduling mechanism. In particular, we describe the implementation of task creation, activation, delays and rendezvous. In the next section, we give an overview of the user-mode scheduler. In the following section, the highly parallel queues used to implement scheduling are described. How SMARTS uses these queues to implement the creation and activation of tasks, time management and rendezvous management is described in sections §4, §5 and §6 (respectively). The implementations are illustrated with code fragments, and in §7, a proof of their correctness is sketched. The complete code for SMARTS is given in [1]. Finally, the performance of SMARTS and the impact of Ada9X, the pending revision of the language, changes to the tasking model are assessed.

2 User-Mode Scheduling

When an Ada program is run, SMARTS binds an operating system processes to each Ultracomputer processor. The processes can be considered as virtual processors as they execute Ada tasks. Scheduling is self-service in that each process "helps itself" to the ready-to-run tasks that are stored in global queues. User-mode scheduling avoids the inefficiencies due to any mismatch of the semantics of language tasks and operating system processes. Calls to scheduler routines, such as `block` and `unblock`, are inserted into the code generated for the tasks. SMARTS supports several scheduling disciplines, including round-robin and preemptive. A discussion of the implementation of these is beyond the scope of this paper, and we therefore restrict it to a prioritized run-until-blocked scheduling discipline, wherein a scheduler executes the ready task with highest priority until it blocks or terminates.

To detect when the schedulers should terminate (perhaps because the program has deadlocked), a global counter `NUM_RUNNABLE` is kept of all active tasks, that is, tasks currently being executed, tasks on ready queues and tasks suspended at delay statements. The inclusion of the later tasks may seem puzzling, but they must must be counted since they can become active without the intervention of another task, i.e., by a timer interrupt. The code for blocking and unblocking tasks that are not suspended at delays is given in figure 1 and discussed below. When blocking and unblocking delayed tasks, `NUM_RUNNABLE` need not be updated.

```
procedure block(T : in out TCB) is
begin
   if fetch&add(T.NUM_EVENT, -1) > 0 then
      return; -- An event is pending.
   else
      switch_out(T);
      if fetch&add(NUM_RUNNABLE, -1) /= 1 then
         NEW_TASK := get_task;
         if NEW_TASK /= null then
            switch_in(NEW_TASK);
            return;
```

```
        end if;
      end if;
      stop_timer(VALUE); -- It's over, cancel any pending interrupts.
    end if;
end block; procedure unblock(T : in out TCB; E : in EVENTS) is
begin
    TASK.EVENT := E;
    if fetch&add(T.NUM_EVENTS, 1) = -1 then -- No more pending events.
      fetch&add(NUM_RUNNABLE, 1);
      ready_enqueue(T, READY_QUEUE);
    end if;
end unblock;
```

Figure 1. Blocking and Unblocking Tasks.

The blocking and unblocking of tasks is coordinated by modifying various fields in their *task control blocks* (TCBs). TCBs contain all of the information necessary for the schedulers to manage tasks throughout their lifetime, i.e., their state. A task can be one of six states: active, blocked (waiting on a rendezvous and/or a delay), terminatable (waiting on an a select with a terminate alternative), abnormal (aborted, but not yet complete) completed (waiting for dependents to terminate) and terminated.

To coordinate task transitions from active to blocked, TCBs contain three fields, EVENT, NUM_EVENT, and STATUS. (The other state transitions are discussed in [7] and [1], wherein the task termination mechanism of SMARTS is described.) The EVENT and STATUS fields of a task are closely related: The STATUS of a task is its current activity. The EVENT of a task is the action that caused a blocked task to become unblocked. The STATUS of the task is set only by the task itself. Other tasks inspect the STATUS of a task when they want to engage in an activity with the task. The EVENT of a task is set by scheduler that unblocks it. The number of pending or outstanding events for a task is recorded in its NUM_EVENTS counter. NUM_EVENTS is used to determine when a task should block or be unblocked. When a task must wait for an event its NUM_EVENT is (atomically) decremented, when an event occurs its NUM_EVENT is (atomically) incremented. If after decrementing, NUM_EVENTS is less than 0 the task blocks, and if after incrementing, NUM_ is 0 the task is made ready.

The events relevant to scheduling, rendezvous and time outs are: CREATED, ACTIVATED, ENTRY_CALL, START_RDV, END_RDV, TIME_OUT, TERMINATE and ABORT. TIME_OUTs occur when delays expire, and TERMINATEs when the terminate alternative of a select statement is taken. The other events have their obvious meanings.

On a parallel machine, competing events can occur when tasks attempt to rendezvous. In particular, *a)* ABORT, START_RDV, and TIME_OUT, *b)* ABORT, END_RDV, and TIME_OUT, and *c)* ABORT and TERMINATE. These conflicting events must be resolved so that only one occurs, and hence, causes a task to become unblocked. Resolving these conflicts without the aid of a central scheduler or locking, both of which are serial bottlenecks on large-scale parallel machines, is non-trivial. However, the SMARTS implementation is highly parallel. Their resolution is discussed in the rest of this paper. Briefly, for *a)* and *b)*, each event disables the others, and for *c)*, a flag ABNORMAL is set by the aborter and later inspected by the task (at synchronization points).

3 Highly Parallel Queues

The efficiency of an Ada scheduler is highly dependent on the cost of its queue handling [9]. There is a ready queue for each task priority, a dependent queue for each master block, a queue of callers for each entry, and a time queue for each scheduler. These queues can be classified by their number of concurrent enqueuers and dequeuers: ready queues have many enqueuers and dequeuers, dependent and entry queues have many enqueuers (activators or callers) and a sole dequeuer (the master or owner), while time queues have a sole enqueuer and dequeuer (the scheduler). The nodes of ready and dependent queues are TCBs. Entry and time queues have special node types, called `ENTRY_NODE`s and `TIME_NODE`s. These two queues also support interior removals, as entry calls and delays must sometimes be cancelled.

All of the queues are implemented as lists of nodes linked by pointers. The `FIRST` and `LAST` node pointers of the the list are updated with `fetch&store`s. To enqueue a node, the instructions `PREVIOUS := fetch&store(LAST, NODE); PREV.NEXT := NODE;` are executed. To dequeue a node, the instruction `NODE := fetch&store(FIRST, FIRST.NEXT);` is executed. Note that entire linked lists can be enqueued in the same number of instructions as a single node (by substituting `NODE` with `LAST_N` and `FIRST_N` in the first and second code fragments).

Many implementation details must be dealt with, such as empty queue re-initialization and concurrent dequeuers; however, by using an optimistic strategy (wherein anomalous events are detected and subsequently corrected), these add surprisingly little overhead. The code for a ready queue is given in figure 2; the other queues are similar, yet simpler. In each case, queue operations take less than ten instructions in the absence of contention.

```
procedure ready_enqueue_list(FIRST_N, LAST_N : in TCB, Q : in out QUEUE) is
begin
   PREVIOUS := fetch&store(Q.LAST, LAST_N);
   if PREVIOUS = null then -- Queue was empty.
      Q.FIRST := FIRST_N;
      Q.FIRSTMULT := FIRST_N.MULT; -- Dequeues enabled.
   else
      PREVIOUS.NEXT := FIRST_N;
   end if;
end ready_enqueue_list;
function ready_dequeue(Q : in out QUEUE) return TCB is
begin
   while Q.LAST /= null loop -- Until work to do.
      if Q.FIRSTMULT > 0 and then fetch&add(Q.FIRSTMULT, -1) > 0 then
         OLD_FIRST := Q.FIRST;
         I := fetch&add(OLD_FIRST.MULT, -1);
         if I = 1 then -- Item now empty, so start new one.
            Q.FIRST := OLD_FIRST.NEXT;
            if Q.FIRST = null then -- Queue empty, so reset LAST.
               OLD_LAST := fetch&store(Q.LAST, null);
               if OLD_LAST /= OLD_FIRST then -- Intervening enqueues missed.
                  while OLD_FIRST = null loop
                  end loop; -- Wait till nodes fully linked.
```

```
                read_enqueue_list(OLD_FIRST.NEXT, OLD_LAST, Q); -- Re-enqueue.
            end if;
         end if;
      end if;
   end if;
   case OLD_FIRST.STATUS of
   when INITIALIZE => -- Initialize array.
      initialize(OLD_FIRST.TCB_PTRS(I), I, OLD_FIRST);
   when ACTIVATE => -- Activate array.
      return OLD_FIRST.TCB_PTRS(I);
   when TERMINATE => -- Termination wave of an array.
      T := OLD_FIRST.TCB_PTRS(I);
      if fetch&store(T.RDV, false) = true
      and then fetch&add(T.NUM_EVENTS, 1) = 0 then
         return T; -- We must terminate.
      else -- Task terminating itself (without blocking).
         fetch&add(NUM_RUNNABLE, -1); -- Was incremented for each TCB.
      end if;
   when others => -- Single-item TCB, so execute.
      return OLD_FIRST;
   end case;
  end loop;
  return null; -- The queue is empty.
end ready_dequeue;
```

Figure 2. Ready Queue Operations.

Ready and dependent queue enqueues and dequeues execute concurrently, and only an entry queue dequeue (by the owner) locks out enqueues (by callers of that entry). (The sole enqueuer and dequeuer of time queues are the same scheduler.) An optimistic scheme, wherein removed nodes are flagged as such, and left as place holders, allows nodes to be removed from the interior of entry and time queues without locking out other operations. (Note that interior removals are the only concurrent operations on time queues.) More specifically, nodes have a `TAG` field that is set to `ENQUEUED` when the node is enqueued. Dequeuers and removers try to claim the node by executing `fetch&store(NODE.TAG, DEQUEUED)` and `fetch&store(NODE.TAG, REMOVED)` (respectively). The one that returns `ENQUEUED` is successful. If a task needs to reuse a node that has been left as a place holder before it reaches the head of the queue, then it creates a new one. (A related queue described in [11] re-uses nodes "in place" obviating the need for their dynamic allocation. This optimization lowers queue operation overhead and permits a greater degree of parallelism, but the resulting queue is not FIFO.)

Ready queues are multi-item queues, that is, they allow a single item on the queue to represent multiple (nearly) identical items. The multiplicity `MULT` of multi-item is decremented when an item is dequeued. Only when its `MULT` reaches 0 is the item actually removed from the queue.

Multi-item TCBs, called `SMART_NODE`s, are used perform operations (e.g., initialization, activation and termination) on an array of tasks in parallel. Once a task is created it is given its own TCB. The ENTRY_NODE of the task is placed on an entry queue when the task calls the corresponding entry, and its TIME_NODE on a time queue when the task executes a delay. When the rendezvous occurs or the timer expires, the TCB of the task is placed back on the appropriate ready queue. If the task is aborted, it is also placed on a ready queue so that it can do any necessary house cleaning before completing.

4 Task Creation and Activation

In SMARTS, families of tasks are created and activated together using a mechanism that is similar to the stack of block frames (BFs) used by the uniprocessor Ada/Ed compiler [4]. (The tasks in a family have the same parent and master tasks.) In this section, we describe how a family of tasks are created and activated in parallel. To avoid serial bottlenecks, when a parent task elaborates an array of tasks, a SMARTS_NODE is created. By placing the SMARTS_NODE on a ready queue, operations, such as TCB initialization and activation, are performed on the array in parallel by the schedulers.

BFs contain the fields necessary to coordinates the dependents of a master block. (So that they can be handled uniformly, each task has both a master task and a master block.) The ones that are relevant to task creation and activation are: FIRST_DEP, LAST_DEP, NUM_DEPS and TASKS_DECLARED. FIRST_DEP and LAST_DEP implement the queue of the direct dependents of the BF. For compatibility, it uses the same queue algorithm as the ready queues. TASKS_DECLARED points to the current set of unactivated tasks that have been created in the same context (i.e., they have the same parent and master block); these task are linked by NEXT pointers.

The primary fields of a TCB used for task creation and activation are: PRIORITY, SAVE_PRIORITY, SIBLING, and WHO. The WHO field is set to the TCB of its parent (activator) when the task is created. The TCBs of the dependent tasks of BF are linked by SIBLING pointers. PRIORITY and SAVE_PRIORITY are required to activate tasks at the maximum of the task's and its parent priority.

The parent of a family of task being created together allocates storage for their TCBs. For each array of tasks, a contiguous block is allocated, and their SMARTS_NODE is placed on a ready queue so that the TCB fields will be initialized in parallel. (The information for initialization is found in the SMARTS_NODE or in the task type template.) The parent initializes the other TCBs. The family of tasks to be activated are linked by NEXT pointers, so their parent can place them on a ready queue with a single enqueue. Before enqueueing a family of N tasks, the parent sets its MULT counter to N.

The schedulers that activate the tasks append their TCBs onto the dependent queues of the parent BF. This can be accomplished without locking as the parent only accesses this queue after it has completed or been aborted. After a task is activated, the MULT of its parent is (atomically) decremented, and if the value reaches 0, its parent is unblocked (i.e., the NUM_EVENT of its parent is incremented).

5 Time Management

Time management in SMARTS assumes that there is a global clock and that each processor has a local timer. Each scheduler has a time queue where it stores the TIME_NODESs of the tasks whose delay it executes. The queue is sorted in ascending order of delay expiration, which is stored as an absolute time (to minimize slippage). Thus the processor only sets a physical timer for the first node on the queue.

The TIME_NODE_PTR of the TCB of a task points to its current TIME_NODE. A TIME_NODE contains four fields: WHEN, TAG, NEXT and TASK_PTR. WHEN is the absolute time that the delay is to expire. As described in §3, TAG allows concurrent interior removals, so that delays can be cancelled when a rendezvous occurs or the task is aborted. NEXT points to the next TIME_NODE on the time queue, and TASK_PTR to the TCB of the owner of the TIME_NODE.

When a task executes a delay, its TIME_NODE is placed on the time queue of the scheduler that is executing it. The correct position in the queue is found using a simple linear search. For scientific code, we believe that few tasks will execute delays, so that time queues will not be long enough to justify a more sophisticated search method (with a better time complexity).

After a time out occurs, the scheduler attempts to disable any conflicting events, e.g., rendezvous or abort. (The resolution of these events is given §7.) The TCB of the task is placed on the appropriate ready queue if no other events have occurred. All the nodes at the front of the queue that have been removed (i.e., their delays cancelled) are then dequeued, and a timer is set for the new head.

6 Rendezvous Management

The select statement of Ada allows tasks to wait conditionally on an entry call or multiple accept statements. Select alternatives may be guarded, delays or terminates. Thus there are several events that can occur concurrently when a task executes a select statement, and their highly parallel implementation is non-obvious. We will refer to the task that declares an entry as its owner, and without loss of generality, consider simple accept statements as selects with only one alternative and a delay of 0.

In SMARTS, entry queues can be accessed concurrently and rendezvous can be initiated by either the owner or the caller of an entry. We outline this parallel implementation below; its details and code can be found in [1] (where the implementation of interrupt entries is also given).

The resolution of the conflicting events that can occur when a task executes a select statement is treated more formally in §7. In short, a flag RDV is used to coordinate rendezvous: when an owner executes a select, it sets its RDV flag. Once the flag is set no event involving the owner can happen without first reseting the flag. This includes rendezvous initiated by the owner, rendezvous initiated by the caller, the expiration of a delay, selection of a terminate alternative and an abort.

There is separate queue of ENTRY_NODEs for each entry implemented with FIRST and LAST pointers. The ENTRY_NODEs are linked by NEXT pointers, and have a TAG field to permit their interior removal. Each queue also has a counter COUNTER that tracks the number of callers and a boolean GUARD that is set when entry guard is true. To resolve owner/caller/remover conflicts, a queue is protected by a readers/writer lock that allows concurrent enqueues and removals, or an exclusive dequeue. It is implemented using atomic increments and swaps. An owner never changes entry queue data structures (e.g., GUARD) without first obtaining its writer-lock.

Accept statements must be executed at the maximum priority of the caller and owner. The priority of the owner is saved in the SAVE_PRIORITY field of the caller's TCB. The accept can be executed at the maximum priority of the callers on the queue, by using an array of counters. Whenever a task is enqueued, it increments the counter for its priority. Rendezvous are executed at the priority level of the highest non-zero counter.

```
function owner_rdv(OWNER : in out TCB; CALLER : out TCB; E : out ENTRY)
return boolean is
begin
   for each I in OWNER.OPEN loop
      if OWNER.RDV = false then -- Set by caller or aborter.
         return false;
      else
         writer_lock(OWNER.ENTRIES(I).OC_LOCK);
         COUNT := fetch&add(OWNER.ENTRIES(I).COUNTER, -1);
         if COUNT = 0 or else fetch&store(OWNER.RDV, false) = false then
            fetch&add(OWNER.ENTRY(I).COUNTER, 1); -- No task waiting or
            OWNER.ENTRY(I).GUARD := true;         -- already set.
            writer_unlock(OWNER.ENTRIES(I).OC_LOCK);
         else -- Pending caller and we reset flag.
            CALLER := entry_dequeue(OWNER.ENTRY(I));
            writer_unlock(OWNER.ENTRIES(I).OC_LOCK);
            return true;
         end if;
      end if;
   end loop;
end function owner_rdv;
```

Figure 3. Owner Attempting to Rendezvous.

When an owner executes a select after setting its RDV flag, it inspects the queue of each open entry in turn. Each queue is write-locked while the owner searches for a caller. If the owner finds a non-empty queue then it attempts to reset its RDV flag thereby committing itself to a rendezvous with the first caller. An entry caller, after obtaining a read-lock, increments COUNT and checks the GUARD. If it is the first caller and GAURD is set, then the caller attempts to reset the flag; otherwise, if the call is not conditional, then it enqueues itself. When a caller discovers that a rendezvous is possible, i.e., resets RDV, it sets the WHO and WHAT fields of the owner (to itself and the entry) before unblocking the owner. The code for an owner attempting a rendezvous is given in figure 3, and for a caller in figure 4.

```
function caller_rdv(CALLER, OWNER : in out TCB; E : in out ENTRY)
return boolean is
begin
   read_lock(E.OC_LOCK); -- Lock out the owner.
   if fetch&add(E.COUNTER, 1) = 0 and then E.GUARD = true
   and then fetch&store(OWNER.RDV, false) = false then
      fetch&add(E.COUNTER, -1);
      CALLER.STATUS := ACTIVE; -- We're the first caller of an open entry.
      read_unlock(E.OC_LOCK);
      OWNER.WHO := CALLER;
      OWNER.WHAT := E;
      flush(VOLATILE); -- Shared data synchronization point.
      if OWNER.STATUS = TIMED_SELECT then
         timed_unblock(OWNER, RDV_EVENT);
      else
         unblock(OWNER, RDV_EVENT);
      end if;
      return true; -- Will block awaiting end of rendezvous.
   end if;
   return false; -- Will be enqueued if non-conditional.
end caller_rdv;
```

Figure 4. Caller Attempting to Rendezvous.

7 Absence of Race Conditions

The interaction of termination waves (of quiescent tasks waiting on a terminate alternative), time outs, aborts and rendezvous is complex. In this section, we explain how race conditions, which might cause a task to be incorrectly unblocked, between the actors (caller, owners, masters, timer handlers and aborters) that participate in these events are avoided. First the actions of termination waves, time outs, aborts and rendezvous are resolved, and then those of callers and owners.

A task T waiting on a select with a terminate alternative cannot be involved in a termination wave while there exists tasks that can call T. Nor can T be involved in a time out (delay and terminate alternatives are exclusive). T can, however, be aborted. To avoid a potential race with aborters to unblock T, when the master is participating in a termination wave it must reset the T.RDV. Only if the flag is successfully reset, does the master unblock t (with a TERMINATE event).

When a task T executes a selective wait, its TIME_NODE is enqueued to the time chain of the scheduler executing it. When the delay of a TIME_NODE expires, if the delay has not been canceled, then the TIMER_HANDLER also tries to reset T.RDV or to remove T from an entry queue. If the timer does not succeed, then the time out fails; a rendezvous or an abort is already underway.

When a task T is aborted its ABNORMAL flag is set. All tasks check their ABNORMAL flags at abort synchronization points. If T is executing a select, then the aborter will attempt to reset T.RDV. If T is executing an entry call, then the aborter attempts to remove T from the entry queue; if the aborter does not succeed, then it waits until the entry call has completed.

Since only one of the actors succeeds in resetting the RDV flag or removing the entry node there is no race condition: whatever actor succeeds unblocks the task. It remains to be shown that rendezvous are achieved when possible, that is, that callers and owners interact correctly. Since a rendezvous can be discovered by a caller or an owner, we must ensure that they do not "miss" each other.

Protecting each entry queue with a readers/writer lock ensures that an entry queue dequeue by its owner and a removal by a timer handler or aborter cannot happen concurrently. Similarly, they ensure that an owner cannot concurrently dequeue while callers enqueue. Consider, also, the following observation regarding the owner `O` and caller `C` of an entry `E`: *1)* `O` decrements `E.COUNTER`, and if non-zero, attempts to reset `O.RDV`. *2)* If unsuccessful, `O` increments `E.COUNTER` and then sets `GAURD`. *3)* `C` increments `E.COUNTER`, and if zero, attempts to reset `O.RDV`. *4)* If successful, `C` decrements `E.COUNTER`.

1) and *3)* imply that once `O` has decremented `E.COUNT` and reset `O.RDV`, `O` will rendezvous with the first task on the entry queue. *2)* and *4)* imply that once `C` has incremented `E.COUNTER` and reset `O.RDV`, `C` will rendezvous with `O`. *1)* also implies that `O` will attempt to reset `O.RDV` when it finds a non-empty queue, and *3)* that `C` will attempt to reset `O.RDV` when it is the first caller. Finally, only one of the first callers of `O`'s entries will succeed in resetting `O.RDV`.

8 Performance

Although SMARTS is targeted to large-scale multiprocessors, it is as efficient as its uniprocessor predecessor: it contains roughly the same number of lines and executes at roughly the same speed. Indeed after being striped of comments the length of the two tasking modules are within 2 lines of each other. (Both are interpreters, so lines of code is a suitable metric for performance comparison.)

Since SMARTS self-schedules Ada tasks on its schedulers, the tasks do not incur the overhead of full-blown operating system processes or threads. Hence, we do not have to conclude that "Ada tasks are not lightweight constructs that can be casually invoked," as was the epitaph of an implementation of Ada tasks using Mach threads [10], which are lighter weight than traditional operating system processes. (When threads rather than operating system processes are used as virtual processors, then the overhead of creating virtual processors is reduced by an order of magnitude [11].)

Using highly parallel queues, the schedulers provide run-time support for Ada tasks in a bottleneck-free manner. By placing a single `SMARTS_NODE` onto a ready queue, the initialization, activation and termination of an array of tasks is preformed in parallel. The implementation of time management is also serialization-free in the sense that a task can be removed from the interior of a time queue while other tasks are being enqueued, dequeued and removed. Moreover, each scheduler can perform enqueues and dequeues to its time queue concurrently. The only serialization in rendezvous management is while a task attempts to rendezvous with the callers of its entries (note that callers of other entries can proceed in parallel).

Our highly parallel implementation of the Ada tasking model makes it possible for computationally intensive numeric applications to be written using Ada's rich set of tasking features without sacrificing performance. Thus, these applications can benefit from Ada's support for programming in the large while harnessing the power of future large-scale parallel machines.

9 Impact of 9X Proposed Changes

A revision of Ada, called Ada 9X (as it is to be finalized this decade), is underway. The current proposed revision is described in [12]. Most of the changes to Ada's tasking model can easily be incorporated into SMARTS without increasing its complexity; indeed, some tasking features can be supported more efficiently (e.g., aborts whose use has been restricted). There is one major exception, however: *selective entry calls*, i.e., the ability to wait on multiple entry calls. To wit, our highly parallel rendezvous mechanism breaks when a task can be on more than one entry queue at a time.

Over the years, languages (such as Occam and Ada) have been criticized for this lack of symmetry between entry calls and accept statements; however, the omission was deliberate due to the implementation penalty: it is much more difficult to retract messages than it is to refuse to accept them (fan-out versus fan-in). Allowing multiple outstanding entry calls requires coarse-grained locking: a rendezvous lock must be held throughout selects, and rendezvous cannot be achieved without holding both the owner's and the caller's locks. Time-outs for conditional delays, terminate alternatives, and aborts may also have to obtain the lock.

This implementation is not disastrous, except perhaps for highly parallel machines, and has some advantages, for instance, being easier to prove correct. Moreover, the impact is mitigated in [12] by the inclusion of *protected records*, which provide passive synchronization mechanisms that are potentially more efficient than task rendezvous. Protected records encapsulate data with their operations, which can be functions, procedures or entry calls. Only functions can operate on the data concurrently. Protected records allow atomic read-modify-write instructions to be specified at the Ada-level, and are better-suited to application programming than rendezvous. (The '83 Ada tasking model was primarily aimed at real-time embedded systems.) Unfortunately, in the current 9X proposal selects can contain calls to protected entries, and their overhead is increased accordingly.

Treating language features, such as entry calls, uniformly leads to a clean design. But over-generality also has its cost. The two types of entry calls are different, one is active and the other passive. As the goal of protected records is to provide low-overhead passive synchronization, their use may have to be more restricted than tasks.

Important questions are therefore: Will selective protective entry calls be common enough to justify the additional locking overhead? What about selective entry calls in general?

Acknowledgements

Many people contributed to the design and implementation of SMARTS. The most influential of these is my thesis advisor, Edmond Schonberg, under whose tutelage SMARTS was designed. Other people on the NYU Ada project, most notably Robert Dewar, and on the NYU Ultracomputer project, most notably Jan Edler, Jim Lipkis and Edith Schonberg, also contributed. SMARTS owes much to the uniprocessor run-time system, designed by Philippe Kruchten and Jean-Pierre Rosen, on which it is based. SMARTS was implemented by Anne Dinning, Bernard Banner and Kurt Behnke. The contributions of all of the above are gratefully acknowledged.

References

[1] S. Flynn Hummel, "SMARTS—Shared-memory Multiprocessor Ada Run-Time Supervisor," *Ph.D. Thesis*, New York University, Dec. 1988.

[2] R. B. K. Dewar, G. A. Fisher Jr., E. Schonberg, R. Froehlich, S. Bryant, C. F. Gross, and M. G. Burke, "The NYU Ada Translator and Interpretter," *Proc. of the IEEE Compsac '80 Conf.*, Oct. 1980.

[3] P. Kruchten, "The Ada Machine,," Ada/Ed Documentation, 1985.

[4] J.-P. Rosen, "The Ada Task Management System," Ada/Ed Documentation, 1985.

[5] A. Gottlieb, "An Overview of the Ultracomputer Project," in *Experimental Computing Architectures*, J. J. Dongarra (ed.), pp. 25-95, North Holland, 1987.

[6] BBN, *Inside the Butterfly GP1000*, Cambridge, MA, Oct. 1988.

[7] S. F. Flynn, E. Schonberg and E. Schonberg, "The Efficient Termination of Ada Tasks," *Ada LETTERS*, vol. VII. pp. 55-76, Nov./Dec. 1987.

[8] S. Flynn Hummel, R. B. K. Dewar and E. Schonberg, "A Storage Model for Ada on Hierarchical-Memory Multiprocessors," *Proc. Ada-Europe Int. Conf.*, pp. 205-214, Cambridge University Press, June 1989.

[9] A. Ardö, "Hardware Support for Executing Ada Tasking," *Proc. Hawaii Int. Conf. on Software Systems Sciences*, pp. 194-202, Jan. 1988.

[10] T. D. Newton, "An Implementation of Ada Tasking," Carnegie-Mellon University Tech. Report CMU-CS-87-169, Oct. 1987.

[11] S. Flynn Hummel and E. Schonberg. "Low-Overhead Scheduling of Nested Parallelism," IBM Journal of Research and Development, Nov. 1991.

[12] Intermetrics, Inc., *Ada 9X Mapping Volume II Mapping Specifications Version 4.0, IR-MZ-1250-2*, Dec. 1991.

STRAda
An Ada transformation and distribution system

G.Bazalgette, D.Bekele, C.Bernon,
M.Filali, J.M Rigaud, A.Sayah

IRIT-Université Paul Sabatier
118, Route de Narbonne
F-31062 TOULOUSE Cedex
email: bekele@irit.fr

Abstract

In this paper, the authors introduce STRAda: a transformation and distribution system for Ada programs. The aim of the system is to allow users to run Ada programs on a distributed architecture, i.e. over a network comprising several nodes.
The problem is addressed from a transformational standpoint: Ada program text is transformed into another kind of Ada text which in turn uses primitives from the STRAda kernel built on top of a distributed operating system: UNIX.
We discuss design and implementation of the STRAda kernel and the kinds of transformations we have taken into consideration.

1 Introduction

The development of parallel and/or distributed applications is generally addressed from two different angles:

- from the language angle, using a programming model which is independent of any underlying physical system,
- from the system standpoint, using an abstract representation of underlying physical resources.

Generally speaking, both angles are not supported by existing distributed programming environments. Thus:

- the task is either addressed from the language angle and the programs written lack the advantages of the sophisticated environment the underlying operating system provides,
- or the system approach is adopted and the resulting programs lack the degree of expression and structure afforded by a high level programming language.

The essential goal set for **STRAda** **[BBB91]** (**S***ystème* de **T***ransformation* et de **R***épartition* **Ada**) was to combine these two ways of addressing distributed system development. We adopted a transformational approach to achieve this goal. Our aim was not to define a new programming language or distributed system but rather to develop a way of transforming a program written in an existing language into a program for an existing distributed system. In the case in question, we opted for the language Ada and the UNIX operating system.
This paper begins with a brief reminder of the basic concepts of parallelism and distributed processing in Ada and UNIX. The authors then define the STRAda kernel and address the transformation issue i.e, the change from the Ada model to the UNIX model. Lastly, the reasons of STRAda choices will be discussed.

2 Working framework and objectives

The Ada language and the UNIX system are well known standards in the programming language and operating system fields. Further on, we will be introducing the idea of parallelism, communication and distribution in the Ada language and the UNIX system. Several solutions will then be discussed and the general outlines of the STRAda project presented.

2.1 Parallelism, communication and distribution in Ada and UNIX

In Ada, the unit of parallelism is the task. Communication between tasks is performed through rendezvous or shared variables. In this language the idea of distribution is not explicitly stated. However, the rendezvous concept can easily be adapted to distributed processing.

In the UNIX system, the unit of parallelism is the process. Several types of communications and protocols are provided by the system. We opted for socket communication because of its transparency with regard to distribution. Moreover, this type of communication is in fact intended for implementing applications designed on the client-server model, which is compatible with the philosophy governing Ada tasks.

2.2 Existing approaches to the problem

Although Ada does not exclude the distribution aspect of an application, it does not include the basic concepts necessary to a simple implementation of this aspect. However it does explicitly provide parallelism or other advanced software engineering concepts. A number of investigations have been brought to bear on this aspect of programming, addressing the issues from various different angles. A classification system developed by

Bishop and Hasling [BH90] sums up the various existing angles:

1 - How many Ada programs are involved?
Either a single Ada program is partitioned for distribution over the network or several Ada programs are run locally at each node and communicate with each other across an independent message system.

2 - How is communication among nodes expressed?
Communication can be explicitly expressed by the programmer of the application, or it can be implicit and transparent to the programmer since it is generated by the translator or tool dedicated to this service.

3 - What is the degree of liberty left to the programmer as far as the unit of distribution is concerned?
A number of constructions in the language could be considered to comply with the profile of a distribution unit, the most important being packages and tasks, although subroutines and even variables could also be distributed.

4 - How is the distribution map specified?
Distribution of units to the various nodes can be explicitly described, using a dedicated language for instance, or automatically dynamically analyzing the topography of the network used.

The authors define several ways of addressing the problem according to the choices made with respect to these criteria. The disadvantage of the most fundamental approach (several Ada programs running locally) [DC90] may be that checking among programs running on several nodes could fail. However, this pitfall could be avoided by using dedicated communication packages.
The next two classes involve single Ada programs and imply constraints on distribution units. Communication can either be explicit [HW90, AD90] or implicit [VKT90, AL90, DFSS90].
The last class explored involves Ada applications in which no constraints are made on distribution units. The most advanced project in this area is the APPL project [JKIC89, JE90, EJ90].

2.3 STRAda and related options

The basic goal of the project is researching and developing a minimal distribution kernel capable of implementing all the most specific features of Ada. The STRAda project is part of the class of applications consisting of a single program with constraints on the distribution units and implicit communication.
The unit of distribution chosen is the task. This choice is justified by the target architecture: a network of workstations. A smaller unit of distribution, such as that adopted by APPL seems to us to be more suitable for the purposes of massively parallel architectures (such as a transputer network for instance).
In the interests of obtaining a minimal kernel, we opted for message passing as the

communications mode. A certain number of aspects of the language are not implemented in this kernel, such as variable sharing and task termination. In section 5 we will discuss the implementation of the above in terms of services offered by the minimal kernel.

Implementation involves translating the source code of one Ada program into another Ada program (figure 1)

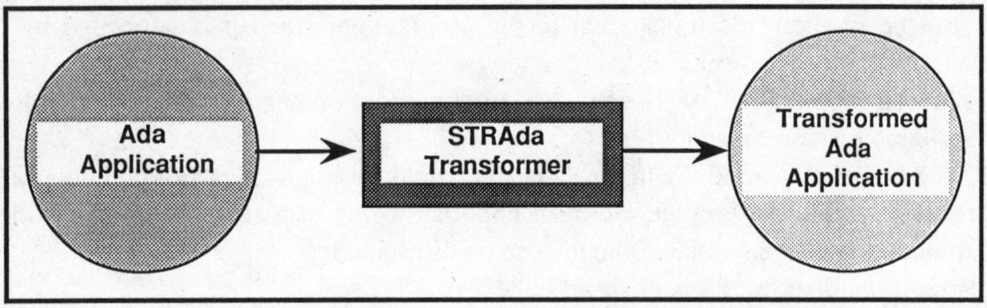

Figure 1: Program transformation

In the transformed program, all constructions involving parallelism and communication have been replaced by calls to STRAda kernel services (figure 2).
A minimal kernel, specific to the Ada language, and reuse without modification of existing systems (Ada compilers, UNIX operating system, etc.) are some of the most interesting aspects of the STRAda project.

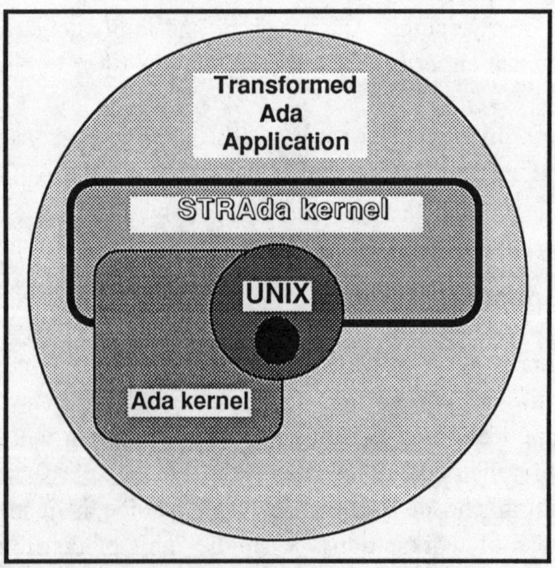

Figure 2: STRAda operating environment

3 Defining a distributed kernel specific to Ada

In this section, the associations we have made between the concepts and mechanisms of Ada and the UNIX system will be introduced. We begin by presenting the parallel processing aspect and then discuss synchronization and distribution.

3.1 Parallelism

We naturally associated a UNIX process to each Ada task. From a purely practical standpoint, such a choice may seem costly and we could have opted for multiplexing several tasks inside the same UNIX process, as most compilers do (pseudo parallelism). However, the implementation strategy we adopted has the following advantages:

- it makes for real parallelism inside an Ada program running on multiprocessor UNIX workstations,
- it provides for better reuse of the underlying operating system (UNIX) since synchronization of an Ada task is directly expressed in terms of synchronisation of the underlying process.

In the STRAda system, parallelism and distribution are implemented by a remote task creation procedure. Currently, the node where the task resides is explicitly given when the task is created.

3.2 Synchronization and communication

In order to implement the distributed version of Ada synchronization and communication instructions, we naturally chose the socket method. We associated a socket and a port with each Ada entry. The UNIX primitives (*sendto, recvfrom, select)* are used to receive or send from one of the entries or select any one entry from a set of entries.

Currently, each Ada task manages its own rendezvous; here we could have imagined a more efficient strategy whereby each node would have a unique rendezvous server.

The solution chosen has its limits but also the enormous advantage of allowing for direct use of the UNIX communication system.

3.3 STRAda kernel architecture and implementation

The STRAda kernel consists of:

- a package supplying tasks with services for parallelism, communication and synchronization,

- a set of tasks called Creation-Server, each executed on a node in the application (figure 3).

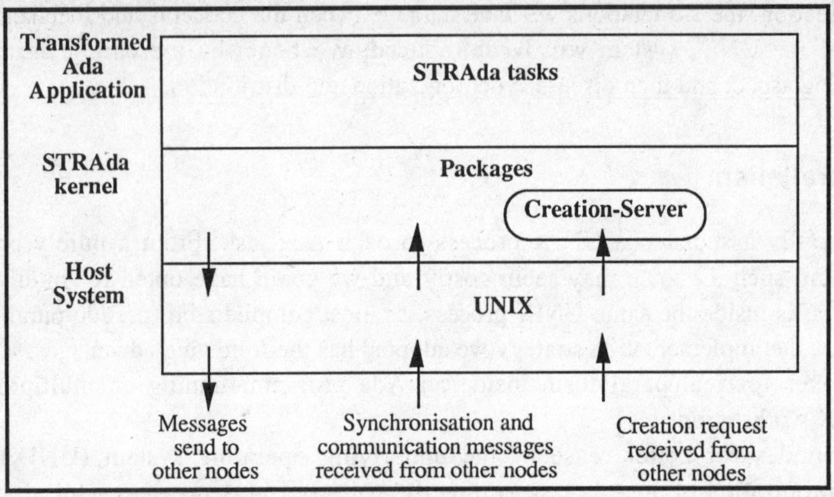

Figure 3 : STRAda architecture

An application task is synchronized or communicates using the dedicated Ada language instruction set (task declaration or dynamic task creation, call from an entry or acceptance of a rendezvous at an entry, the Ada *select* instruction, etc.). These subroutines then use the socket mechanism to dialog directly with a remote task or with a Creation-Server task. The part played by each Creation-Server task consists in initializing the tasks to be performed on their respective nodes. Each initialization involves creating a UNIX process and allocating a unique name to the process. Thus, to create a task on node S, the mother task requests the node's Creation-Server task via the STRAda package which in turn sends it the information used to synchronize or communicate directly with the task created (entry points represented by UNIX sockets). The table 1 sums up the package content:

4 Transforming the Ada model into the UNIX model

In this section, we will give an overview on implementation of the various transformations. We begin with a brief presentation of the tool used: the Cornell Synthesizer Generator [RT89b] (for a detailed presentation with examples, please refer to [RT89a]). We then discuss transformation principles and the relevant choices made.

STRAda primitive	Function performed
CREATE	Creates a task
CALL	Calls a task entry
ACCEPTTT	Accepts a rendezvous with data exchange (does not lock in the caller)
ACCEPT_DO	Accepts a rendezvous with data exchange (locks in the caller until rendezvous terminates)
ACCEPT_END	Terminates rendezvous processing by the task called up (releases caller)
SELECTTT	Accepts one rendezvous among several ones

Table 1

4.1 The Cornell Synthesizer Generator

The Cornell Synthesizer Generator (CSG) is a tool which generates a syntax editor from an attributed abstract syntax. The programming language used for the CSG is Synthesizer Specification Language (SSL). In SSL, abstract trees are specified using the phylum concept. A phylum is a type of tree whose nodes are recursively built using determined operators and phyla. For the STRAda project we chose the abstract syntax DIANA [EBGW83] (Descriptive Intermediate Attributed Notation for Ada). This choice was made for the following reason: DIANA can be considered to be a standard for internal representation of Ada programs. Integration of STRAda with other tools such as Anna [KBL80] is thus feasible. Another important aspect of CSG is that abstract trees can include synthesized or inherited attributes [DJL88]. These attributes are generally used for semantic checking. In the STRAda project, we use them to synthesize other programs.

4.2 Transformation principles

The principles implemented in transforming an Ada program are discussed in this section. Let us remember that the purpose of transformation is to replace all the Ada instructions involving parallelism and synchronization with equivalent instructions which make calls to the STRAda kernel. We considered the following transformation types:

- global functional transformation whereby the abstract tree of a program is entirely transformed by an SSL function;
- local attribute transformation whereby each node of the abstract tree of an Ada program synthesizes a transformed node. In this case, global transformation is the attribute of the root of the program abstract tree.

We stress the fact that whatever type of transformation is adopted, we obtain a new Ada program.

a Functional transformation

As mentioned in the previous section, the SSL language of the CSG is used to define and manipulate abstract syntax trees. In our case, the abstract syntax tree to be transformed is DIANA representation of the Ada program. Transformation can be defined as being a recursive function applied to the abstract tree of a program: for each node type N, we define a transformation function which transforms N and then recursively invokes the functions associated with the son node types of N.
Although theoretically possible, this strategy cannot be implemented at the present time using the CSG. In general, a transformation function references attributes associated with a node of the abstract tree e.g. the node inherited environment, whereas reference to an inherited or synthesized attribute in an SSL function is not possible in the current CSG version.

b Transformation by attribute calculation

In transformation by attributes, only local equations are defined which are used to associate an attribute with each node: the attributes in fact represent the node transformation. On the condition that no circularity exists, the definition of one attribute can make reference to other attributes.
This is the implementation we adopted. An interesting aspect is that the abstract tree of the initial Ada program is not modified; the Ada program of the application to undergo transformation is the attribute associated with the root of the original Ada tree.

c Transformation examples

The examples below aim at illustrating the transformation of an Ada program into an equivalent Ada program which makes calls to the STRAda kernel. Let us begin with a simple example which only comprises the *accept* instruction. In the second example, the instruction *select* is translated.

Example 1

```
type MESSAGE is array (1..N) of character;

accept GET (INFOR : out MESSAGE ) do
  INFOR := BUFFER;
end GET;
```

This Ada text is translated into the Ada text below:

```
declare
  INFOR : MESSAGE ;
begin
  ACCEPT_DO(TASK_BOX.ENTRY_GET, TASK_NAME);
  INFOR := BUFFER;
```

```
  ACCEPT_END
     (TASK_BOX.ENTRY_GET,
      TP_OUT => (TAB_PARAM'first=>(INFOR'address,INFOR'size)),
      CALLER_NAME => TASK_NAME);
end;
```

Example 2

The UNIX primitive *select*, which queues a message at a set of ports, is used to easily translate the Ada *select* instruction. Let us consider the following Ada text:

```
select
  when S>0 =>
      accept P;
      S := S - 1;
  or
      accept V;
      S := S + 1;
end select;
```

This Ada text will be translated into the Ada text below:

```
declare
  ENTRY_LIST       : LIST_OF_ENTRIES (1..MAX);
  NB               : integer := 0;
  SELECTED_ENTRY   : ENTRY_NAME;
begin
  -- guards evaluation and accepted entry list calculation
      --   when S>0 =>accept P;
  if S>0 then
      NB := NB + 1;
      ENTRY_LIST(NB) := ENTRY_P;
  end if;

      -- accept V;
  NB := NB + 1;
  ENTRY_LIST(NB) := ENTRY_V;

      -- select
  SELECTED_ENTRY := SELECTT (ENTRY_LIST (1..NB), NO_WAIT);
  case SELECTED_ENTRY is
      when ENTRY_P =>
          ACCEPTT(SELECTED_ENTRY);
          S := S - 1;
      when ENTRY_V =>
          ACCEPTT(SELECTED_ENTRY);
          S:= S + 1;
      when others =>
          raise Tasking_error;
  end case;
end;
```

5 Discussion

In this section we will discuss the approach adopted for the STRAda project. As we have already seen, the approach is first and foremost a transformational one. Our aim was not to define a new language or system but rather to concentrate on the transformation of certain constructions of an existing language into the equivalent constructions of an existing system. This angle interests us for several reasons:

- it allows for reuse of compilers and well-known, widely used systems which makes for good portability,
- it can easily be adapted to other systems: transformation into Chorus [ZBCGM81], Mach [JR86] or other real-time kernels could also be considered.

As far as implementation is concerned, we have so far ignored the problem posed by shared variables, task termination, and time management (the *delay* instruction). We advance the following remarks on shared variables:

- certain distributed systems now provide for abstraction of distributed memory over a network,
- the minimal STRAda kernel lets us foreshadow a scheme whereby shared variables are implemented like distributed variables encapsulated in the tasks accessed remotely and where transformations are used to substitute access to these shared variables by invoking entries defined by these tasks.

However, the issue of task termination is more complex since this involves implementing an algorithm adapted to Ada. The issue is currently being investigated.

6 Conclusion

A prototype of the STRAda project is currently under development. We have experimented on several classic parallel programs, e.g. an adaptation of the problem of philosophers in a physically distributed environment.

As we saw in section 3.3, distribution of tasks rests with the programmer: it is his job to associate a processing node with each task created. An interesting study would consist in developing this aspect in distributing an Ada program.

A practical facet of the problem which interests us is that involving transformations for existing systems or real-time kernels. This would enable us to write or reuse applications written in a high level language as well as to reuse existing real-time kernels dedicated to certain architecture types.

Lastly, from the theoretical standpoint, it would be interesting to validate the relevant transformations.

We will conclude by observing that the STRAda project has enabled us to address and establish a link between several areas of Computer Science. We have worked on the system and language aspects, and the task has proved to be extremely enriching.

7 Bibliographie

[AD90] C. Atkinson and A. Di Maio
From DIADEM to DRAGOON
Distributed Ada: developments and experiences, pages 105-136, Cambridge University Press 1990

[AL90] A. Ardö and L. Lundberg
The MUMS Multiprocessor Ada Project
Distributed Ada: developments and experiences, pages 235-258, Cambridge University Press 1990

[B86] M.J. Bach
The Design of the UNIX Operating System
Prentice-Hall International Editions 1986

[BBB91] G. Bazalgette, D. Bekele, C. Bernon
STRAda: Un système de transformation et de répartition Ada.
DEA-Université Paul Sabatier TOULOUSE France 1991

[BH90] J.M. Bishop and M.J. Hasling
Distibuted Ada - the Issues
Distributed Ada: developments and experiences, pages 1-14, Cambridge University Press 1990

[DC90] B. Dobbing and I. Caldwell
A pragmatic approach to distributed Ada for transputers
Distributed Ada: developments and experiences, pages 200-221, Cambridge University Press 1990

[DFSS90] R. Dewar, S. Flynn, E. Schonberg and N. Shulman
Distributed Ada on Shared Memory Multiprocessors
Distributed Ada: developments and experiences, pages 222-234, Cambridge University Press 1990

[DJL88] P. Deransart, M. Jourdan, B. Lorho
Attribute Grammars: Definitions and Bibliography.
Springer Verlag, aug 1968

[EBGW83] A. Evans, K.J. Butler, G. Goos, and Wulf W.A.
DIANA reference manual. Technical report TL 83-4.
Tartan laboratories incorporated, feb 1983

[EJ90] G. Eisenhauer and R. Jha
Honeywell Distributed Ada - implementation
Distributed Ada: developments and experiences, pages 158-176, Cambridge University Press 1990

[HW90] A.D. Hutcheon and A.J. Wellings
The York distributed Ada Project
Distributed Ada: developments and experiences, pages 67-104, Cambridge University Press 1990

[JE90] R. Jha and G. Eisenhauer
Honeywell Distributed Ada - Approach
Distributed Ada: developments and experiences, pages 137-157, Cambridge University Press 1990

[JKIC89] R. Jha, M. Kamrad II, and D.T. Cornhill
Ada program partitioning language: a notation for distributed Ada programs.
IEEE Transitions on software engineering, 15(3):271-280, mar 1989

[JR86] M.B. Jones and R.F. Rashid
Mach and machmaker: kernel and language support for object oriented distributed systems.
In N. Meyriwitz, editor, OOPSLA Proc. on object-oriented programming systems, languages and applications, pages 67-77. ACM, sep 1986

[KBL80] B. Krieg-Brückner and D.C. Luckham.
Anna: towards a language for annotating Ada programs.
SIGPLAN, 30(3):228-238, nov 1980

[KS91] F. Kordon, P. Sens
Répartir des programmes Ada sur un ensemble homogène de machines UNIX, une expérience de réalisation
Ada, premier bilan d'utilisation, pages 123-135, Congrès Ada France nov 1991.

[MRA87] Manuel de Référence du langage de programmation Ada
Alsys, fev 1987

[RT89a] T.W. Reps and T.Teitelbaum
The Synthesizer Generator, A System for Constructing Language-based Editors.
Springer Verlag, 1989

[RT89b] T.W. Reps and T.Teitelbaum
The Synthesizer Generator Reference Manual.
Springer Verlag, third edition,1989

[VKT90] A. Volz, P. Krishnan and R. Theriault
Distributed Ada: a Case Study
Distributed Ada: developments and experiences, pages 15-57, Cambridge University Press 1990

[ZBCGM81] H. Zimmermann, J. S. Banino, A. Caristan, M. Guillemont and G. Morisset
Basic concepts for the support of distributed systems: The Chorus Approach
IEEE Catalog NO. 80-83218, pages 60-67, Apr 81
Computer Society Press

AMPATS

A Multi Processor Ada Tool Set

Karlotto Mangold

ATM Computer GmbH

Bücklestr. 1 - 5

D7750 Konstanz

Abstract:

In this paper an approach is presented which supports the distribution of an Ada Program. The idea is to handle functional units, defined during system design, as distributable units during system integration. These partitions are marked by a specific pragma. A preprocessor is analyzing the source code and producing so called Virtual Nodes. As these virtual nodes are communicating via remote procedure calls instead of rendezvous, the preprocessor automatically changes the rendezvous between tasks located in different virtual nodes into the appropriate remote procedure calls. A configuration tool handles a configuration description and integrates all virtual nodes mapped onto one processor into one Ada program. This approach allows the re-arrangement of virtual nodes not only without changes in the source code, but also without any recompilation.
In the second part the handling of the tool set is described and parts of an example are presented to show the use and usefulness of these tools.

Introduction

Ada[1], although being one of the most modern third generation programming languages, does not have any language constructs to support the implementation of distributed systems. Since the last ten years the importance of distributed computer systems for implementing embedded system has grown very fast. Therefore an extension of the language, allowing an efficient distribution of an Ada application onto a multi-processor-system is required in chapter 8 of the Ada9X Requirements Document[2]. A most relevant overview of "Distributed Systems and Ada" with a lot of references is given in [3]. According to the classification given in [3] we would like to classify AMPATS in class 2 which is "a system with explicit partitioning in agreement with Ada language concepts". In this paper we will not repeat earlier publications, but only give the necessary preconditions for presenting the implemented concepts.

Problems in distributing Ada

An Ada program - consisting of several Ada tasks - is only designed to describe concurrencies among tasks executed on a single processing unit. There are no constructs in the language to distribute a program to more than one central processing unit. Nevertheless there is at least one model using full Ada on a distributed system using an automatic load-sharing approach (class 1 in [3]). Due to the elaboration rules, the visibility and naming rules, an Ada program can be distributed onto several CPUs within a tightly coupled system if there exists one and only one task-scheduler within the system and if the data objects declared in the Ada program are mapped to a global memory which is accessible from each CPU. Implementing an application system into such an architecture causes the problem, that the workload on the bus for communication between the different CPUs and the global memory is dependent on the task distribution and therefore at least non-deterministic and non-predictible.

The functionality of the underlying operating system is often used to map an Ada application onto a multi-processor system. Unfortunately these constructs are not part of the language but are specific to the operating system so that this solution is normally not portable even if the approach, using packages, is in accordance with Ada and its principles.

Using these communication packages tasks had to use different communication mechanisms dependent whether they are located on the same processor or on different processors. A consequence of this approach is the fact that such a distribution must be done during the design phase of a project. At this time the workload of the used processors is often unknown. Therefore such a distribution of an application only very seldom leads to a uniform workload on the used processors. If, at a later stage of the project, the distribution - as a result of practical experience - must be modified, a lot of changes in the implemented software is necessary. Such an approach contradicts all modern principles of software engineering which should be fulfilled by using Ada as an implementation language. To overcome these problems we have developed an approach to distribute an Ada program without the disadvantages mentioned above. As a result of these investigations it is possible to use only Ada constructs within the application program. The distribution is supported by a set of tools which allow the distribution of the application in a very simple way without changes in the source code and even without recompilation.
This toolset, called AMPATS, is presented in the following paragraphs.

A First Approach

During the first steps of implementing a distributed system the design and specification phases lead to a separation of the complete system into functional units. These units often interact with each other like components of a loosely coupled system. The Ada approach forces the implementor either to map each functional unit onto one Ada-program, using non-Ada-communication between these programs. The other solution is to map all functional units onto one Ada-program, using the Ada Rendezvous to communicate between the tasks of this program. Obviously the second approach causes problems in distributing such a program onto several processors of a multi-processor-system.
Unfortunately the most effective way of distributing an application among the processors of a multi-processor-system often becomes obvious only during system integration, when all the implementation and testing has already been finished. If changes in the distribution are necessary at such a late stage both approaches need redoing a lot of work already done.
Based on the concepts of virtual nodes and shared objects we structure the whole application system into functional units. These units and their communication needs were defined according the following rules:

- Minimizing the access to data and code outside a functional unit.
- Maximizing the runtime necessary to execute the code of such a functional unit.

These two rules produce an efficient relation between communication- and execution-time.

Normally such a functional unit consists of several Ada-packages and Ada-tasks. This view seems to be a quite natural approach to the top down definition of a software system. Most of the existing CASE-tools support or require such a structuring of the problem. At this level of system design we don't decide the final distribution of the application system. We only define units which can be distributed according to the workload situation among the processors of a multi-processor-system.
The advantages of such support of "late" distribution are obvious.

The Communication Model

Inter-task communication is done in Ada by the Rendezvous-concept. In this asymmetric operation an entry call is issued by the caller or master task and the entry call is accepted by the slave task. This communication model is rather close to a client-server-model, where the caller is the client and the slave task acts as a server.

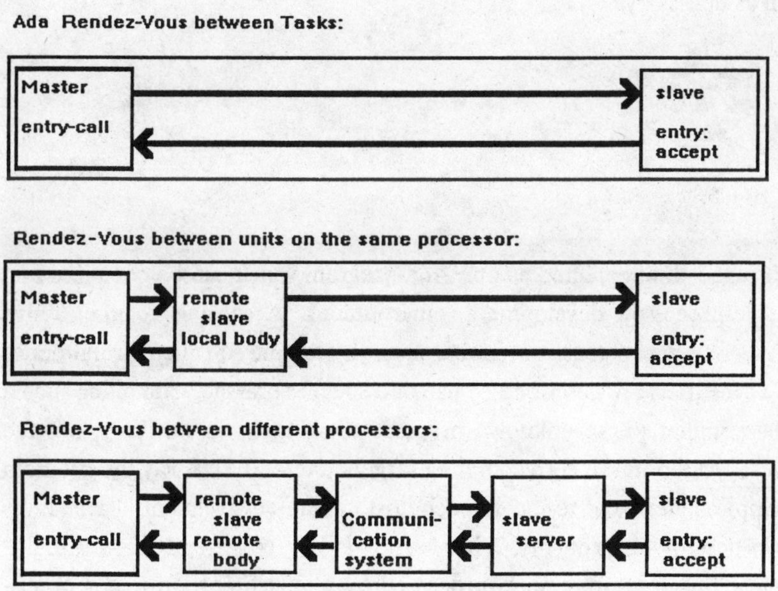

Figure 1: The Communication Model

Since the whole approach aims to automatic distribution, it is necessary to use the Rendezvous between all tasks of the application system, independently whether they are located in the same or in different functional units and also independently whether these virtual nodes are allocated in the same or in different processors. To ensure the synchronization which is part of the rendezvous between tasks on different processors a remote procedure call is used. The three different communication models are shown in figure 1.

With this approach the Rendezvous can take place between tasks in different functional units, even if they are distributed among different processors. To support the communication among units on the same processor a program is implemented consisting of a package "remote slave" together with a local body which executes the rendezvous via an entry call directed to an entry in the other Ada program. If an entry of a task is called from a task located on another processor an additional server task is installed on the same processor as the slave task. The master task issues an entry call via the same package "remote slave", but instead of the local body the remote body is used. This remote body addresses the additional server task via the underlying communication sub-system. All software components mentioned here to establish the communication between the master- and the slave task are part of the runtime library and automatically added to the application program as necessary.

The Solution

The application software is implemented as one Ada-program which can be compiled and tested in each single-processor development environment. According to the above mentioned criteria the system can consist of global data objects and so called virtual nodes or functional units. These units are described by use of a specific pragma. Compiling such a system with an Ada-compiler, these unknown pragmas are flagged as warnings, but the Ada-program can be executed in the corresponding target-system. In this way the program can be developed, implemented and tested in each host system environment. There is no need for any multi-processor functionality. Directed towards a target system with multi-processor functionality, this Ada-program is processed by a specific preprocessor or distribution tool. This tool checks the program units according to the defined virtual nodes. It replaces entry calls between tasks located in different virtual nodes by calls to library routines which work as described in figure 1. The result of this preprocessor are modified source files with Ada program units which can be separated.

These Ada-program units can be compiled and mapped onto the multi-processor-system.

The only requirement is, that each functional unit must be mapped onto one processor. A functional unit cannot be distributed among different processors. But of course it is possible to implement more than one functional unit on the same processor.
The physical communication mechanisms, available between the different processors are totally independent from the concepts and the tools presented here. There is only the requirement, that remote procedure calls are supported by the used communication system. To demonstrate this independence, we have implemented two possible systems. The first approach was a distributed system of two or more identical CPU-boards in one chassis, connected via the VME-bus respectively the VSB-bus. The second system consists of a SUN IV and a Motorola 68030 based computer. The connection between these two components is built up via an Ethernet using TCP/IP-protocols and the remote procedure calls. Other communication systems are just under consideration.
The Ada-software to communicate between these units is automatically generated by this distribution tool. There are three different communication packages. One for inter-unit communication on the same processor , another for communication between different processors and the third one for both requirements. These packages can be compiled and stored in the library as all other Ada-packages.
A second tool, the configuration tool, is used to combine the distributable units according to the specific configuration and to distribute the application and the necessary communication packages according to a distribution specification.

The Tool-Set

Implementing AMPATS for a Motorola 680x0 based multi-processor-system we developed a tool set consisting of three components. The interaction of these components in the development system is shown in figure 2.

The three components are:
The **preprocessor**, implemented in Ada, running on SUN IV with SUN-OS or on VAX with VMS, is analyzing the source code and checking the distribution rules to separate the application program into distributable Ada program units. This separation is done according to the logical units described by the pragma "virtual_Node". The preprocessor also automatically changes the entry calls of tasks into remote procedure calls, if the called entry is located in another virtual node. In addition to the separated application packages the necessary communication packages are generated according to figure 1. This preprocessor is implemented in Ada and consists of about 20.000 lines of Ada source code.

As the preprocessor only interfaces the library system and the source code files, it can easily be ported onto another host system.
The **configuration tool** is dedicated to the multi-processor-system. The configuration tool is reading a configuration description consisting of distribution lists. There is one list for each processor containing those virtual nodes which are to be mapped onto this processor. The output of the configuration tool is one Ada source program for each processor. Each of these generated programs is treated as the main program calling all necessary units in that way, that linking of this program will automatically link all units used on this processor and activating this program will also activate all virtual nodes. The configuration tool is implemented on the base of the above mentioned development systems. Therefore it is dependent on the job-control language and the command input into the linker. Due to its small size (about 1000 lines of Ada-code) it is possible to modify this tool according to the requirements of other development and/or target systems.

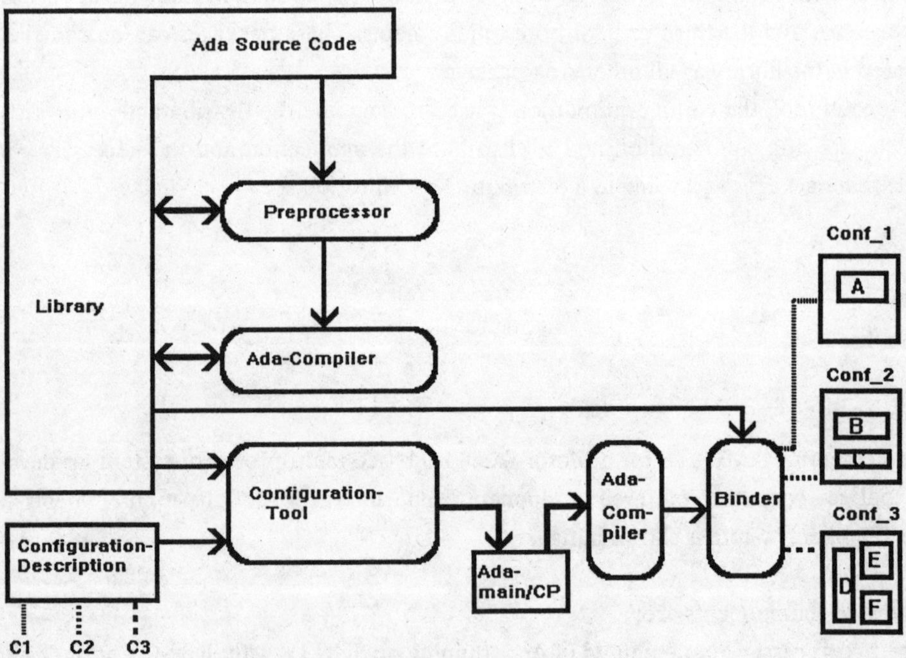

Figure 2: AMPATS in the development-system

The **communication package** is an addition to the target system. It offers the functions of a remote procedure call and a remote copy facility. To achieve a good system performance this package is implemented in a target dependent way. Up to now the communication system is implemented for use in two very different system architectures. The first implementation was directed to a multi-processor-system where several of Motorola's 680x0 processors are installed in one VME-bus chassis. The communication is done between identical real-time kernels residing on each CPU-board. The VME-Bus and/or the VSBus are used as communication lines. The second implementation was to connect a VME-Bus based single processor system and a SUN IV workstation via Ethernet using TCP/IP protocols. In both cases the RPC-package is implemented as an extension to the target system. The two very different communication mechanisms show that the principles used for distributing the application are independent from the available communication lines. As this functionality of remote procedure calls is available in a lot of different systems, the whole tool-set can easily be ported.

As already mentioned, the target system is either a homogeneous multi processor system based on 680x0 processors with the VME-bus as physical communication layer, or a heterogeneous multi-computer-system with an LAN as physical communication layer. A Multibus II based multi-processor system is just under consideration.

In figure 2 there are three different distribution descriptions called C1, C2 and C3 to explain the principal work of the tool. If the tool is invoked, the result is - depending on the input - one of the three configurations named Conf_1, Conf_2 and Conf_3. It is assumed, that Conf_1 is a single processor configuration containing the whole application in one Ada-program called A. Conf_2 is a two processor configuration with the two Ada-programs B and C, each on one of the processors. The third configuration Conf_3 consists of three processors with the three programs D, E and F.

Performance issues

To measure the overhead of this approach, the execution times of two Rendezvous are compared. The first one took place between two tasks within one functional unit, which is the normal Ada Rendezvous between two tasks. The second one is done between two tasks located in different logical units on the same processor. The overhead of this Rendezvous between different functional units is about 15 %. Obviously a Rendezvous performed via the underlying communication system between different processors is dependent on the performance of the used communication system and leads to totally different results depending whether the VME-Bus or the Ethernet-line is used. This communication overhead is also dependent an the used protocols.

An Example

In the first part an example of a distributable Ada program using generic virtual nodes is presented in part. To keep the example readable, only the specifications of the packages are presented. In the second part an example for the distribution description is given together with the automatically generated Ada-programs calling the virtual nodes.

```
-- Ada program with distributable units, virtual nodes
pragma virtual_Node;
with Apple_Node;
package Apple_1 is new Apple_Node;
-----------------------------------------------------------------
pragma virtual_Node;
with Apple_Node;
package Apple_2 is new Apple_Node;
-----------------------------------------------------------------
pragma virtual_Node;
with Apple_Node;
package Apple_3 is new Apple_Node;
-----------------------------------------------------------------
pragma virtual_Node;
with Apple_Node;
package Apple_4 is new Apple_Node;
-----------------------------------------------------------------
pragma virtual_Node;
with Apple_Node;
package Apple_5 is new Apple_Node;
-----------------------------------------------------------------
pragma virtual_Node;
with Graphics; use Graphics;
package Apple_master is

    task Distributor is
        entry start(ix,iy: Interval_Type; Criterion: Float;
            Iterations: Integer);
        entry Apple_line(py: out Float; ix: out Interval_type;
            y: out Y_Range; Criterion: out Float;
```

```
            Iteration: out Integer );
      end Distributor;
      -----------------------------------------------------------
      procedure start;
      -----------------------------------------------------------
end Apple_Master;
-----------------------------------------------------------------
pragma virtual_Node;
generic package Apple_Node is
      task Worker is
            entry start;
      end Worker;
      ------------------------------------------------------------
      procedure start;
      ------------------------------------------------------------
end Apple_Node;
-----------------------------------------------------------------
pragma virtual_Node;
package Display is
      task Driver is
            entry write ( s: String);
      end Driver;
      ------------------------------------------------------------
      procedure start;
      ------------------------------------------------------------
end Display;
-----------------------------------------------------------------
```

Here you see the specification of seven distributable units. Five of them are instantations of the same generic package called Apple_Node. For explanation purposes in a double processor system, the packages DISPLAY, APPLE_MASTER, APPLE_1, and APPLE_2 are to be mapped onto processor 1, whereas the packages APPLE_3, APPLE_4, and APPLE_5 are mapped onto processor 2. This distribution is described as follows:

Processor #1:

```
CONFIG /NODE_LIST = p1.nodes            A1
```

where p1.nodes is:

```
DISPLAY          /local       /callable         /server=5
```

```
        APPLE_MASTER      /local      /callable       /server=3
        APPLE_1           /local
        APPLE_2           /local
```

The generated Ada program is:

```
    with MEM;
    with RMT_DISPLAY, SRV_DISPLAY;
    with RMT_APPLE_MASTER, SRV_APPLE_MASTER;
    with RMT_APPLE_1, RMT_APPLE_2;
    procedure A1 is
    begin
        SRV_DISPLAY.ASG_START (5);
        SRV_APPLE_MASTER.ASG_START(3);
        MEM_SYNCHRONIZE;
        RMT_DISPLAY.START;
        RMT_APPLE_MASTER.START;
        RMT_APPLE_1.START;
        RMT_APPLE_2.START;
    end A1;
```

-- Processor #2:

```
CONFIG /NODE_LIST = p2.nodes                A2
```

where p2.nodes is:

```
        APPLE_3           /local
        APPLE_4           /local
        APPLE_5           /local
```

The generated Ada program is:

```
    with MEM;
    with RMT_APPLE_3, RMT_APPLE_4, RMT_APPLE_5;
    procedure A2 is
    begin
        MEM_SYNCHRONIZE;
        RMT_APPLE_3.START;
        RMT_APPLE_4.START;
        RMT_APPLE_5.START;
    end A2;
```

The purpose of the program listed above is to calculate and display the well-known Mandelbrot-set [4] for demonstration purposes. This distribution was done to use the additional computing power of the computers involved..

Conclusion

As mentioned at the beginning of this paper distribution of Ada programs is a requirement to Ada9X. After implementing AMPATS the Ada9X Mapping Specification [5] was published. In the Annex G chapter 3 of this document the distribution of Ada programs is described. Although the syntactic form of distribution in Ada9X is different from the pragma used in AMPATS, a first look at the concepts used in Ada9X gives the impression, that the basic principles are at least very similar. Therefore we are pretty sure that using AMPATS opens the principles of distribution in Ada9X to the user in an Ada_83 environment.

References

[1] Reference manual for the Ada Programming Language, ANSI/MIL-STD 1815 A, Washington D.C., 1983

[2] Ada9X Project Report, Ada9X Requirements, December 1990, Washington D.C., 1990.

[3] Baumgarten, U.: Distributed Systems and Ada - Current Projects and Approaches Comparative Study's Results - in Ada: The Choice for '92, Proceedings of the Ada-Europe International Conference Athens, Greece, May 1991, pages 260 - 278, 1991.

[4] Mandelbrot, B. B.: Die fraktale Geometrie der Natur, Basel, 1987.

[5] Draft Ada9X Project Report, Ada9X Mapping Document Volume II, Mapping Specification, December 1991, Washington D.C., 1991.

A Practical Use of the Ada Rendez-Vous Paradigm in Distributed Systems

M.Bayassi, H.Bitteur, JF.Jézéquel, P.Legrain

CoreliS Technologie
31, avenue Général Leclerc
92340 Bourg-La-Reine FRANCE
Phone : 33 1 46 64 86 86
Fax : 33 1 46 64 77 39

1. Abstract

This is the result of a work done to generalize the Ada Rendez-Vous mechanism, when developing an application distributed among several processes and machines, while keeping a clear separation between the objects semantics and the physical communication issues. The proposed mechanism is based upon a Client-Server architecture, coping with several types of Server (Mono and Multi Client), and requiring only any validated Ada-83 compiler and a task-to-task communication layer.

We describe how such an architecture can be developped using Object-Oriented Design methods, and how its components can afterwards be distributed on different machines in a transparent manner. We show that its implementation depends upon nothing but the Ada Server Specification. We have therefore developed a tool (using Alex and Ayacc utilities to create a simple Ada grammar parser and a generator) capable of automatically building the additionnal bricks needed by the mechanism. The implementation-dependent features dealing with physical communication are kept encapsulated in a generic layer, the only piece to modify should another communication layer be chosen.

2. Context

2.1. Usual Client - Server Architecture

Using an Object-Oriented Design method, we usually come up with a decomposition of the application into high level active objects, lower level passive objects, and abstract data types. The high-level active objects often lead to packages encapsulating Ada tasks, and providing procedures and functions mapped to the task entries. Communications between the high-level active objects are thus actually implemented by Ada Rendez-Vous.

The diagram below shows the typical case of two high-level objects in a Client Server Architecture.

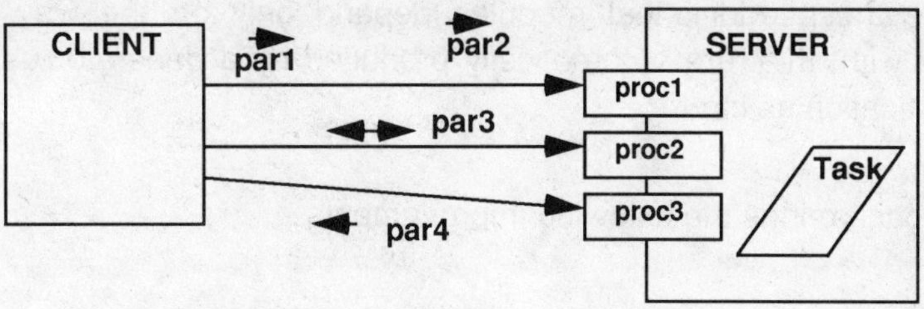

2.2. Issues in a distributed environment

Problems arise when the Client object and the Server object are no longer in a unique address space : this is the case of a configuration based upon several processes, whether these processes are located on the same machine or not.

The obvious low-level solution is to rely on some external means of inter-process communication, as with any RPC (Remote Procedure Call) utility. The main drawback is that the code needed for data encoding and decoding, as well as the use of the communication primitives, is often embedded in the application code.

This leads to a more obscure code for the objects, but worse than that, tends to freeze the overall configuration, since any later modification of the configuration would imply to update the very code of the existing objects. Moreover, this approach is not compatible with the management of different configurations of the same application, for example on different sites.

2.3. Rationale of our approach

The bottom-line of our approach is to avoid any interaction between the design and coding of the application objects, and the items needed to make them communicate around any given configuration.

As described later in this paper, the specifications and bodies of application objects are kept unchanged, we only act upon additionnal modules, refferred to as virtual client and virtual server, which in turn make use of the given communication layer. And since these additionnal modules depend only on the way the Server is interacted with, they are automatically produced by a generator using the Server Ada specification as input.

This approach brings the following improvements :

a) **Test and Integration** : Since most Ada debugging environments can be used only at a process level, this allows the application to be tested as a whole in one process, using directly the Ada Rendez-Vous. Once it is tested enough, we can distribute the Clients and the Server, using the tool, without any recompilation of the application objects, and so with no potential introduction of bugs.

b) **Configuration evolution** : The user is able, in the integration phase, to change his implementation and distribute Clients and Servers on different machines (e.g. if a machine resources can no longer accommodate both Clients and Servers). Managing different configurations of the same application is also made easier since there is only one version of the application objects to manage.

c) **Clear separation between application and configuration** : The design of the application does not have to take into account the development of specific layers to support communication between the high-level objects. The designer has just to keep in mind that these objects communicate using the Rendez-Vous paradigm.

d) **Low dependency upon physical communication** : The generic packages, which are the building blocks of the solution, can be modified to support any low-level communication layer. The specifications of such components do not have to be changed (all they need is an Open, a Send, a Receive, and a Close procedures).

3. Distributing the Clients and the Servers

3.1. Different types of Servers

Using one or several tasks inside the Server body is just an implementation issue, only the way the Server actually interacts with its Clients is relevant. This behavior has important impacts when we want to distribute high-level objects on distinct machines.

We listed three possible Server behaviors :

1) The **Mono-Client** mode, which is the simplest of all. The server has only one client at any moment, i.e only one task requests a service at any given time.

2) The **Multi-Client / Mono-Service** mode.The server has several concurrent clients, but serves only one client at a time.

3) The **Multi-Client / Multi-Service** mode. The server has several clients, and is able to serve more than one client at a time.

To actually support these kinds of interactions, it is well known that the server may require zero, one or several internal tasks. But we will see in the next sections that the communication bricks are also impacted.

3.2. Description of the mechanism

The main objective that led us in our work was to have NO changes to apply in either the Client or the Server source code, whether these objects were both located in the same process or not. The idea was to develop a layer in the Client process, and a layer in the Server process, each layer playing each other role.

Thus, in the Client process, we replace the Server body with an alternate body. The client still retains the visibility on the Server, whose specification is not changed. This ensures that the application will behave the same, whether implemented on several processes or not. This alternate Server body is called the Virtual Server, and its role is further described in the next paragraph.

In the Server process, we create a Virtual Client, a new package to play the Client role in this process. This virtual client directly calls the actual server.

To summarize, we come up with two processes, the (actual) Client and the Virtual Server in one, and the Virtual Client and the (actual) server in the other, the physical communication being handled at both ends by the virtual entities.

At initialization time, for example when packages are elaborated, the Virtual Server establishes a communication link with the Virtual Client, using the chosen communication layer. The Virtual Client encapsulates at least one task, waiting for messages to be sent by the Virtual Server.

Now, let's have a look at a typical interaction, when the Client requests a service from the Server. The Client actually calls the Virtual Server, which in turn encodes this request, using the values of parameters passed along by the Client (only parameters of mode "in" and "in out" are coded for this direction). The message is then sent using the communication layer. At the other end, the Virtual Client receives the message, decodes it, and calls the corresponding service provided by the actual server, with the parameters found in the message.

When the interaction between the Virtual Client and the (actual) Server is over, the Virtual Client gets back the parameters of "in out" and "out" mode, encodes them in a return message, and sends it back to the Virtual Server.

The Virtual Server, which was waiting for the answer, decodes the message and then returns the "in out" and "out" parameters to the client.

This general mechanism is illustrated by the diagram below.

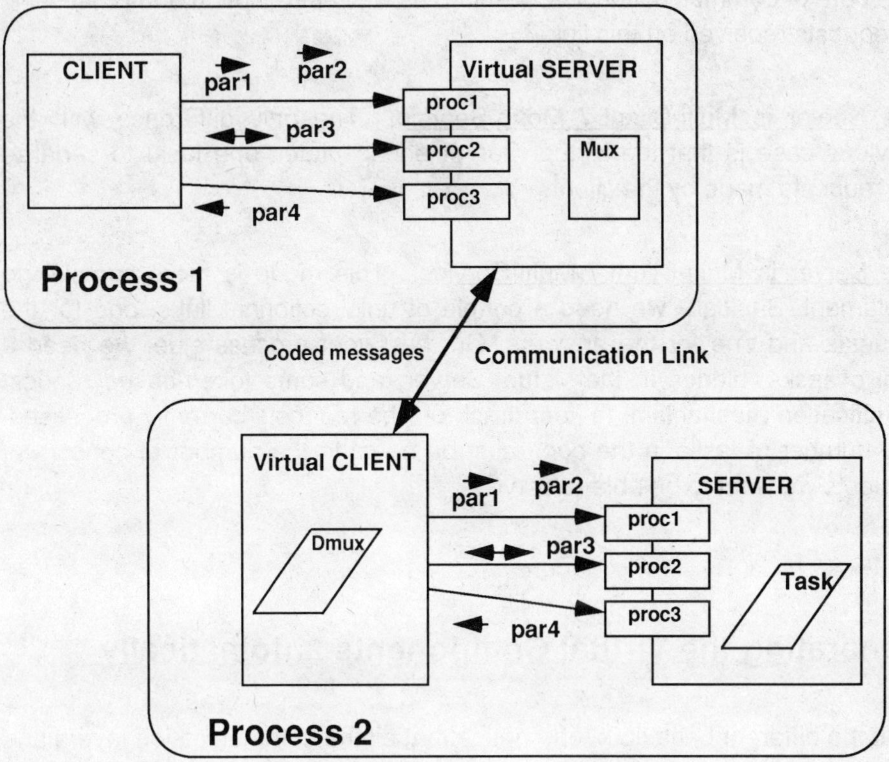

3.3. Impacts of the Server behavior

Notice that in fact the two virtual components depend only upon the Server specification, the Server behavior (see previous paragraphs about the different types of servers), and the chosen communication layer.

The virtual components described above must behave as if they were the actual components, and accordingly the implementation varies with the interactions modes :

1) The Server is Mono-Client : In this mode, the Virtual Server has no need of a task. The procedure calls provided by the server (in the client process) are executed under the client control. The Virtual Client needs only one task, to take care of communication link opening, as well as reception and processing of requests received on this link.

2) The Server is Multi-Client / Mono-Service : The only difference with the previous case is that the Virtual Server encapsulates one task, to serialize the requests made by the clients.

3) The Server is Multi-Client / Multi-Service : This mode is more complex to implement. Basically we need a couple of unidirectionnal links, one for the requests and one for the answers. On the Client process side, we need a pool of tasks, hidden in the Virtual Server, and some token-based request identification mechanism, to keep track of the requests currently processed. The number of tasks in the pool must be equal to the number of concurrent requests we want to be able to serve.

4. Generating the Virtual Components automatically

Looking at the different behaviors, one notice that all the communication layers and the tasks can be encapsulated within generic packages, and that the coding / decoding algorithms can be generated automatically.

4.1. Identification of needed components

* A coding / decoding component for the Virtual Server, depending on the Server Specification and the Server behavior,

* A coding / decoding component for the Virtual Client, depending on the Server Specification and the Server behavior,

* A behavioral component, instance of a generic component, depending on the Server behavior (for the Virtual Server and the Virtual Client),

* A communication component, instance of a generic component, depending on the chosen communication layer.

4.2. Development of the Tool

The idea was to develop a tool to automatically generate the coding/decoding components (for the Virtual Server and Virtual Client), and the instances of the generic behavioral and communication components. The synoptic of this tool is given below :

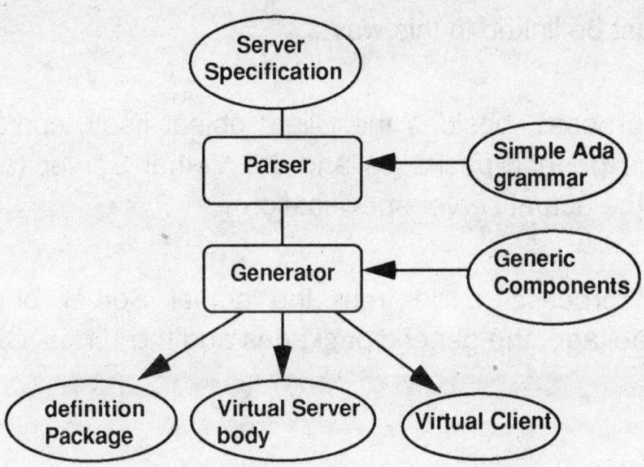

The Server specification must be a correct Ada package specification. To specify the way this Server is going to be interacted with, we chose to add the following specialized Pragma at the end of the Server specification :

```
pragma Concurrency
   (Usage      => [Mono_Client | Multi_Clients],
   [Processing => <number>]);
```

The "processing" parameter stands for the number of simultaneous requests the server can service.

Here are some hints about the implementation of the tool :

* The Parser was developed using Alex and Ayacc, with a minimal Ada grammar, including the specific "Concurrency" pragma.

* The Generator was developed by hand as a specific program.

* The Definition package exports two variant records, one for the "in" and "in out" messages, one for the "in out" and "out" messages.

* The Virtual Server and the Virtual Client contain the coding / decoding algorithms, and the instances of the various generic building blocks.

The packages must be linked in this way :

a) The Client process, besides the Client object itself, contains the Definition package, the generic packages and the Virtual Server (actually, it's only a body using the actual server specification),

b) The Server process, apart from the actual Server object, contains the Definition package, the generic packages and the Virtual Client.

4.3. Examples of actual results

The tool was developed and used both on IBM/PC with Alsys/First-Ada and VAX/VMS with DEC/Ada environment. The tool was itself generated by means of the Alex and Ayacc utilities from Irvine University.

Using the the Ada specification corresponding to the Server shown on the previous diagrams, the tool needs 2 seconds on a MicroVAX III to generate the following Ada files.

Here is the starting point, coded by hand, since it is nothing but the Ada specification of the Server object. This file is used as input by the tool, all other Ada files presented after this one were automatically generated :

```
with Some_Definitions;   use Some_Definitions;
package Server_Pkg is
    procedure Proc1 (Par1 : in      Par1_Type;
                     Par2 : in      Par2_Type);
    procedure Proc2 (Par3 : in out Par3_Type);
    procedure Proc3 (Par4 :    out Par4_Type);
end Server_Pkg;

pragma Concurrency(Usage       => Multi_Clients,
                   Processing => 2);
```

Following is the Definition file generated to declare the messages exchanged back and forth between Virtual Server and Virtual Client. Notice that the packages "withed" and "used" by the Server's Spec are forwarded to this unit. The Translation_Pkg provides functionalities similar to environment variables but in a portable way.

```
with Some_Definitions;   use Some_Definitions;
with Translation_Pkg;    use Translation_Pkg;

package Def_Server_Pkg is

    Service_Name_In  : constant String
                     := Translated("Server_Pkg_In");
    Service_Name_Out : constant String
                     := Translated("Server_Pkg_Out");

    type Service_Type is
       (Proc1_S1,
        Proc2_S2,
        Proc3_S3);

    type Message_In_Type
       (Service : Service_Type := Service_Type'First) is
        record
            case Service is
                when Proc1_S1 =>
                    Par1_P1 : Par1_Type;
                    Par2_P2 : Par2_Type;
                when Proc2_S2 =>
                    Par3_P3 : Par3_Type;
                when Proc3_S3 =>
                    null;
            end case;
        end record;
```

```
    type Message_Out_Type
        (Service : Service_Type := Service_Type'First) is
        record
            case Service is
                when Proc1_S1 =>
                    null;
                when Proc2_S2 =>
                    Par3_P3 : Par3_Type;
                when Proc3_S3 =>
                    Par4_P4 : Par4_Type;
            end case;
        end record;
end Def_Server_Pkg;
```

Here-under is the body of the Virtual Server, remember that there is no need for a specific Virtual Server spec, since it shares the actual Server's specification :

```
with Def_Server_Pkg; use Def_Server_Pkg;
with Gen_Multi_Clients_Multi_Services_Pkg;
package body Server_Pkg is
    package Communication is
        new Gen_Multi_Clients_Multi_Services_Pkg
            (Message_In_Type  => Message_In_Type,
             Message_Out_Type => Message_Out_Type,
             Service_Name_In  => Service_Name_In,
             Service_Name_Out => Service_Name_Out,
             Maximum_Simultaneous_Requests =>  2);
    use Communication;

    procedure Proc1 (Par1 : in Par1_Type;
                     Par2 : in Par2_Type) is
        Message_In  : Message_In_Type  (Proc1_S1);
        Message_Out : Message_Out_Type (Proc1_S1);
    begin
        Message_In.Par1_P1 := Par1;
        Message_In.Par2_P2 := Par2;
        Remote_Call (Message_In, Message_Out);
    end Proc1;

    procedure Proc2 (Par3 : in out Par3_Type) is
        Message_In  : Message_In_Type  (Proc2_S2);
        Message_Out : Message_Out_Type (Proc2_S2);
    begin
        Message_In.Par3_P3 := Par3;
        Remote_Call (Message_In, Message_Out);
        Par3 := Message_Out.Par3_P3;
    end Proc2;

    procedure Proc3 (Par4 : out Par4_Type) is
        Message_In  : Message_In_Type  (Proc3_S3);
        Message_Out : Message_Out_Type (Proc3_S3);
    begin
        Remote_Call (Message_In, Message_Out);
        Par4 := Message_Out.Par4_P4;
    end Proc3;
begin -- Server_Pkg
    Communication.Connect;
end Server_Pkg;
```

The specification part of the generated Virtual Client looks like :

```
package Frontal_Server_Pkg is
    procedure Start;
    procedure Stop;
end Frontal_Server_Pkg;
```

And finally we obtain the body of the generated Virtual Client :

```
with Server_Pkg;                use Server_Pkg;
with Def_Server_Pkg;            use Def_Server_Pkg;
with Gen_Multi_Services_Pkg;

package body Frontal_Server_Pkg is

    procedure DeMux(Message_In  : in  Message_In_Type;
                    Message_Out : out Message_Out_Type) is
        Temp_Out : Message_Out_Type(Service=>Message_In.Service);
    begin
        case Message_In.Service is
            when Proc1_S1 =>
                Server_Pkg.Proc1(
                    Par1 => Message_In.Par1_P1,
                    Par2 => Message_In.Par2_P2);
            when Proc2_S2 =>
                Temp_Out.Par3_P3 := Message_In.Par3_P3;
                Server_Pkg.Proc2(
                    Par3 => Temp_Out.Par3_P3);
            when Proc3_S3 =>
                Server_Pkg.Proc3(
                    Par4 => Temp_Out.Par4_P4);
        end case;
        Message_Out := Temp_Out;
    end DeMux;

    package Communication is new Gen_Multi_Services_Pkg
        (Message_In_Type   => Message_In_Type,
         Message_Out_Type  => Message_Out_Type,
         DeMux             => DeMux,
         Service_Name_In   => Service_Name_In,
         Service_Name_Out  => Service_Name_Out,
         Maximum_Simultaneous_Requests =>  2);

    procedure Start is
    begin
        Communication.Open;
    end Init;

    procedure Stop is
    begin
        Communication.Close;
    end Close;
end Frontal_Server_Pkg;
```

5. Conclusion

5.1. Known limitations

On top of the limitations of any distributed environment, concerning for example the notion of time-out or exceptions, we must be aware of the following restrictions :

* The parameters must contain no access type, since an access value is meaningless in another address space,

* In an heterogeneous environment, the same data type may be represented differently from one machine to another, and would have to be handled in the coding/decoding units,

* All parameters must be constrained, since requests are encoded in Ada records,

* Care must be taken with "out" parameters, if some of their attributes (such as P'Length) are used by the Server : It is safer in that case to make them "in out" parameters, to force the receiving structure to be passed along from the Client to the Virtual Client,

* And finally, the communication layers are slow, when compared with a usual procedure call.

5.2. Practical results

Despite these limitations, this approach has been applied to a real-size industrial project, in which there were many clients and servers, nearly each of them in a different process. The final configuration was known after the design phase. The tests and first integration phase were held on one machine, using the Ada Rendez-Vous, allowing to test the functionalities of the various objects, and the interaction between them. Then the tool was applied on the servers, with the desired modes, and it led automatically to the operationnal code with no modification but the specialized pragma.

Lecture Notes in Computer Science

For information about Vols. 1–529
please contact your bookseller or Springer-Verlag

Vol. 530: D. H. Pitt, P.-L. Curien, S. Abramsky, A. M. Pitts, A. Poigné, D. E. Rydeheard (Eds.), Category Theory and Computer Science. Proceedings, 1991. VII, 301 pages. 1991.

Vol. 531: E. M. Clarke, R. P. Kurshan (Eds.), Computer-Aided Verification. Proceedings, 1990. XIII, 372 pages. 1991.

Vol. 532: H. Ehrig, H.-J. Kreowski, G. Rozenberg (Eds.), Graph Grammars and Their Application to Computer Science. Proceedings, 1990. X, 703 pages. 1991.

Vol. 533: E. Börger, H. Kleine Büning, M. M. Richter, W. Schönfeld (Eds.), Computer Science Logic. Proceedings, 1990. VIII, 399 pages. 1991.

Vol. 534: H. Ehrig, K. P. Jantke, F. Orejas, H. Reichel (Eds.), Recent Trends in Data Type Specification. Proceedings, 1990. VIII, 379 pages. 1991.

Vol. 535: P. Jorrand, J. Kelemen (Eds.), Fundamentals of Artificial Intelligence Research. Proceedings, 1991. VIII, 255 pages. 1991. (Subseries LNAI).

Vol. 536: J. E. Tomayko, Software Engineering Education. Proceedings, 1991. VIII, 296 pages. 1991.

Vol. 537: A. J. Menezes, S. A. Vanstone (Eds.), Advances in Cryptology – CRYPTO '90. Proceedings. XIII, 644 pages. 1991.

Vol. 538: M. Kojima, N. Megiddo, T. Noma, A. Yoshise, A Unified Approach to Interior Point Algorithms for Linear Complementarity Problems. VIII, 108 pages. 1991.

Vol. 539: H. F. Mattson, T. Mora, T. R. N. Rao (Eds.), Applied Algebra, Algebraic Algorithms and Error-Correcting Codes. Proceedings, 1991. XI, 489 pages. 1991.

Vol. 540: A. Prieto (Ed.), Artificial Neural Networks. Proceedings, 1991. XIII, 476 pages. 1991.

Vol. 541: P. Barahona, L. Moniz Pereira, A. Porto (Eds.), EPIA '91. Proceedings, 1991. VIII, 292 pages. 1991. (Subseries LNAI).

Vol. 542: Z. W. Ras, M. Zemankova (Eds.), Methodologies for Intelligent Systems. Proceedings, 1991. X, 644 pages. 1991. (Subseries LNAI).

Vol. 543: J. Dix, K. P. Jantke, P. H. Schmitt (Eds.), Nonmonotonic and Inductive Logic. Proceedings, 1990. X, 243 pages. 1991. (Subseries LNAI).

Vol. 544: M. Broy, M. Wirsing (Eds.), Methods of Programming. XII, 268 pages. 1991.

Vol. 545: H. Alblas, B. Melichar (Eds.), Attribute Grammars , Applications and Systems. Proceedings, 1991. IX, 513 pages. 1991.

Vol. 546: O. Herzog, C.-R. Rollinger (Eds.), Text Understanding in LILOG. XI, 738 pages. 1991. (Subseries LNAI).

Vol. 547: D. W. Davies (Ed.), Advances in Cryptology – EUROCRYPT '91. Proceedings, 1991. XII, 556 pages. 1991.

Vol. 548: R. Kruse, P. Siegel (Eds.), Symbolic and Quantitative Approaches to Uncertainty. Proceedings, 1991. XI, 362 pages. 1991.

Vol. 549: E. Ardizzone, S. Gaglio, F. Sorbello (Eds.), Trends in Artificial Intelligence. Proceedings, 1991. XIV, 479 pages. 1991. (Subseries LNAI).

Vol. 550: A. van Lamsweerde, A. Fugetta (Eds.), ESEC '91. Proceedings, 1991. XII, 515 pages. 1991.

Vol. 551:S. Prehn, W. J. Toetenel (Eds.), VDM '91. Formal Software Development Methods. Volume 1. Proceedings, 1991. XIII, 699 pages. 1991.

Vol. 552: S. Prehn, W. J. Toetenel (Eds.), VDM '91. Formal Software Development Methods. Volume 2. Proceedings, 1991. XIV, 430 pages. 1991.

Vol. 553: H. Bieri, H. Noltemeier (Eds.), Computational Geometry - Methods, Algorithms and Applications '91. Proceedings, 1991. VIII, 320 pages. 1991.

Vol. 554: G. Grahne, The Problem of Incomplete Information in Relational Databases. VIII, 156 pages. 1991.

Vol. 555: H. Maurer (Ed.), New Results and New Trends in Computer Science. Proceedings, 1991. VIII, 403 pages. 1991.

Vol. 556: J.-M. Jacquet, Conclog: A Methodological Approach to Concurrent Logic Programming. XII, 781 pages. 1991.

Vol. 557: W. L. Hsu, R. C. T. Lee (Eds.), ISA '91 Algorithms. Proceedings, 1991. X, 396 pages. 1991.

Vol. 558: J. Hooman, Specification and Compositional Verification of Real-Time Systems. VIII, 235 pages. 1991.

Vol. 559: G. Butler, Fundamental Algorithms for Permutation Groups. XII, 238 pages. 1991.

Vol. 560: S. Biswas, K. V. Nori (Eds.), Foundations of Software Technology and Theoretical Computer Science. Proceedings, 1991. X, 420 pages. 1991.

Vol. 561: C. Ding, G. Xiao, W. Shan, The Stability Theory of Stream Ciphers. IX, 187 pages. 1991.

Vol. 562: R. Breu, Algebraic Specification Techniques in Object Oriented Programming Environments. XI, 228 pages. 1991.

Vol. 563: A. Karshmer, J. Nehmer (Eds.), Operating Systems of the 90s and Beyond. Proceedings, 1991. X, 285 pages. 1991.

Vol. 564: I. Herman, The Use of Projective Geometry in Computer Graphics. VIII, 146 pages. 1992.

Vol. 565: J. D. Becker, I. Eisele, F. W. Mündemann (Eds.), Parallelism, Learning, Evolution. Proceedings, 1989. VIII, 525 pages. 1991. (Subseries LNAI).

Vol. 566: C. Delobel, M. Kifer, Y. Masunaga (Eds.), Deductive and Object-Oriented Databases. Proceedings, 1991. XV, 581 pages. 1991.

Vol. 567: H. Boley, M. M. Richter (Eds.), Processing Declarative Kowledge. Proceedings, 1991. XII, 427 pages. 1991. (Subseries LNAI).

Vol. 568: H.-J. Bürckert, A Resolution Principle for a Logic with Restricted Quantifiers. X, 116 pages. 1991. (Subseries LNAI).

Vol. 569: A. Beaumont, G. Gupta (Eds.), Parallel Execution of Logic Programs. Proceedings, 1991. VII, 195 pages. 1991.

Vol. 570: R. Berghammer, G. Schmidt (Eds.), Graph-Theoretic Concepts in Computer Science. Proceedings, 1991. VIII, 253 pages. 1992.

Vol. 571: J. Vytopil (Ed.), Formal Techniques in Real-Time and Fault-Tolerant Systems. Proceedings, 1992. IX, 620 pages. 1991.

Vol. 572: K. U. Schulz (Ed.), Word Equations and Related Topics. Proceedings, 1990. VII, 256 pages. 1992.

Vol. 573: G. Cohen, S. N. Litsyn, A. Lobstein, G. Zémor (Eds.), Algebraic Coding. Proceedings, 1991. X, 158 pages. 1992.

Vol. 574: J. P. Banâtre, D. Le Métayer (Eds.), Research Directions in High-Level Parallel Programming Languages. Proceedings, 1991. VIII, 387 pages. 1992.

Vol. 575: K. G. Larsen, A. Skou (Eds.), Computer Aided Verification. Proceedings, 1991. X, 487 pages. 1992.

Vol. 576: J. Feigenbaum (Ed.), Advances in Cryptology - CRYPTO '91. Proceedings. X, 485 pages. 1992.

Vol. 577: A. Finkel, M. Jantzen (Eds.), STACS 92. Proceedings, 1992. XIV, 621 pages. 1992.

Vol. 578: Th. Beth, M. Frisch, G. J. Simmons (Eds.), Public-Key Cryptography: State of the Art and Future Directions. XI, 97 pages. 1992.

Vol. 579: S. Toueg, P. G. Spirakis, L. Kirousis (Eds.), Distributed Algorithms. Proceedings, 1991. X, 319 pages. 1992.

Vol. 580: A. Pirotte, C. Delobel, G. Gottlob (Eds.), Advances in Database Technology – EDBT '92. Proceedings. XII, 551 pages. 1992.

Vol. 581: J.-C. Raoult (Ed.), CAAP '92. Proceedings. VIII, 361 pages. 1992.

Vol. 582: B. Krieg-Brückner (Ed.), ESOP '92. Proceedings. VIII, 491 pages. 1992.

Vol. 583: I. Simon (Ed.), LATIN '92. Proceedings. IX, 545 pages. 1992.

Vol. 584: R. E. Zippel (Ed.), Computer Algebra and Parallelism. Proceedings, 1990. IX, 114 pages. 1992.

Vol. 585: F. Pichler, R. Moreno Díaz (Eds.), Computer Aided System Theory – EUROCAST '91. Proceedings. X, 761 pages. 1992.

Vol. 586: A. Cheese, Parallel Execution of Parlog. IX, 184 pages. 1992.

Vol. 587: R. Dale, E. Hovy, D. Rösner, O. Stock (Eds.), Aspects of Automated Natural Language Generation. Proceedings, 1992. VIII, 311 pages. 1992. (Subseries LNAI).

Vol. 588: G. Sandini (Ed.), Computer Vision – ECCV '92. Proceedings. XV, 909 pages. 1992.

Vol. 589: U. Banerjee, D. Gelernter, A. Nicolau, D. Padua (Eds.), Languages and Compilers for Parallel Computing. Proceedings, 1991. IX, 419 pages. 1992.

Vol. 590: B. Fronhöfer, G. Wrightson (Eds.), Parallelization in Inference Systems. Proceedings, 1990. VIII, 372 pages. 1992. (Subseries LNAI).

Vol. 591: H. P. Zima (Ed.), Parallel Computation. Proceedings, 1991. IX, 451 pages. 1992.

Vol. 592: A. Voronkov (Ed.), Logic Programming. Proceedings, 1991. IX, 514 pages. 1992. (Subseries LNAI).

Vol. 593: P. Loucopoulos (Ed.), Advanced Information Systems Engineering. Proceedings. XI, 650 pages. 1992.

Vol. 594: B. Monien, Th. Ottmann (Eds.), Data Structures and Efficient Algorithms. VIII, 389 pages. 1992.

Vol. 595: M. Levene, The Nested Universal Relation Database Model. X, 177 pages. 1992.

Vol. 596: L.-H. Eriksson, L. Hallnäs, P. Schroeder-Heister (Eds.), Extensions of Logic Programming. Proceedings, 1991. VII, 369 pages. 1992. (Subseries LNAI).

Vol. 597: H. W. Guesgen, J. Hertzberg, A Perspective of Constraint-Based Reasoning. VIII, 123 pages. 1992. (Subseries LNAI).

Vol. 598: S. Brookes, M. Main, A. Melton, M. Mislove, D. Schmidt (Eds.), Mathematical Foundations of Programming Semantics. Proceedings, 1991. VIII, 506 pages. 1992.

Vol. 599: Th. Wetter, K.-D. Althoff, J. Boose, B. R. Gaines, M. Linster, F. Schmalhofer (Eds.), Current Developments in Knowledge Acquisition - EKAW '92. Proceedings. XIII, 444 pages. 1992. (Subseries LNAI).

Vol. 600: J. W. de Bakker, K. Huizing, W. P. de Roever, G. Rozenberg (Eds.), Real-Time: Theory in Practice. Proceedings, 1991. VIII, 723 pages. 1992.

Vol. 601: D. Dolev, Z. Galil, M. Rodeh (Eds.), Theory of Computing and Systems. Proceedings, 1992. VIII, 220 pages. 1992.

Vol. 602: I. Tomek (Ed.), Computer Assisted Learning. Proceedigs, 1992. X, 615 pages. 1992.

Vol. 603: J. van Katwijk (Ed.), Ada: Moving Towards 2000. Proceedings, 1992. VIII, 324 pages. 1992.